HISTORY
OF RUSSIA

Sergei Mikhailovich Soloviev

The
Academic International Press
Edition
of
Sergei M. Soloviev

History of Russia From Earliest Times

G. EDWARD ORCHARD
General Editor

Contributing Editors

HUGH F. GRAHAM	PATRICK J. O'MEARA
JOHN D. WINDHAUSEN	PETER C. STUPPLES
ALEXANDER V. MULLER	T. ALLAN SMITH
K.A. PAPMEHL	MARTHA L. LAHANA
RICHARD HANTULA	ANTHONY V. KNOWLES
WALTER J. GLEASON, JR.	HELEN Y. PROCHAZKA
WILLIAM H. HILL	ALEXANDRA S. KORROS
G. EDWARD ORCHARD	GARY J. MARKER
LINDSEY A.J. HUGHES	MARIAN J. RUBCHAK
NICKOLAS LUPININ	RALPH M. CLEMINSON
GEORGE E. MUNRO	CATHY J. POTTER
DANIEL L. SCHLAFLY, JR.	BRIGIT A. FARLEY
ANTHONY L.H. RHINELANDER	

SERGEI M. SOLOVIEV

History of Russia

Volume 2

Early Russia, 1054-1157

Edited, Translated and With an
Introduction by

Ralph M. Cleminson

2002
Academic International Press

The Academic International Press Edition of S.M. Soloviev's
History of Russia From Earliest Times in fifty volumes.

Volume 2. *Early Russia, 1054-1157*
Unabridged translation of the text of Chapters 1-5 of Volume 2 of
S.M. Soloviev's *Istoriia Rossii s drevneishikh vremen* as found in
Volume I of this work published in Moscow from 1959-1966, with
added annotation by Ralph M. Cleminson.

Copyright © 2002 by Academic International Press

ISBN: 0-87569-238-9

Composition by Ethel Chamberlain

Printed in the United States of America

A list of Academic International Press publications is found at
the end of this volume.

ACADEMIC INTERNATIONAL PRESS
PO Box 1111 • Gulf Breeze FL 32562-1111 • USA

www.ai-press.com

CONTENTS

WEIGHTS AND MEASURES

Linear and Surface Measure

Arshin: 16 vershoks, 28 in. (diuims) 72.12 cm
Chetvert (quarter): 1/4 arshin, 1/2 desiatina,
  1.35 acres (sometimes 1.5 desiatinas or c.
  4.1 acres)
Desiatina: 2,400 square sazhens, 2.7 acres,
  1.025 hectares
Diuim: 1 inch, 2.54 cm
Fut: 12 diuims, 1 foot, 30.48 cm

Obza (areal): c. 10 chetverts, 13–15 acres
Osmina: 1/4 desiatina, 600 sq. sazhens, .256
  hectare
Sazhen: 3 arshins, 7 feet, 2.133 m
Vershok: 1.75 in., 4.445 cm, 1/16 arshin
Verst: 500 sazhens, 1,166 yards and 2 feet, .663
  miles, 1.0668 km
Voloka (plowland): 19 desiatinas, 20 hectares, 49 acres

Liquid Measure

Bochka (barrel): 40 vedros, 121 gallons,
  492 liters
Chetvert (quarter): 1.4 bochkas, 32.5 gallons
Korchago (wine): Rus, unknown

Kufa: 30 stofy
Stof: Kruzhka (cup), 1/10 vedro, c. 1.3 quarts, 1.23
  liters
Vedro (pail): 3.25 gallons, 12.3 liters, 10 stofy

Weights

Berkovets: 361 lbs., 10 puds
Bezmen: c. 1 kg, 2.2 lbs.
Chetverik (grain measure dating from 16th
  century): 1/8 chetvert, 15.8 lbs.
Chetvert (grain measure): 1/4 rad, 3.5 puds,
  126.39 lbs., c. 8 bushels
Funt: 96 zolotniks, .903 lbs., 14.4 oz., 408.24
  kg
Grivenka: 205 grams
Kad: 4 chetverts, 14 puds, 505.56 lbs.
Kadka malenkaia: 12th-century, small measure

Kamen (stone): 32 funt
Korob (basket): 7 puds, 252 lbs.
Osmina (eighth): 2 osmina to a chetvert (dry
  measure)
Polbezmen: c. 500 g, 1 lb.
Polosmina (sixteenth): 1/2 osmina
Pud: 40 funts, 36.113 lbs. (US), 40 lbs. (Russian),
  16.38 kg
Rad: 14 puds, 505.58 lbs.
Zolotnik: 1/96 lbs., 4.26 grams

Money

Altyn: 6 Muscovite dengas, 3 copecks
Bel: Rus, pure silver coin
Chervonets (chervonnyi): gold coin of first
  half of 18th century worth c. 3 rubles
Chetvertak: silver coin equal to 25 copecks or
  1/4 ruble (18–19th centuries)
Copeck: two Muscovite dengas
Denga: 1/2 copeck
Grivna: 20 Muscovite dengas, 100 grivnas
  equals 1 ruble, 10 copecks
Grosh: 10 peniaz
Grosh litovsky (Lithuanian grosh): 5 silver
  copecks
Kopa grosh: 60 groshas, one Muscovite
  poltina, 1/2 ruble
Kuna: 12th-century Rus coin comparable to
  Westerns denarii or Eastern dirhems.
  Varied in value by region. Replaced late
  14th century by the denga or serebro
  (silver). Also a marten skin.
Moskovka: 1/2 copeck
Muscovite denga: 200 equals 1 ruble
Novgorod denga: 100 equals 1 ruble
Novgorodka: 1 copeck

Peniaz: 10 equals one grosh (Lithuania)
Poltina (poltinnik): 50 copecks, 100 dengas,
  1 ruble
Poltora: 1 1/2 rubles
Polupoltina (-nik): 25 copecks, 50 dengas
Rezan: 12th century Rus coin. 50 rezan equals one
  grivna kuna
Ruble: 100 copecks, 200 dengas
Shiroky grosh (large silver coin): 20 Muscovite
  copecks
Veksa: 12th-century Rus small coin equal to one
  squirrel pelt (belka)

Foreign Denominations
Chervonnyi: c. 3 rubles
Ducat: c. 3 rubles
Dutch efimok: "lion dollar" or levok, 1 thaler, 2.5
  guilders
Efimok: foreign currency, 1 thaler, .75-1 ruble, 1
  chervonets or chervonnyi
Levok: Dutch silver lion dollar
Thaler (Joachimsthaler): c. 1 ruble, 1/3 chervonets
  or chervonnyi

Note: Weights and measures often changed values over time and sometimes held more than one value at the same time. For details consult Sergei G. Pushkarev, *Dictionary of Russian Historical Terms from the Eleventh Century to 1917* (Yale, 1970).

0   200 miles

Onega

N. Dvina

Volkhov • Ladoga • Beloozero

• Novgorod

Pskov • Staraia Russa

• Yaroslavl

• Rostov *Volga*

Suzdal •

Kliazma • Vladimir

• Murom

Bulgar •

W. Dvina

Volga

Neman

Polotsk • Smolensk

Gdansk

Minsk

Dnieper

• Novgorod Seversky

Vistula

W. Bug

Pripiat

Turov • • Liubech

Seim

Vladimir-in-Volhynia •

• Chernigov

Don

Cracow •

• Cherven Kiev •

Peremyshl •

• Pereiaslavl

Ros

Dniester

Bug *Dnieper*

Prut • Peresechen

Dnieper

• Sarkel

Volga

Itil •

• Bîrlad • Oleshie

Don

Kuma

Kerch •

• Tmutorokan

Danube

Dorystolum

Sardica Preslav •

Sugdaea

Cherson

B L A C K   S E A

Constantinople •

• Trebizond

© Academic International Press 2001

LAND OF RUS

B   A   L   T   I   C   S   E   A

PREFACE

This volume is a complete translation of the first five chapters of the second volume of S.M. Soloviev's *Istoriia Rossii s drevneishikh vremen* (History of Russia from Earliest Times, 29 volumes, St. Petersburg, 1851-1879). It corresponds to Book I, pp. 343-499 of the fifteen-volume edition published in Moscow in 1959 to 1966.

The chapters of the original are of uneven duration and some of them excessively long. Therefore the editor has inserted additional chapter breaks. Chapters I and II correspond with those in Soloviev's original Volume II, and to pages 343-349 and 350-370 respectively of Book I in the Moscow edition. Chapter III in the original has been divided into Chapters III and IV in the translation, corresponding to Book I, pages 371-401 and 401-410. Soloviev's Volume II, Chapter IV, similarly has been divided into Chapters V and VI of the translation, corresponding to Book I, pages 411-456 and 456-499 respectively. The final chapter, Volume II, Chapter V, in the original, corresponds to Chapter VII in the translation and Book I, pages 500-527 in the "gray" edition.

The aim of the translation has been to reproduce the work in a form and style appropriate to an English text of this register. This means that, while aiming for scrupulous accuracy in conveying Soloviev's meaning, I have felt free to modify his syntax, sentence structure, etc., in conformity with the usage of English-language scholarly prose. In a similar manner Soloviev's paragraphs, which are extremely long, have been broken into smaller units, and sectional headings have been provided at intervals within the chapters, all of which will, it is hoped, assist the reader in his use of the book.

Every effort has been made to avoid using unfamiliar Russian terminology. Where a Russian term has passed into normal English usage it is retained in its standard English form, for example boyar. Otherwise an equivalent English term is used, and if necessary this is signalled in a footnote at its first occurrence. In fact there are very few instances in the present volume, which does not deal with the minutiae of legal or administrative affairs, where such specialized terminology occurs.

Similar considerations have informed the treatment of proper names. Where a Russian personal name differs only slightly from its English equivalent, the latter is preferred, so, for example, Aleksandr is rendered as Alexander. Names that differ substantially, such as Ivan or Viacheslav, are retained in their Russian form, and not turned into John and Wenceslas. Established English forms, where they exist, are always used for kings, emperors and other historical personages from other countries, including the Greek clergy who served in the Land of Rus. Otherwise, native usage is followed within the typographical limitations of the edition. Polovetsian names are given in the form used by Soloviev, which is that of his sources the chronicles, without any attempt to reconstruct their Turkic original, as this could only be hypothetical.

Geographical names have their usual English forms where there is one, otherwise their native forms, except for Ukrainian and Polish localities which in the eleventh and twelfth centuries were within the Land of Rus. In these cases I have felt that it would be less confusing to the English-speaking reader to follow the usual practice of histories of Russia written in English and use the Russian forms, which are also those used by Soloviev. The reader thus will find the familiar Chernigov, Galich and Peremyshl on these pages, rather than the more strictly accurate Chernihiv, Halych and Przemysl.

The Library of Congress system of transliteration has been used, omitting diacritics and ligatures and with certain modifications as follows. Initial "Ia-" and "Iu-" are rendered as "Ya-" and "Yu-" ("Yury Yaroslavich"). The diphthongs "-ai," "-ei" and "-oi" are replaced in final position by "ay," "ey" and "oy" ("Supoy," etc.). In personal names the final "-ii" and "-iia" are replaced by "-y" and "-ia" ("Dolgoruky," "Maria"). Before vowels the soft sign is indicated by "-i-" ("Soloviev"); elsewhere it is omitted.

Soloviev's original *History* was furnished abundantly with footnotes, and more were provided by the editors of the edition of 1959-1966.

Almost all of these have been omitted in the present translation, referring as they do largely to primary sources. Any reader requiring these presumably would have access to Soloviev's original text anyway. Footnotes giving more general information, notably about geographical locations, have been retained, and additional notes are supplied giving brief information on persons, events and circumstances that may not be immediately familiar to the general reader.

Professor G. Edward Orchard's watchful editorial supervision, exercised with exemplary patience during this volume's extended gestation, has rescued it from a number of shortcomings proceeding from my inexperience and oversights. For any that remain I can only beg the reader's indulgence.

R.M. Cleminson

INTRODUCTION

The period covered by this volume, from the middle of the eleventh century to the middle of the twelfth, is unmarked, as far as the Land of Rus is concerned, by great events. There is nothing to match the baptism of Rus of the tenth century, nor the Mongol invasions of the thirteenth. No radical transformation of the land takes place, nor does history take any new direction over these years. Nor is it a period of stagnation. The Land of Rus was by no means the same at the end of it as it was during the reign of Yaroslav the Wise, for the land and its institutions evolved steadily during this century, which perhaps presents the classic image of Kievan Rus. If no great events characterize the age, there was certainly no shortage of small ones. Indeed at times it seems to be a mad cascade of battles and campaigns, accessions and depositions, alliances and betrayals.

By the beginning of the period in question the Land of Rus already was forged into what was recognizably a state in medieval terms. The two long reigns of St. Vladimir (980-1015) and his son Yaroslav the Wise (1019-1054), combined with the adoption of Christianity as the official religion of the country, provided the conditions of stability and progress in which something like a national identity could develop from the tribal groupings and warrior bands of earlier times. This emergent nation consisted fundamentally of the Eastern Slavs, but its ruling caste was not Slavonic in origin. It was descended from the Scandinavian adventurers and colonists known to the Slavs as Rus (from the Finnish ruotsi, meaning Swede), whose forays into Eastern Europe were part of the same Nordic expansion as produced the Viking raids in the West, which themselves led to the establishment of Norman states in Normandy and Sicily.

As they established themselves amongst the Slavs, the Rus were assimilated to the native population. As early as the first half of the ninth century they were beginning to adopt Slavonic names and to speak Slavonic dialects. The last of the Kievan princes to maintain intimate ties with Scandinavia was Yaroslav the Wise, married to the daughter of Olof

Skötkonung, whose court was for a time home to the great Viking leader Harald Hardrada who fell at Stamford Bridge trying to wrest the crown of England from Harold Godwinson. In the following generations the princes' outlook was directed more to the South and West than to the North, and although in the time of Yaroslav's sons some distinction still occasionally was made between the Rus and the rest of the population, the name was coming more and more to be applied to the people as a whole.

It is important to remember that amongst the Slavs at this period national designations referred to peoples rather than countries. The Rus were a people; when they wanted to refer to the geographical area that they inhabited, they called it Russkaia zemlia, the Land of Rus. The Greeks, whose concept of the nation was more advanced, coined the word Rossia for it, although the better informed Byzantine writers also refer to *"he rossike ge,"* the Land of Rus, and this Greek word in turn was borrowed by the Russians when at the beginning of the sixteenth century they began to feel the need for such a term to describe their own country. In the eleventh century, though, the name Rus had no such geographical or ethnic limits. Although the Eastern Slavs even then were not a homogeneous people, all could identify themselves as Rus, and the Land of Rus was all the territory that they inhabited or ruled.

There was, to be sure, even at this stage some tendency towards a localization of the term. There is a particular tendency to identify it with the heartland of Norse colonization around Kiev, so that the Novgorod chronicles, for example, frequently speak of someone going "to Rus" when they mean that he went to Kiev or the surrounding territories. The same sort of thing happened elsewhere in the Land of Rus (in its broad sense) at other focuses of national identity. Thus we find a "Red Rus" (Rus Czerwona) on the Polish marches, and it would not be long before the prince of Galich would be styling himself rex Russiae. The Byzantines, finding that their Rossia was dividing into two political entities with their respective centers in Vladimir-Suzdal and Galich, distinguished them as "the Great" and "the Little," which is the origin of the term "Little Russia" for Ukraine. The last and most successful appropriation of the name was by the Great Russian state based on Moscow, but no hint of this was yet in evidence.

The Land of Rus was always a fragile political unit, and the forces tending towards its dissolution are illustrated amply by the century following the death of Yaroslav, who indeed maintained the unity of his realm simply by eliminating his rivals for power, and the settlement he made for his heirs had as its object avoidance of the fratricidal strife attending his own accession. In this there was a degree of success in that at least Yaroslav's own death was not followed by the bloodshed that ensued upon his father's or his grandfather's decease. The price was the perpetual presence in the realm of a number of actual or potential contenders for power. Only when Kiev was in the hands of an individual such as Vladimir Monomakh, so much more powerful than the other princes that none of them realistically could challenge him, did the Land of Rus enjoy unity and stability.

A great deal of Soloviev's attention is devoted to the principles of succession in Kievan Rus and his analysis, though refined and developed by more recent scholarship, remains fundamentally valid. Central to the question is the fact that the Land of Rus, like other Northern and Eastern European lands at this time, was not regarded as the possession of a monarch descending lineally to a single heir, but rather as the patrimony of the entire ruling kindred, each member of which had a legitimate interest in the country.

Yaroslav's problem was thus to ensure that each of his heirs received an adequate share of the inheritance but was not thereby encouraged to strive for supremacy over his brethren and their exclusion from their patrimony. His solution was to divide his realm amongst his three eldest surviving sons, each of whom received a major principality and its dependencies for himself and his descendants. Iziaslav was to have Turov, Sviatoslav obtained Chernigov, while Vsevolod received Pereiaslavl. No such provision was made for their younger brothers Viacheslav and Igor, perhaps on account of their youth. Although on their father's death they received Smolensk and Vladimir-in-Volhynia respectively, these seem to have been personal, and alienable, possessions without dynastic significance. The two most important principalities, Kiev and Novgorod, were excluded from the division of the realm. They remained the patrimony of the whole family, to be ruled by the grand prince, its senior member.

The inheritance of the grand-princely throne, as well as of the individual patrimonies, was governed by the principle of lateral succession,[1] that is to say, the inheritance passed not (necessarily) from father to son, but always to the next most senior member of the family, whoever that might be. This ensured that he who ruled the patrimony of any particular kindred was in fact the senior member of that kindred. If a prince was survived by brothers, he was succeeded by the eldest of them; if not, he was succeeded by the most senior of the next generation, be he son or nephew, whose father had at some time ruled the domain in question. This last provision is most important, meaning that no one had rights of inheritance over lands never ruled by his own father.

The intention of Yaroslav's settlement is thus clear. His sons' rights of inheritance were assured by the division of the realm whereas Kiev and Novgorod, possession of which ensured a preeminence of power, were attached to the grand-princely dignity and excluded from the permanent possession of any particular line. Yaroslav perhaps remembered that both he and his father Vladimir had used Novgorod as the base from which they had launched their successful wars against their own brothers. The princes thus were evenly matched in terms of their own patrimonies yet each could hope eventually to inherit Kiev legitimately in the natural course of events, and these considerations would act as a disincentive for any to encroach upon another's rights.

Given the essential concept of the realm as the possession of the whole family, and that of the nature of seniority within the family, both of which were central to the princes' understanding of their position, this system does seem to provide in theory for the logical and just regulation of succession. Certainly the princes do not seem to have been able to devise anything better. When Yaroslav's grandsons met to resolve their differences at Liubech in 1096 their decision was that "each should retain his patrimony," in other words that they abide by the provisions of Yaroslav's settlement.

Moreover, the system was not peculiar to the Land of Rus. Almost exactly the same provision was made for the sons of Bolesław Krzywousty. When he died in 1138, Poland was divided amongst them into hereditary patrimonies, while the chief city of Cracow and certain other territories were excluded from the division and were to be held by the senior prince. The consequences for Poland were very similar to the consequences of Yaroslav's division for the Land of Rus. Professor Pritsak has indicated similar systems of inheritance amongst various Turkic peoples, and even the division of Charlemagne's empire amongst his sons and the subsequent patterns of succession suggest similar attitudes towards the realm and its rulers' rights over it.

Although it may have seemed in principle the best means of regulating the succession, this system of inheritance proved far from ideal in practice. Its most obvious weakness perhaps was that the princes could not be expected to die in order of seniority. It frequently occurred that a prince died without having succeeded to his inheritance, thus leaving his sons excluded from the succession. These dispossessed princes, or izgoi, often constituted a disturbing element within the body politic. If their father died possessed of a patrimony of his own they at least could divide it amongst themselves, reproducing on a smaller scale the division of the whole realm amongst the sons of Yaroslav. In such a case their legitimate interests henceforth were confined to their own patrimony. The result was the emergence of a number of local dynasties and the fragmentation of the Land of Rus into a multiplicity of principalities whose rulers were likely to put their own immediate interests above those of the realm as a whole. If the dispossessed princes had no adequate inheritance of their own they must either be content with whatever provision might be made for them by the rest of the family, who were hardly disposed to enrich them at their own expense, or win a principality for themselves by their own enterprise, energy and force of arms. If successful, they also established local dynasties; whether successful or not, they troubled the land considerably by their efforts.

The system of inheritance prevailing in the Land of Rus thus contained the seeds of its inevitable fragmentation, a process which continued with each succeeding generation. Moreover, although it went some way towards regulating the order of succession, it did not limit it. At any time there were a number of princes claiming the right to succeed should they find themselves the senior member of the clan.

Therefore it is crucially important to realize that the criteria for determining the seniority were not clearly defined, especially as the family grew larger and more diffuse. Descent alone certainly meant very little. When Vladimir Monomakh died in 1125 there were still living two sons of Sviatopolk, his predecessor on the throne of Kiev, namely Briacheslav and Iziaslav. Their right to be included within the succession is indisputable, and they were moreover representatives of the senior line of the descendants of Yaroslav the Wise, being the grandsons of Iziaslav, the eldest of his sons reigning in Kiev after him. Yet it does not seem to have occurred to anyone that they should succeed Monomakh. The reason is plain. Whatever their descent, Briacheslav and Iziaslav were by no means the senior representatives of their own generation. That position belonged without doubt to Monomakh's son Mstislav, who was twenty-eight years older than Briacheslav, the elder of the two, and even more senior in terms of power. Accordingly it was he that became the next grand prince.

Briacheslav and Iziaslav died not long afterwards, in 1127 or 1128, and with them the rights of the descendants of Iziaslav Yaroslavich to Kiev. As for the descendants of the other two sons of Yaroslav the Wise who had reigned there, the position of the junior line, the descendants of Vsevolod and his son Vladimir Monomakh, was secure, while that of the descendants of Sviatoslav was anomalous. Sviatoslav predeceased his elder brother Iziaslav by two years, which might be considered, on the one hand, to exclude his sons from the succession. On the other hand, he actually had reigned as grand prince in Kiev, having deposed his brother, and his sons therefore could expect to inherit the city of which he had enjoyed the real possession. This uncertainty was the cause of much contention within the Land of Rus, for the descendants of Monomakh naturally were disposed to ignore the claims of their cousins of Sviatoslav's line, who were equally inclined to aspire to the senior throne when one of them attained a position of seniority within the family. This in fact was realized by Vsevolod Olgovich in 1139.

Even in the countries of Western Europe where there was a clearly defined system of lineal succession a weak ruler always was vulnerable to usurpation by a mightier kinsman, but there it was usually clear on whose side right lay. Among the princes of Rus the right to the senior throne was determined not by lineal descent, but by de facto seniority within the family. When this was clear and indisputable, as in the reign of Vladimir Monomakh, there was order within the realm. At other times internecine strife was inevitable as the various contenders for the seniority strove to establish themselves. This was the consequence of a state of affairs where it was not the throne of Kiev that bestowed preeminence among the princes, but preeminence of power that gained the throne.

Soloviev himself seems to shrink from such a conclusion, reluctant to see the chaotic feuding of the eleventh and twelfth centuries as inherent within the constitution of Rus. It would perhaps seem to derogate from the dignity of the realm to ascribe these events to endemic weakness rather than to the ambition of contumacious individuals. Soloviev tends, in fact, to take "the state" somewhat for granted, and to assume the existence of a Rus nation without exploring the question of what such an entity might be, or considering the similarities and differences which might exist between it and other surrounding national units.

Soloviev actually does little to provide a European, still less an Asiatic, context for his history of the Land of Rus. His discussion of other countries aims not to describe the wider historical processes of the age, rather is confined to events taking place there in so far as they impinge directly upon the affairs of the Land of Rus, and more particularly upon Kiev. This focus on Kiev is indeed a reason why he devotes so little attention to other European powers, for the Kievan lands had no common borders with them. It was in Galich that the influence of Hungary and Poland was chiefly felt, and in Novgorod that the interests of Rus enmeshed, for good or ill, with those of Sweden and the other peoples of the Baltic.[2]

Even more serious, in terms of a complete understanding of the nature of the Land of Rus, is Soloviev's silence about the Byzantine empire. This too is explicable, for their relations at this period were chiefly in the ecclesiastical and commercial spheres, both of which Soloviev evidently saw as outside the scope of his work. Byzantium was the creator of the Land of Rus, for it was the wealth of that realm that drew the first Northmen along the Dnieper trade route "from the Varangians to the Greeks," and the Byzantine trade was still essential to the prosperity of Kiev. The Land of Rus was further bound to Byzantium by its acceptance of Eastern Rite Christianity as its official religion.[3] The church in Rus was still young in the eleventh century. Indeed it is doubtful whether the new faith extended much beyond the towns and the immediate protection of the princes. Christianity was still dependent on Constantinople. The head of the church in Rus, the metropolitan of Kiev, was a Greek appointed by and from Constantinople; the very rare exceptions, such as Hilarion in 1052, are clear deviations from normal practice. The metropolitan was responsible for appointing the other bishops in the land, many of whom were also Greeks. Only in the case of Novgorod did the citizens enjoy some autonomy in their choice of bishop, but even this never was recognized formally by the metropolitanate.

By their adoption of Eastern Rite Christianity the princes of Rus moreover included their land within the Byzantine Commonwealth,[4] and accepted the Byzantine outlook regarding the nature of their country and its position in the world. The officially acknowledged culture of the country was henceforth Byzantine, and this heritage did much to determine the perceptions of its princes and its chroniclers.

Least of all has Soloviev to say about those peoples who did not create a realm, the Finnic tribes of the North and the Turkic nomads of the steppes, whose religion and way of life placed them outside the oikoumene of civilized nations. Since history as written by Soloviev was essentially the history of the state, peoples failing to evolve corresponding institutions are effectively left outside the historical record, especially since they left no written histories. Soloviev mentions them almost exclusively in the context of the princes' wars, in campaigns undertaken against them or in alliance with them.

This is particularly noticeable in Soloviev's treatment of the Polovetsians. The position of Kiev near the southern edge of the wooded steppe meant that its territories stood on the border between two ways of life, the sedentary culture of the forest zone and the nomadic ways of the steppe. The first was represented by the Slavs, and by their Baltic and Finnic neighbors further north, and the latter by a succession of Turkic peoples, the dominant group during the period covered by this volume being the Polovetsians, also known as Kipchaks or Cumans. The clash between these two types of culture, which has been regarded as one of the cardinal processes of history, is manifested in the frequent Polovetsian raids upon the Land of Rus, and the reprisals undertaken by the princes of Rus against the Polovetsians.

It should not be thought that the division between the two modes of existence was absolute. The Torks, one of the smaller Turkic peoples, with their town of Torchesk, seem to have taken some steps along the way towards a settled way of life. The chronicles' description of the behavior of Prince Sviatoslav (964-972), his incessant campaigning, his raids on richer lands, and his preference for the banks of the Danube over his own town of Kiev suggest that he had succumbed to the lure of the steppe. In later days the pages of the chronicles and of Soloviev bear occasional references to the brodniki (pl.), apparently Slavs who adopted the nomadic way of life.

Soloviev sees this interaction primarily in terms of the clash of cultures. The "barbarians of the steppes" are fundamentally the enemies of the Land of Rus, an alien race whose relationship to the Rus was essentially and immutably hostile. Yet in reality the people of the steppes were Kiev's closest neighbors. There was extensive intermarriage between ruling families, and individuals of Turkic race appear in the retinues of the princes of Rus. The Polovetsian language was known in Rus, and it seems clear that there was constant contact between the two peoples, by no means always of a hostile nature. Even if it was in principle reprehensible to bring down the godless sons of Hagar on the Land of Rus, the shifting alliances between khans and princes rarely were overruled by national loyalties.

Soloviev, in describing the Polovetsians as hostile and alien to the Land of Rus, faithfully reflects the attitude of his sources, the chronicles, which express an implacable enmity between the two peoples even as they record events that belie it.[5] It must be remembered that the chronicles have come down to us in recensions later than the Tartar invasions and hegemony, and that they reflect attitudes developed over those years; that subsequent centuries of Russian history have done little to promote feelings of affinity with the peoples of the East; and that Asiatic elements were the last thing that Soloviev, a Westernizer in the intellectual climate of nineteenth-century Russia, was looking for in the origins of the Russian nation. He is more likely to have been projecting back onto the eleventh century the nineteenth-century image of Russia as the last bastion of European civilization against the Asiatic hordes.

It must be said that nineteenth-century preoccupations do color Soloviev's presentation of the middle ages. The very title of his work, *The History of Russia from Earliest Times,* suggests that in describing the history of the Land of Rus he was concerned with the origins of the modern Russian state. It is perhaps the weakest point in his approach to the medieval period that he sees it in terms of what was to come afterwards. He shares the rectilinear view of Russian history that dominated both nineteenth-century and Soviet historiography, and which essentially perceives the Russian state as a single entity shifting its center from Kiev to Vladimir to Moscow. This in turn affects both the focus of his attention and his evaluation of events and personalities.

In the first place, this is seen in the way Soloviev effectively identifies the Land of Rus with the principality of Kiev. Partly, it is true, this arises from his reliance on Kievan sources, but this is far from sufficient to account for the concentration of his narrative on the grand-princely seat to the neglect of other centers of population and political activity in the realm. This is particularly striking in a period when Kiev's importance was declining and that of other cities such as Suzdal, Galich and Smolensk was increasing. There is nothing in Soloviev's narrative to suggest this. Rather it gives the impression that Suzdal was an obscure outpost in the

North and Galich a troublesome frontier province. This in turn makes it hard to understand why, for example, Yury Dolgoruky is such a dominant figure as prince of Suzdal, or why Galich affairs figure so largely in the *History*.

One reason is Soloviev's exclusion of economic history from his study. Modern scholarship generally attributes the shifts in power in twelfth-century Rus to shifts in the patterns of economic activity, notably the trade routes, which tended to favor the North and West at the expense of Kiev. Soloviev thus leaves unexplained the processes by which Suzdal and Galich developed into centers of political power in their own right, with their own interests, particularistic aspirations and institutions. For a number of reasons the process of individualization is more marked in Galich. Its geographical position meant that its rulers and people were concerned with relations with Hungary and Poland at least as much as with the other principalities of Rus, and both these nations intervened actively in Galich affairs. There were also dynastic ties with these nations. The social structure of this land also reveals closer ties with the nations to the West, and the Galich boyars, more influential than in other principalities, in some ways resemble the Hungarian nobility as much as they do the followers of the other princes of Rus. Furthermore, Galich was ruled by princes who had no title to the Kievan throne, and who were the more concerned with establishing the power and independence of their own patrimony.

The position in Suzdal was quite different. Even further from the nations of the West than Kiev, it also was far removed from the peoples of the steppes and their depredations that loomed so large in the affairs of Kiev and its immediate neighbors. This in itself may have contributed to its rise. Being distant from the arena of the princely feuds, which chiefly concerned the older established cities of the South, it had little involvement in them until the days of Yury Dolgoruky, by which time it was sufficiently powerful to play a role of its own. The character of the northern towns remained distinct, and the difference between the produce of the two regions, indicating the inhabitants' activity and their trading orientations, is reflected in the exchange of gifts between Iziaslav of Kiev and his brother Rostislav of Smolensk in 1148.[6]

Since Suzdal remained in the hands of the princes of the ruling dynasty, its rulers' aspirations continued to be linked to the Kievan succession. Yury Dolgoruky held the throne of Kiev for three brief and insecure periods between 1149 and his death in 1157. Even during his lifetime his son Andrei Bogoliubsky realized that the family's true interests lay with its firm power base in the North, not with the ancient senior throne. It was Andrei who brought the political structures of the land into line with reality by choosing in 1169 to rule as grand prince in Vladimir, reducing Kiev to the status of a junior principality.

The way Soloviev describes, or fails to describe, these processes is determined by his conception of the Russian state, and his attitude to the Land of Rus as the first stage of its development. He views the Land of Rus as a single entity the unity of which is maintained, despite its division into more or less autonomous principalities, by the fact that the entire land is regarded by the princes as the heritage of the whole family, and that each prince's tenure is conditional upon his seniority within the clan. He does not draw the logical conclusion that when any territory became the patrimony of any group within the family, and when that group's rights of inheritance became restricted to its patrimony and ceased to embrace the land as a whole, the identification of the whole land with the whole family was effectively broken and the basis for its unity destroyed. On the contrary, Soloviev constantly stresses the singularity of the land, and presents the development of Galich in the direction of independent statehood, for example, not as a process naturally arising from the constitution of Rus, but rather one contradicting its essential character.

The reason would appear to be his teleological view of the Land of Rus as the forerunner of the modern Russian state, which caused him to endow it prematurely with certain characteristics of what it became, and make it a unitary entity centered upon Kiev. The entire volume is written from the Kievan point of view, and Soloviev tends to view any developments tending against the political unity of the Land of Rus and the dominance of the grand prince of Kiev in a very negative light. Historical processes are evaluated less by their effectiveness in coping with prevailing conditions than by the extent to which they furthered the anticipated end.

This is clearly seen in Soloviev's attitude to the two dominant figures of the age, Vladimir Monomakh and Yury Dolgoruky. His admiration for Vladimir is evident throughout, notwithstanding his sober assessment of his achievements as essentially conservative, re-establishing the order of his grandfather's reign rather than contributing anything new to the constitution of the land. The fact remains that Vladimir was a successful ruler, and his greatest successes were achieved after he acceded, in strict order of seniority, to the throne of Kiev. His indisputable dominance in terms of real power enabled him to act as an effective leader of the whole Land of Rus, and he used his position to conduct successful military campaigns against the Polovetsians. In short, he was Soloviev's ideal prince. He also has the great advantage of having been portrayed favorably by the medieval chroniclers and, alone among the princes of Rus, appears to posterity not merely through the record of the chronicles but also through a partly autobiographical composition of his own, the Admonition, which enables us to see him much more as a living personality.

Yury, by contrast, appears as a brooding presence in the North, for whom Soloviev has an undisguised antipathy. Based outside Kiev, he appears from time to time in arms undermining the authority of the grand prince and threatening the unity of the princes. Viewed from a different perspective, Yury's achievements may appear more enduring than his father's. While the lure of Kiev may have brought no good to him or anyone else, the establishment of the ascendancy of Suzdal represented both Yury's personal accomplishment as a ruler and assured the future of the Land of Rus.

In spite of Soloviev's identification of the fortunes of Rus with those of Kiev there is one other center to which he does devote some attention. This is Novgorod.[7] Riurik's city could not be ignored, and its position amongst the cities of Rus was a unique one. Novgorod and Kiev were from the earliest times the two most important cities of Rus, and both were excluded from the partition of the land at the death of Yaroslav, remaining subject to the grand prince alone. Thus it was excluded from the system of succession, never becoming the dominion of any individual prince, and retained its formal allegiance to the grand prince throughout its existence. Because of its great distance from Kiev he could not rule it in person, instead ruled it through his representatives, the prince and the posadnik, or mayor.

The prince of Novgorod did not rule in his own right, like the other princes. Indeed in many senses he did not rule at all, for his functions were strictly circumscribed, and came to be confined largely to military and certain judicial matters. Novgorod typically was given to one of the junior princes, very often a son of the prince of Kiev, who was thus assured of his cooperation. With the passage of time, as the authority of the grand prince grew less absolute, the city came to have more of a say in the appointment and dismissal of its prince, though never to the extent of obtaining an entirely free choice. The prince continued to be "given" by the grand prince at the citizens' petition, though the extent to which the grand prince could impose a prince of his own choice, whom the citizens were obliged to tolerate, was legally undefined and depended upon the realities of power.

In this way the changing fortunes of the rest of the land were reflected in Novgorod. Thus when Iziaslav Yaroslavich regained the throne of Kiev on the death of his brother Sviatoslav in 1076 he removed Sviatoslav's son Gleb from Novgorod and replaced him with his own son Sviatopolk. Novgorod itself, however, never became an object of contention in the same way as Kiev, nor did it intervene in the feuding in the South. Even so its citizens were not averse to making use of the rivalries of the other princes to support rival candidates for their own leadership.

The most important individual in the government of Novgorod was the posadnik, or mayor, as the word is usually translated in reference to Novgorod, where he was an individual elected by the citizens from among their own number. Originally he was a burgrave or viceroy appointed by the grand prince, and the word continued to have this meaning elsewhere in the Land of Rus, where a prince appointed a posadnik in any city he could not administer in person or entrust to a junior member of his house. In Novgorod, where the prince was an appointee, and sovereignty vested in a distant absentee, power became concentrated in the hands of an oligarchy dominated by the city's commercial interests. These operated through the veche or town assembly, an institution which may be older than the Land of Rus itself but which seems to have carried little political weight in the princely patrimonies.

This shift of power away from the grand prince to the citizens, which was decisive during the first half of the twelfth century, was the result of the decline in the authority of the Kievan prince over the whole Land of Rus and the special features of Novgorod and its life. Novgorod's wealth was founded upon trade, especially the Baltic trade, and its life was ruled by commercial interests as nowhere else in the Land of Rus. In this respect it has been compared with the Hanseatic towns or the city-states of the Adriatic. Soloviev, as ever, omits these considerations from his narrative, and concentrates on the visible manifestations of political life, the changes of prince or mayor. Still, the fact that Novgorod in many ways lived its own life, moved by forces other than those that governed the rest of the Land of Rus, means that his account of events there often seems poorly integrated into the rest of his history.

An awareness of the limitations or perhaps rather the limits of Soloviev's *History,* however necessary for the modern reader, should not make us disregard what he in fact produced. This is effectively the record of the public acts of the princes. On these pages there are no women, no priests, unless like Bishop Anthony of Chernigov they are unwise enough to dabble in politics, no merchants and no husbandmen. There is little explicit analysis. "Proceeding haphazardly in their exposition of the basic facts," wrote P.N. Petrov in 1886, "confining themselves to a paraphrase of the various recensions of the chronicle, our historians, not excluding Karamzin himself, have touched only lightly upon the reasons for events, and unfolded their development in a one-sided manner, often attributing to the arbitrary actions of an individual that which was the direct result of the irreversible progress of circumstances of which they were unaware."[8] Though this is harsh criticism, perhaps excessively so, Soloviev cannot be entirely immune from it. The concept of the scope of history that emerges from his pages is not modern, not even that of his own time, but a medieval one, that of his sources the chronicles.

It is of course admirable that Soloviev drew his history almost entirely from primary sources, specifically the first three volumes of the *Complete Collection of Russian Chronicles,* which were published in the 1840s and thus available to him when he was working on this volume. They contain the Laurentian, Hypatian and Novgorod First, Second and Third chronicles, collectively some of the most valuable sources for the history of Rus. The Laurentian and the Hypatian chronicles are the oldest texts, written respectively in 1377 and the middle of the fifteenth century, of the so-called Primary Chronicle, also known as the Tale of Bygone Years, which reflects the interests of the Kievan dynasty, and also forms the nucleus of many subsequent compilations and continuations. It is associated with the name of Nestor, a monk of the Caves monastery in Kiev, and though it would be wrong to regard him as the "author" of the chronicle, it is certainly possible that he was responsible for a redaction of the material believed to have been made in Kiev in 1111. This redaction, no longer extant, would have incorporated earlier historical writings, and itself would have undergone considerable modification in subsequent years to produce the surviving texts.[9] The Novgorod chronicles, of almost comparable antiquity, are particularly valuable for material relating to the North.

None of the chronicles were histories of the modern type, compiled at a single time by a single writer. On the contrary, each reached its present form as a result of a long process of compilation and revision. The chroniclers reproduced and added to the work of their predecessors, sometimes combining more than one source, sometimes expanding and sometimes abridging their material, all of which was itself the product of just such a process. Their revisions were, moreover, by no means mechanical, but reflected the circumstances of the chronicles' composition. Most frequently a chronicle was compiled at the court of a particular prince, in which case the chronicler would be at pains to present events in a manner favorable to that prince, his ancestors and political pretensions. Such considerations informed his editorial activity, determining which elements in his sources he chose to reproduce in his own chronicle, and which to omit, which events to recount in detail, and which to pass over briefly. The history of a single text thus can be immensely complex. For example, one of the stages in the development of the Primary Chronicle is held to be a redaction made in 1116 during Vladimir Monomakh's reign at Kiev, in which the material is presented in a light reflecting that prince's position.

We must not accuse the chroniclers of falsifying history. On the contrary, they seem in general to have been most conscientious in presenting the facts as they understood them, albeit in a manner agreeable to their patrons. Yet it follows that the more editorial activity the narrative has undergone, the further it is removed from the events it recounts. This is particularly serious in respect of some of the other sources available to Soloviev, of which the two he used the most extensively seem to have been the Nikon Chronicle,[10] a vast seventeenth-century compilation which achieves comprehensiveness at the expense of considerable editorial intervention, and was published in St. Petersburg between 1767 and 1792, and the notoriously unreliable Joachim Chronicle which Soloviev seems to have known through the work of the eighteenth-century historian V.N. Tatishchev.[11]

Twentieth-century scholarship, beginning with the work of A.A. Shakhmatov around the turn of the century, has been very largely concerned with the textual history of the chronicles, using this to determine the reliability of the different texts. This, of course was unavailable to Soloviev. He does from time to time exhibit an awareness that the chronicles were written from a particular point of view, yet the only yardstick he can use to judge their reliability is his own conception of the Russian state and its historical development. This may represent a certain advance in sophistication over the meticulous documentation of his predecessor Karamzin,[12] but it does not necessarily result in sounder judgment. By and large Soloviev had to use the sources in their raw state, and for the most part he is content to retell in modern form the story told by the chronicles. If he does not attempt to transcend his material it is because, were he to do so, his history probably never would have been written.

Soloviev is one of the pioneers of modern historiography. He began to write his *History of Russia* in 1848 and continued to work on it until his death thirty-one years and twenty-nine volumes later, by which time he brought the narrative into the eighteenth century. It is obvious that the task he set himself was sufficiently vast even if he confined himself, as he did, to the narration of political events. This was, after all, the fundamental task. No historical scholarship is possible until it has been established as far as it can be what actually happened. For the century following the death of Yaroslav the Wise, a period characterized by a plethora of events of little individual significance for which even Karamzin doubted his ability to hold his readers' attention, this does indeed mean unraveling and synthesizing the chronicle accounts. This Soloviev has done, and this is his achievement, which remains valid.

HISTORY OF RUSSIA

Volume 2

Early Russia

1054-1157

I

CONCERNING PRINCELY RELATIONS

At his death Yaroslav I[1] left five sons, and a grandson by his eldest son Vladimir.[2] Polotsk was ruled by the descendants of Iziaslav, St. Vladimir's eldest son.[3] As the princes increased in number and received lands of their own, relations between them occupy the most prominent place in the chronicle account. What then was the nature of these relations?

In Western Europe at this time, in Latin and Germanic countries, feudal relations predominated. Rights and duties of feudal lords with respect to their overlords are known. In the other Slavonic countries the same system of relations between greater and lesser princes obtained as in Rus, but neither from Rus nor from any other of these countries do we have any document setting out the rights and duties of princes towards each other or towards the chief prince. The only means of learning the nature of the relations between princes is therefore to search the chronicles to see if they provide any indication of these rights and duties, whether the princes themselves say anything of the principles governing their relations.

The common ancestor of almost all the princely lines was Yaroslav I, who is regarded as the author of the first written civil code, the so-called Rus Justice,[4] so it might be expected that he would give his sons some code of behavior towards one another. Indeed the chronicles do record what purport to be Yaroslav's dying words, his testament to his sons. According to the chronicler, this is what he said to them before his death. "Now I am leaving this world, children. Love one another, for you are brothers, sons of the same father and mother. If you live in love for one another, God will be with you. He will subject all your enemies to you, and you shall live in peace. If you hate one another and quarrel, you will perish and will destroy the land of your fathers and grandfathers, which they obtained with such great labor. Therefore live in peace, obeying one another. My throne of Kiev I bequeath to my eldest son, your brother Iziaslav. Obey him as you have obeyed me, and regard him as occupying my place." Distributing the rest of the lands to his other sons, he instructed them to remain within their own territories, not to expel each other from them. Addressing his eldest son Iziaslav, he added, "If anyone does any wrong to his brother, help him who is wronged."[5]

INDIVISIBILITY OF THE CLAN

These are all his instructions, all their rights and duties! The princes are to love one another, obey one another, obey their eldest brother like a father. There is not a word about the rights of the younger brothers, not a word about their duties as subordinate rulers towards their eldest brother as sovereign of the whole land. Attention is called only to ties of blood and to family obligations. No mention is made of political ties or any political hierarchy. Love one another and do not quarrel, says Yaroslav, because you are children of one father and one mother. What if the princes are no longer children of the same father and mother, when they are first, second and third cousins, or even further removed? What motives will they have for loving one another and not quarrelling? When the ties of blood and family weaken and surcease, what will replace them? There is nothing to replace them, though hereditary ties are indeed powerful. Let us not forget that the descendants of Yaroslav ruled over tribes only recently emancipated from the patriarchal way of life which long held sway over them. Even after a century or a century and a half, when the princes multiplied and their lines diverged, they still all called themselves brothers without distinguishing degrees of kinship. The chronicles make no use of the terms "cousin" or "second cousin" in discussing princely relations. To this day the Russian language has no distinctive words denoting these relationships in the way that other languages do.[6]

SIGNIFICANCE OF THE CLAN ELDER OR GRAND PRINCE

The princes preserve the idea of the unity and indivisibility of their house, which is expressed in the fact that they all had one senior prince, who was always the senior member of the whole family. This meant that any member of the family might achieve the seniority, which was not tied exclusively to any one branch. In this way the house of the princes of Rus, despite all its ramifications, continued to be a single family—a father with children, grandchildren and so on.[7]

RIGHTS TO SENIORITY

What information is then to be obtained from the words of the chronicler, or from the words of the princes themselves as he records them, concerning the princes' attitude to their common overlord, their so-called father? The senior prince, like a father, was responsible for looking after the interests of the whole family, deliberating and taking counsel for the whole Land of Rus, for his own honor and that of all his kin. He held the right to judge and punish the junior princes, distributed lands to the princes, found husbands for their orphaned daughters. The junior princes were supposed to display the deepest respect and submissiveness to the senior, to regard him indeed as their father and be obedient to him, appear before him when summoned and take up arms when commanded. The relationship of junior princes to the senior was expressed by the junior prince riding at the elder's stirrup, having him as his lord, being at his disposal, and looking up to him.

LOSS OF SENIORITY RIGHTS

Still, all these definitions of rights and duties are of the same sort as those in Yaroslav's testament. The junior prince is to regard the senior as his father in deed and obey him like a father. The senior prince must love the junior like a son and care for the entire family as for his own soul. All rights and duties are conditioned by the sense of kinship, by familial love on either side, between fourth cousins, for example! As soon as this condition disappeared all ties and all subordination collapsed because there was no relationship other than that of kinship. The junior princes obeyed the senior as long as it seemed that he was behaving as a father to them, but if he behaved otherwise they took up arms. "You are our elder brother," they then said, "but if you wrong us and give us no lands, we will seek them for ourselves." Or "He is the oldest among us, but does not know how to get along with us." On one occasion the senior prince, irritated by the junior princes' disobedience, commanded them to vacate the principalities he had bestowed upon them. "You drive us from the Land of Rus without cause...," was their reply. "Hitherto we have honored you as a father, in love. If you send such messages to us, as are addressed not to princes but to subjects and commoners, do as you see fit. Let God judge among us all." They then had recourse to the judgment of God, that is, to war and open resistance. These words express clearly the idea of the sort of relations that our princes of old wished to have with their senior prince, since they contrast these relations with the sort they reject, demanding that he treat them as a father treats his children, not as an overlord treats his vassals or subjects. Family relationships are clearly and directly opposed to political relationships.

Thus did the princes themselves express their concept of relations between them. Now let us see how princely relations were envisaged by the remainder of the population, how the chronicler, as a representative of his literate contemporaries, expressed them. On one occasion when a junior prince disobeyed the senior prince and began hostilities the chronicler, condemning the junior prince, says that he failed to fulfill his obligations. Yet how does he understand these obligations? "This prince did wrong," he says, "to open hostilities against his uncle, and then against his father-in-law." In the chronicler's eyes the prince was wrong because he broke the obligations of kinship towards his uncle and father-in-law, and that is sufficient.

On occasions when the junior princes' own interests were not affected they behaved very respectfully towards the senior prince. If the senior prince asked his advice, the junior prince considered it a great honor. "Brother," said he, "you are older than I. Let it be as you decide, and I shall be ready to do your will. Yet since you do me the honor of asking my advice, this is what I counsel," and so on. When the junior princes' interests were affected, it was another matter. If the senior prince took it into his head to say "You have called me father, and as a father I have the right to punish you," the junior prince naturally replied that a good father does not punish his sons without cause, that he must declare what he did wrong before punishing him. Thus when Monomakh[8] and the sons of Sviatoslav[9] heard of the blinding of Vasilko,[10] they sent to Sviatopolk, the senior prince, saying "Why have you blinded your brother? Even if he was guilty, you ought to have accused him before us and to have punished him only after proving his guilt."

The senior distributed lands to the junior princes. When he really was their father, he could do this as he saw fit both during his lifetime and in the testament determining the distribution of lands after his death. When he was their father in name only he could not act arbitrarily because at the slightest offense a junior prince considered himself justified in seizing his due by force of arms. In fact the senior prince undertook nothing without conferring with the junior princes, or at least with those nearest to himself in seniority. This explains the plural verbs in the chronicles, *they* installed, *they* expelled, and so on, which indicate decisions taken by the whole family. Normally the senior prince *took counsel* with the junior princes in the distribution of lands. The princes also met to legislate or formulate the rules to govern their own behavior. Later, when the various princes' rights to the seniority grew confused, they sometimes came to agreements amongst themselves that if such and such a prince received the seniority he must surrender to another a certain territory. The unity of the princely house also was maintained by the fact that each of its members hoped that he in turn would achieve the seniority and the possessions pertaining to the grand-princely throne of Kiev. Seniority was founded upon physical seniority. Therefore an uncle had precedence over a nephew, an elder over younger brothers, a father-in-law over a son-in-law, an elder sister's husband over younger brothers-in-law, an older wife's brother over a younger sister's husband. Although during the period when kinship relations predominated amongst the princes we do find instances of nephews fighting against uncles (their fathers' younger brothers), they never dared put forward any claims of inheritance. Their pretensions, based upon mere circumstance must, with one exception, always give way to the rights of even the youngest uncles. We do find on occasion that certain princes and certain entire branches of the princely house were excluded from the succession, and that this exclusion was acknowledged as lawful. How could this come about? This may be determined by examining the way in which a prince attained the seniority and was promoted towards it.

At first the family consisted of father, sons, grandsons and so on. When the father died his place in the family was taken by the eldest brother. He became a father to the younger brothers, and consequently his children became their brothers, being promoted from the rank of grandsons to that of sons, because they no longer had a grandfather, the head of the family being their immediate father. Indeed, their uncles did address them as brothers. Their cousins, however, remained at the rank of grandsons, as minors[11] in precedence, because they still had two generations senior to them. Their eldest uncle was regarded as their fathers' father, and thus had the position of their grandfather. When this eldest brother died, the next brother took his place, becoming father to the remaining brothers. His own children were promoted from grandsons to sons and attained their majority. In this manner gradually all the young princes by means of their fathers' seniority attained their majority and themselves moved nearer to the senior position. Should a prince die before attaining the headship of the family, his sons remained at the rank of grandsons forever as minors, without means of further advancement. Thus it can be understood why a son could never attain the seniority if his father was never the head of the family. This is how the princes understood the order of their progress to seniority. "As our ancestors ascended the ladder to the grand principality of Kiev," they said, "so we also must ascend to it step by step." Further ascent became impossible once a rung was removed from the ladder. Princes thus excluded from the succession were included among the "dispossessed princes."[12]

Every member of the princely house in the right circumstances might attain the seniority and receive the senior throne of Kiev, which thus remained the common patrimony of the house. Did the other principalities remain the permanent inheritance of particular princely lines, or did they, according to the various degrees of seniority, pass from princes of one branch to those of another as they ascended the ladder? To answer this question we must look at how the princes behaved in the early days when the system of relations was not yet confused by various circumstances.

At the death of Yaroslav's fourth son Viacheslav, who was prince of Smolensk, his principality did not pass to his sons, rather was given to Yaroslav's fifth son Igor, previously prince of Volhynia, a clear sign that the principalities were not hereditary and that the princes moved from one to another according to their seniority, ascending step by step. Later, when Sviatoslav Yaroslavich[13] received the seniority and the throne of Kiev after his brother's expulsion his next brother Vsevolod, until then prince of Pereiaslavl, moved to Chernigov in place of Sviatoslav. A particular principality became the hereditary patrimony of an individual branch of the princely house only when a prince, for reasons described, lost the right to continue his progress up the ladder of seniority. Then, once he received a principality from his kin he and his posterity were confined to it forever, for movement from one principality to another was dependent upon progress up the ladder of seniority, from which dispossessed princes were excluded. This is how the separate principalities of Polotsk, Galich, Riazan and later Turov were formed. The descendants of Yaroslav's second son Sviatoslav, better known as the descendants of Oleg, also through force of circumstances very nearly were reduced to the lamentable condition of dispossessed princes. The principality of Chernigov itself was on the point of becoming a separate patrimony had not the descendants of Oleg eventually forced the descendants of Vladimir Monomakh to recognize their right to the succession. The inevitable result was that the Dnieper principalities once again became the common inheritance of both lines. A descendant of Oleg ascended the throne of Kiev, a descendant of Monomakh took his place in Chernigov.

PATRIMONY

In spite of this we encounter the word *patrimony* in the chronicles. Princes not excluded from the succession used this word to denote particular lands. In what sense did they use it, in its proper meaning of an hereditary possession, or some other? In 1097 the grandsons of Yaroslav met and decided that each retain his own patrimony. Sviatopolk was to have his father's land of Kiev, Vladimir Monomakh his father's land of Pereiaslavl, and the sons of Sviatoslav were to have Chernigov. These arrangements can hardly be understood if the word *patrimony* is taken to mean the hereditary possessions of a single line because in that sense Kiev was just as much the other princes' patrimony as it was Sviatopolk's, as both Vsevolod and Sviatoslav had ruled there. If Kiev here is not called Sviatopolk's patrimony in the sense of a hereditary possession exclusively for him and his descendants, there are no grounds for assuming that the word has a different meaning when it is applied to Pereiaslavl and Chernigov as the patrimonies of Monomakh and the sons of Sviatoslav. Another example from the eastern bank of the Dnieper is that in 1151 two descendants of Oleg,[14] Sviatoslav Olgovich and his nephew Sviatoslav Vsevolodovich, said to Iziaslav Davydovich "We have two patrimonies, one is that of my father Oleg, and the other is that of your father Davyd. You, brother, are a son of Davyd, and I am a son of Oleg so you, brother, take what belonged to your father Davyd, give what was Oleg's to us, and we will share it between ourselves." As a result Iziaslav Davydovich remained in Kiev, and gave the Novgorod Seversk lands to Oleg's family. Chernigov was just as much Sviatoslav Vsevolodovich's patrimony as Iziaslav Davydovich's because his father, Vsevolod Olgovich, was prince of Chernigov, and when Iziaslav became prince of Kiev he yielded his patrimony of Chernigov to Sviatoslav Olgovich.

What then was a patrimony? A prince's patrimony was a principality ruled by his father, which he too had a right to rule if he occupied the same position on the ladder of seniority as his father occupied when he ruled it. The right to rule was determined by the degree of seniority, by kinship reckonings.

SENIOR AND JUNIOR PRINCIPALITIES

There remains the question of the relation of the junior principalities to the senior. Relations between senior and junior princes were familial. The junior princes desired to be called the senior prince's sons, on no account subjects. This outlook also must have determined their attitude with regard to their lands. Rejecting subject status, they must also reject the payment of tribute as its most evident token. Nor could they allow any political submission of their principalities to the grand prince who, as a result, could not have the status of head of a realm, supreme ruler of the land, prince of all Rus with power to grant estates to be held by his vassals on a temporary or hereditary basis. The principalities were completely independent of each other and of Kiev, were separate lands. At the same time, together they constituted a single undivided whole by virtue of the ties of kinship between the princes, who regarded the whole land as their patrimony, the indivisible possession of the whole family.

II

THE SONS OF YAROSLAV I, 1054-1093

LINEAGE OF THE HOUSE OF RIURIK

After the death of Yaroslav I rule by the family as a whole long remained in force in Rus, though the territories occupied by the first Varangian-Rus princes were divided between two princely lines or *tribes* of the Riurik clan. The first consisted of the descendants of Iziaslav, St. Vladimir's eldest son, who received from his father the principality of Polotsk, which had belonged to his maternal grandfather Rogvolod.[1] Iziaslav died while his father was still alive, consequently never having been head of the family or grand prince. As a result his descendants could not progress towards the seniority and move from one principality to another. They were confined to Polotsk, which was confirmed as theirs under Yaroslav. The second line consisted of the descendants of Yaroslav Vladimirovich, who took possession of the remaining Rus territories. Yaroslav left five sons. The eldest, Iziaslav,[2] took *his father's place* in relation to his younger brothers Sviatoslav, Vsevolod, Viacheslav and Igor. There was also their nephew Rostislav, son of Yaroslav's eldest son Vladimir, who as a result of his father's untimely death had no hope of the seniority.[3] He and his descendants had to be content with whatever territory fate or their elder relatives' decision bestowed upon them.

When the heirs of Yaroslav divided their inheritance the four eldest took up residence along the Dnieper, the other three in the South. Iziaslav received Kiev, Sviatoslav obtained Chernigov, Vsevolod got Pereiaslavl. Viacheslav, the fourth, established his throne in Smolensk. Vladimir-in-Volhynia fell to the fifth, Igor. As for the Northern and Eastern lands more distant from the Dnieper, in the end Novgorod became a dependency of Kiev, the whole territory east of the Dnieper from Murom to Tmutorokan was under the princes of Chernigov, while Rostov, Suzdal, Beloozero and the lands along the Volga were subject to the princes of Pereiaslavl. "In the end," because Beloozero, for example, at one time belonged to Sviatoslav. Rostov likewise did not become immediately the possession of Vsevolod of Pereiaslavl, as the sons of Yaroslav at first gave it to their nephew Rostislav Vladimirovich. This is how the heirs of Yaroslav divided the Land of Rus.

Another of St. Vladimir's sons was still alive. Sudislav spent twenty-two years in the dungeon where his brother Yaroslav imprisoned him. This forgotten old man, evidently childless and therefore representing no threat, was set free by his nephews in 1058, swearing that he would undertake nothing against their interests. Sudislav made use of his freedom only to become a monk and died not long afterwards, in 1063.

When Yaroslav enjoined brotherly love upon his sons he must have remembered all too well the actions of his own brother Sviatopolk.[4] He appears to have attributed the enmity amongst the sons of Vladimir to the fact that they had different mothers. This circumstance led Vladimir to favor his younger sons, causing hatred and fratricide. Since his sons all had the same mother Yaroslav gave no preferential treatment to his favorite, his third son Vsevolod,[5] enjoining him to wait his turn until God allowed him to receive the senior throne by right and not by violence.

FURTHER DIVISIONS OF PRINCIPALITIES

Indeed it was long before the brothers had any cause to quarrel. In 1056 Viacheslav died, whereupon his throne of Smolensk was given to Igor, until then prince of Vladimir, and Rostislav Vladimirovich moved from Rostov to Vladimir. In 1053 Igor Yaroslavich died at Smolensk. It is not known how the brothers disposed of his throne, only that their nephew the *dispossessed prince*[6] Rostislav Vladimirovich was dissatisfied with their decision. He had no hope of becoming senior prince and may have been uncomfortable at being perpetually dependent upon his uncles. A valiant warrior, as the chronicle says, he was attracted by Tmutorokan and the freedom of the steppes, from among whose ethnically diverse inhabitants a valiant leader could always assemble a bold retinue. It was here that the famous Mstislav had reigned. Thence Mstislav led his Caucasian hordes into Rus, forcing his elder brother to share their father's inheritance equally with him. Such a career must have been tempting for the bold Rostislav, who as a dispossessed prince might win a rich territory only by the sword, with no hope of acquiring the means for such a venture anywhere but Tmutorokan. After Viacheslav's death the sons of Yaroslav sent Igor to Smolensk and their nephew Rostislav to Vladimir-in-Volhynia. Now that Igor had died in Smolensk, Rostislav probably hoped to be transferred there by his uncles. That did not happen, so Rostislav had grounds for offense.

Whatever the case, in 1064 he fled to Tmutorokan. Neither was he alone, for he was accompanied by two well-known and well-born individuals, Porey and Vyshata, the sons of Ostromir, mayor[7] of Novgorod, to whom Iziaslav entrusted the government of Novgorod during his absence. Porey and Vyshata were the best known of Rostislav's companions, though evidently he was accompanied by a significant number of fortune seekers or malcontents, as on his arrival in Tmutorokan he could expel his cousin Gleb Sviatoslavich and take his place. Gleb's father Sviatoslav marched against Rostislav who, reluctant to make war on his uncle, abandoned the city, allowing Sviatoslav to reinstate his son. Nevertheless as soon as Sviatoslav went home, Rostislav again expelled Gleb, this time becoming undisputed ruler of Tmutorokan.

He attacked the surrounding peoples, Circassians[8] and others, exacting tribute from them. The Greeks, alarmed at having such a neighbor, sent the governor[9] of Cherson[10] on a mission to him. Rostislav received him unsuspecting, with honors befitting a distinguished man and an ambassador. At a banquet with Rostislav and his retinue the governor took a goblet and proposed to drink Rostislav's health. "Drink," said the prince, whereupon the governor downed half of what was in the goblet and passed the rest to Rostislav, first touching the edge of the cup and slipping into it the poison concealed beneath his fingernail and which, by his calculations, would cause Rostislav's death eight days later. After the banquet the governor returned home and announced to the people of Cherson that Rostislav would die on a certain a day, which indeed happened. The chronicler adds that the governor subsequently was stoned to death by the people of Cherson. According to the same chronicle Rostislav was tall, handsome, valiant in battle and generous to the poor. His throne of Tmutorokan reverted to Gleb Sviatoslavich.

VSESLAV OF POLOTSK

The Greeks and the princes of Rus were rid of the bold dispossessed prince, yet now that there was nothing to fear from the Southeast the clouds of war gathered in the Northwest, where there arose the descendant of another dispossessed prince, Vseslav of Polotsk, bloodthirsty and merciless, reputedly born by wizardry.[11] He may have begun hostilities while Rostislav was yet alive and his uncles' attention turned to the South, for in 1065 he conducted an unsuccessful siege of Pskov. In 1066 he followed his father's example and attacked Novgorod, taking prisoners and removing the bells from the Holy Wisdom.[12] "This was a time of great misfortune," adds the chronicle, "for he took away even the candelabra."[13]

Iziaslav, Sviatoslav and Vsevolod, the sons of Yaroslav, assembled an army and marched against Vseslav in bitterly cold weather. When they came to Minsk the inhabitants shut themselves up behind the fortifications. The brothers nevertheless captured the town, put the men to the sword and took the women and children into captivity.[14] Then they went on to the Nemiza river, where they encountered Vseslav at the beginning of March. Despite heavy snow there was a fierce battle in which the sons of Yaroslav eventually were victorious with many casualties, and Vseslav fled.

In summer, the following July, Iziaslav, Sviatoslav and Vsevolod invited Vseslav to negotiations, solemnly swearing they would do him no harm. Vseslav believed them. Crossing the Dnieper, he entered Iziaslav's tent, where he was seized. Iziaslav took him to Kiev, imprisoning him and his two sons.

ADVENT OF THE POLOVETSIANS

It seemed that the sons of Yaroslav, free of Rostislav and Vseslav, could look forward to a lasting peace. It turned out otherwise. A bloody star, harbinger of bloodshed, appeared in the sky, the sun stood like the moon, fishermen drew a horrible monster from the Setomlia river. All this boded no good, said the people. Indeed a foreign nation appeared, at this time an ordinary occurrence on the steppes east of the Dnieper, the replacement of one nomadic people's power by that of another. The Uzes, Cumans or Polovetsians,[15] a people of Turkic origin and language, took the place of the Pechenegs,[16] whom they conquered. The year after Yaroslav's death the Polovetsians under their khan Bolush appeared within the principality of Pereiaslavl, though on this occasion he concluded a peace with Vsevolod and retired into the steppe.

The sons of Yaroslav, hitherto undisturbed from this quarter and not yet preoccupied with internecine squabbles, decided to inflict a final defeat on the barbarians on their frontier, a people called the Torks.[17] No clashes with them are recorded in the chronicles before the death of Yaroslav. Only once did their hired cavalry participate in Vladimir's campaign against the Bulgars, but as early as 1059 Vsevolod attacked and defeated them. Then in 1060 the three sons of Yaroslav, and Vseslav of Polotsk, assembled what the chronicle calls an innumerable army and attacked the Torks with cavalry and boats. On hearing of this the Torks were afraid and fled into the steppe, whither they were pursued by the princes, who killed many and led others into captivity, settling them in the various towns of Rus. The rest perished in the steppe of cold, hunger and disease.

The steppes soon sent avengers for the Torks. The next year the Polovetsians came to make war on the Land of Rus. Vsevolod went out to meet them but was defeated. The Polovetsians ravaged his land and departed. This, says the chronicle, was the first evil inflicted by godless and heathen foes. In 1068 the Land of Rus again was invaded by the Polovetsian hordes. This time the three sons of Yaroslav went to intercept them on the Alta river, were defeated and fled, Iziaslav and Vsevolod to Kiev, Sviatoslav to Chernigov.

REBELLION IN KIEV AGAINST IZIASLAV YAROSLAVICH

Returning to their city, on September 15 the people of Kiev called a popular assembly in the marketplace and sent a message to their prince. "The Polovetsians are scattered throughout the land. Give us weapons and horses, and we will fight them again." Iziaslav refused. Then the people mutinied against the chiliarch Kosniachko, who as commander of the urban and rural levies had failed to give them victory. Now he was failing to take their part, not leading them in battle, dissuading the prince from providing them with arms and horses.

The crowd left the assembly and went up the hill to Kosniachko's house. Not finding him at home, they paused for deliberation at Briachislav's house, saying "Come, let's release our folk from prison." They set off in two groups, one to the prison, the other over the bridge to the prince's court. Iziaslav was sitting with his retinue in the front hall of his house when the people approached and disputed with him. They stood down below, and he spoke to them out of the window. Evidently some said they would do better with a different prince, who would lead them against the Polovetsians, because one of the boyars, a certain Tuki the brother of Chudin, said to Iziaslav "You hear, prince, what they are shouting. Send to strengthen the guard about Vseslav."

At that point the other half of the populace, having opened the prison, came to the prince's court. "Things look bad, prince," said the retinue. "Trick Vseslav into approaching the window, so that we can stab him." When Iziaslav refused, his retinue's fears were realized. The crowd moved off with shouts to where Vseslav was held. When Iziaslav saw this he fled from his court with his brother Vsevolod, whereupon the people took Vseslav from his prison and placed him in the middle of the prince's court, in other words they proclaimed him prince. At the same time they plundered Iziaslav's treasury, taking countless gold and silver. Iziaslav fled to Poland.

Meanwhile the Polovetsians devastated Rus, reaching Chernigov. Sviatoslav assembled a small army and marched against them in the direction of Snovsk. Though the Polovetsians were very numerous, Sviatoslav was not deterred. He drew up his troops, and said "Let us give battle, there is nothing else for us to do." The men of Chernigov attacked, and Sviatoslav was victorious, although he had only three thousand men, against the Polovetsians' twelve thousand. Some were slain, others drowned in the Snov river, and their prince was captured by the Rus.

IZIASLAV RETURNS TO KIEV

Vseslav had reigned for seven months in Kiev when in the spring of 1069 Iziaslav appeared on the territory of Rus with King Bolesław of Poland.[18] Vseslav went out as if to meet him but fled secretly from Belgorod by night to Polotsk, evidently fearing a war on two fronts, for the other sons of Yaroslav would hardly be on his side in his struggle with Iziaslav. So the sorcerer succeeded only in touching the golden throne of Kiev with his lance, and "turning into a wolf, he fled by night from Belgorod, wrapped in a blue mist."[19]

The men of Kiev, left without a prince, called an assembly and sent a message to Yaroslav's sons Sviatoslav and Vsevolod. "We did wrong," they said, "to drive away our prince, who now leads the Poles against us. Come to your father's city! If you will not, we have nothing left to do but burn the city and flee to the land of the Greeks." "We shall send a message to our brother," Sviatoslav replied, "and if he goes with the Poles to destroy you, we shall oppose him by force of arms, nor shall we permit him to destroy our father's city. If he comes in peace, let him come with a small retinue."

The men of Kiev were reassured, and Sviatoslav and Vsevolod sent to Iziaslav. "Vseslav has fled," they said. "Do not lead the Poles against Kiev, for there is no opposition to you there. If you will not cease from anger and wish to destroy the city, know that we are concerned for our father's throne." When he heard what his brothers had to say, Iziaslav took with him only Bolesław and a small company of Poles, sending his son Mstislav on ahead to Kiev. When Mstislav arrived there he had those he held responsible for liberating Vseslav put to death, seventy men in all, and others blinded, some of whom were in fact innocent. When Iziaslav himself arrived the people did homage to him and he resumed his throne on May 2. Bolesław II's Poles suffered the same fate as their predecessors who followed Bolesław I to Rus.[20] They were billeted around the countryside where the inhabitants took to murdering them secretly, forcing Bolesław to return home. Iziaslav's restoration is apparently connected in the chronicle with the record of his having moved the market from the Podol quarter to the hill.

FURTHER WARS AGAINST VSESLAV OF POLOTSK

After the execution of the men of Kiev who liberated Vseslav, Iziaslav lost no time in making war on him. He expelled him from Polotsk, installing his son Mstislav in his place, and when Mstislav died, replaced him with his second son Sviatopolk. The chronicle records that Vseslav fled, but does not say where. Since he appeared before Novgorod in 1069 with an army made up of the Finnic tribe of the Vod,[21] it is evident that it was among them he found refuge and succor.

The prince of Novgorod at this time was Gleb, son of Sviatoslav of Chernigov, whom we have encountered at Tmutorokan. The men of Novgorod sent an armed force against the Vod, and God favored them. There was a fierce battle in which many of the Vod fell, but out of Christian charity they set Prince Vseslav free. Even after this defeat Vseslav did not give up his warlike career. The brave prince attracted adventurers from all parts, gathering a retinue to expel Sviatopolk from Polotsk. Even though he was defeated by another son of Iziaslav at Golotichesk, he held on to his father's throne.

IZIASLAV'S SECOND EXPULSION FROM KIEV

Iziaslav opened negotiations with him, the subject of which is unknown, but which provided the occasion for Iziaslav to be expelled from Kiev a second time, this time by his own brothers. This second expulsion was connected with the first. Iziaslav had returned to Kiev on conditions laid down by his brothers. He could not gain acceptance in the city, whereas the citizens inevitably were well disposed towards Sviatoslav, who restrained his brother's anger, and who with his tiny army defeated the Polovetsian hordes, driving them from Rus. Iziaslav's son Mstislav executed the men of Kiev who set Vseslav free, the innocent along with the guilty, but that was not the end of the matter.

Persecutions continued, the victims finding refuge with Sviatoslav in Chernigov. Thus St. Anthony, founder of the Caves monastery,[22] who as a friend of Vseslav had incurred the grand prince's wrath, was taken secretly by night and sheltered in Chernigov by Sviatoslav. Even if Sviatoslav did this only out of love and respect for the holy man, Iziaslav for his part could not but be offended by his brother's friendship with someone he regarded as his enemy. These circumstances must have given rise to ambitious thoughts in the mind of Sviatoslav, encouraging him to believe in the possibility of their success, and turning Iziaslav against his brother.

This was the beginning of enmity amongst the sons of Yaroslav. Their military campaigns were no longer the joint undertakings of yesteryear. Iziaslav made war on Vseslav alone, opened negotiations with him alone. By the very nature of interprincely relations this last action must have aroused his brothers' indignation and suspicion. "Iziaslav is plotting against us with Vseslav," said Sviatoslav to Vsevolod, "and if we do not forestall him, he will drive us out." So Vsevolod was turned against Iziaslav. The chronicle regards Sviatoslav as the guilty party, saying that he deceived Vsevolod because of his desire for more power. Whatever the case, the younger brothers turned against the elder. Iziaslav once more was obliged to leave Kiev, and Sviatoslav became prince there, giving Chernigov to Vsevolod. Iziaslav's unresisting departure indicates that everyone in Kiev was on Sviatoslav's side. The chronicle recounts that Sviatoslav and Vsevolod first set themselves up in the village of Berestovo. Then, after Iziaslav left, Sviatoslav entered Kiev.

EVENTS IN POLAND AND BOHEMIA

Iziaslav and his sons went to Poland again. It appears that this time he did not leave Kiev in haste, for he had time to take a large amount of his property, saying "With gold I shall find warriors," forgetting the words of his grandfather Vladimir, that a retinue can win gold, but gold cannot win a retinue. Iziaslav gave the Polish magnates rich gifts which they accepted, but they did not give him any help, and even expelled him from their country. This is understandable, considering the condition of the Western Slavonic nations at this period. Bolesław the Brave's interventions in Bohemian affairs ended just as unsuccessfully as his interference in the quarrel between the princes of Rus.[23] The Poles were driven from Bohemia, and the Bohemian princes Jaromír and Oldřich ruled the country although they did not rule for long in peace. Oldřich, in the words of an old Czech song, "was a glorious warrior, to whom God gave both power and might, and placed clear wisdom in his warlike head." In 1012 he expelled Jaromír, for what reason neither the ballad nor the chronicles say.

Emperor Conrad II[24] was displeased at the appearance of a single ruler of the Czechs, and repeatedly summoned Oldřich before him. When he at length appeared he was exiled to Regensburg. Jaromír again ruled Bohemia together with his nephew Břetislav, Oldřich's son. Meanwhile the emperor offered his captive the opportunity to return home and share power with his elder brother. Oldřich swore to relinquish half the kingdom to his brother, yet as soon as he returned he had Jaromír blinded. After Oldřich's death his son Břetislav I became the sole ruler of the country. This vigorous prince took advantage of the unsettled state of Poland after the death of Bolesław the Brave to expand his possessions at the Piasts' expense, for which he is celebrated as the restorer of Bohemian glory.

The death of Břetislav I gave rise to the same situation in Bohemia as obtained at the same time, in 1054, in Rus upon the death of Yaroslav I. Power was exercised by the whole princely house, the supreme throne occupied by the senior member of the family. After Břetislav's death the "grand prince," that is, the head of the ruling family (Dux principalis), was his eldest son Spytihněv II. His other sons were called Vratislav, Conrad, Jaromír and Otto. Like with us the sons of Yaroslav, the sons of Břetislav did not live long in amity. The second, Vratislav,[25] had at first to seek refuge in Hungary from his elder brother, later was reconciled and returned home, succeeding him in 1061. Vratislav II was succeeded according to custom not by his son but by his next brother, Conrad I, whose reign lasted merely eight months. He was the last of the sons of Břetislav. After his death in 1092 power passed to the next generation, Břetislav I's grandsons.[26]

In Poland Casimir the Restorer[27] was succeeded in 1058 by his son Bolesław II, the Bold.[28] Two years earlier Emperor Henry III[29] died. The unrest which followed during the minority of his son and successor Henry IV,[30] followed by this emperor's struggles with the German princes and the papacy, meant that Poland for a long period was free from imperial influence. Bolesław the Bold took advantage of this in order to regulate his relations with neighboring countries to Poland's honor and advantage. He helped Iziaslav regain Kiev, and it was through his help that the Hungarian king Béla[31] came to the throne. Béla's sons also maintained their position in Hungary thanks to Polish arms. Bolesław was almost constantly at war with the Czechs. At the time of Iziaslav's second appearance at the Polish court in 1075 Bolesław was fighting Vratislav of Bohemia, who was closely allied with Emperor Henry IV. Probably these circumstances prevented Bolesław from offering any aid to Iziaslav who, forced to leave Poland, took the advice of his grandfather the margrave of Saxony and went to Mainz to seek aid from Bolesław's enemy Emperor Henry IV. In this manner the strife amongst the princes of Rus gave the emperor the opportunity to extend his influence to this country, though this influence could never be very strong, first because Rus was so far away, second because the emperor's circumstances were such that even Poland could break free of his tutelage.

IZIASLAV'S WESTERN ALLIANCES AND SECOND RESTORATION

Receiving rich presents from Iziaslav, Henry IV sent to Sviatoslav demanding that he return Kiev to his elder brother, threatening war if he opposed him. It goes without saying that there was no intention of acting upon this threat. According to the chronicle, when Sviatoslav received the German envoys he boastfully showed them his treasure. The envoys, seeing the gold and silver and rich cloths, repeated the ancient words of St. Vladimir. "This is nothing, for it is all dead. Better is a retinue, with which more than this can be won." The chronicle adds that Sviatoslav's riches, like those of Hezekiah king of Judah,[32] were all dispersed after his death. These words indicate that their contemporaries and immediate posterity disapproved of the sons of Yaroslav heaping up wealth and trusting in it, in contrast to their grandfather's example when, according to the prevailing opinion of the age, a good prince must not keep back anything for himself but distribute everything to his retinue, with whose help he would never lack riches.

Since Iziaslav turned to Bolesław's enemy Henry IV for help it was obvious that Sviatoslav should, out of common interest, hasten to conclude an alliance with the Polish prince. Indeed the young princes Oleg Sviatoslavich and Vladimir Vsevolodovich went to the Poles' assistance and made war on the emperor's allies the Bohemians. Unsuccessful at Henry's court, Iziaslav turned to the other potentate of the West, Pope Gregory VII,[33] sending his son to Rome with a plea to restore him to his throne by the power of St. Peter. Just as Iziaslav at Mainz promised allegiance to the emperor, so his son at Rome promised submission to the Apostolic See.

The result of these negotiations was Gregory's letter to Bolesław enjoining him to return the treasures he took from Iziaslav. Perhaps it was also at the Pope's instigation that Bolesław at last helped Iziaslav against his brothers. Not that there is any need to assume papal persuasion to explain this course of action. It can be accounted for perfectly adequately by another narrative, according to which Prince Vratislav of Bohemia, hearing of Bolesław's alliance with the younger sons of Yaroslav, and of Oleg and Vladimir's movements towards his borders, sued for peace and obtained it at the price of a thousand grivnas of silver. Bolesław informed Oleg and Vladimir, who replied that to return home without accomplishing anything would shame their fathers and their land. Hence they advanced to *vindicate their honor* and "went through" the Czech land for four months, in other words devastated it. To them also Vratislav made proposals of peace, thus the princes of Rus, having vindicated their honor and taken a thousand grivnas of silver, made peace.

There is no doubt that this action angered Bolesław, who decided to assist Iziaslav again. Meanwhile Sviatoslav died in 1076. Vsevolod succeeded him in Kiev in the winter. In the summer he had to march out against Iziaslav, who was advancing with his Polish troops. The two brothers met in Volhynia and made peace. Vsevolod ceded Kiev and the seniority to Iziaslav, himself remaining in his old principality of Chernigov. The Poles hardly can have offered their assistance for nothing, which lends credence to reports that Iziaslav paid for it with the towns of Red Ruthenia.[34]

FURTHER CONFLICTS AMONG THE PRINCES

Peace between the sons of Yaroslav did not bring peace to the Land of Rus, for there were many nephews hungry for land. Vseslav had no intention of sitting quietly in Polotsk. He threatened Novgorod, evidently taking advantage of Sviatoslav's death and the expected war between Iziaslav and Vsevolod. In the winter of 1076 Vsevolod's son Vladimir went to Novgorod to assist its prince Gleb, doubtless against Vseslav. In the summer, after making peace and coming to an agreement with Iziaslav, Vsevolod and his son Vladimir made war on Polotsk. In the winter there was another campaign. Momomakh and his cousin Sviatopolk Iziaslavich attacked Polotsk and burned it. At the same time Monomakh and the Polovetsians devastated Vseslav's lands as far as Odrsk. This is the first record of Polovetsian mercenaries participating in the internecine strife between the princes.

While the princes had to be on constant guard against the enchanter Vseslav in the Northwest, a new threat of war appeared in the Southeast from the barbarians of the steppes and the dispossessed princes who led them into Rus. Besides Vladimir of Novgorod two other of the younger sons of Yaroslav, Viacheslav and Igor, died leaving sons to whom, according to custom, neither patrimonies nor other territories were granted. These dispossessed princes grew up and sought lands for themselves. At the time Sviatoslav died and Vsevolod led his retinue against Iziaslav, Boris, son of Viacheslav of Smolensk, taking advantage of his uncle's absence to seize Chernigov, maintained his position there only for eight months before fleeing to Tmutorokan, then ruled by Roman, one of Sviatoslav's sons.

Sviatoslav left five sons: Gleb, Oleg, Davyd, Roman and Yaroslav. During their father's lifetime Gleb was prince of Novgorod, Oleg of Vladimir-in-Volhynia, and Roman of Tmutorokan. Where Davyd ruled is unknown, while Yaroslav was still very young. Roman of Tmutorokan received Boris Viacheslavich, then had to give refuge to his own brothers because Iziaslav refused to give any lands to Sviatoslav's sons. Gleb was driven from Novgorod, Oleg expelled from Vladimir. Gleb perished in the Far North, in the lands of the Chud beyond the portage.[35] Oleg at first sought refuge in Chernigov with his uncle Vsevolod, from whom he could expect more favor than from Iziaslav. Vsevolod was either unable or unwilling to provide him with territory, whereupon he joined his brothers in Tmutorokan, the perpetual refuge of exiles and malcontents. Expelling their nephews, the sons of Yaroslav distributed the principalities to the benefit of their own sons. Sviatopolk Iziaslavich received Novgorod, his brother Yaropolk obtained Vyshgorod, while Vladimir Vsevolodovich Monomakh was installed at Smolensk.

The exiled princes could not sit idly in Tmutorokan. In 1078 Oleg and Boris led the Polovetsians into the Land of Rus, attacking Vsevolod, who resisted them at the Sozhitsa (Orzhitsa) river. There the Polovetsians defeated the Rus, the land losing many famous men. Ivan Zhiroslavich, Tuki the brother of Chudin, Porey and many others were slain. Oleg and Boris entered Chernigov, thinking themselves victorious. They brought great evil upon the Land of Rus, says the chronicle.

Vsevolod came to his brother Iziaslav at Kiev and told him his misfortune. "Brother," replied Iziaslav, "do not be sorrowful. Remember what happened to me! Was I not driven out the first time, and my possessions plundered? What wrong did I commit, that I deserved to be driven out by you, my own brothers? Did I not wander dispossessed through foreign lands, not knowing what evil I had done? Therefore, brother, let us not be sorrowful. If we are to have any part in the Land of Rus, we will gain or lose together. I will lay down my life for you."

Comforting Vsevolod with these words, he commanded a general muster from the greatest to the least. Indeed there was no alternative, for it was not to be expected that the sons of Sviatoslav would leave their chief enemy Iziaslav in peace. Iziaslav set off on campaign accompanied by his son Yaropolk, and Vsevolod with his son Vladimir, who was at Smolensk when he heard of the exiled princes' invasion. Hastening to his father's aid, he cut his way through the Polovetsian forces to Pereiaslavl, where he joined his father, just returned from the battle on the Sozhitsa.

The sons and grandsons of Yaroslav marched to Chernigov, where the citizens shut the gates against them even though Oleg and Boris were not within. According to one report they had gone to Tmutorokan to gather a fresh army. Chernigov had a double ring of fortifications. The princes assailed the outer wall, while Monomakh forced the eastern gate. When the outer city was burned, the citizens took refuge within the inner fortifications. The sons of Yaroslav did not have time to attack them there because news came that Oleg and Boris were approaching. Hearing this, Iziaslav and Vsevolod departed from Chernigov early in the morning and went to meet their nephews, who discussed what to do next. "We cannot withstand four princes," said Oleg to Boris. "We had better send to our uncles and ask for peace." "You stand and watch," replied Boris, "and I will take them all on." They advanced, encountering the sons of Yaroslav at the village of Nezhatina Niva. The armies engaged and there was a fierce battle. First Boris Viacheslavich was killed. Then Iziaslav, who stood with the infantry, was mortally wounded in the shoulder with a lance. Despite the death of the two princes, one on either side, the battle continued until eventually Oleg fled, with great difficulty reaching Tmutorokan on October 3, 1078.

Iziaslav's body was brought in a boat to Gorodets, where all the people of Kiev came out to meet him. Then they continued the journey by sledge accompanied by priests and monks, their chanting inaudible because of the noise of weeping and wailing made by all the inhabitants of Kiev. Yaropolk followed the body with his retinue. "Father, father," he lamented, "many cares you had in this life, suffering much hardship at the hands of the people and your brothers, but it is not your brother that has killed you now, though you have laid down your life for him."

Iziaslav was buried in a marble sarcophagus in the church of the Mother of God. According to the chronicle, Iziaslav was fair of face, tall and stout, good-tempered, hated injustice and loved righteousness. There was no guile in him, he was straightforward and not vindictive. How much harm the men of Kiev did him! Although they drove him out and plundered his home, he did not render evil for evil. While it might be said that he put to death those who set Vseslav free, in fact it was not he who did this, but his son. Then his brothers drove him out, and he was a wanderer in an alien land. When he regained his throne, and Vsevolod came to him defeated, he did not say "What did you do to me?" He did not render him evil for evil, but comforted him, saying "Brother, you have shown your love for me, placed me on my throne and called me your elder, so I shall not remember past wrongdoing. We are brothers, and I will lay down my life for you," as indeed he did. He did not say "You have done me much evil, so now it is your turn," or "Go where you will," rather took brotherly pity upon him, and showed him great love.

The fact that he gave his life for his brother, a shining example to the warring princes, deeply moved the chronicler and perhaps, given the prevailing spontaneity of feeling, all his contemporaries. The chronicler is careful to answer the objection concerning the execution of Vseslav's liberators and lay the blame upon Mstislav, which must mean that this objection was raised at the time. A monk of the Caves monastery could not have been unaware of the persecutions that followed, affecting even St. Anthony. Iziaslav forgave Vsevolod because evidently he had not been greatly to blame previously, and had made amends since. In any case

Iziaslav had to take up arms against his nephews for his own safety. Yet he could not forgive the sons of Sviatoslav, even though they were not guilty of their father's offense. He deprived them of their lands, thereby storing up misfortune for himself and for the Land of Rus.

REASONS FOR INTERNECINE STRIFE

Be that as it may, the first senior or grand prince after Yaroslav fell in civil strife. All the feuding in Iziaslav's time came about because fatherless nephews did not receive lands. Thanks to the absence of any hereditary rights over individual principalities, the uncles regarded their fatherless nephews as dispossessed princes, whose position made them dependent on the generosity of their elders who compelled them to be satisfied with whatever they chose to give them. As a result they either did not give them any lands, or gave insufficient to satisfy them. While the absence of rights of inheritance was to the uncles' advantage, it was to the nephews' disadvantage. Since their fathers' premature deaths deprived them of all hope of the seniority, they wanted at best to achieve what their fathers had, or at the very least some other more or less significant principality so as not to be excluded from all share in the Land of Rus. In other words, the first domestic strife in Rus came about because of the lack of hereditary rights over individual principalities and the fatherless princes' ambition to establish such rights and their elders' efforts to prevent them. The attempt by dispossessed princes to gain a principality was easily made. Rus bordered upon the steppe, which was full of different barbarian hordes among whom it was easy to raise an army by promise of booty. For this reason Tmutorokan, on the other side of the steppes, served as a constant haven for the dispossessed princes, who came back with retinues to win themselves lands.

We have followed the career of the dispossessed prince Rostislav Vladimirovich. His sons were left in the same position as their father, and consequently had the same ambitions. We have seen the fate of the dispossessed prince Boris Viacheslavich, who apparently had neither sons nor brothers. There remained the sons of Igor Yaroslavich, also dispossessed princes. Iziaslav attempted to reduce the sons of Sviatoslav to the same condition, although they had grounds for rejecting it, for their father was grand prince and died on the senior throne. Though Iziaslav considered Sviatoslav's seniority illegitimate and avenged himself on his persecutor's sons by depriving them of their lands, Vsevolod had no right to do so. Iziaslav was not expelled by Sviatoslav alone, but by Sviatoslav and Vsevolod together. Vsevolod recognized Iziaslav's expulsion as legitimate, acknowledging Sviatoslav's seniority right until the latter's death. What grounds could he have for considering Sviatoslav's sons dispossessed princes and depriving them of their lands? Nevertheless Vsevolod was hostile to the sons of Sviatoslav on account of his recent exile. Enjoying the victor's privilege, he had no intention of inviting them back to Rus. Thereby he sowed the seeds of a new conflict for himself and his posterity.

VSEVOLOD AND SONS OF SVIATOSLAV

Vsevolod took the throne of Kiev, the throne of his father and his brother, taking all the principalities of Rus under his rule. He made his son Vladimir prince of Chernigov, his nephew Yaropolk Iziaslavich prince of Vladimir-in-Volhynia, adding Turov to his possessions. The princes left out of this division of the lands could not leave him in peace for long. In 1079 Roman Sviatoslavich appeared with a force of Polovetsians at Voin. Vsevolod advanced towards them, halted at Pereiaslavl, and made peace with the Polovetsians. It goes without saying that he gave something tangible in place of Roman's promises. Not only did the Polovetsians fail to accomplish the purpose for which Roman brought them, they killed him on the way back, according to one credible source as a result of a quarrel he picked with their princes over their deception. Subsequent information in the chronicles makes it clear that it was not strictly the Polovetsians who killed him, rather the Khazars. This means that Roman's army was ethnically diverse, and that the Khazars continued to exist as a separate people after the destruction of their empire, playing some part in the affairs of the Azov and Black Sea steppes.

After killing Roman, naturally the Khazars and Polovetsians could not live in peace with his brother Oleg. Therefore, says the chronicle, they exiled him over the sea to Constantinople, whence he was sent to Rhodes. It is quite clear that the Khazars and Polovetsians could not have done this without the agreement of the emperor, who also must have found the dispossessed Rus princes troublesome neighbors. This is clear from the fate of Rostislav. Probably also Vsevolod was aware of Oleg's exile, for he took advantage of it by sending his burgrave Ratibor to Tmutorokan.[36]

Tmutorokan did not long remain without dispossessed princes. A year later Igor Yaroslavich's son Davyd fled there from the territories of Vladimir-in-Volhynia, as did Rostislav Vladimirovich's son Volodar. They expelled Ratibor and settled in Tmutorokan. Their stay was short-lived.

A year later Oleg returned from exile, seized Davyd and Volodar, and made himself prince of Tmutorokan again. He killed the Khazars responsible for his brother's death and his own exile, and let Davyd and Volodar go.

Deprived of their refuge in Tmutorokan, these two princes had to devise other means of winning lands. In 1084 the sons of Rostislav fled from Yaropolk, says the chronicle, which implies that they had been living with him in Vladimir without lands of their own. It is not stated where they went but they came back with an army and drove Yaropolk out of Vladimir. Whom did they bring? Where did they find their retinue? How could landless princes drive Yaropolk from his principality? Though the chronicle supplies no answers to these questions, its short account makes it clear how easy it was to assemble a retinue. It is also clear that the sons of Rostislav could not have expelled Yaropolk without some powerful supporters within Vladimir. Vsevolod sent his son Monomakh against them, expelling them from Vladimir and reinstalling Yaropolk. It seems from the chronicle as though all this happened all at once whereas Monomakh's own words make it clear that the struggle against the sons of Rostislav took some time to finish, for he fought against the sons of Iziaslav over Mikulin, in present-day Galich, and then twice against Yaropolk at Brody, once in spring and once in winter.

FURTHER STRIFE AMONG PRINCES

Davyd Igorevich was more fortunate than the sons of Rostislav. He left with his retinue for the mouth of the Dnieper, where he seized some Greek merchants and robbed them of all their goods. Since the prosperity of Kiev, and hence the grand prince's treasury, depended on the Greek trade, Vsevolod was constrained to put an end to Davyd's depredations by promising him a principality. He did indeed give him Dorogobuzh in Volhynia.[37]

Vsevolod's initiative did not put an end to, but rather intensified the strife between the princes. Yaropolk Iziaslavich, prince of Volhynia, considered himself injured by the fact that Dorogobuzh was given to Davyd, which he took as meaning that Vsevolod intended to diminish his principality. He therefore harbored resentment against Vsevolod and gathered an army, at the instigation of evil counsellors adds the chronicle. When Vsevolod learned of this he sent his son Vladimir against him, and Yaropolk fled to Poland, leaving his mother in Lutsk, which surrendered to Monomakh. This allowed him to capture Yaropolk's wife, mother, retinue and all his possessions, and make Davyd Igorevich prince of Vladimir. The Cherven towns, which later formed part of the principality of Galich, probably passed into the possession of the sons of Rostislav at this time because the eldest, Riurik, is mentioned later as prince of Peremyshl. Very probably the sons of Rostislav conquered these towns from the Poles, Yaropolk's allies, not without Vsevolod's acquiescence. The next year Yaropolk returned from Poland and made peace with Monomakh, becoming prince of Vladimir again. This turn of events probably was assisted by Monomakh's previous friendship with Yaropolk, and by old Vsevolod's gratitude to his father Iziaslav and consequent disinclination to quarrel with his sons, the eldest of whom was to inherit the seniority after his own death.

MURDER OF YAROPOLK IZIASLAVICH

Yaropolk did not enjoy his restoration for long. After only a few days in Vladimir he set off for Zvenigorod, a town in Galich. As he was reclining on a wagon during the journey a certain Neradets, apparently one of his retinue riding beside him on horseback, struck him with his sabre. Yaropolk raised himself up, pulled the sabre out of the wound, saying "Alas, this enemy has finished me!" Neradets fled to Riurik Rostislavich in Peremyshl, and Yaropolk died of the wound.[38] His servants took his body to Vladimir, and thence to Kiev, where he was buried in St. Peter's church, which he had founded. There was much weeping in Kiev at Yaropolk's funeral. The chronicler also mourns his passing, saying that he suffered many misfortunes, was exiled by his brothers without cause, wronged, robbed and finally murdered. He was, says the chronicle, quiet, meek, humble, a lover of his brethren, gave a tithe of his goods every year to the church of the Mother of God in Kiev, and prayed for a death like that of Boris and Gleb.[39] God heard his prayer, concludes the chronicler.

The chronicle is less explicit on the reason for the murder. Neradets, it says, was incited by the devil and by evil men. It must be remembered that, as mentioned earlier, the sons of Rostislav could not have taken Vladimir without assistance from their supporters within, who consequently must have been Yaropolk's enemies. Those who earlier wanted him exiled cannot have been pleased with his restoration. The murderer fled to Riurik Rostislavich in Peremyshl. This circumstance by itself is sufficient to cast suspicion on the sons of Rostislav, even if there was no certainty that they actually were implicated in the murder. Davyd Igorevich was later to say in so many words that Yaropolk was killed by the sons of Rostislav.

It would seem at first sight that the sons of Rostislav, or at least one of them, Riurik, had insufficient reason to instigate such an action. Suspicion might fall rather on Davyd Igorevich, both because of his character, and because he had the most to lose by Yaropolk's return to the throne of Vladimir. Yet the chronicles contain not the slightest hint of Davyd's involvement. When Davyd himself mentioned the complicity of the sons of Rostislav in the murder in later conversation with Sviatopolk, it could hardly have been a new invention on his part. If Davyd's contemporaries suspected him, neither the chronicler nor Sviatopolk Iziaslavich nor the Kievans at their assembly, nor the princes at their council would have failed to mention it on the occasion of Davyd's crime against Vasilko.[40]

If the chronicler does not accuse the sons of Rostislav directly this means that there was insufficient evidence against them. The chronicler quite deliberately draws attention to the fact that Neradets fled to Riurik Rostislavich. As to their possible motives, all that can be said is that the sons of Rostislav formerly lived under Yaropolk's protection, found the means to expel him, and themselves then were expelled in his favor. This could very well have engendered mortal enmity, for the sons of Rostislav may have considered they would never be secure in their principality while their enemy was prince of Vladimir.

It is also worth bearing in mind that Yaropolk departed for Zvenigorod after a very short sojourn at Vladimir. It is not known why he undertook this journey, or even to whom Zvenigorod belonged at this period. Very likely it belonged to the sons of Rostislav, and that when the chronicle says he departed for Zvenigorod it indicates a warlike expedition. Finally as to the character of Riurik Rostislavich, all that can be said is that he expelled Yaropolk from Vladimir and later received his murderer, neither of which actions says much for his moral fiber.

EVENTS AT THE END OF VSEVOLOD'S REIGN

In the same year, 1046, Vsevolod himself undertook a campaign against the sons of Rostislav at Peremyshl, which must have been connected with the previous events. As later events made clear, the sons of Rostislav were difficult enemies to deal with. The campaign ended inconclusively, the sons of Rostislav still in their principality. This put a temporary end to unrest in Volhynia, yet in addition to this unrest and the struggle in the

East with the sons of Sviatoslav, the struggle with Vseslav of Polotsk continued. As soon as Vsevolod became senior prince Vseslav *burned round about* Smolensk, that is, the settlements outside the walls, while Monomakh rode out of Chernigov *on two horses* (that is, each member of his retinue took with him a change of horses) in hurried pursuit. The sorcerer Vseslav was hard to catch. Monomakh, not finding him at Smolensk, pursued him into the territory of Polotsk, pillaging and burning as he went. Later Monomakh led the men of Chernigov and the Polovetsians in a surprise raid on Minsk where, in his own words, he did not leave a single servant or a single head of cattle.

Vsevolod, the last of the sons of Yaroslav, died in 1093 at the age of sixty-four. According to the chronicle, he was a religious man from his youth, a lover of justice, generous to the poor, respectful towards the bishops and priests, but especially fond of the monks, to whom he gave all they needed. He was also temperate in character, which won him his father's affection. The chronicle adds that Vsevolod had much more trouble in Kiev than in Pereiaslavl, his difficulties all being connected with his nephews who wanted lands. One asked for this principality, another for that, and he spent his time pacifying them and distributing the lands amongst them.

Sickness and old age were added to these concerns. He began to favor the young and take counsel with them. They in turn tried to estrange him from his former, older retinue. The prince's justice ceased to reach the people, his agents robbed the people and exacted unjust fines when administering justice, and the sick Vsevolod knew nothing about it.[41]

There is no need to believe that these *young men* were necessarily young in years. It is indeed unlikely that Vsevolod in his declining years abandoned his contemporaries and surrounded himself with young men. The consequences suggest rather that by "young men" the chronicle means new people, the new retinue brought from Pereiaslavl and Chernigov, as opposed to the original. When the princes moved from one principality to another, from a junior to a senior throne, they took their retinue with them, naturally preferring it to the old retinue left by the former prince in their new principality. This worked to the disadvantage of the people because the newcomers were not concerned for the welfare of what was for them a strange land. They sought to grow rich at the expense of the citizens, also harming the old boyars, whom the newcomers deprived of their important offices and the prince's goodwill, *overtaking* them, to use a later expression.[42] The words of the most prominent citizens of Kiev, that their land was impoverished by war and venality, testify to the corruption of Vsevolod's agents.

CONDITION OF THE COUNTRY AT VSEVOLOD'S DEATH

In this manner the first generation of Yaroslav's descendants left the stage. Even under this first generation the land was torn by domestic strife as a result of the expulsion of their fatherless nephews. Even under the first the order of succession was disrupted, adding to the number of dispossessed princes, consequently to domestic strife, claiming the lives of three princes. Movement of princes from principality to principality according to clan reckonings already demonstrated to the people the disadvantages of such a system, particularly in the reign of Vsevolod, whose incoming followers ruined the Kievan territories. The land was also ruined by war, incursions of steppe barbarians continued. At the head of the Polovetsian invaders the people saw Rus princes seeking territories in the Land of Rus, which their allies devastated with impunity. The time began when internecine conflict was sown and grew throughout the land, when the princes' quarrels shortened the lives of men, when in the Land of Rus instead of the cry of the plowman was heard the croaking of ravens over the bodies of the slain, and the speech of jackdaws gathering in search of prey.[43]

CONFLICTS WITH EXTERNAL ENEMIES

Foreign relations were dominated as before by the struggle with the steppe barbarians, chiefly the Polovetsians. Wars with them have been mentioned in the context of interprincely strife. They also often invaded on their own account. It was in fighting them successfully for the sake of the Land of Rus that Vsevolod's son Monomakh established his reputation and gained the people's affection. He won twelve battles against the Polovetsians during his father's reign alone. If the Polovetsians assisted the princes of Rus in their domestic conflicts, Monomakh in his campaigns against the barbarians also occasionally enlisted the aid of barbarians of other tribes. We have seen how the sons of Yaroslav, before they started fighting each other, inflicted a crushing defeat on the Torks, forcing many to settle within the territory of Rus and acknowledge themselves its subjects. In 1080 the Torks settled around Pereiaslavl, whom the chronicle calls Pereiaslavl Torks, took up arms in a bid to reassert their independence. Vsevolod sent his son Monomakh, who defeated them.[44]

There was also constant fighting in the North with the Finnic and Lithuanian tribes. Iziaslav's victory over the Goliad[45] belongs to the first years of his reign, indicating that the population of the present Mozhaisk and Gzhatsk regions previously were not subject to him, which is not surprising, as they are situated far from the main routes along which Rus power expanded.

In 1055 the mayor Ostromir led the men of Novgorod against the Estonians and took possession of the town of Osek Dekipiv (meaning the Sun Hand). In 1060 Iziaslav himself attacked the Sosola[46] and made them pay tribute, but they soon expelled the tax gatherers, burning the town of Yuriev and the local settlements as far as Pskov. The men of Pskov and Novgorod marched against them and in the ensuing battle lost a thousand men, while the Sosola lost a countless multitude. In the Northeast there was a clash with the Bulgars, who took Murom in 1088.

In the West the sons of Rostislav were involved in conflict with the Poles, in which the third son Vasilko particularly distinguished himself. Bolesław II the Bold took advantage of disorders within the Holy Roman empire to restore Poland to its former glory which it lost at the death of Bolesław I the Brave. Despite successes against external enemies, Bolesław could not overcome the enemy within. His assumption of the title of king,[47] his attempts to increase his power at the expense of his nobles and his severe treatment of them, and the murder of Bishop Stanisław of Cracow[48] earned him the hatred of the aristocracy and clergy. As a result Bolesław was exiled and his brother, the weak Władysław Herman,[49] ascended the throne. Władysław put his entire trust in the palatine Sieciech, whose avarice and violence aroused general indignation. The discontented Poles rebelled, led by Władysław's illegitimate son Zbigniew. The Czechs intervened in the struggle. At the same time Władysław had to carry on a prolonged struggle with the Pomeranian Slavs.[50] Naturally in such circumstances not only was Poland powerless to influence Rus affairs, it could not even prevent Vasilko Rostislavich and the Polovetsians from devastating its territories.

MEMBERS OF PRINCES' RETINUES

After considering the activities of the princes in the domestic and foreign affairs of Rus we should give some attention to other prominent individuals, members of the princes' retinues, whose names are preserved here and there in the chronicles. In the first place there is Ostromir, mayor of Novgorod. His son Vyshata accompanied Rostislav Vladimirovich on his flight to Tmutorokan, which is all that is known about him. Another of Rostislav's companions was a certain Porey. A man of this name was killed fighting the Polovetsians at the battle on the Sozhitsa in 1078. If this was the same man, he must have joined Vsevolod's retinue after Rostislav's death.

There was a chiliarch Kosniachko in Kiev in 1067 under Iziaslav, with whom he probably fled. The same Kosniachko was with Iziaslav at the time of the ratification of the Law Code, when Sviatoslav of Chernigov was assisted by Pereneg, and Vsevolod of Pereiaslavl by Nikifor. If Kosniachko was chiliarch in Kiev, it may be surmised that Pereneg had the same office in Chernigov and Nikifor in Pereiaslavl. If this is so, it is interesting that the chiliarchs, who had a close relationship with the populace of the cities, were involved in the establishment of the Law Code.

It is not known who was chiliarch in Kiev after Iziaslav's first and second restorations, or under Sviatoslav, but under Vsevolod in 1089 the office was held by Yan, son of Vyshata, the famous chiliarch of Yaroslav's time. It appears that this same Yan collected tribute in the North in Sviatoslav's time.

The chronicles also record the names of two brothers *Chudin* and *Tuki*, whose names indicate their Finnic origins. After Iziaslav's first restoration Chudin governed Vyshgorod (1072). Tuki was active at the time of Iziaslav's first expulsion. It was he who advised Iziaslav to strengthen the guard about Vseslav, which shows that he must have belonged to Iziaslav's retinue. By the time of Iziaslav's second restoration he appears as a follower of Vsevolod, whom he accompanied on his campaign against the Polovetsians, and was slain in the battle on the Sozhitsa. The implication is that he left Iziaslav's retinue and joined Vsevolod's. Perhaps he was involved in the events at Kiev as a member of Vsevolod's retinue who fled to Kiev with Iziaslav from the field of battle. In that case it is curious that one brother took service under Iziaslav and another under Vsevolod.

Also slain at the battle on the Sozhitsa was Ivan Zhiroslavich, also a member of Vsevolod's retinue, as was Ratibor, whom he appointed burgrave of Tmutorokan when he was prince of Kiev.[51] It is impossible to establish the allegiance of Bern, who is mentioned in connection with the translation of the relics of St. Boris and St. Gleb. Probably he belonged to the retinue of Sviatoslav of Chernigov.

III

REIGN OF SVIATOPOLK IZIASLAVICH, 1093-1113

PREVIOUS CAUSES OF DISSENSION

Less than half a century had passed since the death of Yaroslav I before his sons' generation gave way to that of his grandsons. Internecine strife caused by the attempts of fatherless princes to obtain a part of the Land of Rus and their uncles' opposition began under the first generation, intensifying when Iziaslav was driven out by his brothers. Returning after the death of Sviatoslav, he deprived Sviatoslav's sons of their former lands, forcing them to seek refuge in distant Tmutorokan and, according to some sources, Murom. With the arrival on the scene of Yaroslav's grandsons the earlier causes of internecine strife remained. Therefore the same pattern of events as appeared under the rule of Yaroslav's sons were to be expected.

CHARACTER OF VLADIMIR MONOMAKH

Vladimir Monomakh and his brother Rostislav were in Kiev at the time of their father's death and burial. In the words of the chronicle "If I take my father's throne," thought Vladimir, "I shall have to fight a war with Sviatopolk because it was previously occupied by his father." Therefore, having thus considered, he summoned Sviatopolk[1] from Turov, himself going to Chernigov, while his brother Rostislav went to Pereiaslavl.[2] If Monomakh regarded the seniority and the rights of Sviatopolk Iziaslavich as the only obstacle to his occupation of the throne of Kiev it is clear that he did not see any other obstacles. In particular he did not expect any opposition on the part of the citizens of Kiev, being assured of their desire to have him as prince. There is no doubt that he won the affection of the people, for which he is particularly renowned in our ancient history. Monomakh is by no means one of those historical figures who look to the future, break down the old order and fulfill the new demands of society. His was a purely conservative character. He did not rise above the conceptions of his age, did not go against them, did not want to change the existing order. Rather by his personal valor and rigorous performance of his duties he concealed the shortcomings of the existing order, making it not merely tolerable for the people, but capable of satisfying their social requirements.

Society, disturbed by the strife among the princes, suffering so much as a result, required of a prince, first and foremost, that he fulfill kinship obligations to the letter, not *quarrel* with his brothers, pacify his warring kin and bring order to family affairs by wise counsel. Monomakh, at a time of violent hostility amongst brothers, won a reputation for brotherly love. To the pious, Monomakh was a model of piety. Contemporary sources record that everyone was impressed by his fulfillment of religious duties. To restrain the chief evil, strife amongst the princes, they all must keep the oaths they swore to each other. Monomakh would on no account break an oath.

Under other princes the people suffered by being denied the prince's justice while his agents and servitors despoiled them without his knowledge. Monomakh would not suffer the strong to harm either the lowly serf or the poor widow, and he *judged* the people himself. In accordance with the rough manners of the time the strong were not accustomed to restrain their wrath, whereas those who incurred it were liable to pay with their lives. Monomakh instructed his sons to spare the innocent and the guilty alike, and not to cause Christian souls to perish. While other princes gave themselves over to debauchery, Monomakh was distinguished by his chastity. Since avarice in a prince was particularly disliked, it gave rise to great dissatisfaction that St. Vladimir's grandsons and great-grandsons abandoned his principles and heaped up riches, burdening the people. In this respect also Monomakh was the model of a good prince. Contemporary sources testify that he was generous to all from his youth. He never hid his treasures, never counted his money, rather distributed it with both hands.

At the same time his treasury was always full because he combined generosity with good management, did not rely on his servants, and looked after his household affairs personally. More than any of his contemporaries he resembled his great-grandfather, the *gracious* prince Vladimir. "If you go anywhere in your lands," he instructed his children, "do not allow your servants to wrong the people in the villages or in the fields, lest they curse you afterwards. Wherever you go or stay, give food and drink to the poor. Above all honor the stranger, no matter whence he comes, be he of high or low degree, or an emissary. Give him good lodging, food and drink, for the traveller creates a man's reputation, good or ill, throughout the whole earth."[3] Vladimir himself followed the advice he gave his children. He himself served his guests, and while they ate and drank their fill he merely beheld them.

After the princes' feuds, the other great source of loss to the land were the Polovetsian[4] invasions. Monomakh was a defender of the Land of Rus from his early youth and fought for it against the heathen. His reputation was above all that of one who suffered (labored) for the Land of Rus. In those days, the youth of the nation, Monomakh's heroic exploits and remarkable deeds could not fail to excite general admiration, especially when directed to the nation's good. He spent the greater part of his life away from home, most of his nights being spent on the damp ground. He made eighty-three distant journeys. Whether at home or abroad, at war or at the chase, he did everything for himself, allowing himself no ease either day or night, in heat or cold. He rose before dawn, went to church, took counsel with his retinue, judged his people, went hunting or about some other business, lay down to sleep about midday and then resumed his activity.

A child of his age, Monomakh loved to try his huge strength as much on wild beasts as on the Polovetsians. He had a passion for the chase. He bound wild horses in the wilderness with his bare hands. More than once he was tossed by an aurochs, gored by a reindeer, trampled by an elk, had the sword torn from his side by a boar, was bitten by a bear and brought down together with his horse by a wolf. "I have not fled to save my life, nor have I spared myself," he said. "Children, fear neither battle nor beast, but acquit yourselves like men. Nothing can harm you, except that God permit it. If your death is ordained by God, neither father, mother nor brethren can prevent it. The care of God is better than the care of man."[5]

Monomakh combined this courage, daring and insatiable thirst for activity with common sense, acuity and capacity to look to the future and turn things to his advantage. These fine qualities he inherited from his parents, the good Vsevolod and his Greek princess. Amongst Monomakh's kin there were princes no less brave, no less active, like for example the sorcerer Vseslav of Polotsk or Sviatoslav's sons Roman and Oleg. Yet Monomakh's bravery and striving always were directed towards the good of the Land of Rus. The people became accustomed to this, used to trusting in the valor, good sense and good purpose of Monomakh, used to feeling secure behind his shield, and therefore grew strongly attached to him and all his posterity. Finally, respect for Monomakh was increased by the fact that in addition to his personal qualities he was descended through his mother from the imperial line. This appears to have been particularly important for the Greek-born metropolitans and for the clergy in general.

ACCESSION AND CHARACTER OF SVIATOPOLK IZIASLAVICH

The people of Kiev must have wanted Monomakh to be their prince, all the more so as they knew him well and knew his best side, whereas Sviatopolk Iziaslavich always lived in the Far North and only recently, after the death of his brother Yaropolk, came from Novgorod to Turov, no doubt in order to be nearer to Kiev in the event of Vsevolod's sudden death. We have seen the reasons which led Monomakh to decline the senior throne. He was afraid that Sviatopolk would insist upon his rights and maintain them by the sword. He must have known the possible consequences of such violations of rights, and also must have feared that if Sviatopolk threatened him from the West, neither would the sons of Sviatoslav leave him in peace in the East.

The citizens of Kiev could not fail to respect Monomakh's motives for refusing the throne, neither could they fail to sympathize with his respect for seniority. Moreover they had no right to reject Sviatopolk because they did not yet know his character, so when at Monomakh's invitation he arrived in Kiev from Turov they went out and did homage to him and received him with joy. Their joy must have been short-lived. In temperament the son of Iziaslav presented a striking contrast to the son of Vsevolod. Sviatopolk was cruel, grasping, hungry for power but lacking in wisdom and resolution, and his sons were like him.

WAR WITH THE POLOVETSIANS

The people of Kiev immediately received a demonstration of the new prince's incompetence. At that time the Polovetsians attacked the Land of Rus. Hearing of Vsevolod's death they sent envoys to Sviatopolk with offers of peace, or rather an offer to let him buy peace. Monomakh tells his children that he made peace with the Polovetsians twelve times, giving them large quantities of cattle and cloth in the process. The chronicle says that in this instance Sviatopolk took counsel not with the great retinue of his father and uncle, in other words not with the boyars of Kiev, but with those who came with him,[6] that is, with the retinue he brought from Turov, or more probably from Novgorod. This is again an evident complaint that the old boyars were *overtaken*[7] by the newly-arrived retinue of the new prince, which was inevitable so long as the principalities were not hereditary. On his retinue's advice Sviatopolk incarcerated the Polovetsian emissaries. He either begrudged the cattle and cloth necessary for buying peace, or was ashamed to begin his reign in such a manner.

When they heard their envoys were in prison the Polovetsians began hostilities and besieged the city of the Torks in great numbers.[8] Sviatopolk took fright, decided for peace, and released the envoys. The Polovetsians no longer wanted peace and continued the war. Sviatopolk gathered an army, but the wise advised caution. "Do not go out against them," they said, "you have too few men." "My own eight hundred servants are enough to withstand them," he replied. He was encouraged by the foolish to set out, yet those who had more sense told him "Even if we gathered eight thousand, they would barely be enough. Our land is impoverished through war and venality. You would do better to send to your cousin Vladimir for help."

Sviatopolk heeded them and sent to Vladimir, who gathered his army and also summoned his brother Rostislav from Pereiaslavl to Sviatopolk's aid. Vladimir came to Kiev and conferred with Sviatopolk at St. Michael's monastery,[9] and the two argued and disputed. "Why are you quarreling," their wise men upbraided them, "while the heathen destroy the Land of Rus? Settle your differences later, now go and face the heathen and either make peace or wage war." Vladimir was for peace and Sviatopolk was for war, then they finally agreed, swore an oath to each other, and the three princes, Sviatopolk, Vladimir and Rostislav marched out to Trepol.

Before they crossed the Stugna they called the retinue to a council of war. Vladimir proposed staying where they were and making peace because of the enemy's strength. He was supported by Yan and other wise men but the men of Kiev, who wanted to cross over and fight, prevailed. The army crossed the river, which was then in spate. Sviatopolk, Vladimir and Rostislav, having armed their retinue, opened the attack. Sviatopolk commanded the right wing, Vladimir the left and Rostislav the center. They passed Trepol and crossed over the earthwork when the Polovetsians showed themselves with their archers to the fore. The princes of Rus raised their standards between two earthworks and sent their archers forward across the earthwork. The Polovetsians came up to the earthwork, raised their banners, attacked Sviatopolk and broke his ranks. Sviatopolk stood firm, but when his men fled, he fled too. Then the Polovetsians attacked Vladimir, and after fierce fighting Vladimir and Rostislav also fled. They reached the Stugna and forded it, but during the crossing

Rostislav drowned before the eyes of his brother, who himself almost perished trying to save him. The sorrowing Vladimir, having lost his brother and most of his retinue, came to Chernigov, and Sviatopolk fled first to Trepol, where he took refuge until evening, and then reached Kiev by night. Seeing they had won, bands of Polovetsians scoured the country, while others returned to their siege of the Torks.

The Torks put up a fierce resistance from within the town, killing many Polovetsians, but the enemy did not reduce their attacks and cut off the water supply, hoping to overcome the defenders by hunger and thirst. The Torks sent a message to Sviatopolk that unless he supplied them with bread they would surrender. Sviatopolk sent bread but his wagons could not reach the town through the besiegers. After nine weeks outside Torchesk the Polovetsians split their forces. One detachment continued the siege, while the other marched on Kiev. Sviatopolk came out to meet them at the Zhelan.[10] The armies engaged, and again the Rus fled, this time with even greater losses than at Trepol. Sviatopolk returned to Kiev with only two companions, and the Polovetsians returned to Torchesk. The wicked sons of Ishmael, says the chronicle, burned the villages and threshing floors and churches, slaughtered the inhabitants, tortured the survivors and led them into captivity. The towns and villages were deserted, where once horses and sheep and oxen grazed there was desolation, and the fields were overgrown and the home of wild beasts.[11] When the victorious Polovetsians returned to Torchesk the inhabitants, weakened by hunger, surrendered. The Polovetsians, having captured the town, burned it and enslaved the inhabitants, distributing them among the encampments of their friends and kin. Sorrowful, exhausted with hunger and thirst, haggard, blackened, naked, barefoot, torn with thorns, the Rus captives trudged across the steppe, recounting to each other with tears where they were from, which town or which village.[12]

OLEG SVIATOSLAVICH MAKES WAR ON CHERNIGOV

Sviatopolk, seeing that he could gain nothing by force, made peace with the Polovetsians, for which he had to pay them everything they demanded, and he married the daughter of their khan Tugorkan.[13] In the same year, 1094, the Polovetsians appeared again, this time led by Oleg Sviatoslavich from Tmutorokan.[14] The serious defeat his cousins suffered at the hands of the Polovetsians the previous year encouraged Oleg to hope not only for a part of the Land of Rus, but all his father's domains, to which he and his brothers had every right. The relationship between Yaroslav's grandsons was now the same, as regards their position in the family, and consequently also as regards their rights to territory, as previously it was between his sons. Now Oleg had no wish to regard himself as a dispossessed prince. He came to Chernigov and besieged Monomakh in the fortress. The outskirts of the city and the monasteries were burned.

Monomakh's retinue fought the Polovetsians for eight days and prevented them from entering the city. In the end Monomakh had pity on the Christian blood being shed, and on the burning villages and monasteries. Saying "The heathen shall not boast," he relinquished Chernigov to Oleg, whose father once reigned there, himself departing to his father's principality of Pereiaslavl.

This is Monomakh's own account of his motives. It is hard to say to what extent he also was motivated by the impossibility of maintaining a long resistance with his small retinue which at the time of his departure from Chernigov numbered less than a hundred, including their wives and children. He had lost most of his retinue, including all his boyars, at the battle on the Stugna. Later he ransomed those taken prisoner, but evidently these were very few. With this little retinue Vladimir rode from Chernigov to Pereiaslavl through the Polovetsian ranks. The barbarians licked their lips like wolves, he says, but dared not attack.

Oleg became prince of Chernigov and the Polovetsians plundered the surrounding country. The prince offered no resistance, and indeed gave them leave, for he had no other means of rewarding the allies who won him his father's throne. "This was the third time," says the chronicle, "that he led the heathen into the Land of Rus. God forgive him this sin, for many Christians were slain, and others taken captive and scattered through many lands." The people of Rus did not forgive Oleg. As much as Monomakh was loved for his sufferings for the Land of Rus and for defending it from the heathen, so much was Oleg hated for causing it to be devastated by the Polovetsians. Seeing the disastrous consequences of Oleg's wars, they overlooked the wrong done to him, forgetting that he had to use force to obtain his father's place, from which his cousins excluded him.

VLADIMIR MONOMAKH IN PEREIASLAVL

Monomakh led an unenviable existence in Pereiaslavl. "Three summers and three winters," he complained, "my retinue and I spent in Pereiaslavl,

AN ENCOLPION FOUND AT CHERNIGOV

Eleventh Century

suffering much distress by war and hunger." There were continual
Polovetsian attacks on the already devastated principality. On one occasion Monomakh defeated the Polovetsians and took prisoners. In 1095
two Polovetsian khans, Itlar and Kitan, came to discuss peace with him,
or rather to haggle for how much the prince of Pereiaslavl was prepared
to give for it. Itlar and his chief men entered the city. Kitan remained with
the army between the earthworks, and Vladimir gave him his son Sviatoslav as hostage for the safety of Itlar, who was lodged in the house of
the boyar Ratibor. One of Sviatopolk's boyars, Slavata, sent to Vladimir
from Kiev on some business, persuaded Ratibor and his household to
approach Monomakh and obtain his consent to Itlar's murder. "How can
I do that when I have sworn an oath to him?" answered Vladimir. "Prince,"
they replied, "it would be no sin. The Polovetsians always swear oaths to
you, yet they continue to ravage the Land of Rus and shed Christian blood."

Vladimir listened to them, and sent a detachment of his retinue and
Torks to the earthworks by night. First they rescued Sviatoslav, then
massacred Kitan and all his retinue. This was on a Saturday night. Itlar
was spending the night at Ratibor's house, not knowing what had
happened to Kitan. Early on the Sunday morning Ratibor made ready a
group of armed men and told them to heat a cottage, while Vladimir sent
one of his servants with a message to Itlar and his men. "When you have
put on your shoes," he said, "and broken your fast in the warm cottage in
Ratibor's homestead, come to me." Itlar agreed, and the Polovetsians,
entering the cottage, were locked up there. Meanwhile Ratibor's men
climbed onto the roof and made a hole in it. Olbeg Ratiborovich drew his
bow and shot an arrow straight into Itlar's heart. Itlar's retinue also were
killed with arrows.[15]

HOSTILITY BETWEEN OLEG SVIATOSLAVICH AND HIS COUSINS

Sviatopolk and Vladimir then sent to Oleg in Chernigov, calling on him
to join them in making war on the Polovetsians. Oleg promised to join
them and set out, but separately. Clearly he did not trust them. What had
happened to Itlar may have been one of the reasons. Sviatopolk and
Vladimir attacked the Polovetsian camp and took it, carrying off cattle,
horses, camels and slaves to their own country. Oleg's cousins were
highly irritated by his mistrust, and sent their message to him after the
campaign. "You have not gone with us against the heathen who ravaged
the Land of Rus. Now Itlar's son is with you. Kill him, or give him up to

us, for he is the enemy of the Land of Rus." Oleg did not do as they said, and enmity arose between them.[16]

No account is found in the surviving chronicle manuscripts of the movement of Oleg's brother Davyd in the North, which is probably connected with these events. Only Tatishchev's digest of the chronicles[17] recounts that the other sons of Sviatoslav were princes of Murom in Vsevolod's time, which is highly probable. After Vsevolod's death Monomakh evidently was forced not only to give up Chernigov to Oleg, but also Smolensk to Davyd.

At the end of 1095 hostility again broke out between Oleg and his cousins Sviatopolk and Vladimir, who moved on Smolensk, removed Davyd and gave him Novgorod. Thence Vladimir's son Mstislav, installed there by his grandfather Vsevolod even before Sviatopolk left, moved to Rostov. They probably did not want the principalities of the sons of Sviatoslav to adjoin each other, making it easier for the princes to take concerted action. Sviatopolk and Vladimir therefore must install one of their own relatives in Smolensk, which divided from each other the territories of the sons of Sviatoslav. Indeed there is one account which says that Vladimir placed his son Iziaslav there. Davyd, perhaps with his brother's agreement, remained in Novgorod only a short time before returning to Smolensk, although he seems to have intended to hold on to Novgorod. This was because when the people of Novgorod during his absence invited Mstislav Vladimirovich back from Rostov and reinstated him, Davyd at once returned from Smolensk to Novgorod. The citizens warned him not to come, and he was forced to turn back to Smolensk. Iziaslav, expelled by him from there, attacked the territories of the sons of Sviatoslav, first Kursk, then Murom, where he seized Oleg's burgrave and made himself prince with the consent of the inhabitants.

The next year, 1096, Sviatopolk and Vladimir sent a message to Oleg. "Come to Kiev," they said, "and let us order the affairs of the Land of Rus before the bishops, the abbots, our fathers' men and the citizens, that henceforth we may together defend the Land of Rus against the heathen." Oleg replied that he "would not go to be judged by bishops, abbots or common people."[18] Having earlier feared to go on campaign with his brothers, how could he now decide to go to Kiev, where he knew that the clergy, the prince's retinue and townsmen were ill-disposed to him? Could he entrust himself to their decision? In any case a prince who was accustomed to rely on his sword alone, to settle his affairs by no other means, thought it a humiliation to go to judgment before bishops and commoners. In any case, Oleg's proud reply made him very unpopular in Kiev. The chronicler reproaches the prince of Chernigov for his haughtiness and magniloquence, also blaming his evil counsellors.

Sviatopolk and Vladimir declared war on him. "You will not accompany us against the heathen," was their message to him, "nor will you come to council with us, your intentions towards us must be evil, and you are disposed to aid the heathen. So God be our judge!" The princes rode to Chernigov against Oleg, who fled before them and shut himself up in Starodub, evidently to be nearer to his brothers' territories, whence he hoped to receive succor more swiftly. Sviatopolk and Vladimir besieged Starodub for thirty-three days. They attacked fiercely, but the defense also was resolute. Finally the defenders were exhausted. Oleg came out of the town to sue for peace, which his cousins granted. "Go to your brother Davyd," they said, "and come with him to Kiev, to the throne of our fathers and our grandfathers, for it is the first of the cities of our land. There it is that we should gather and order our affairs." Oleg promised to come, kissing the cross. He departed from Starodub to Smolensk, but the people of Smolensk would not receive him, and he was forced to go to Riazan.

Seeing that the sons of Sviatoslav had no intention of coming to Kiev to settle matters, Sviatopolk and Vladimir prepared to attack Davyd in Smolensk, but they made peace with him. Meanwhile Oleg led Davyd's army out of Riazan in an attack on Monomakh's son Iziaslav in Murom. Hearing of Oleg's approach, Iziaslav sent for the men of Suzdal, Rostov and Beloozero and collected a large army. Oleg sent to him, saying "Go to your father's principality of Rostov. This is my father's principality, and here I desire to rule and arrange matters with your father. He has driven me out of my father's city, and will you here deny me my own bread?"[19] Iziaslav, relying on his large army, would not listen to him but Oleg, says the chronicle, relied on the justice of his cause, for now he was in the right.

This comment of the chronicler's is very interesting. Since Oleg was deprived of Chernigov and Murom as a result of the war his cousins began against him, contemporary opinion must have considered the war itself unjust. Otherwise the chronicler would not have vindicated Oleg. On the contrary, he would have regarded loss of his lands as just punishment for his crimes. Oleg and Iziaslav fought before the walls of Murom, and in the fierce battle Iziaslav was killed. His army fled in all directions, some into the forest and the rest into the town. Oleg entered Murom and was accepted by the citizens. Seizing the men of Suzdal, Beloozero and Rostov and putting them in irons, he fell upon Suzdal, which capitulated. Oleg pacified the town, taking some of its citizens into captivity and settling others in various places after depriving them of their property. From Suzdal he proceeded to Rostov, which also surrendered. In this manner he subdued the whole land of Murom and Rostov, placed his burgraves in the towns and exacted tribute.

At this time there came to him an emissary from Mstislav Vladimirovich in Novgorod. "Leave Suzdal and go to Murom," was his message, "and do not rule a land that is not yours. My retinue and I will send to my father and reconcile you with him. Even though you have killed my brother, it cannot be helped. Both rulers and boyars fall in battle."

Oleg refused to make peace, intending to take Novgorod as well. He sent his brother Yaroslav to stand guard on the Medveditsa river, taking up his own position in the open country outside Rostov. After consulting the people of Novgorod, Mstislav sent out with an advance guard Dobrynia Raguilovich, who immediately arrested Oleg's *tax collectors*.[20] As soon as Yaroslav heard they were taken, he fled to Oleg by night, warning him of Mstislav's advance. Oleg retreated towards Rostov, pursued by Mstislav, then moved towards Suzdal with Mstislav still in pursuit. Oleg burned Suzdal and fled towards Murom. Mstislav arrived at Suzdal and paused there to send Oleg a renewed offer of peace. "I am younger than you," he said. "Resume relations with my father, dismiss your retinue, and I will do as you say." The reason why Mstislav was so humble in his dealings with Oleg is that he was Oleg's godson.

Seeing he would have difficulty overcoming Mstislav by force, Oleg decided to use cunning. He sent a peaceable answer to Mstislav who, hoping for peace, billeted his retinue about the countryside. Oleg unexpectedly appeared on the Kliazma. Mstislav was at dinner when he was informed of the approach of Oleg, who thought that his nephew, taken unawares, would flee, but he did not. In two days a retinue consisting of the men of Novgorod, Rostov and Beloozero rallied to him. These he positioned in front of the town, then when Oleg arrived neither side wanted to take the offensive. The two armies faced each other for four days, while Monomakh sent his other son Viacheslav with a force of Polovetsians to Mstislav's assistance. On the fifth day Oleg deployed his retinue and advanced on the town. Mstislav moved forward to meet him, giving Monomakh's banner and a troop of infantry to the Polovetsian Kunuy and placing him on his right flank. The battle was joined, with

Oleg's men against Mstislav's and Yaroslav's against Viacheslav's. Mstislav and the men of Novgorod passed through a fire. Catching up with the enemy on the Kolakcha river, they gained the upper hand, while Kunuy and his infantry attacked Oleg's rear, raising Vladimir's banner. Oleg and all his men were filled with terror and ran away.

Oleg fled to Murom, where he left his brother Yaroslav and a garrison, himself proceeding to Riazan. Mstislav followed him to Murom, where he made peace with the citizens and set free his men from Rostov and Suzdal whom Oleg earlier took captive. Mstislav pursued Oleg to Riazan, but Oleg fled again, and Mstislav made terms with the citizens of Riazan, who also freed their prisoners. From Riazan he sent his third offer of peace to Oleg. "Do not run," he said. "Send to your cousins and sue for peace, for they will not deprive you of the Land of Rus. I too will intercede with my father." Oleg promised to do as he said, and Mstislav returned to Suzdal and thence to Novgorod, whence he did indeed write to Monomakh to intercede on behalf of his godfather.[21]

PEACE NEGOTIATIONS BETWEEN OLEG AND VLADIMIR

When Monomakh received his son's letter, he wrote to Oleg. "I write to you at the urging of your godson, who has sent one of his men to me with a letter, saying 'Let us come to terms and be reconciled. My brother has gone to judgment, but let us not be his avengers. Rather let us entrust ourselves in all things to God. They will stand before the judgment of God, and we shall not destroy the Land of Rus.' Beholding such humility in my son, I was touched and filled with the fear of God, thinking 'If my son in the folly of his youth so humbles himself, what shall I do?' I am a sinful man, the most sinful of men. I have listened to my son and written to you. I shall see by your letter how you have received mine, with good-will or derision. I have written to you first, in the expectation of humility and penitence. Our Lord is no man, but the God of all creation. He does whatever He desires in the twinkling of an eye, yet endured reviling, spitting and blows. He submitted to death, the Lord of life and death.

"What are we sinful people? Today we live, tomorrow we are dead. Today we enjoy honor and glory, tomorrow we lie forgotten in our graves, while others divide what we have gathered. Consider, O brother, our fathers. What did they take with them, other than what they did for the good of their souls?

"It was for you to write such words first to me, cousin. When my child and yours[22] was killed before your very eyes, you beheld his blood and his body faded like a newly-opened flower, like a lamb at the slaughter, as you stood by him. 'Alas,' you should have thought, 'what have I done? For the sake of the injustice of this vain world I have taken this sin upon my soul and been the cause of my father and my mother's tears.' Then, like David, you should have said 'for I acknowledge my faults, and my sin is ever before me.'[23]

"You should have repented then before God, and sent letters of consolation to me, and also sent my daughter-in-law, for she is responsible for nothing, whether good or evil. I would have embraced her and wept with her for her husband and for their marriage instead of singing wedding songs, since I for my sins saw neither their first joy nor their wedding. For God's sake send her to me as soon as you can, let her abide with me like a turtledove mourning upon a dry tree, and God will be my comfort. This is the road that our fathers' children have travelled. Now God has called him to judgment. Had you done then according to your intentions, you would have taken Murom, not Rostov. You would have sent to me and we would have come to terms. Consider for yourself whether it was for me to write to you first, or you to me?

"As for what you said to my son, 'Send to your father,' I sent ten times. It is no wonder that a man died in battle, for so our forefathers died before. He should not have sought what was not his, bringing shame and sorrow upon me,[24] but he was urged on by his servants for their own gain and his ruin.

"If you desire to repent before God and make peace with me, write a sincere letter and send it to me with an envoy or a priest. Thus you will receive your principality honorably. It will turn our heart towards you, and we shall live better than before. I shall not be an enemy or an avenger to you. I did not wish to see your blood at Starodub. God forbid that I should see blood shed by your hand, or by the hand of any of my brethren, with my consent. If I lie, may God and the Holy Cross call me to account. If I sinned in marching on Chernigov against you on account of your friendship with the heathen, I repent. Now your godson and his young brother sit by you and eat their grandfather's bread, and you rule your own principality. So arrange matters, if you will. If you wish to kill them, they are in your power.

"I do not desire evil, I desire the good of my brethren and of the Land of Rus. Your patrimony, that you now strive to take by force, we offered you freely at Starodub. God is my witness that we came to terms with your brother, but he cannot make terms without you. We have done nothing evil, but have told him to send to his brother so that we may come to terms. If any of you does not desire the welfare and peace of Christian people, may his soul know no peace from God in the next world. It is not out of necessity that I write to you, for I suffer no misfortune. I write to you for God's sake, because my soul is dearer to me than the whole world."

CONGRESS OF LIUBECH

From this letter it is evident that it was Monomakh who wrote first to Oleg. The extremity to which Oleg was driven by Mstislav's assaults, and the sense of Monomakh's letter, must have convinced him of the necessity of a sincere rapprochement with his cousins. Thus in 1097 the princes— Sviatopolk, Vladimir, Davyd Igorevich, Vasilko Rostislavich, Davyd Sviatoslavich[25] and his brother Oleg—met to *make peace* at Liubech, which was in the principality of Chernigov, on the far side of the Dnieper. This may have been an additional concession to Oleg's suspicions. "Why should we destroy the Land of Rus," said the princes, "through our mutual hostilities? The Polovetsians despoil our lands and are glad when we quarrel. Let us then henceforth live with one heart and preserve the Land of Rus."

Apart from Vasilko Rostislavich the princes were all cousins, grandsons of Yaroslav. It was easy for them to agree, as all they had to do was to divide the principalities as they were divided amongst their fathers, whose places they now occupied. The root of all the hostilities was that the sons of Sviatoslav were denied the lands to which they were fully entitled by their position in the family as sons of the second son of Yaroslav. Now the princes decreed that each line rule its own patrimony. Sviatopolk was to have Kiev, with all the territories that always had belonged to it, and Turov. Vladimir received all Vsevolod's lands, that is, Pereiaslavl, Smolensk and the lands of Rostov, while Novgorod also remained under the rule of his son Mstislav. Oleg, Davyd and Yaroslav, the sons of Sviatoslav, received the principality of Chernigov.

There remained the dispossessed princes, Davyd Igorevich and the sons of Rostislav. In their case it was decided to hold to the decisions of Grand Prince Vsevolod and leave Davyd in possession of Vladimir-in-Volhynia, Volodar Rostislavich in Peremyshl and Vasilko in Terebovl. The princes confirmed their agreement with an oath. "If any of us attacks any of the others," they said, "we shall all resist him, and the Holy Cross also will be against him." "May the Holy Cross," they all repeated, "and the whole Land of Rus be against him." Parting with a kiss, the princes returned to their homes.

Absence of a hereditary system and of direct succession to the principalities was the main cause of the internecine strife arising in the first generation of Yaroslav's descendants and continuing in the second. At the Liubech congress the princes did away with this main reason by trying to confirm each member of the family in possession of the lands belonging to his father in the first generation. Indeed the meeting at Liubech did mark the end of the eastern struggle with the sons of Sviatoslav for Chernigov.[26]

BLINDING OF VASILKO ROSTISLAVICH

It was not the end of the western struggle in Volhynia, the seat of dispossessed princes, the sons of Rostislav and Davyd Igorevich. The youngest of the sons of Rostislav, Prince Vasilko of Terebovl, was distinguished by his particularly enterprising spirit.[27] He made a name for himself in his wars with Poland, which he ravaged with the Polovetsians. Now he started new campaigns. Hordes of Berendey, Pechenegs and Torks[28] answered his call. He prepared to lead them against Poland, conquer it and avenge the Land of Rus for the campaigns of both the Bolesławs.[29] Then he wanted to attack the Danube Bulgars[30] and force them to resettle in Rus. Finally, he wanted to attack the Polovetsians and either win glory or lay down his life for the Land of Rus. It is understandable that Davyd felt uncomfortable with such a prince for a neighbor, particularly since he did not know his real intentions, aware only of his warlike preparations and the approach of barbarian armies. He may well have thought that the martial Vasilko had designs first of all upon his own principality. The enmity between the sons of Rostislav and Yaropolk, the previous prince of Volhynia, was well known, as was the suspicion of their complicity in his murder.

There were those who took possibility for reality. It might have seemed strange that the two valiant princes, Monomakh and Vasilko, did not employ their valor and glory to enlarge their own power and dignity at the expense of the lesser princes. Three members of Davyd's retinue, Turiak, Lazar and Vasil, informed their prince that Monomakh and Vasilko were plotting against him and Sviatopolk, that Monomakh desired to rule in Kiev and Vasilko in Volhynia. Davyd was frightened. He was threatened with loss of his lands and exile, which he already had experienced. His men's words were plausible. Moreover we do not know what evidence they offered to support their allegations, nor even to what extent they were supported by the behavior of Monomakh and Vasilko at Liubech.

While the princes settled matters and made peace their men observed them and discussed the proceedings. God knows what conclusions they reached. In any case the chronicler and contemporary opinion in general apparently held that Davyd's men were chiefly to blame. Davyd himself is accused only of being too ready to believe their lying words in his fright. From Liubech he rode to Kiev with Sviatopolk, telling him as fact what he heard from his men. "Who killed your brother Yaropolk?" he asked. "Now he is plotting against you and me with Vladimir, so look to yourself!" Sviatopolk was perplexed, and did not know whether to believe him. "If you are telling the truth," he answered, "God be your witness, if you speak out of envy, God be your judge."

Then Sviatopolk's sorrow for his brother combined with concern for himself to make him wonder "What if it be true?" Davyd tried to convince him that it was true, and they considered together what to do about Vasilko, while Vasilko and Vladimir were completely unaware. "If we don't seize Vasilko," said Davyd, "you won't reign in Kiev nor I in Vladimir." Sviatopolk agreed.

At this point Vasilko arrived in Kiev, went to pray in St. Michael's monastery, where he also dined, and returned to his encampment. Next morning he received an invitation to Sviatopolk's nameday celebrations.[31] Vasilko declined, saying that he could not delay his journey, fearing war at home. Davyd sent urging him to accept. "Do not go away," he said, "do not disobey our elder brother." Vasilko still refused. "See," then said Davyd to Sviatopolk, "he refuses to have anything to do with you even when he is in your principality. What will he be like when he goes home? You will see that he will take your towns of Turov, Pinsk and the rest. Then you will remember what I have said. Summon the men of Kiev, seize him and deliver him to me."

Sviatopolk did as he said and sent to Vasilko, saying "If you do not want to stay until my nameday, at least come and see me now, and we will sit with Davyd a while." Vasilko promised to come, mounted his horse and was on his way, when one of his men met him. "Prince," said he, "do not go, for they intend to seize you." Vasilko did not believe him. "Seize me?" he thought. "They have sworn an oath to me. Have we not agreed that if any of us attack another, all will be against him, and the Holy Cross as well?" With this he crossed himself, saying "The Lord's will be done," and went on his way.

He came to the prince's court with few companions. Sviatopolk came out to meet him and brought him indoors. Davyd came, and they sat down. Sviatopolk again asked Vasilko to stay for the feast. "I have sent my wagons on," replied Vasilko, "I cannot possibly stay." Davyd was sitting there meanwhile as if dumb. Then Sviatopolk asked Vasilko at least to have breakfast with them. Vasilko agreed, and Sviatopolk went out. "Sit here," he said, "and I will see to it." Vasilko tried to converse with Davyd, who was so frightened that he seemed deaf and dumb. After a little while Davyd asked the servants "Where is my brother Sviatopolk?" They said that he was standing in the outer hall. "Sit here," said he to Vasilko, "while I go to him." As soon as Davyd left the room, the doors were locked upon Vasilko, who was bound with a double chain and had a guard set about him for the night.

Next morning Sviatopolk summoned the boyars and the citizens, telling them everything he had heard from Davyd, how Vasilko killed his brother, and now was plotting with Vladimir to kill him and take possession of his city. "You must look to your own safety, prince," the boyars and commoners replied. "If Davyd has spoken the truth, Vasilko must be punished, if falsely, he must answer before God." The abbots heard of it and interceded with Sviatopolk for Vasilko, but Sviatopolk said "It's all up to Davyd." Seeing that the people interceded for Vasilko and that Sviatopolk hesitated, Davyd urged that he be blinded. "If you do not," he said to Sviatopolk, "and let him go, neither of us will retain our principalities." According to the chronicle, Sviatopolk was for letting Vasilko go, but Davyd was utterly opposed, fearing the prince of Terebovl as he did. In the end Sviatopolk handed Vasilko over to Davyd.

They brought him in chains on a cart to Belgorod by night, and shut him up in a small cabin. Looking round, Vasilko saw Sviatopolk's shepherd, a Tork by the name of Berendi, sharpening his knife. Guessing he was about to be blinded, he "lifted up his voice to God with weeping and lamentation." Then Snovid Izechevich, Sviatopolk's groom, and Davyd's groom Dmitry, sent by their princes, entered and unrolled a carpet. They seized Vasilko and tried to knock him down, but he struggled with them so vigorously that the two of them could not overcome him. Only with the help of some others did they succeed in bringing him down and tying him up. Then they took a board off the stove an laid it on his chest. Snovid and

Dmitry sat on either end, but they could not keep him still, so two others took another board and also sat on it, and Vasilko's ribs began to crack. The Tork approached with his knife and tried to put his eye out, but missed, cutting his face. Finally he blinded him in both eyes and Vasilko lost consciousness.

They picked him up on the carpet and laid him on the cart like a corpse, taking him to Vladimir. When they crossed the bridge at Vzdvizhensk, Snovid and his men stopped, took off Vasilko's bloody shirt and gave it to the priest's wife to wash while they had dinner. When the priest's wife had washed the shirt, she put it back on Vasilko and wept over him as over a dead man. Vasilko regained consciousness and asked where he was. "In the town of Vzdvizhensk,"[32] replied the priest's wife. Then he asked for water, and when he drank, he came to himself completely and, feeling for his shirt, said "Why did you take it off me? Would that I had died and stood before God in that bloodstained shirt." Meanwhile Snovid and the rest finished their meal and continued the journey to Vladimir, where they arrived on the sixth day. Davyd also arrived there with them as if, the chronicle says, he had brought back some game from the hunt. He set a guard of thirty men about Vasilko, with two of the prince's servants at their head.[33]

REACTION TO THE BLINDING OF VASILKO

When Monomakh was told of Vasilko's capture and blinding he was horrified and wept. "Such an evil," he said, "has there never been in the Land of Rus, neither in our grandfathers' nor in our fathers' time."[34] He at once sent to Davyd and Oleg Sviatoslavich. "Come to Gorodets," he commanded, "let us put right the evil that has come to pass in the Land of Rus and among our brethren. A knife has been thrown in our midst. If we leave it, there will be yet greater evil. Brother will slay brother, the Land of Rus will perish, and our enemies the Polovetsians will come and take it." Davyd and Oleg were also grievously dismayed, they wept, assembled their armies, and at once marched to join Vladimir. Then the three of them sent to Sviatopolk. "Why have you done this evil in the Land of Rus," they demanded, "and thrown down the knife in our midst? Why have you blinded your brother? If he was guilty of anything, you ought to have accused him before us and then punished him according to his fault. Now tell us, what did he do to deserve this?" "Davyd Igorevich told me that Vasilko killed my brother Yaropolk," Sviatopolk replied, "and that he was planning to kill me and seize my lands, that he was plotting with

Vladimir to make Vladimir prince of Kiev and himself prince of Volhynia. I had no choice but to protect myself. In any case it was not I who blinded him, but Davyd. He took him to his own city, and blinded him on the way." "It is no justification for you that Davyd blinded him," objected the envoys of Monomakh and the sons of Sviatoslav, "it was not in Davyd's city that he was taken and blinded, but yours." With this they left him.

Next day the princes intended to cross the Dnieper and attack Sviatopolk, who prepared to flee from Kiev, but the citizens would not let him. They sent Vladimir's stepmother, Grand Prince Vsevolod's widow, and Metropolitan Nicholas[35] as their envoys to Vladimir. In the citizens' name they implored the princes not to make war on Sviatopolk. "If you fight among yourselves the heathen will rejoice and seize the Land of Rus, which your fathers and grandfathers obtained. They conquered the Land of Rus with great labor and valor, and sought other lands for themselves, but you will destroy the land that you have."

"Truly, our fathers and grandfathers preserved the Land of Rus," said Vladimir, weeping, "and we are about to destroy it." He consented to their plea. The princess and the metropolitan returned to Kiev, proclaiming that there would be peace.[36] The princes withdrew and exchanged messages. Vladimir and the sons of Sviatoslav sent to Sviatopolk. "Since this is all Davyd's doing" they said, "you, Sviatopolk, must march against him and either capture him or drive him out." Sviatopolk set about doing as they said.

Meanwhile Vasilko was still imprisoned in Vladimir, where the chronicler Vasily, who has left a record of these events, was also present. "One night," he says, "Prince Davyd sent for me. I came, and found him seated amongst his retinue. The prince bade me sit down and spoke. 'Tonight Vasilko has said to his guards "I hear that Vladimir and Sviatopolk are marching against Davyd. If Davyd would listen to me, I would send one of my boyars to Vladimir, and he would turn back." So, Vasily, go to your namesake[37] Vasilko and tell him that if he sends his man and Vladimir turns back, I will give him his choice of towns, Vsevolozh, Shepol or Peremyshl.'[38] I went to Vasilko and told him what Davyd said. 'I said no such thing,' he replied, 'but I trust in God, and I will send someone so that blood shall not be shed for my sake. One thing, though, surprises me. He offers me one of his towns, but my town is Terebovl, and that is my country. Send me Kulmey,' he continued, 'and I will send him to Vladimir.'"[39]

Davyd, evidently afraid to entrust the negotiations to a man of Vasilko's choice, sent Vasily back to tell Vladimir that Kulmey was not to be found. Vasilko sent his servant to the meeting and said to Vasily "I hear that Davyd wants to hand me over to the Poles. Evidently he has not had enough of my blood and wants more, for I have done much harm to the Poles and intended to do even more, wreaking vengeance on them for the Land of Rus. If he does hand me over to the Poles, I am not afraid of death, but I tell you that God has brought this misfortune upon me justly for my pride. When I heard that the Berendey, the Pechenegs and the Torks were rallying to me, I thought to myself 'When they come to me, I shall say to my brothers Volodar and Davyd "Give me your lesser retinues, and you drink and be merry."' For I thought to march on Poland in the winter, and conquer it in the summer and avenge the Land of Rus. Then I wanted to conquer the Bulgars of the Danube and settle them in my own lands. After that I intended to ask permission of Vladimir and Sviatopolk to make war on the Polovetsians and either win glory for myself or lay down my life for the Land of Rus. I had no intention of doing anything against Sviatopolk or Davyd. I swear by God and His coming that I have planned no evil against my brethren. God has brought me low and humbled me for my pride."

WAR BETWEEN DAVYD AND THE SONS OF ROSTISLAV

In the spring, before Easter, Davyd set forth to occupy Vasilko's principality. At Buzhsk[40] on the border he was met by Vasilko's brother Volodar. Davyd dared not do battle with him but shut himself up in Buzhsk, where Volodar besieged him, saying "Why have you done evil, and why do you not repent? Come to your senses after doing so much harm!" Davyd tried to put the blame on Sviatopolk. "Was it I that did it? Was it done in my city? I was afraid that they would lay hands upon me and do the same to me. I had no choice but to join in, because I was at his mercy." "Which of you is guilty, God knows," replied Volodar. "Release my brother to me, and I will make peace with you." Davyd was delighted and released Vasilko to Volodar. They made peace and parted.

The peace was short-lived. According to some accounts Davyd refused to return to the sons of Rostislav the towns which he occupied immediately after the blinding of Vasilko, hence they attacked him at Vsevolozh the following spring. Davyd shut himself up in Vladimir, and Vsevolozh was taken "by the lance" (by storm) and burned. When the inhabitants fled from the fire Vasilko had them massacred, thereby, remarks the chronicler, taking his revenge upon the innocent. Then the sons of Rostislav proceeded to Vladimir, where they besieged Davyd and sent a message to the citizens. "We have not come against you or against your city, but against our enemies Turiak, Lazar and Vasil, who incited Davyd to do such an evil deed. Give them up, or if you want to fight for them, we are ready."

The citizens called an assembly. "Give up those men," said they to Davyd, "for we are not prepared to fight for them, but we would fight for you. If you refuse, we will open the gates, and you can look out for yourself." "They are not here," replied Davyd, for he had sent them to Lutsk. The men of Vladimir ordered them brought from there. Turiak fled to Kiev, and Lazar and Vasil returned to Turiisk.[41] When they learned that they were in Turiisk, the men of Vladimir demanded of Davyd "Give them up to the sons of Rostislav, or else we will surrender at once." Davyd sent for Vasil and Lazar and gave them up. The sons of Rostislav made peace. The next morning before departing they hanged their prisoners and shot them with arrows. "This was the second time that Vasilko took vengeance," remarks the chronicle, "which he ought not to have done, for God should have been his avenger."[42]

Sviatopolk promised his cousins to march against Davyd and drive him out in the autumn of 1097, but it was not until 1099 that he went to Brest on the frontier to confer with the Poles. It is probably a reliable report that describes how he was afraid to attack Davyd, making up his mind only when he saw that the prince of Vladimir was defeated by the sons of Rostislav. Even then he wanted a Polish alliance first, and made a treaty with the sons of Rostislav too, swearing peace and friendship.

When Davyd heard that Sviatopolk was at Brest, he too applied to Prince Władysław Herman of Poland[43] for assistance. Thus the Poles became mediators in the struggle. They promised to help Davyd too, receiving fifty grivnas of gold in return. Władysław told him to go to Brest, where Sviatopolk invited him to confer, promising to reconcile them. Davyd did as he said and accompanied him, but Władysław found the alliance with Sviatopolk more profitable. The prince of Kiev also gave him rich gifts, and agreed to give his daughter in marriage to Władysław's son. For this reason Władysław told Davyd that he found it impossible to incline Sviatopolk towards peace. He advised him to go home, though he also promised him military support should he be attacked by his cousins.

Davyd returned to his throne of Vladimir while Sviatopolk, concluding his agreement with the Poles, went first to Pinsk, whence he summoned his army, and then to Dorogobuzh, where he waited for it to join him. Then he led it against Davyd in Vladimir, besieging the city for seven weeks. Davyd still would not surrender, expecting help from the Poles. When he realized none was forthcoming, he sent to Sviatopolk asking permission to leave the city. Sviatopolk agreed, and they swore an oath to each other. Davyd then left for Cherven and Sviatopolk entered Vladimir. It is evident from this narrative that Davyd made an agreement with Sviatopolk relinquishing Vladimir to him, contenting himself with Cherven. Having expelled Davyd from Vladimir, Sviatopolk turned his attention to Volodar and Vasilko. "They are ruling the principality of my father and brother," said he, and attacked them.

The progress of this war is an excellent demonstration of Sviatopolk's character. First he long feared to attack Davyd. He only made his move when assured of safety from the Poles, after Davyd failed in his war with the sons of Rostislav. When he eventually secured Vladimir he remembered that under his father Iziaslav the entire principality of Volhynia belonged to Kiev. Subsequently it was ruled by his brother Yaropolk, and that according to the Liubech accord each prince was to rule his patrimony. Sviatopolk therefore marched against the sons of Rostislav, forgetful of his recent agreement and oath.

It was not easy to dislodge the sons of Rostislav from their principality. They resisted Sviatopolk and took with them the cross he kissed when he swore his oath, meeting him on the border of their dominions, at Rozhne plain.[44] Before the battle began Vasilko lifted up the cross and called out to Sviatopolk "This is what you kissed. First you took away my eyes, now you would take away my life, so let this cross judge between us." It was said afterwards that many God-fearing people saw the cross appearing in the air above Vasilko.

The battle was fierce, with many casualties on both sides. Eventually Sviatopolk, finding himself hard pressed, fled to Vladimir. Volodar and Vasilko, having won the battle, halted. "It is enough for us" they said, "if we stand upon our border," and went no further.[45] Meanwhile Sviatopolk fled to Vladimir with his two sons Mstislav and Yaroslav, his two nephews the sons of Yaropolk, and Sviatoslav, or Sviatosha, son of Davyd Sviatoslavich. He made his son Mstislav prince of Vladimir. Sending his other son Yaroslav to Hungary to persuade the king to attack the sons of Rostislav, he returned to Kiev.

Yaroslav persuaded the Hungarians to attack Volodar's territory. King Kálmán[46] came with two bishops and encamped upon the Vagr river not far from Peremyshl, and Volodar shut himself up in the town. At the same time Davyd came back from Poland, whither he had fled from Cherven before the outbreak of hostilities between Sviatopolk and the sons of Rostislav. He seems not to have found any help in Poland, and the common threat now united him with the sons of Rostislav. Therefore, leaving his wife with Volodar, he set off to hire Polovetsian mercenaries. On the way he encountered their famous khan Boniak, and together they attacked the Hungarians. At midnight, when all the army slept, Boniak arose, went alone into the steppe, and howled like a wolf. A wolf answered him, then another and another, and Boniak returned and said to Davyd "Tomorrow we shall have victory over the Hungarians."[47]

The next morning Boniak deployed his men. He had three hundred, and Davyd one hundred, and he divided them all into three regiments. He sent Altunopa ahead against the Hungarians with a detachment of fifty men, placed Davyd beneath the standard, and divided his company into two halves, fifty men in each. The Hungarians were ranged in a series of detachments, one behind the other.[48] Altunopa's troop rode up as far as the first of them, shot their arrows, and withdrew. The Hungarians pursued them, and when they rode past Boniak's position, he attacked their rear. At the same time Altunopa turned back, so that the Hungarians were caught between two enemy detachments and cut off from their own main army. Boniak threw them into confusion, as a falcon brings down a jackdaw, as the chronicler puts it.[49]

The Hungarians fled, and many drowned in the Vagr and the San, because they ran down the hillside beside the San, pushing each other into the water. The Polovetsians pursued them, killing them for two days. Among the victims were a bishop and many lords.[50] Sviatopolk's son Yaroslav fled to Poland. Davyd took advantage of the victory to seize Suteisk and Cherven,[51] coming suddenly to Vladimir and occupying the surrounding villages. Mstislav Sviatopolchich shut himself up in the citadel with a garrison consisting of men of Brest, Pinsk and Vygoshev.

Davyd besieged the citadel and made many assaults. Once during a furious exchange of arrows between the besiegers and defenders Mstislav wanted to join the archers, then an arrow which flew in through a slit in the earthworks struck him in the chest, and he died the following night. His death was kept secret for three days, and on the fourth it was announced at the popular assembly. "The prince is dead," said the people. "If we surrender now, Sviatopolk will kill us all." They sent a message to him, saying "Your son is slain, and we perish from hunger. If you do not come, the people will want to surrender."[52]

Sviatopolk sent them his commander Putiata. When he arrived with his men at Lutsk, where Sviatosha Davydovich was, he found Davyd Igorevich's envoys with him. Sviatosha had sworn to let Davyd know when Sviatopolk attacked him. Now, being afraid of Putiata, he seized Davyd's envoys and marched against him together with the Kievan commander. Sviatosha and Putiata reached Vladimir at midday, attacked the sleepy Davyd and slaughtered his retinue, while the men of Vladimir made a sortie from the citadel on the other side. Davyd and his nephew Mstislav fled. Sviatosha and Putiata secured the town and installed Sviatopolk's burgrave Vasil there. They then departed, Sviatosha to Lutsk and Putiata to Kiev. Meanwhile Davyd again fled to the Polovetsians. Again he encountered Boniak on the way and they went together to besiege Sviatosha in Lutsk. Sviatosha made peace and went to his father in Chernigov. Davyd took Lutsk, whence he proceeded to Vladimir, expelled Sviatopolk's burgrave Vasil and resumed his previous throne, while his nephew Mstislav went to the coast to waylay merchants.[53]

CONGRESS AT VITICHI

Immediately after the account of Mstislav's departure for the coast in the year 1100 the chronicle records a new congress of all the princes in Vitichi or Vitichev.[54] Present were Sviatopolk, Vladimir, Oleg and Davyd Sviatoslavich. Davyd Igorevich also arrived, saying "Why have you summoned me? Here I am. Who has any complaint against me?" "You yourself sent to us," replied Vladimir, "saying that you desired to come to us and complain of the injury done to you. Now that you have come, and are sitting on the same carpet as your brethren, why do you not make your complaint? Which of us has given you cause for complaint?" Davyd made no reply.

Then they all arose, mounted their horses and departed, each encamping separately with his retinue, while Davyd remained alone. They did not admit him to their company and considered his case without him. Having considered, they sent their men to him. Sviatopolk sent Putiata, Vladimir sent Orogost and Ratibor, Davyd and Oleg sent Torchin. "We do not want to give you the throne of Vladimir," the princes' representatives declared, "because you have thrown down the knife amongst us, such as never has happened before in the Land of Rus. We shall neither imprison you nor do you any other harm. Go, rule in Buzhsk and Ostrog, and Sviatopolk will give you Dubno and Chartoryisk as well. Vladimir will give you two hundred grivnas, and Davyd and Oleg likewise two hundred grivnas."

Then the princes sent to Volodar Rostislavich. "Take your brother Vasilko," they said, "and share with him the principality of Peremyshl or, if you do not agree, send Vasilko to us, and we shall maintain him. Also release our serfs and bondsmen." The sons of Rostislav would not obey, each holding on to what he had. The princes were on the point of compelling them by force to agree but Monomakh refused to go with them, unwilling to break the oath he swore to the sons of Rostislav at Liubech.[55]

Here we must supply certain elements which the chronicle omits from the chain of events. Davyd, as we have seen, remained victorious over Sviatopolk and maintained his hold on Vladimir. Sviatopolk, unable to overcome him, had to call on his other cousins. They entrusted to him the punishment of Davyd who, for his part, apparently also called on them to defend him against Sviatopolk. As the chronicle says, the princes made peace with one another at Vitichi on August 10, which evidently means that they decided through their representatives to meet all together in one place, which they did on August 30.

Davyd was invited to attend and dared not refuse, for he could not hope to vanquish the combined forces of all the princes as he previously had overcome Sviatopolk. Moreover, according to some accounts, the princes' message was couched in friendly terms, promising to confirm him in possession of Vladimir. Indeed a very clement sentence was pronounced upon him, for to lay hands upon a prince who appeared at a conference of his brethren of his own free will would have been a perfidy sufficient to destroy the possibility of holding such a conference ever again. To deny him a principality would have meant continuing the war, and Davyd had proved his skill at extricating himself from the most difficult of circumstances. Therefore they decided to give him an adequate principality, punishing him only by taking away the throne of Vladimir, which was given to Sviatopolk as his patrimony on the basis of the accord of Liubech, while Sviatopolk gave Davyd also Dorogobuzh, where he died.

Thus the princes' conference put an end to a struggle begun under Yaroslav's immediate successor, which had continued for almost half a century. The dispossessed princes and their descendants could not establish themselves in separate patrimonies anywhere. Only the sons of Rostislav secured a separate principality, subsequently giving it real historical significance. The descendants of Viacheslav Yaroslavich left the scene in the first generation, and Igor's in the second. Subsequently they appear only as princelings of insignificant lands with no capacity for independent action.

Full rights were enjoyed only by the descendants of Yaroslav's three eldest sons, after the vain attempt to reduce the sons of the second, Sviatoslav, to the status of dispossessed princes. It required a long struggle for them to attain their father's status and territory. It was not easy to foresee the disparity in the distribution of territory between the three lines, nor the advantage obtained by the son of Vsevolod thanks to his own abilities and favorable circumstances. Monomakh kept in his family the principalities of Pereiaslavl, Smolensk, Rostov and Novgorod. Sviatopolk did not receive Vladimir-in-Volhynia until after the Vitichi accord, while Novgorod the Great, which always was closely linked with Kiev, eluded him. The dominions of the sons of Sviatoslav were the smallest of all, for they received nothing in addition to their original patrimony, and moreover there were three of them.

DISPOSITIONS CONCERNING NOVGOROD

It would seem that Sviatopolk was very dissatisfied that Novgorod did not belong to his family, yet it was impossible to take it from Monomakh without some kind of recompense. Therefore he decided to sacrifice Volhynia in order to obtain Novgorod, and agreed that Monomakh's son Mstislav should move to Vladimir-in-Volhynia, while his own son Yaroslav, hitherto prince of Vladimir, should take his place in Novgorod. At this point the men of Novgorod for the first time resisted the will of the princes. Novgorod's dependence upon Kiev was disadvantageous to its citizens insofar as it entailed repercussions of all the vicissitudes and divisions of Rus within its walls.

The expulsion of Iziaslav from Kiev inevitably resulted in changes in Novgorod. Sviatoslav's son Gleb became its prince, then he too was forced to leave Novgorod as a result of the second triumph of Iziaslav, who sent his son Sviatopolk there. Towards the end of Vsevolod's reign Sviatopolk left Novgorod for Turov to be nearer to Kiev, and Vsevolod sent his grandson Mstislav to Novgorod. Then Sviatopolk and Monomakh withdrew Mstislav and sent Davyd Sviatoslavich instead. When Davyd left Novgorod, Mstislav came back again.

Thus in the forty-seven years from 1054 to 1101 there were six changes of prince in Novgorod. Two of them left of their own free will, the rest departed as a result of a change of grand prince or the grand prince's agreement with the others. Now, in 1102, the princes again demanded that the citizens of Novgorod part with Mstislav Vladimirovich and accept a son of Sviatopolk in his place. The men of Novgorod firmly refused. In so doing they probably knew that by disobeying Sviatopolk they were doing what Monomakh wanted. They could not have kept his son as their prince against his will, nor could they have quarrelled with the two most powerful princes of Rus while remaining themselves without a prince.

A strange scene was enacted at the prince's court in Kiev in the presence of Sviatopolk. Mstislav Vladimirovich appeared, accompanied by the envoys of Novgorod. "Vladimir has sent his son, and the men of Novgorod are sitting here," Monomakh's envoys announced to Sviatopolk. "Let them take your son to Novgorod, and let Mstislav go to Vladimir." "Prince," said the men of Novgorod to Sviatopolk, "we are sent to say to you that we want neither Sviatopolk nor his son. If your son has two heads, send him to us. Mstislav was given to us by Vsevolod. We have raised him to be our prince, while you departed from us." Sviatopolk argued with them for a long time, but they would not be won over, and when they left they took Mstislav back with them to Novgorod.[56]

The reason for Novgorod's reference to Vsevolod's decision was presumably that at Liubech the princes themselves determined to conform to his last arrangements, while what they said about having raised Mstislav for themselves probably reflected a desire to have a permanent prince, raised in their city, which was precisely what the princes' clan reckonings and disputes so far prevented. Finally, by reproaching Sviatopolk for having departed from them, the men of Novgorod intended to express their dissatisfaction that he preferred Turov to their city, suggesting that by leaving Novgorod voluntarily he resigned all right to it.

FATE OF YAROSLAV YAROPOLCHICH

No sooner did the accord of Vitichi put an end to the old strife arising from the position of the dispossessed princes than new discord arose, for there were also dispossessed princes in the second generation of Yaroslav's descendants. Sviatopolk had a nephew Yaroslav, his brother Yaropolk's son. In 1101 he "shut himself up" in Brest against his uncle, a sure sign that his uncle did not wish to allow him any territory, while he hoped to secure at least Brest for himself by force. Sviatopolk attacked, forced him to surrender and brought him to Kiev in chains. The metropolitan and the abbots persuaded Sviatopolk to set him at liberty after he took an oath at the tomb of Boris and Gleb, probably swearing not to make any more attempts on his uncle's territory and to live peacefully in Kiev. Even so, the next year Yaroslav left his uncle. His cousin Yaroslav Sviatopolchich pursued him, captured him by deceit on the other side of Brest, by the Polish border, and brought him to his father in chains. This time the son of Yaropolk was kept in captivity, and died in exile the same year.[57]

EVENTS IN THE PRINCIPALITY OF POLOTSK

The famous warlock Vseslav of Polotsk gave the sons of Yaroslav no more trouble in his old age, and let them proceed with their affairs without interference. His death in 1101 marked the end of Polotsk as a power. His sons, of whom there were seven, seem to have lost no time in plunging into disagreements in which the sons of Yaroslav intervened. Thus it is recorded that in 1104 there was a campaign against Gleb in Minsk to which Sviatopolk sent Putiata, and Vladimir sent his son Yaropolk. Oleg marched himself in company with Davyd Vseslavich, which shows that the campaign was undertaken for the benefit of Davyd, who was allied even earlier with the descendants of Yaroslav. It came to nothing.

WAR WITH THE POLOVETSIANS

Such were the princes' relations amongst themselves under the first grand prince of the second generation after Yaroslav. As for external relations, we have seen that the populace feared the princes' squabbles chiefly because of the opportunities they opened to the heathen Polovetsians. This fear was also the main stimulus towards peace amongst the princes themselves. The southern part of Rus, as a borderland of Europe, was forced, like the Greek Pontic colonies of old, to maintain a constant state of armed readiness.

How very inauspicious in this respect was the beginning of the reign of Sviatopolk, who set the precedent of matrimonial alliance with the Polovetsian khans. After the killing of Itlar and the princes' successful steppe campaign of 1095 the Polovetsians appeared on the Ros, the effective border between Rus proper and the steppe. They besieged Yuriev, one of the towns founded there by Yaroslav I, which was named in his honor.[58]

The barbarian siege, which lasted a whole summer, was very nearly successful. Sviatopolk, according to the chronicle, *pacified* them. In other words he bought them off, in spite of which they remained within the bounds of Rus and did not recross the Ros into the steppe. The people of Yuriev, seeing this and weary of living in constant jeopardy, fled to Kiev, and the Polovetsians burned the abandoned town, an event that well illustrates the condition of the Southern Rus borderlands at that time. Sviatopolk had a new town built on Vitichi hill, fifty-six versts from Kiev along the Dnieper. He named it Sviatopolch, telling the people of Yuriev and their bishop to live there. Their numbers were swelled further by refugees from other areas bordering the steppes, troubled by fear of the Polovetsians.

In the next year, 1096, taking advantage of the absence of Sviatopolk and Monomakh who were occupied with their wars against the sons of Sviatoslav in the North, the Polovetsians did not confine themselves to destroying border fortresses. Their khan Boniak, who established such a dire reputation in our chronicles, appeared outside Kiev, devastated the surrounding countryside and burned the prince's country residence at Berestovo. On the eastern side of the Dnieper another khan, Kuria, laid waste the country about Pereiaslavl.[59] The success of Boniak and Kuria tempted Sviatopolk's father-in-law Tugorkan, who also besieged Pereiaslavl. By this time the princes had returned from campaign and attacked the Polovetsians at Pereiaslavl, defeating them and killing Tugorkan and his sons and princes. Sviatopolk had Tugorkan's body taken and buried at Berestovo.

While the princes were occupied east of the Dnieper, the *mangy predator* Boniak unexpectedly returned to Kiev, which he very nearly succeeded in entering, and burned the surrounding villages and monasteries, including that of the Caves. "They came to our monastery," says the chronicler, who was a witness of these events, "while we were sleeping in our cells after matins. Suddenly they raised a shout about the monastery and planted two banners before the gates. We fled out of the back[60] of the monastery and others climbed up on the buildings, while the godless sons of Ishmael broke down the gates and went through the cells, breaking down the doors and removing everything they could lay their hands on. Then they burned the church of the Mother of God, and entered the chapel by the tomb of St. Feodosy, taking the icons. They burned the doors, reviling God and our religion." At the same time they burned the Red Court that Vsevolod built at Vydubets Hill.[61]

Once the princes resolved their differences at Vitichi, they could take the offensive against the Polovetsians. In 1101 Sviatopolk, Monomakh and the three sons of Sviatoslav met at the Zolotcha river on the right bank of the Dnieper in order to attack the Polovetsians, who sent emissaries in the name of all their khans to treat for peace. "If you want peace," the princes of Rus told them, "let us meet at Sakov."[62] The Polovetsians met them at the appointed place. They made peace, both sides taking hostages.

Nevertheless the princes of Rus did not give up the idea of campaigning against the barbarians, and the chronicler consistently describes this idea as "good," inspired by God. In 1103 Vladimir suggested to Sviatopolk a spring campaign against the heathen.[63] When Sviatopolk discussed this with his retinue they said that it was not the right time to take the men from the fields. Sviatopolk told Vladimir that they should take counsel with their retinues about it. They agreed to meet at Dolobsk (near the lake of the same name) on the left-hand side of the Dnieper above Kiev, where Sviatopolk, Vladimir and their followers gathered in one tent. After a long silence, Vladimir opened the discussion. "Brother, you are the elder, it is for you say what steps we should take for the Land of Rus." "It would be better for you to speak first, brother," replied Sviatopolk. "How can I speak?" said Vladimir. "Both our retinues will be against me, and will say that I want to ruin the tillers of the soil and their land. I am surprised only that, in your concern for the peasants and their horses, you do not consider that when the peasant goes out to plough with his horse in the spring a Polovetsian comes and shoots him with his bow and arrow, taking his horse and wife and children, and burning his barn. You do not think of this." "Indeed," replied the men, "it is so." "I am ready," said Sviatopolk, rising. "This is a great deed" said Vladimir, "that you are performing for the Land of Rus."[64]

They also sent to the sons of Sviatoslav to summon them to join the campaign, saying "Let us go against the Polovetsians, whether we live or die!" Whereas Davyd responded, Oleg sent a message that he was unwell. Besides these elder princes there were four younger on campaign, namely Davyd Vseslavich of Polotsk, Mstislav the nephew of Davyd Igorevich of Volhynia (a dispossessed prince), Sviatopolk's nephew Viacheslav Yaropolchich (another dispossessed prince), and Monomakh's son Yaropolk Vladimirovich. The princes took both mounted troops and footmen who travelled along the Dnieper in boats, while the cavalry rode along the bank. When they passed the rapids the infantry disembarked at Khortitsa island, and the cavalry mounted their horses, traversing the steppe for four days.

When the Polovetsians learned that the Rus were marching against them, they gathered together to take counsel. "Let us make an offer of peace," said Urusoba, one of their khans, "for they will fight fiercely against us after all the harm we have done their land." "If you are afraid of the Rus, we aren't," replied the young men. "We will beat them and ride into their land to take their cities, for who will defend them against us?"

Meanwhile the princes and warriors of Rus were at prayer and made vows, some to have prayers said for the dead, others to give alms to the poor and others to supply the monasteries with necessities for the brethren. The Polovetsians sent Altunopa, famed among them for his courage, forward with an advance guard. The Rus also sent out to test the enemy's strength a forward detachment which encountered Altunopa's men and utterly destroyed them. Then the two main armies met, and that of Rus was victorious, killing twenty khans. Khan Beldiuz was taken alive and brought to Sviatopolk. He offered a ransom of gold and silver, horses and cattle. Sviatopolk sent him to Vladimir. "How many times," asked Vladimir, "have you sworn not to make war, yet have made war upon the Land of Rus? Why did you not teach your sons and kinsmen to keep their oaths, instead of shedding Christian blood? Your blood be upon your own head." He commanded his execution, and Beldiuz was hacked to pieces.

Then all the princes met and Vladimir said "This is the day that the Lord has made, let us rejoice and be glad therein. The Lord has delivered us from our enemies and subjected them to us. He has crushed the serpents' heads and given them as food for the people of Rus." Then the warriors took many cattle, sheep, horses, camels and tents, with many goods and slaves. They took the Pechenegs and Torks subject to the Polovetsians, and returned to Rus with great booty, glory and triumph. Sviatopolk thought that he would be free of the Polovetsians for a long time and ordered the rebuilding of the town of Yuriev which previously they had burned.[65]

Nevertheless the dread Boniak was still alive, and the following year made his presence felt when he came to Zarub, which was on the western side of the Dnieper opposite the mouth of the Trubezh, defeating the Torks and Berendey. The following year, 1106, Sviatopolk was forced to send three of his commanders against the Polovetsians plundering the land about Zarechsk, in order to regain what they took. In 1107 Boniak seized several herds of horses near Pereiaslavl, and the Polovetsians advanced accompanied by many other khans and took up a position near Lubeny[66] on the Sula. When Sviatopolk, Vladimir, Oleg and four other princes made a surprise attack on them the Polovetsians were so frightened that they fled without even raising their banner. Those who had time to find mounts fled on horseback, the rest on foot, and the princes of Rus pursued them as far as the Khorol river and captured their baggage. Sviatopolk came to matins at the monastery of the Caves on the feast of the Dormition [August 15] and was congratulated by the monks on his victory.[67]

Despite these successes Monomakh, Oleg and Davyd Sviatoslavich arranged a meeting the same year with two khans and accepted their daughters as brides for their sons. A campaign led by the three princes Sviatopolk, Vladimir and Davyd in 1110 ended fruitlessly, as they were forced to return from the town of Voin on account of the cold and a murrain amongst the horses.

The following year, at the "counsel and desire" of Monomakh, the princes decided to make a foray against the Polovetsians on the Don, where Vladimir's commander Dmitro Ivorovich fought in 1109, capturing three Polovetsian encampments.[68] Sviatopolk, Vladimir, Davyd and his sons set out on the second Sunday of Lent. By Friday they reached the Sula, and by Saturday were at the Khorol, where they abandoned their sledges.

On the Sunday of the Veneration of the Cross[69] they marched from the Khorol to the Psel. They continued to the Goltva river, where they waited for the rest of their army before setting off to the Vorskla. Here, on the Wednesday, they kissed the cross with many tears, and after traversing many rivers they reached the Don on the Tuesday of the sixth week. Here they put on their armor and advanced in battle formation on the Polovetsian town of Sharukan. Vladimir ordered his priests to ride at the head of the army chanting prayers. The inhabitants of Sharukan came out to meet the princes with fish and wine. The army spent the night there. The next day, Wednesday, it proceeded to another town, called Sugrov, which they burned. On Thursday they left the Don. On Friday, March 24, the Polovetsians assembled and marched against the Rus. The princes placed all their hope in God, says the chronicler. "This is where we shall die," the princes said one to another. "Let us stand firm." They embraced and, raising their eyes to Heaven, called upon God Most High.

God helped the princes of Rus. After fierce fighting the Polovetsians were defeated, and many of them fell. Joyfully did the army of Rus celebrate the raising of Lazarus and the Annunciation the next day [March 25], and on the Sunday they advanced further. On the Monday of Holy

Week another large Polovetsian force assembled and engaged the army of Rus on the Salnitsa river. When the Rus fell upon the Polovetsians it was like the sound of thunder, the battle was fierce, and many fell on both sides.

At length Vladimir and Davyd and their men joined the fray, the Polovetsians fled before them, falling before Vladimir's army, struck down invisibly by an angel. Many saw how their heads flew, struck off by an invisible hand. Sviatopolk, Vladimir and Davyd glorified God, Who gave them such a victory over the heathen. The Rus took great booty of cattle and horses and sheep, also many prisoners. "How is it," the victors asked their captives, "that you were such a great force, yet you could not fight us and fled so soon?" "How could we fight you?" was the reply. "There were others in terrible shining armor who rode above you and helped you." These, explains the chronicler, were angels sent by God to the aid of the Christians. It was also an angel who put it into Vladimir's heart to urge his brethren to attack their enemies. Thus with God's help the princes returned home to their people with great glory. Their fame was carried into far countries, as far as the Greeks, the Hungarians, Poles and Czechs, even as far as Rome.[70]

The chronicle account of the princes' Don campaign against the Polovetsians is given here in full detail in order to demonstrate the importance attached to this campaign at the time. The times of Sviatoslav of old had passed out of memory. Since then none of the princes had campaigned so far east. Against whom did they fight? Against those dreadful enemies who more than once stood before the walls of Kiev and Pereiaslavl, from whom whole towns fled. The Polovetsians now were defeated, not within the territory of Rus, not on its borders, but deep within their own steppes. This explains the religious enthusiasm with which the chronicle describes the event. Only an angel could have inspired Monomakh with the thought of such a vital enterprise, an angel helped the princes of Rus to overcome their innumerable enemies. If the fame of this campaign carried into far countries it can be imagined how it was celebrated within Rus and how much glory attached to the prince whom the angel inspired to persuade his cousins to undertake the campaign. Monomakh enjoyed the special protection of Heaven. It was in front of his troops, it was said, that the Polovetsians fell, cut down by the invisible angel. The people long preserved the memory of Monomakh as the chief and only hero of the Don campaign, the tradition of how he drank the water of the Don from his golden helm, driving the accursed sons of Hagar beyond the Iron Gates.

STRUGGLE WITH OTHER NEIGHBORING PEOPLES

The princes, and primarily Monomakh, took this glorious advantage of the cessation of their internal feuding. The chief interests of the Land of Rus were linked to the struggle with the Polovetsians and the relations between the princes. Yet from its distant borders in the North and East and West came news of struggles with other surrounding tribes. The men of Novgorod under Prince Mstislav fought the Chud west of Lake Peipus. The princes of Polotsk and Volhynia fought with the Yatviags[71] and the Latvians, sometimes victorious and sometimes defeated. And Sviatoslav's youngest son Yaroslav, who appears to have been prince of Murom, waged an unsuccessful war on the Mordvinians.

LINKS WITH HUNGARY

Under Sviatopolk the history of Rus finds links with that of Hungary. The invasion of the Magyars and their establishment in the plains of Pannonia among the ruins of the Moravian state[72] was of enormous significance for the West Slavonic peoples. Emperor Leo the Wise[73] has left a curious description of Hungarian tactics, which is reflected in accounts of the Hungarians (and indeed the Polovetsians) occurring in Russian chronicles. "From early childhood," says Leo, "the Hungarians are accustomed to ride and dislike going on foot. They bear long spears on their shoulders and bows in their hands, and have great skill in the use of these weapons. Accustomed to fight with arrows, they dislike hand-to-hand combat, and prefer to fight at a distance. In battle they divide their troops into small detachments, which they place at a small distance from each other."

This foreshadows the disposition of the Hungarian forces in the battle with Davyd Igorevich and the Polovetsian Boniak. At the end of the tenth century they abandoned their nomadic way of life and devastating raids on their neighbors. They adapted to a sedentary mode of existence and to nationhood, which they acquired at the same time as the Christian religion. Prince Géza[74] and his son were baptized in 994. The son, St. Stephen,[75] commanded the immediate baptism of all his subjects, provoking among those who wished to remain pagan a revolt which was only suppressed after a bloody defeat inflicted on them by the prince's army.

After the death of Stephen the first king of Hungary, who was childless, the various princes of the Árpád dynasty began feuding amongst themselves, giving the western emperors the opportunity to make the kings of Hungary their vassals. The Hungarian lords sought to extend their power at the expense of the monarch's. This also allowed the possibility of several further pagan revolts. Only at the end of the eleventh century, in the reigns of St. László[76] and Kálmán,[77] did Hungary begin to recover from its domestic dissensions, grow strong at the expense of neighboring lands and intervene in their affairs. Hence the alliance between Kálmán and Sviatopolk against Davyd and the sons of Rostislav, cemented by the marriage of one of the king's sons to Predslava, daughter of the prince of Kiev. Not long before his death Kálmán himself married Monomakh's daughter Evfimia but a year later, accused of infidelity, the young queen was sent back to her father in Rus where she gave birth to a son, Boris, who long was to trouble Hungary with his claims.[78] Kálmán died early in 1114 and was succeeded by his son Stephen II.[79]

DEATH OF GRAND PRINCE SVIATOPOLK

At the beginning of 1113 in Kiev there was an eclipse of the sun.[80] According to the chronicle it was a portent of Sviatopolk's death, which occurred on April 16, not long after that of Davyd Igorevich in May of the previous year. The chronicle records lamentation for the death of Sviatopolk amongst his boyars and retinue, but says not a word about any popular grief. His widow distributed much wealth amongst the monasteries, priests and poor, causing general astonishment at such an unprecedented scale of almsgiving. Sviatopolk was a religious man. Before departing for war or on a journey he always went to the monastery of the Caves to worship at the tomb of St. Feodosy and ask the abbot's prayers. Nevertheless the chronicler adds nothing else in his praise, in spite of his habit of saying a good word for each prince at his death.

Further information explaining this silence may be gleaned from the lives of the saints of the Caves monastery. On one occasion the price of salt rose in Kiev, and the monks of the Caves helped the people in their need. Sviatopolk, hearing of this, plundered the monks' supply of salt in order to sell it on his own account at a high price. He was denounced for his avarice and cruelty by the abbot John, whom he first exiled but then allowed to return in order not to excite Monomakh's hostility.

Sviatopolk's son Mstislav was like his father. When he heard that two monks discovered some buried treasure in the monastery he tortured them mercilessly to make them reveal its whereabouts. This Mstislav was the son of a concubine who, according to some accounts, had great influence on the weak-willed Sviatopolk. The hagiographer says that the people suffered much violence at the hands of the prince. Families of local lords were exterminated without cause, many deprived of their property, and there was great disorder, robbery and lawlessness.

IV

MONOMAKH AS GRAND PRINCE, 1113-1125

KIEV ELECTS VLADIMIR MONOMAKH

This was the Kievans' experience of Sviatopolk's reign. It is not surprising that the line of Iziaslav finally lost all its popularity amongst the ordinary people. The sons of Sviatoslav were never popular. We have seen what sort of a reputation Oleg Gorislavich[1] had, and his failure to participate in the other princes' most celebrated campaigns did nothing to improve it. His elder brother Davyd was a nonentity. If he did less harm to the Land of Rus than his brother, it was because he was less energetic.

However great Sviatopolk's importance, it would have been eclipsed by that of Monomakh, who was in the forefront for the whole of Sviatopolk's reign. To him the people looked for all good things. For the chronicler he was the favorite of heaven, inspired in his dealings and the fountain of good undertakings. He enjoyed a *de facto* seniority, for when listing the princes the chronicle always names him in second place, immediately after Sviatopolk and before the sons of Sviatoslav. What hope had they now of receiving the seniority on Sviatopolk's death? Under the poorly defined conditions regulating the ruling family it would have been unreasonable to expect Sviatopolk's place to be taken by anyone other than Monomakh.

When Sviatopolk died the people of Kiev, who wanted Monomakh as his successor, acted just as the people of Novgorod when the princes wanted to remove their beloved Mstislav.[2] They summoned an assembly, decided Vladimir should be prince, and informed him of their decision. "Come, prince," they said, "and take the throne of your father and grandfather." When Monomakh heard of Sviatopolk's death he wept bitterly, and did not come to Kiev. As the reason why he did not visit when Vsevolod died was his respect for Sviatopolk's seniority, so clearly now he acted out of the same motives, respecting the seniority of the sons of

Sviatoslav. The Kievans had their own ideas. They plundered the house of the chiliarch Putiata, according to one account because he was on the side of the sons of Sviatoslav. Then they plundered the houses of the hundredmen and the Jews. This confirms the report that Sviatopolk, for his own personal profit, gave large privileges to the Jews, which they used to the disadvantage of the people and thus made themselves highly unpopular.

After this bout of looting the people of Kiev sent another message to Vladimir. "Come to Kiev, prince," they said, "for if you do not, much evil will befall. Not only will Putiata's house be plundered, or those of the hundredmen or the Jews. People will turn on Sviatopolk's widow, on the boyars and the monasteries. You will be answerable before God if the monasteries are plundered." At this Vladimir came to Kiev. The metropolitan, the bishops and all the people came out to meet him and received him with great honor. There was general rejoicing and the disturbances died down.

Thus after the first senior prince of the second generation the order of succession broke down as a result of the personal qualities of Vsevolod's son. Sviatoslav's line lost the seniority and was forced to confine itself to Chernigov, which thus was transformed into a patrimony separate from the rest of the territories of Rus, like that of the sons of Iziaslav at Polotsk. There was no feuding over this at first. The sons of Sviatoslav were in no position to quarrel with Monomakh, so for a time they nursed their resentment in secret.

Immediately after becoming grand prince Monomakh called a meeting of his men, to which Oleg Sviatoslavich also sent a representative, at which it was decided to set a limit to the rate of interest. This is directly connected with the circumstances of his election, for it is very probable that Sviatopolk allowed the Jews to charge excessive rates, thus inciting the people against them.[3]

WAR WITH GLEB OF MINSK AND YAROSLAV OF VOLHYNIA

Although the sons of Sviatoslav pressed no claim and there was no war with them, Monomakh's reign was not free of domestic strife. Under Sviatopolk there was a campaign against Gleb Vseslavich of Minsk[4]. This prince evidently inherited the spirit and hostile attitude of his father and grandfather towards the line of Yaroslav, and he was not afraid to attack the powerful Monomakh. He laid waste part of the land of the Dregovichians[5] which belonged to the principality of Kiev, burned

Slutsk,[6] and when Vladimir demanded that he cease his depredation, instead of repenting and submitting, he answered with reproaches.

Then in 1116 Vladimir, trusting in God and his rights, as the chronicle said, marched on Minsk together with his sons, also with Davyd Sviatoslavich and the sons of Oleg. Monomakh's son Viacheslav, prince of Smolensk, took Orsha and Kopys. Davyd and Vladimir's other son Yaropolk, who succeeded his father at Pereiaslavl, took Drutsk by storm, and Vladimir himself besieged Gleb in Minsk. Monomakh decided to capture Minsk no matter how long it took, therefore he built solid living quarters in his camp. Seeing these preparations for a long siege, Gleb grew fearful and sent messengers to sue for peace. Vladimir, unwilling to shed Christian blood during Lent, came to terms. Gleb came out of the town with his children and retinue, did homage to Vladimir and promised to obey him, whereupon Vladimir, after instructing him as to how he should conduct himself henceforth, allowed him to keep Minsk and himself returned to Kiev.

Vladimir's son Yaropolk of Pereiaslavl had no thought of giving up his captives, the people of Drutsk. More than any other prince he suffered from a lack of population in his steppe territory, so often overrun by the Polovetsians. For this reason he took the people of Drutsk back to the principality of Pereiaslavl, where he built the town of Zhelin for them.[7] Apparently the prince of Minsk did not obey Vladimir for long. In 1120 he was deprived of his city and brought to Kiev, where he died the same year.[8]

The other feuding took place in Volhynia. Sviatopolk enjoyed good relations with Vladimir. To strengthen a friendship which could prove very useful to his son Yaroslav, he arranged a marriage between him and Vladimir's granddaughter, the daughter of Mstislav of Novgorod. This marriage turned out to be, if not the only, then at least one of the most important reasons for the enmity between Yaroslav and Monomakh. It is recorded that in 1118 Monomakh, accompanied by Davyd Sviatoslavich and Volodar and Vasilko Rostislavich, made war on Yaroslav in Vladimir-in-Volhynia. After a two-month siege Yaroslav submitted and did homage to Vladimir, who admonished and commanded him to be ready to appear before him whenever summoned. Vladimir then returned in peace to Kiev.

Some chronicles say that the reason for Monomakh's attack was Yaroslav's ill-treatment of his wife, which is very probable if Yaroslav inherited his father's temperament. According to other versions, also very probable, Yaroslav's hostility towards Monomakh, and particularly towards the sons of Rostislav, was inflamed by the Poles, their old enemies, who had not forgiven Vasilko his devastating incursions and conquests. Like his father, Yaroslav could not forget that the territory ruled by the sons of Rostislav once was part of the principality of Volhynia. Thus his interests coincided with those of the Polish prince. They also were connected by marriage. Władysław Herman[9] and Sviatopolk agreed on a marriage alliance at Brest, and Sviatopolk's daughter Sbyslava was betrothed to Władysław's son Bolesław Krzywousty,[10] which marriage was deferred as they were both minors.

In 1102 Władysław Herman died. Even during his lifetime he divided his kingdom between his two sons, the legitimate Bolesław and the bastard Zbigniew. When his magnates asked him which was to be the senior, he replied "It is for me to divide my lands, because I am old and weak, but only God can exalt one above the other or give them wisdom and justice. My will is that you serve him who is the more just and the more valiant in the defense of his fatherland." These words recorded in the Polish chronicle are very remarkable, indicating the vagueness of the notions of inheritance then prevailing in the Slavonic countries.

Bolesław proved to be the better of the brothers. Unlike his father, he was distinguished for his courage and energy. He observed his father's agreement with Sviatopolk and married his daughter Sbyslava, as a result of which relationship Yaroslav of Volhynia constantly assisted Bolesław in his feud with his brother Zbigniew.[11] It is therefore not surprising that the princes of Poland and Volhynia decided to act in concert against the sons of Rostislav. Monomakh could hardly tolerate this, especially as he was related by marriage to the sons of Rostislav, since his son Roman was married to Volodar's daughter. Obviously he must stand up for Volodar and his brother. First, says the chronicle, he tried to persuade Yaroslav. Then he called him to judgment before the princes, and finally, when Yaroslav would not heed him, he declared war, the outcome of which has been described, following the account given in the chronicles which have come down to us.

Significantly the chronicles also record that before beginning the campaign against Yaroslav, Monomakh called his son Mstislav from Novgorod and installed him as prince of Belgorod, not far from himself in Kiev. This could have made Yaroslav think that Monomakh intended Mstislav to inherit the seniority after his death, while Monomakh may have taken this step precisely because of Yaroslav's unfriendly actions.

Yaroslav's enforced submission did not last long. He soon repudiated his wife, thus provoking another attack by Monomakh. It is obvious that Yaroslav never would have dared make an open break had he not already assembled a considerable force, and were he not expecting support from Poland and Hungary, for he was also related to the king of Hungary. His own boyars deserted him and he was forced to flee first to Hungary, then to Poland.

Monomakh first made his son Roman prince of Vladimir-in-Volhynia and then, when he died, his next son Andrei. That these events were connected with the Polish war is demonstrated by the expedition into Poland, using Polovetsian troops, made by Andrei in 1120, shortly after he became prince of Vladimir. The following year Yaroslav and the Poles prepared to invade Cherven, while Monomakh took steps to ensure the security of his frontier towns. Cherven was commanded by the famous Foma Ratiborovich, who compelled Yaroslav to return empty-handed.

The Poles' most dangerous enemy was evidently Volodar Rostislavich, who not only led the Polovetsians into Poland but was allied with their other dangerous enemies, the Pomeranians and Prus. Unable to defeat him by force, the Poles decided to capture him by trickery. One of Bolesław's courtiers at this time was a renowned warrior called Peter Vlast, said to have been a Dane.[12] At the council Bolesław called to discuss Volodar's invasion Vlast declared himself against open war, because of Volodar's alliance with the Polovetsians, Pomeranians and Prus, who might all attack Poland simultaneously. He advised that Volodar be taken by stealth, offering his own services for the enterprise. Bolesław accepted the offer. Vlast went to Volodar accompanied by thirty men, pretending to be an exile and Bolesław's sworn enemy. He won Volodar's complete confidence. On one occasion, when they were hunting together the prince, in pursuit of his quarry, rode far away from the town, and his retinue were scattered through the forest, only Vlast and his men remained near him. They seized their moment, fell upon Volodar, captured him and swiftly carried him away to the Polish frontier.

Bolesław achieved his aim. Vasilko Rostislavich emptied his own treasury and his brother's in order to ransom Volodar. More important, they both undertook to act in alliance with the Poles against all enemies. There is no other explanation for both brothers' presence with the Polish army in its invasion of Rus in 1123. In that year Yaroslav marched on Vladimir with a force of Hungarians, Poles, Czechs and both sons of Rostislav, Volodar and Vasilko. He had a great army, says the chronicle.

Monomakh's son Andrei was prince of Vladimir, and Monomakh himself assembled his army in the principality of Kiev, sending his eldest son Mstislav on ahead to Vladimir with a small force. The siege nevertheless was raised before Mstislav arrived.

Early on Sunday morning Yaroslav approached the city walls with two companions and shouted to Andrei and the citizens. "This is my town," he cried. "If you do not open the gates and come out and bow to me, tomorrow you shall see me attack the town and take it." While he was yet riding before the walls two Poles, doubtless in Andrei's service (which was not unusual at the time), came out of the town secretly and hid by the roadside. As Yaroslav, returning, passed their hiding place, they suddenly burst out onto the road and struck him with a lance. His companions barely got him back to the camp, where he died the following night.

King Stephen II of Hungary would have continued the siege but the leaders of the individual contingents of his army opposed him, refusing to shed the blood of their warriors to no purpose. As a result all Yaroslav's allies returned to their various homes, sending to Vladimir envoys bearing gifts and requesting peace.

"Thus died Yaroslav," the chronicler elaborates concerning this event, "alone before such a great force. He died through pride, because his hope was not in God but in his great army. Now behold what his pride achieved. Consider, brethren and retainers, on whose side is God, on that of the proud or the humble? While Vladimir gathered his men in Kiev, he wept before God on account of Yaroslav's violence and pride. God aided the faithful Prince Vladimir because of his honorable life and his humility, whereas the young prince rose up in his pride against his grandfather, and then again against Mstislav his father-in-law."

These words are significant because they express the contemporary view of relations between the princes. The chronicler considers Yaroslav to blame because he was a young man whose pride caused him to oppose his grandfather and father-in-law, purely familial relationships, to the exclusion of all others. Moreover, what is said about the relationship between Mstislav and Yaroslav is also significant in that Yaroslav is described as "young" in relation to Mstislav, and is condemned for his arrogance towards him. Is not this a hint of the clash of the father-in-law's and son-in-law's rights to seniority? Did not Yaroslav's pride consist primarily in that, although he was a young man and Mstislav's son-in-law, he attempted to take precedence over him as the son of Yaroslav's eldest grandson? It seems very probable.

In any case with Yaroslav's death the elder line of the descendants of Yaroslav the Wise lost its right to the seniority, for if he was considered young in comparison with Mstislav, his younger brothers Iziaslav and Briachislav, both of whom died in 1127, could hardly be serious rivals. The descendants of Sviatopolk lost not only Volhynia, but also Turov, which also passed to Monomakh's family. All the sons of Sviatopolk had left in these parts was Kletsk. Finally Monomakh and his family were favored everywhere with the goodwill of the people. Yaroslav could not resist Monomakh in Vladimir, for his boyars deserted him. When he attacked Vladimir the citizens had no thought of abandoning the son of Monomakh.

RELATIONS WITH GREEKS AND POLOVETSIANS

This was the end of the princely feuding of Vladimir's reign, and of the Polish wars connected with it. As for the other European powers, we have records of Monomakh's dealings with the Byzantine empire. Monomakh's daughter Maria married Leo, son of the emperor [Romanus] Diogenes.[13] After Romanus lost his throne to the Comnenoi in one of Byzantium's regular coups, Leo initiated an armed rebellion against Alexius Comnenus[14] in 1116, in which no doubt he had his father-in-law's advice and support. His intention was to acquire territory. He already had secured the submission of several towns along the Danube, when two Arabs, agents of Alexis, assassinated him at Dorostolon.[15]

Vladimir wanted at least to retain Leo's conquests for his grandson Basil. He sent his commander Ivan Voitishich, who placed burgraves in the towns along the Danube, but Dorostolon was in the hands of the imperial forces. Monomakh's son Viacheslav and his commander Foma Ratiborovich marched to the Danube to take the town, then were compelled to return without achieving anything. Other sources say that their army did have some success in Thrace, laying waste to it. To put an end to the war Alexius Comnenus sent Metropolitan Neophytos of Ephesus and other prominent individuals to Monomakh with peace proposals and rich gifts, including a cross made of wood of the Holy Rood, an imperial crown, a cup of sardonyx which had belonged to Emperor Augustus, golden chains and other items. Besides, Metropolitan Neophytos placed the crown on Vladimir's head and called him emperor.

It has been noted that Monmomakh's imperial lineage on his mother's side gave him great consequence, particularly in the eyes of the clergy. In twelfth-century writings he is referred to as *tsar*.[16] It is hard to say what connection this has with the foregoing, whether a cause or an effect, but it should be said that there is nothing inherently improbable. It is also very likely that advantage was taken of this opportunity in Kiev to give the beloved prince and his children even more right to the position they had obtained, to the disadvantage of the senior branches of the family. In any case there was no renewal of hostilities against Byzantium and in 1122 there was a further matrimonial alliance, this time between a daughter of Monomakh's son Mstislav and a prince of the house of the Comnenoi.

Naturally the position of the Polovetsians and the other steppe hordes was not strengthened by Monomakh's accession. When they learned of Sviatopolk's death they prepared to cross the eastern borders, but Monomakh, in cooperation with Oleg and his sons and nephews, put them to flight. In 1116 there was further aggression by Rus when Monomakh sent his son Yaropolk and Davyd sent his son Vsevolod to the Don, where they took three Polovetsian towns. It appears that the series of successful campaigns conducted by the princes of Rus weakened the Polovetsians and gave their subject peoples, the Torks and the Pechenegs, hope of regaining independence. They revolted against the Polovetsians and there was a dreadful battle on the banks of the Don lasting two days and two nights, ending in defeat for the Pechenegs and the Torks. They fled to Rus and were settled on its marches.

The movements in the steppes continued. The following year the Belovezhtsy[17] left the banks of the Don and also came to Rus, making the marches of Rus settled by a mixture of barbarian peoples who later play an important rôle in our narrative. At first the newcomers were very turbulent and found it hard to forget the ways of the steppe and live amicably with the sedentary population. In 1120 Monomakh had to expel the Berendey from Rus, while the Torks and Pechenegs fled of their own accord. After this Yaropolk crossed the Don to do battle with the Polovetsians, but failed to find them. Not for nothing is there a tradition that Monomakh drove them all the way to the Caucasus.

The men of Novgorod and Pskov continued to make war on the Chud west of Lake Peipus. In 1116 Mstislav took the town of Odenpe or Medvezhia Golova and many of the surrounding settlements, returning home with great booty. In 1122 his son Vsevolod defeated the Häme, a Finnic tribe,[18] but the journey was hard because of food shortages. In the Northeast the previous defeats of the princes of Murom at the hands of the Bulgars and the Mordvinians were replaced by successes. In 1120 Monomakh's son Yury, made prince of Rostov by his father, attacked the

Bulgars[19] along the Volga, defeated them and returned home with great booty, honor and glory.

DEATH OF VLADIMIR MONOMAKH

Thus the people's hopes for the blessed reign of Vladimir were justified from one end of the land to the other. Monomakh, who shone like the sun upon the Land of Rus, in the words of the chronicle, died in 1125 after ruling Kiev for twelve years. His fame spread among the nations, and especially he was a terror to the heathen. He loved his brothers and the poor and suffered (labored) well for the Land of Rus. The clergy mourned him as a good and holy prince who honored monks and priests, supplied their wants and built and adorned churches. When he entered a church and heard the singing, he could not restrain his tears. Therefore God heard all his petitions and he lived in prosperity. The whole people mourned him, like children mourning for their father or their mother.

PRINCELY RETINUES AND YAROSLAV'S GRANDSONS

Having examined the activities of the second generation of Yaroslav's descendants, we should also look at those of their entourage. After Sviatopolk came to Kiev from Turov there were two retinues in Kiev, the old, which had served Iziaslav and Vsevolod, and the new, which Sviatopolk brought. The chronicler is clearly biased towards the old retinue, regarding its members as wise and experienced, and calling the members of the new retinue unwise. It is curious to note that the wise men of the old retinue were constant partisans of Monomakh and his policies. The chronicler gives pride of place to Yan Vyshatich, active in the time of the first generation. The last mention of him is in 1106, when together with his brother Putiata and Ivan Zakharich they drove away the Polovetsians and took their booty from them. After this is the record of Yan's death at the age of ninety. "He lived according to the law of God," says the chronicler, "no less than the righteous men of old. I heard many things from him that I have recorded in the chronicle."[20] It is hard to establish whether this was indeed Yan Vyshatich or someone else called Yan, because had it been the former the chronicler would surely have added something about his public deeds.

There are many more mentions of his brother Putiata, chiliarch of Kiev under Sviatopolk. Under Vsevolod, Yan was chiliarch of Kiev. Under what circumstances the office passed from the elder to the younger brother during his lifetime is unknown, although it is noticeable that it remains in the family of Yaroslav's chiliarch Vyshata. Putiata was engaged in Sviatopolk's war with Davyd of Volhynia, at the congress of Vitichi and in the campaign against the Polovetsians in 1106. Finally, his house was plundered by the people after Sviatopolk's death because of his attachment to the sons of Sviatoslav. This attachment may have been the result not so much of his personal inclinations as of his attachment to the accepted order of seniority, any breach of which inevitably led to troubles and feuding.

Besides the sons of Vyshata, Yan and Putiata, the chronicle mentions Vasil, Slavata, Ivanko Zakharich and Kozarin among Sviatopolk's Kievan boyars. After Vsevolod's death his man Ratibor, burgrave of Tmutorokan, did not remain in Kiev but took service under Monomakh, enjoying great consequence in Pereiaslavl, as may be seen from the story of the assassination of the Polovetsian khans. He was present at the congress of Vitichi and finally, when Monomakh became prince of Kiev, Ratibor replaced Putiata as chiliarch, in which capacity he took part in the council which changed the law on interest rates, together with Prokopy, chiliarch of Belgorod, Stanislav (Tukievich) of Pereiaslavl, and two other men called Nazhir and Miroslav.

It should be noted once more that the change in the law on interest was made in consultation with the chiliarchs of various cities. The names of two of Ratibor's sons, Olbeg and Foma, are mentioned, as are those of two other of Monomakh's commanders, Dmitro Ivorovich and Ivan Voitishich, the first in connection with the campaign against the Polovetsians over the Don, the second fighting the Greeks on the Danube.[21] Finally, the chronicle names one Orogost as assisting Ratibor at the congress of Vitichi.

Amongst the boyars of the sons of Sviatoslav in Chernigov we find the names of Torchin in the story of the council of Vitichi, and Ivanko who assisted in the change of the law concerning interest. If this Ivanko was the son of Chudin, one of Iziaslav's boyars, it is curious to find him in the retinue of the sons of Sviatoslav. Of the Volhynian boyars, Turiak, Lazar and Vasil were identified primarily as responsible for the blinding of Vasilko. As for the origin of the members of the retinues, the names of Torchin, the boyar of the sons of Sviatoslav at Chernigov, and of Sviatopolk's boyar Kozarin give a clear indication.[22] The names of some of the princes' servants—Torchin, Sviatopolk's shepherd, Bianduk, Monomakh's servant, and Kulmey, Ulan and Kolchko, Davyd of Volhynia's servants— also may indicate their foreign origin.

V

STRIFE AMONG GREAT-GRANDCHILDREN
OF YAROSLAV I, 1125-1148

GRAND PRINCE MSTISLAV

After the death of Monomakh his eldest son Mstislav[1] succeeded him in Kiev. There could be no other contenders for the throne. Oleg Sviatoslavich[2] and his brother Davyd[3] predeceased Monomakh. Their younger brother Yaroslav, prince of Chernigov,[4] was a minor figure, unable to retain seniority even within his own branch of the family. Briachislav Sviatopolchich, whose very seat somewhere in the region of Pinsk is unknown, was even less of a rival for Mstislav. Given the general popularity of Monomakh's family, strengthened by the fact that Mstislav resembled his famous father in all respects, he would not have had to fear even stronger rivals. The chronicle has good reason to recall at the beginning of its account of Mstislav's reign that he defeated his uncle Oleg in his youth.[5] His personal merits were used to justify his supplanting the senior line of Sviatoslav.

MONOMAKH'S OTHER SONS

Monomakh left four sons besides Mstislav, namely Yaropolk,[6] Viacheslav, Yury[7] and Andrei.[8] Yaropolk became prince of Pereiaslavl even during his father's lifetime, and remained there during his brother's tenure of Kiev. He was well suited, possessing the courage essential to a ruler of Pereiaslavl, inevitably involved in constant conflict with the steppe barbarians. The third brother Viacheslav was first prince of Smolensk, then of Turov.[9] Yury was long prince of Rostov, while Andrei had Vladimir-in-Volhynia. Mstislav's eldest son Vsevolod[10] was in Novgorod, and his third son Rostislav[11] in Smolensk, while was his second son Iziaslav[12] was no doubt somewhere near Kiev, for he also was famed for his courage. His father would have had need of him in warfare. It would not be long before he too had his own territory and field of action.

DISSENSIONS AMONG PRINCES OF CHERNIGOV

An important event occurred in Chernigov. Oleg's son Vsevolod[13] made a surprise attack on his uncle Yaroslav. Driving him from the senior throne, he killed and despoiled his retinue. Vsevolod may have regarded Mstislav's occupation of the throne of Kiev over the head of Yaroslav Sviatoslavich as a precedent and justification for his own action. If Yaroslav lost the seniority in the family as a whole, how could he maintain it in his own branch?

In any case Mstislav initially was not disposed to tolerate this assault on his uncles' seniority, especially as apparently he had sworn to uphold Yaroslav in Chernigov. Mstislav and his brother Yaropolk gathered an army to attack Vsevolod. Powerless to resist them by himself, he called on the Polovetsians and released his uncle Yaroslav, allowing him to go to Murom. Seven thousand Polovetsians responded to Vsevolod's call and encamped in the oakwood of Ratimir on the other side of the Vyr.[14] Their messengers to Vsevolod were intercepted on the Lokna[15] and brought before Yaropolk, who gained control of the whole Seim river, placing Kursk under his nephew Iziaslav Mstislavich, and all the other towns under his burgraves.

When the Polovetsians received no news from Chernigov, in fear they turned and fled, a remarkable fact showing how diffident they had become after the campaigns waged beyond the Don by Monomakh, his sons and his commanders. Mstislav then pressed Vsevolod even harder. "What have you gained," he asked, "by bringing the Polovetsians upon us? What good has it done you?" Vsevolod pleaded with Mstislav, bribing his boyars with gifts to further his cause. This continued all summer.

In the winter Yaroslav came to Kiev from Murom and also did obeisance to Mstislav, urging him to attack Vsevolod for his oath's sake, while Vsevolod for his part grew even more insistent. The abbot of St. Andrew's monastery at this time was one Grigory, a friend of Vladimir Monomakh greatly revered by Mstislav and the people. This Grigory would not allow Mstislav to attack Vsevolod for Yaroslav's sake, saying that it was better for him to break his oath than shed Christian blood.[16] Mstislav was at a loss what to do. The metropolitan was absent from Kiev, causing Mstislav to convoke a council of the clergy, submitting the matter to their judgment. They agreed to take the sin of oathbreaking upon themselves. Mstislav followed their decision, broke his promise to Yaroslav, and regretted it for the rest of his life.

Grigory's words and the decision of the council may be regarded as an expression of popular opinion. The citizens were opposed to princely feuding and to all wars not resulting in any immediate advantage or serving to defend the land. The men of Kiev can hardly have been anxious to shed their blood for an unloved prince of Sviatoslav's line. Mstislav may have been swayed not only by clerical opinion but by his relationship with Vsevolod, who was married to his daughter.

Whatever the case, Vsevolod held on to the senior throne in spite of his uncle's rights, the only such instance in the history of Kievan Rus. It was not unprofitable for the descendants of Monomakh, for they retained Kursk and the lands along the Seim, a very important acquisition since it hindered communications between the descendants of Sviatoslav and the Polovetsians. Yaroslav had to withdraw to Murom, where he remained for the rest of his life. His descendants were now dispossessed princes within the line of Sviatoslav. Losing their right to the senior position, they were confined to the principality of Murom, which as a result separated from that of Chernigov. In this way a separate principality, resembling Polotsk or Galich in the West, was created to the east of the Dnieper.

WAR WITH POLOTSK

When he had finished with the princes of Chernigov in the same year of 1127 Mstislav sent his troops against the princes of Polotsk who, say the sources, continued to ravage the borders of the lands belonging to Mono- makh's lineage. Mstislav's army set out along four separate routes, one under his brother Viacheslav from Turov, another under Andrei from Vladimir, a third under Davyd Igorevich's son Vsevolodko from Goroden,[17] and the fourth from Kletsk under Viacheslav Yaroslavich.[18]

These four princes were under orders to march to Iziaslavl, while Vse- volod Olgovich of Chernigov was to go with his brothers to Borisov by way of Strezhev, as was Mstislav's commander Ivan Voitishich with the Torks. Mstislav's own troop was sent to Lagozhsk[19] under the command of his son Iziaslav, while his other son Rostislav led the men of Smolensk to Drutsk. The prince of Polotsk at this time was Davyd Vseslavich,[20] who previously was allied with the princes of Yaroslav's line against Gleb of Minsk.[21] His son prince Briachislav of Iziaslavl[22] was married to one of Mstislav's daughters. Minsk must have passed into the possession of the princes of Yaroslav's line during the reign of Vladimir Monomakh, who took its prince Gleb into captivity, otherwise Mstislav would not have sent his armies past it to more distant objectives.

Probably the loss of Minsk, which still rankled with the descendants of Vseslav, was the main cause of the war. Mstislav commanded all the princes to attack their respective objectives on the same day, but Iziaslav Mstislavich arrived at Lagozhsk ahead of the appointed time. His son-in-law Briachislav of Iziaslavl was leading the men of Lagozhsk to his father Davyd's assistance. Told when he was halfway there that Iziaslav had reached the town, he was so alarmed that he did not know which way to turn, and fell directly into the hands of his brother-in-law, who had been joined by the retinue from Lagozhsk. When the inhabitants of Lagozhsk saw that their warriors were Iziaslav's prisoners, they surrendered to him. After spending two days in the town, Iziaslav joined his uncles Viacheslav and Andrei, who were besieging Iziaslavl.

The inhabitants, seeing that their prince and the men of Lagozhsk came to no harm as Iziaslav's prisoners, offered to surrender to Viacheslav if he would swear not to permit his men to sack the town. Viacheslav agreed. In the evening his chiliarch Ivanko and Prince Andrei's chiliarch Vratislav sent their servants into the town. When the rest of the army discovered this at dawn next day, they all poured into the town and plundered it. All that the princes and their retinues could do was to to defend the property of Grand Prince Mstislav's daughter, Briachislav's wife, having to fight their own men to do so. Meanwhile Mstislav's eldest son Prince Vsevolod of Novgorod advanced on Polotsk from another side. Then the men of Polotsk expelled Davyd and his sons and, taking his brother Rogvolod,[23] sent to Mstislav asking him to confirm Rogvolod as their prince. Mstislav agreed.

This latest turn of the hereditary and implacable enmity between the princes of Polotsk and the descendants of Yaroslav, which contemporary writers could only explain by the legend of Rogvolod and Rogneda,[24] had the same eventual outcome as the previous episode under Monomakh, namely the expulsion of the princes of Iziaslav's line from their territories. During the Polovetsian invasion of 1129 Mstislav sent to the princes of Polotsk calling upon them to lend their aid against the barbarians. It seems that Rogvolod, the friend of the sons of Yaroslav, was no longer living, accordingly the position of senior prince had reverted to Davyd, who together with his brothers and nephews returned an insolent and mocking reply.

Mstislav was prevented from dealing with Vseslav's son at once by war with the Polovetsians. Once these were repulsed he remembered his offense and sent for the "princes of the Krivichians,"[25] as the rulers of

Polotsk were still known. Davyd, Rostislav[26] and Sviatoslav,[27] and their nephews the sons of Rogvolod[28] were placed on three ships and exiled to Constantinople.[29] There is no doubt that the men of Polotsk gave up their princes to save their land from devastation. The chronicler records that Mstislav appointed his burgraves over the towns of Polotsk, which later was ruled by his son Iziaslav, previously prince of Kursk.

RELATIONS WITH NEIGHBORING PEOPLES

As for foreign affairs, the chronicles record continuing wars with the Polovetsians and other barbarian neighbors. The Polovetsians rejoiced over Monomakh's death and immediately attacked the principality of Pereiaslavl. As we have seen, during their successful campaigns in the steppes the princes of Rus took from the Polovetsians some of their Tork and Pecheneg subjects and settled them in their own country, where later they were joined by emigrants from among their kinsfolk in the steppes. The Polovetsians naturally wanted them back, and the chronicle[30] explicitly states that they appeared in order to seize the Torks of Rus.[31]

The brave Yaropolk, prince of Pereiaslavl,[32] was a worthy son of his father, and was used to defeating the Polovetsians in their own steppes under his father's banner. When he heard of the Polovetsian attack and their intentions he ordered the Torks and all the rest of the people to take refuge in the towns, so that when the Polovetsians arrived they could not achieve anything. Finding that Yaropolk was in Pereiaslavl, they pursued their campaign along the banks of the Sula. Yaropolk, *the faithful branch of a faithful root,* as the chronicle calls him, set off in pursuit with the men of Pereiaslavl without waiting for assistance from his brothers. He caught up with them on the right bank of the Uday.[33] Invoking God and *his father,* he attacked the heathen and defeated them. God and his father's prayers came to his aid, says the chronicle. We next hear of the Polovetsians in connection with the events at Chernigov and Polotsk.

Mstislav did not forget his wars against the Chud during his time in Novgorod. In 1130 he sent his sons Vsevolod, Iziaslav and Rostislav against them. The chronicle describes in detail how they slew their enemies, burned their homes and took their wives and children into captivity. Vsevolod of Novgorod's Chud campaign of the following year was much less successful. It was a considerable disaster, says the chronicle,[34] and many good men of Novgorod were killed at "Klin," which is a Russian translation of the Estonian Waija or Wagja, the thirteenth-century name of what is now part of the district of Dorpat.[35]

The Lithuanians were to Western Rus, and especially to Polotsk, what the Polovetsians were to the Southeast. Now that Mstislav had joined Polotsk to his dominions he was obliged also to contend with this enemy, and a campaign against them is recorded in the last year of his reign. Mstislav was accompanied by his sons, by the sons of Oleg and by his son-in-law Vsevolod of Goroden. The campaign was successful and the suburbs of the Lithuanian towns were burned, yet on the way back the men of Kiev, marching separately from the princes' retinues, were attacked by the Lithuanians and suffered heavy losses.

DEATH OF MSTISLAV AND ACCESSION OF YAROPOLK

Mstislav died in 1132. His reign, following the model of his father's, did much to confirm the people's faith in the family of Monomakh. This Mstislav the Great, says the chronicle, inherited the sweat of his father Vladimir Monomakh, who stood in person on the banks of the Don and wiped away much sweat for the Land of Rus, while Mstislav sent his men and drove the Polovetsians across the Don, the Volga and the Yaik. Thus God delivered the land from the heathen. This is an expression of the chief concern of the times, the struggle with the barbarians of the steppes. The people could hope for a long period of relief from their incursions because Mstislav's successor was his brother Yaropolk, a *faithful branch* known for his courage and successful campaigns in the steppes.

There were no rivals to Yaropolk, the only prince who could take the senior throne by right of his father and grandfather. His position in Kiev was strengthened further by the fact that the citizens of Kiev sent for him. Their hopes proved vain, for the peace of Rus ended with Mstislav's death. From the start of Yaropolk's reign feuding broke out again, even within the family of Monomakh, who was such an example of brotherly love. The descendants of Sviatoslav took advantage of this, and the people of Kiev had to endure a prince of a baser line on their throne.

The strife which broke out upon the death of Mstislav the Great was different from before. The main reason for the previous feuds was the position of the dispossessed princes and the fact that princes whose fathers predeceased their grandfathers or senior uncles not only were deprived of the succession and their fathers' principalities, but often did not receive any lands at all. Exclusion from the right to succeed rather than any romantic traditions best explains the unquenched hostility of the descendants of Iziaslav of Polotsk to those of Yaroslav. It also explains the actions of Rostislav Vladimirovich,[36] the conduct and fate of his sons. The reigns of Iziaslav, Vsevolod and Sviatopolk are full of struggles with dispossessed princes, sons of Viacheslav, Igor and Sviatoslav, in the East and West. All these struggles finally were resolved by decisions taken by the princes at their family gatherings.

Now a new type of struggle began, carried on by nephews, the sons of the older brother, against their junior uncles. The first example of this was at Chernigov, where Oleg's son Vsevolod removed his uncle Yaroslav from the senior throne. Mstislav allowed such an infringement of the uncles' rights though he subsequently regretted it all his life, and after his death the mere apprehension of such an action led to a bitter feud within his own family.

Mstislav not only left his throne to Yaropolk, says the chronicle. He entrusted him, under God, with his children. Yaropolk was childless and all the more able to see to their welfare. While Mstislav was alive he agreed with his brother that when he succeeded to the senior throne he immediately would bring his eldest nephew Vsevolod Mstislavich from Novgorod to Pereiaslavl.

It appears from the chronicle that the elder sons of Monomakh claimed their father's authority for this arrangement, basing their claim upon the fact that Monomakh gave Pereiaslavl to them jointly, even though according to the custom of the age this did not give them the right to dispose of it to their sons over the heads of their other brothers. Pereiaslavl belonged to both Vsevolod and Monomakh and, once Chernigov became the particular inheritance of the sons of Sviatoslav, Pereiaslavl was the most senior principality after Kiev for the descendants of Monomakh. It was from Pereiaslavl that Monomakh, Mstislav and Yaropolk all had succeeded to the throne of Kiev. Perhaps by bringing Vsevolod to Pereiaslavl the elder sons of Monomakh indeed intended to give him precedence over his uncles and the possibility of inheriting Kiev next. For this he would need not only to occupy Pereiaslavl, he must become acquainted with and win over the Southern populace, which had such a decisive voice at the time. To this the historian has not the right to render a positive verdict.

In any case the younger sons of Monomakh saw Vsevolod's move to Pereiaslavl as at least a promotion over their heads, especially when they had before their eyes the example of Yaroslav Sviatoslavich of Chernigov, deprived of the senior throne by his nephew with the evident connivance of Mstislav and Yaropolk, the elder sons of Monomakh. It was the two youngest sons, Yury of Rostov and Andrei of Volhynia, who intervened, since the third brother, Viacheslav of Turov, was too weak-willed and limited in outlook to do anything on his own initiative. According to the chronicle Yury and Andrei said in so many words that "our brother Yaropolk wants to give Kiev to his nephew Vsevolod after his death," and took steps to forestall him.

Vsevolod entered Pereiaslavl in the morning and by dinner time was expelled by his uncle Yury, who nevertheless remained there no more than eight days because Yaropolk, remembering the oath he swore to his dead brother, removed Yury from Pereiaslavl. Probably Vsevolod no longer wanted to exchange a secure principality for an insecure one, so Yaropolk brought to Pereiaslavl another son of Mstislav, Iziaslav, hitherto prince of Polotsk, swearing to support him on his new throne.

Mstislav's third son Sviatopolk received Polotsk in place of Iziaslav. The citizens, like those of Novgorod, disliked their princes leaving them for another principality. Declaring themselves abandoned by Iziaslav, they expelled his brother Sviatopolk, summoning one of their former princes, Vasilko Sviatoslavich, Vseslav's grandson, who somehow had remained in Rus or returned from exile.[37] Then Yaropolk saw that after the departure of the valiant Iziaslav, who always knew how to gain popularity, Polotsk was being lost to the descendants of Monomakh. He came to an agreement with his brothers, sending Iziaslav against his will back to Minsk, the only part of the old principality of Polotsk remaining to his family. To console him for this unwanted transfer, Turov and Pinsk were added to his territory with many rich gifts, while Viacheslav was moved from Turov to Pereiaslavl.

FURTHER REDISTRIBUTION OF PRINCIPALITIES

In such a way the younger sons of Monomakh were satisfied. Pereiaslavl passed to the oldest brother after Yaropolk also, his legitimate heir to Kiev. The peace of the family was soon disturbed by Viacheslav. Perhaps he, or rather his boyars, found the principality of Pereiaslavl unprofitable, or maybe he was ill at ease in the borderlands amongst Torks and Polovetsians. Whatever the reason, he abandoned his new lands. The first time he reached the Dnieper and turned back. It is said that he received a message from Yaropolk, saying "Why do you not stay in one place? Why do you wander about like a Polovetsian?" He would not listen to his older brother and abandoned Pereiaslavl again, returning to Turov and displacing Iziaslav. This forced Yaropolk to make new arrangements. He acceded to the request of Yury of Rostov, giving him Pereiaslavl on condition that he cede him the principality of Rostov. This he did, but not in its entirety. It seems he wanted at all cost to keep a safe haven in the North. It also seems that Yaropolk wanted Rostov so that he could pass it to Iziaslav. He may have hoped that this bargain would satisfy his brothers, all now grouped around him in the heartland of Rus, while their nephews, the junior princes, received the more distant Northern provinces.

He was no longer in a position to carry out his intentions. Hostility between uncles and nephews now flared up. Iziaslav, twice ejected from his principality, decided not to await the outcome of any further agreements between his uncles. He entrusted the matter to the judgment of God, as it was understood in those days, in other words he determined to decide it by force of arms. He went to his brother Vsevolod in Novgorod and persuaded him to lead the men of Novgorod into Yury's territory. At this the descendants of Sviatoslav saw their opportunity and concluded an alliance with the dissatisfied sons of Mstislav, though it is not clear from the surviving records from which side the proposal came. They sent for the Polovetsians and took up arms against the sons of Monomakh. "You tried to ruin us," they said. Then the people saw that the happy times of Monomakh and Mstislav were over, that the feuding had begun again. The princes of Chernigov, following their father's example, brought the Polovetsians into the Land of Rus. What was worse, they were joined by Iziaslav and Sviatopolk, sons of Mstislav the Great.

WAR WITH CHERNIGOV

Yaropolk and his brothers Yury and Andrei set off to attack Vsevolod Olgovich, crossed the Dnieper and took the villages around Chernigov. Vsevolod did not come out to do battle with them because his Polovetsian allies had not yet arrived. After encamping around Chernigov for several days, Yaropolk withdrew to Kiev and dismissed his troops without coming to terms with Vsevolod. Probably he thought that it was enough to give him a fright. It turned out otherwise, for once the Polovetsians from the South and the sons of Mstislav from the North joined Vsevolod, he marched on the principality of Pereiaslavl, attacked the villages and towns, killing the inhabitants, got as far as Kiev, and burned Gorodets.[38] The Polovetsians laid waste all the left bank of the Dnieper. Unable to escape to the right bank because the river was covered with ice floes, the people either were killed or taken prisoner. Vast numbers of cattle also were taken. Yaropolk meanwhile was prevented by the ice from crossing over and driving the Polovetsians away. Vsevolod stood with his army in the woods around Gorodets for three days, then returned to Chernigov and opened negotiations with the sons of Monomakh, with whom he made peace.

Probably this was only a truce until a proper princely congress could be convened, because the chronicle immediately begins to set out the demands made by the sons of Oleg. These were that Yaropolk return to them whatever their father ruled in his father's time. "We want that which our father held in your father's time. If you will not give it to us, do not complain afterwards, for if anything happens it will be your fault, the blood will be on your head."

No doubt the sons of Oleg asked for Kursk and the lands along the Seim, which the sons of Monomakh took from them immediately after Yaroslav was expelled by Vsevolod. In answer to this demand Yaropolk assembled the fighting men of Kiev, and Yury those of Pereiaslavl. They remained in readiness before Kiev for fifty days, before making peace with Vsevolod. The youngest brother Andrei Vladimirovich became prince of Pereiaslavl, his place in Vladimir-in-Volhynia being taken by his nephew Iziaslav Mstislavich.

From all this it is evident that the arrangement was a condition for, not a consequence of, the peace agreement with the sons of Oleg. In order to detach their nephews from the descendants of Sviatoslav and to deny them any pretext for hostilities or any justification in the eyes of the people, the brothers satisfied Iziaslav by giving him Volhynia. Yury of Rostov, evidently having discovered how contestable the Southern thrones were and what an unenviable principality was that of Pereiaslavl, constantly assailed by the sons of Oleg and the Polovetsians, no longer desired to exchange his Northern fastness for it. His younger brother's occupation of Pereiaslavl was not dangerous for him, as there were no instances of a younger brother contesting his elder brother's right, as there were of an elder brother's son contesting the right of his uncle. These events occurred in the year 1134.

The sons of Oleg were forced to come to terms against their will by the defection of the sons of Mstislav. This is proved by the fact that the following year, 1135, they attacked the principality of Pereiaslavl. Vsevolod and all his brothers besieged the city and attacked the city gates for three days until they heard that Yaropolk was coming to his brother's aid. Then they withdrew to the upper reaches of the Supoy river and awaited him there.

We have said that Yaropolk inherited his father's courage. When he located the enemy he did not hold back and wait for reinforcements but attacked at once with just his own retinue. This proved a successful tactic and won him great renown against the Polovetsians at the beginning of Mstislav's reign. This is how he acted now. He did not wait for the Kiev regiments, nor did he even put his own men into proper battle order, instead fell upon the sons of Oleg with his brothers and his retinue, thinking that the enemy could not resist their strength. At first both sides fought resolutely, but soon Vsevolod's Polovetsians turned and fled. The chiliarch of Kiev with the best troops of the sons of Monomakh pursued them, leaving the princes to fight the sons of Oleg. After fierce fighting the sons of Monomakh were compelled to surrender the field to the princes of Chernigov, so when the chiliarch and the boyars returned after defeating the Polovetsians they were too late to do anything for their princes and fell straight into the hands of the victorious sons of Oleg, who raised Yaropolk's captured banner and thus deceived them. Yaropolk's losses included not only the capture of many of his best men. Among the slain was also his nephew the Byzantine prince Basil, son of Monomakh's daughter and Prince Leo.[39]

The prince of Kiev went back across the Dnieper and assembled a new army, while Vsevolod crossed the Desna and encamped before Vyshgorod.[40] Although he spent seven days on the banks of the Dnieper he did not make up his mind to cross it. Instead he returned to Chernigov, whence he made unsuccessful peace overtures to the Kievan prince. This happened in late summer. In the winter the sons of Oleg and the Polovetsians crossed the Dnieper and ravaged the whole principality of Kiev, reaching the city itself. There was an exchange of arrows across the Lybed, but they only took two towns, and even those were deserted. The inhabitants of the marches usually abandoned their towns at the threat of invasion. According to the chronicle, Yaropolk assembled a very large army from all over the country but did not lead it against the enemy or engage in any fighting. Fearing the judgment of God, he abased himself before the sons of Oleg, reviled and reproached by his brothers and the rest of the people in order to fulfill the commandment that we should love our enemies. He made a peace agreement with the sons of Oleg in which he gave them what they previously asked, the towns along the Seim that were part of their patrimony.

It is hard to say what precisely made Yaropolk yield. Perhaps he was one of those strongly affected by failure after a long run of success. Perhaps the clergy, led by Metropolitan Michael,[41] strove to put an end to a war which was ruining the country. Yaropolk does indeed deserve the chronicler's praise for his outstanding act of Christian humility for the good of his people. Maybe both factors were at work. Moreover it should not be forgotten that there could be no guarantee of success in the conflict. Vsevolod Olgovich was not exactly a model of rash courage, preferring to retreat when he saw the odds were against him. That he did not retreat at that time implied that Yaropolk's forces were not as great as the chronicler claims, at least in comparison to those of the sons of Oleg. These events occurred in 1135.

The peace could not last. The main reason for the hostility of the sons of Oleg towards those of Monomakh, their exclusion from the seniority, was still unresolved, and moreover they now experienced the possibility of a successful campaign against them, particularly while the sons of Monomakh were disunited. The expulsion from Novgorod of Vsevolod's brother Sviatoslav in 1138 served to start another war. The sons of Oleg again summoned the Polovetsians and ravaged the lands along the Sula belonging to the principality of Pereiaslavl. Andrei Vladimirovich could not withstand them. Not receiving any assistance from his brothers, he was on the point of fleeing Pereiaslavl. When the sons of Oleg discovered that Andrei's brothers were not coming to his aid they reassured him with what the chronicler calls "deceitful" words. The chronicler implies that their intention was to turn him against his brothers and win him over to their own side, convincing him that his brothers showed no concern for him.

The war was intensified by news that Sviatoslav Olgovich was detained at Smolensk on his way from Novgorod. His brother Vsevolod took Priluk with a large force of Polovetsians and was about to take his old road to Kiev when he heard of the enormous army the sons of Monomakh were gathering, and hurried back to Chernigov. Calling on all his brothers and nephews, as well as the men of Kiev and Pereiaslavl, Yaropolk assembled an army of the men of the "upper" lands, from Suzdal, Rostov, Polotsk and Smolensk. He received help from the sons of Rostislav in Galich and from the king of Hungary. Finally, he had large formations of Berendey from the frontier at his disposal. With such an army Yaropolk did not wait for Vsevolod to meet him in the lands of Kiev, he marched after him to Chernigov.

Vsevolod took fright and would have run to the Polovetsians had not the men of Chernigov prevented him. "You want to flee to the Polovetsians," they said, "but that will be the ruin of your principality, and what will you have to come back to? You would do better to forget your pride and ask for peace. We know how merciful Yaropolk is. He does not enjoy shedding blood. For God's sake he will make peace with you, since his is the care of the Land of Rus." Vsevolod did as they said and sued for peace. Yaropolk, says the chronicle, being good and merciful in temper, a God-fearing man like his father before him, after due reflection decided to avoid bloodshed, and they made peace at Moravsk[42] on the right bank of the Desna. A further treaty was concluded between them later in unknown circumstances. These events occurred between 1136 and 1139.

DISSENSIONS IN NOVGOROD

This was the end of the feuding in the South under Yaropolk, though such strife was much in evidence in the North, in Novgorod the Great. In Sviatopolk's time the people of Novgorod insisted on keeping Mstislav Vladimirovich, who had grown up amongst them, as their prince. They did not keep their beloved prince for long, for Monomakh summoned him to the South in 1116, and his son Vsevolod remained in Novgorod. The prince's youth and the death of two mayors, apparently within a year of each other, led to disorders within the city. Certain boyars and the hundredman Stavr plundered the property of two of the citizens. The circumstances of this action are unknown. Therefore, since plunder was sometimes the result of a sentence passed by a court, it is hard to say whether Stavr and the boyars were guilty of banditry or injustice. In any case, Mstislav and Monomakh summoned all the boyars of Novgorod to Kiev. Stavr and his comrades were exiled, the rest were allowed to return to Novgorod, presumably after swearing that there would be no repetition of these events.

It is not known who chose Konstantin Moiseevich as mayor at this point. Probably the prince of Kiev, considering the circumstances. He died the following year and was replaced by one Boris, who certainly was sent by Monomakh. When Monomakh died, his son Mstislav became prince of Kiev and his grandson Vsevolod became prince of Novgorod. In both cases the chronicle uses the same expression, "they set him,"[43] meaning that the citizens wanted them, asked for them, summoned them. The citizens of Novgorod appointed Vsevolod for the second time, because when Mstislav became senior prince he might have placed him in a principality nearer to his own in Southern Rus as his father did. Apparently the citizens of Novgorod made him swear not to leave them.

The following year Vsevolod visited his father in Kiev, but returned to rule in Novgorod afterwards. The same year the office of mayor was given to Miroslav Giuratinich, though the chronicle makes no mention of his predecessor Boris's death. When the chronicle says that *they gave him the office of mayor,* it is not clear whether "they" signifies the princes, Mstislav and Vsevolod, or the citizens. A year later, again without any mention of Miroslav's death, the chronicle records the appointment of his successor, Davyd Dmitrievich, who was both the grand prince's brother-in-law[44] and the son of a former mayor. He died the same year, 1128, and in 1129 one Daniel came from Kiev to take his place.[45] The chronicle mentions the appointment of another mayor, Petrilo, in 1130, again saying that "they gave" him the appointment. At the same time it mentions Vsevolod's campaign against the Chud and his visit to his father in Kiev, but it is hard to tell whether the events are connected.

This was the situation while Mstislav was grand prince. His death was followed immediately by disorders. Although he swore not to abandon the men of Novgorod, Vsevolod was tempted by the throne of Pereiaslavl and rode south, leaving Novgorod without a prince. On previous occasions it was a source of offense to the citizens when a prince left their city for another. Besides the fact that a change of prince threw all their domestic arrangements into disorder, Novgorod must have been offended when a prince preferred Turov or Pereiaslavl to their city, thereby lowering the dignity of the throne of Riurik.[46] The princes themselves, as we shall see, did not forget that Novgorod once was the premier throne of the Land of Rus. It is easy to understand therefore why, when Vsevolod returned to Novgorod after being turned out of Pereiaslavl by Yury, he found the city in disorder, *a great uproar among the people* as the chronicle calls it. Men of Pskov and Ladoga were in the city, and Vsevolod was forced to leave, though the citizens soon changed their mind and brought him back.[47]

It may be supposed that Vsevolod was accepted not on the same conditions as earlier, and that this marks the beginning of the conditions or agreements which Novgorod imposed on its princes. Probably from this time on the mayor ceased to be an appointee of the prince, becoming a civic official, elected by the citizens at their assembly, though not without the prince's involvement. Also at least this early burgraves were chosen for the dependent towns, Miroslav for Pskov and Raguil for Ladoga. This fact may suggest that the men of Pskov and Ladoga came to Novgorod for the express purpose of demanding new burgraves. It is also recorded that beginning at this time Vsevolod lacked his proper influence in Novgorod, nor could he make the citizens send the customary tithes to the Caves monastery in Kiev. Yaropolk was obliged to send his other nephew Iziaslav to collect it.

Meanwhile the situation in the South grew more and more involved. In 1134 Iziaslav Mstislavich came to Novgorod to persuade his brother and the citizens to make war on his uncle Yury and obtain the Rostov principality for the sons of Mstislav, if they were excluded from sharing in the Land of Rus. The men of Novgorod contemplated war with Suzdal, and killed some of their own people, throwing them off the bridge, says the chronicle. This means that, after Vsevolod's proposition, the debate in the popular assembly was extremely violent, one side in favor of supporting the sons of Mstislav and winning territory for them, the other against. The war party being in the majority, it was decided to open hostilities, and the dissident minority found itself in the Volkhov. The sons of Mstislav and the mayor Petrilo rode out to war, but no sooner did they reach the Dubna river[48] than the dissensions of the assembly were repeated in the army. This time the debate was won by those opposed to supporting the nephews against the uncles and making war on Monomakh's son for the sake of his grandsons. They made the prince return and dismissed Petrilo who evidently supported the war. They gave his office to Ivan Pavlovich. Thus appointment of the mayor became dependent upon the relative strength of domestic factions.

Apparently the peace party included some who were ill-disposed to Vsevolod and did not wish to receive him when he returned from Pereiaslavl to Novgorod. When they came home they were defeated again. Their opponents gained the upper hand once more, and Vsevolod set out a second time leading the whole army of Novgorod against Rostov at a time of severe frosts and snowstorms. This was against the urging of Metropolitan Michael, who came to Novgorod at that time. "Do not go, for God will hear my prayers," he threatened. The men of Novgorod detained him and departed. They met the armies of Rostov at Zhdanova hill and were defeated, losing their brave mayor Ivan, also Petrilo Nikolaich, who may have been the previous mayor, and many other good men. The Novgorod chronicle claims that casualties were even heavier amongst the men of Suzdal,[49] whereas the Rostov chronicler claims that his fellow-countrymen defeated the men of Novgorod, killed many, and returned home in great triumph. When the men of Novgorod returned home they freed the metropolitan and elected their former mayor Miroslav Giuriatinich to his old office.

In 1135, having experienced how harmful princely feuding was for them, the men of Novgorod dispatched their mayor Miroslav to the South to make peace between the sons of Monomakh and the sons of Oleg. He returned without accomplishing anything because, as the chronicler says, the whole Land of Rus was in great tumult. Although the princes were not reconciled through the mediation of the men of Novgorod, they all tried to win them over to their side, which meant giving them the right of choice. The men of Novgorod were not slow to take advantage, but they had to decide which side to support. Whom would God help, who would win in the end? It was the sons of Oleg whom God helped at the battle on the Supoy, giving Vsevolod Monomashich's opponents the chance to rebel against him.

In 1136 the men of Novgorod summoned the men of Pskov and Ladoga and considered how to be free of their prince Vsevolod. They imprisoned him in the bishop's court with his wife, children and mother-in-law, setting a guard of thirty men over them day and night. They were not released until the arrival of the new prince, Sviatoslav Olgovich, from Chernigov.

The chronicle gives four grounds for complaint against Vsevolod. (1) He did not take care of the common people. (2) Why did he want to be prince of Pereiaslavl? (3) He was the first to flee at the battle of Zhdanova hill. (4) He involved Novgorod in the princes' internecine strife, first telling them to ally themselves with the sons of Oleg, then urging them to desert them.

It was not easy to expel a son of Mstislav and replace him one of Oleg's because there was a strong party at Novgorod supporting the sons of Mstislav. Novgorod was divided the same way as the Land of Rus was "torn apart," as the chronicler puts it. Disturbances are recorded as early as 1136, the year of Sviatoslav Olgovich's arrival. Though a certain Yury Zhiroslavich, evidently a partisan of Vsevolod, was thrown off the bridge, there were many others of the same persuasion, for an unsuccessful attempt was made on Sviatoslav's life with bows and arrows. Then a few of the more prominent citizens, among them the mayor Konstantin, elected in place of Miroslav Giuriatinich who died in 1135, fled to Vyshgorod, where Vsevolod was sheltered by his uncle Yaroslav. Yakun Miroslavich, probably Miroslav Guiriatinich's son, was elected mayor in Konstantin's place.[50]

Meanwhile the fugitives told Vsevolod that in Novgorod and Pskov he had many friends who were only waiting for him to reappear. "Come, prince," they said, "they want you back." Vsevolod set off, accompanied by his brother Sviatopolk. He was indeed received in Pskov. As he rode past Polotsk the local prince Vasilko came out to meet him in person and sent him on his way with honor, forgetting for the sake of God's commandment all the evil Vsevolod's father Mstislav did to his family. He had no intention of avenging the wrongs his father suffered even though Vsevolod now was in his power. The two princes swore to forget past offenses.

When the citizens of Novgorod learned that Vsevolod was at Pskov, intending to return to reign over them, there were violent disturbances in the city. The majority were against having a son of Mstislav, and Vsevolod's friends were obliged to flee to him at Pskov. Their property was plundered by the majority faction, who also tried to identify Vsevolod's supporters among those boyars who stayed behind. They took fifteen hundred grivnas from those who fell under suspicion, and gave it to the merchants to finance the war. It is noteworthy that Vsevolod's part was taken largely by the boyars, amongst whom a number were found to sympathize with him, while the opposition was largely made up of commoners, neglect of whom was also the first of the accusations made against him.

Sviatoslav assembled all the army of Novgorod, calling on his brother Gleb and the men of Kursk and the Polovetsians for aid, and set out to drive Vsevolod out of Pskov. The men of Pskov immediately displayed that fortitude which was to distinguish them in years to come, all the more so since it was to their advantage to have a prince of their own, thus emancipating themselves from the influence of the senior city. They neither submitted to the men of Novgorod, nor did they expel Vsevolod, instead took precautions against attack, digging earthworks on all sides. Sviatoslav and the men of Novgorod saw that it would be a difficult war, of uncertain outcome, and turned back. "We will not shed the blood of our brothers," they said. "May God determine all by His providence." Vsevolod died the same year, 1137, and the men of Pskov made his brother Sviatopolk their prince.

Meanwhile times were very difficult for the people of Novgorod. The sons of Monomakh and their allies, angry that they had a son of Oleg for their prince, cut trade links with them. They were at peace neither with Suzdal, nor Smolensk, nor Kiev, nor Polotsk. Food grew very dear because supplies were cut off. Dissensions within the princely family helped Novgorod to find a way out of its difficulties. The triumph of the sons of Oleg was caused by disunity within the family of Monomakh, the split between the younger brothers and the elder brothers' sons. In the future this split was to enable the sons of Oleg to re-establish their lost rights by regaining the seniority and Kiev. The fact that the descendants of Yaroslav were split into three camps was extremely important for Novgorod. On one hand, since they always had acknowledged the authority of the most senior prince among the descendants of Yaroslav, they found themselves obliged to change their prince every time the grand-princely throne of Kiev passed from one of the warring lines to another. This in turn exacerbated the domestic troubles stirred by both the enemies and the adherents of the deposed princes. On the other hand, it gave Novgorod a choice between the three lines, thereby inevitably increasing the power, consequence and pretensions of the popular assembly, lending the citizens the appearance of a free people.

Thus in response to the changes which took place in the South to the advantage of the sons of Oleg they expelled their prince, who was of the line of Monomakh. They also could extricate themselves from the awkward position in which this placed them without loss or humiliation, for they could be reconciled to the family of Monomakh without being forced to accept a son of Mstislav. They placed themselves under the protection of Yury of Rostov, accepting one of his sons as their prince. This meant that not only would Yury defend them from the sons of Oleg, but also reconcile them with the descendants of Monomakh, sparing them the humiliation of accepting Sviatopolk, which would have meant acknowledging the ascendancy of Pskov. Finally, having a son of Yury as prince would calm their domestic dissensions because as Monomakh's grandson he was acceptable to the adherents of that family. Because he was not a son of Mstislav, he was acceptable to Vsevolod's enemies. It was well calculated and Rostislav Yurievich was invited to be prince of Novgorod while Sviatoslav Olgovich was dismissed.[51]

SUMMARY OF YAROPOLK'S REIGN

During the reign of Yaropolk the princes were so busy with their domestic quarrels that they conducted no campaigns against the foreign enemy. The Polovetsians, having recovered from the assaults of Monomakh and Mstislav, now could make new incursions into the Land of Rus. In 1138 they devastated the principality of Kursk, and some of their allied detachments appeared even in the Novgorod territories. The Chud also took advantage of the disturbances in Novgorod. Not only did they stop paying tribute, they even overran Yuriev and slaughtered the inhabitants. In 1133 Vsevolod, confirmed as prince of Novgorod for the second time, led a campaign against the Chud and recovered Yuriev.

Yaropolk died in 1139. The chronicle is strongly biased in his favor, for he reminded the people of his father through his courage, the fame of his successful warfare against the Polovetsians, and also evidently through his moral qualities. Yaropolk's excessive daring and self-confidence proved disastrous for him and his family on the Supoy. The unlucky pact he made with his elder brother unleashed the feuding which rent the Land of Rus during his reign. Nevertheless, before blaming Yaropolk for lack of discretion or resolution, the indeterminacy of familial relations should be remembered, the fact that the junior members of the family were by no means entirely obedient to the senior, particularly when he was not their father or even their uncle, rather a member of the same generation, not even the oldest member. Younger brothers and nephews considered themselves perfectly justified in armed resistance to the decisions of the senior prince when these seemed disadvantageous. Yaropolk's position was very difficult. What was he to do with the restless Viacheslav, who kept moving from one principality to another, according to the chronicle bearing the chief responsibility for the feuding? The grand prince's invidious situation was appreciated by the people, who retained their attachment to the faithful scion of the famous Monomakh.

VSEVOLOD OLGOVICH OBTAINS THE THRONE OF KIEV

At Yaropolk's death the seniority passed by right to his brother Viacheslav, who entered Kiev without opposition. As soon as Vsevolod Olgovich heard of Yaropolk's death and Viacheslav's succession he assembled a small retinue and with his brother Sviatoslav and cousin Vladimir Davydovich appeared on the western bank of the Dnieper. He occupied Vyshgorod, where he deployed his troops and marched on Kiev. Arriving at the Kopyrev suburb he set fire to the homesteads in that part of the city, sending a message to Viacheslav inviting him to leave peaceably. Viacheslav sent word through the metropolitan. "Brother," he said, "I have come here in the place of my brothers Mstislav and Yaropolk, according to the testament of our fathers. If you, brother, desire this throne and wish to leave your patrimony, so be it. I shall be subject to you and return to my former land. Kiev shall be yours." So Vsevolod entered Kiev with great honor and glory, says the chronicle.

Thus a son of Oleg, in contravention to established conventions, took possession of the senior throne. What were the reasons for such a remarkable turn of events? How could the descendants of Monomakh allow Sviatoslav's grandson to take Kiev without hereditary right?

At that time the descendants of Monomakh were in a difficult situation. They lacked a leader and were at odds amongst themselves. Viacheslav remained the senior, yet his character made him incapable of promoting family interests or maintaining order and unity. The next brother, Yury of Rostov, was more energetic and capable, though being younger he could not act on his own account, ignoring Viacheslav. Moreover he was not well known in the South, which was very important where the populace was concerned. When they did get to know him, they found that he was not like his father or two elder brothers. Andrei, the youngest son of Monomakh, was regarded as a good prince but, being the youngest of the brothers, could not act as head of the family.

The prince whose personal qualities best fitted him to represent the tribe of Monomakh amongst the people was Iziaslav Mstislavich of Vladimir-in-Volhynia,[52] the eldest son of Monomakh's eldest son. Unusually brave, generous to his retinue, gracious to the people, Iziaslav was a model prince in the eyes of his contemporaries, reminding the people of his celebrated grandfather. Unfortunately he was placed in an antagonistic position in relation to his uncles, from whom he could expect nothing good, either for himself or his children. On the other hand, he was closely related by marriage to Vsevolod Olgovich who, being married to his elder sister, according to contemporary concepts stood in the same relationship to him as an elder brother or father. Vsevolod was aware that his sole opportunity to attain the seniority was through dissensions among the family of Monomakh, so he did what he could to win over Iziaslav, the most valiant.

This he could do easily, owing to his marriage and to their earlier dealings, for he could claim that it was only thanks to him that Iziaslav was reconciled with his uncles and received an important principality. According to some accounts, Vsevolod sent to Iziaslav, saying "After your father Kiev belongs to you (he could say this, having expelled his uncle), but your uncles will not allow you to reign there. You know that in former times they drove you out wherever you were. Had it not been for me, you would not have any principality. Now therefore I shall take Kiev, and you shall be like one of my own brothers. I will give you good lands now, and after my death Kiev will be yours, only do not join with your uncles against me." Iziaslav assented, and they confirmed the agreement by oath. This may explain the indifference of the citizens of Kiev to Vsevolod's occupation of their city, when they certainly could have resisted his "small" retinue. There is no doubt that Vsevolod never would have arrived with such a small force, had he not been sure that there would be no opposition.

Having settled matters with his brothers-in-law the sons of Mstislav, Vsevolod also had to come to some sort of arrangement with his own family, his brothers and cousins, sons of Oleg and Davyd. In order to have the support of both for his occupation of Kiev, says the chronicle, he promised the reversion of Chernigov to his brother Igor and his cousin Vladimir. Still, once he became prince of Kiev he gave it to Vladimir Davydovich alone, thus starting a quarrel between his brothers and his cousins. Other credible sources allege that he promised that as soon as he was in possession of Kiev he would expel the sons of Monomakh from their principalities and give them to his brothers, leaving his cousins in possession of Chernigov. Now, afraid of uniting the sons of Monomakh against him if he took any action, he could not keep his promise to his brothers, and was glad to foment a quarrel between them and his cousins. It is hard otherwise to imagine that he could have deceived them by promising the same to everyone.

WAR BETWEEN LINES OF SVIATOSLAV AND MONOMAKH

In spite of all Vsevolod's cunning, and in spite of the fact that at first he wanted to spare the sons of Monomakh and merely keep them disunited, they were not willing to surrender the seniority to him. As might be expected, Yury was the first to act. He went to his nephew Rostislav Mstislavich of Smolensk,[53] who always was respectful towards his uncles and could thus be a mediator between them and his brothers. The chronicle account implies that the discussions amongst the descendants of Monomakh were initially successful because when Vsevolod made peace overtures towards them and called Iziaslav Mstislavich to a meeting in Kiev, they refused to have any contact with him. They continued their discussions, intending to make war on him.

Vsevolod decided to forestall them, attack them one by one and give their principalities to his brothers, as he promised. He trusted in his own strength, says the chronicler, desiring to rule the whole land. He sent his cousin Iziaslav Davydovich and the princes of Galich, Rostislav's grandsons, with some Polovetsians against Iziaslav of Volhynia and his uncle Viacheslav of Turov, while he and his brother Sviatoslav marched to Pereiaslavl against Andrei. He intended to make Sviatoslav prince of Pereiaslavl, and when he reached the Dnieper he sent a message to Andrei telling him to go to Kursk.

For Andrei it would have been more than a personal humiliation to agree to such a demand and accept an insignificant and distant part of the principality of Chernigov while yielding his father's and grandfather's seat of Pereiaslavl to his enemies. It would have meant dishonoring his entire family, depriving the whole line of Monomakh of the consequence, preeminence and territories won by Vladimir and his two eldest sons. The sons of Oleg were excluded from the succession and should have been confined to the Chernigov territories. Consequently the remaining principalities became the exclusive patrimony of the line of Monomakh. Now the sons of Oleg, in defiance of tradition, attempted by force to deprive them of the lands they had inherited from their father and give them the inferior territories of Chernigov. Considering how all members of the princely family, in order not to inflict any *damage* on the family, were afraid of occupying any place not previously occupied by their seniors, Andrei's reply is not surprising. After taking counsel with his retinue, he sent a message to Vsevolod. "Better for me and for my retinue to die in the land of my father and grandfather," he said, "than for me to be prince in Kursk. My father was prince not of Kursk, but of Pereiaslavl, and I will die in my patrimony. If your lands are too few for you, brother, if the whole Land of Rus is not enough, and you want to take this land also, kill me and take it. While I live, I shall not leave this land. It will not be a wonder among our kin, for such things have happened before. Did not Sviatopolk kill Boris and Gleb for their lands?[54] Yet did he live long to enjoy them? He lost this earthly life, and is tormented eternally in the next."

Vsevolod did not attack Pereiaslavl in person. He sent his brother Sviatoslav, who encountered Andrei's retinue on the way and was defeated. They pursued him as far as Koran,[55] where Andrei called a halt. Vsevolod made peace with Andrei the next day, though it is not known on what conditions. Most probably Andrei agreed to acknowledge his seniority and not take part in the alliance of his brothers, while Vsevolod promised to let him keep Pereiaslavl. When Andrei already had taken the oath, but before Vsevolod did, fire broke out in Pereiaslavl that night. Vsevolod took no advantage of this calamity and sent to Andrei next day. "You see that I have not yet sworn," said he, "so I could have done you harm had I wished. God delivered you into my hands, for you set your own town on fire. I could have done whatever I wanted. Now you have sworn. If you keep your oath, well and good. If not, may God judge you." Having made peace with Andrei, Vsevolod returned to Kiev.

Meanwhile there was war in the West. Some alarm caused the army sent to Vladimir against Iziaslav to turn back at the Goryn river. Then the princes of Galich invited Iziaslav Mstislavich to negotiate, but could not reach agreement. Perhaps they wanted to expand their territory at the expense of the beleaguered prince of Volhynia. The Poles, who were on Vsevolod's side, attacked Volhynia, while Iziaslav Davydovich attacked Turov. Nothing came of it, for both princes, uncle and nephew, remained on their thrones. No help came to them from the North, from either Suzdal or Smolensk. Yury, who was at Smolensk, ordered the men of Novgorod to send a force against Vsevolod, but they would not obey him. His son Rostislav fled from Novgorod to join his father at Smolensk. Yury went back to Suzdal in anger. Fom there he seized Torzhok, which belonged to Novgorod.

The only reason the chronicle gives for Yury's inactivity is that Rostislav dared not assist his kin by himself, while they, left to themselves, had no choice but to send peace proposals to Vsevolod. At first Vsevolod rejected the conditions they proposed, then on reflection decided that he could not do without the sons of Monomakh, agreed to their conditions and swore an oath. The chronicle does not say what these conditions were. Evidently it was agreed that each prince of Monomakh's line retain his principality. It is quite clear why Vsevolod thought that he could not do without the sons of Monomakh, since even with the combined forces of Chernigov, Galich and Poland he could not unseat any of them. Even though there was a split between the Northern and Southern branches, and their actions were separate and purely defensive, they had the people on their side.

FURTHER DISAGREEMENTS AND MOVEMENTS AMONG THE PRINCES

The only thing that kept Vsevolod in Kiev was the enmity which divided the line of Monomakh, though there also were constant dissensions among his own kin. Sviatoslav Olgovich, summoned to be prince of Novgorod a second time, still could not maintain good relations with the citizens and fled to Starodub. Vsevolod called him to Kiev, but the brothers could not agree about their lands. Sviatoslav went to Kursk, holding it in conjunction with Novgorod Seversk. What Igor had is not known. Soon afterwards Vsevolod gave Belgorod to Sviatoslav. Igor continued to be at odds with [Vladimir] Davydovich over Chernigov and made war on him, then had to come to terms.

The death of Andrei Vladimirovich of Pereiaslavl in 1142 gave rise to new changes and troubles. Vsevolod evidently was ill at ease in Kiev, surrounded by territories held by the Monomakh line, and sent to Viacheslav of Turov. "You are living within the principality of Kiev, which belongs to me," he said. "Go to your patrimony of Pereiaslavl." Viacheslav had no excuse not to go, so he went, while Vsevolod made his son Sviatoslav prince of Turov. This could not fail to irritate the sons of Oleg—it made their hearts heavy, says the chronicle—as Vsevolod bestowed a principality on his son, leaving his brothers with nothing.

Then Vsevolod called all his brothers and cousins to meet him and divide the lands. They gathered on the other side of the Dnieper. Sviatoslav Olgovich, Vladimir Davydovich and Iziaslav Davydovich met at Olzhichi, while Igor halted near Gorodets. This means that they did not go all the way to Kiev, preferring to conduct their business across the Dnieper. Sviatoslav went to Igor, asking him "What is our eldest brother giving us?" "He is giving us each a town," Igor replied, "Brest and Drogichin,[56] Chartoryisk and Kletsk, but nothing from his patrimony, the land of the Viatichians."[57] Then Sviatoslav and Igor swore, and the next day the sons of Davyd swore also, that their whole kin would stand against the injustice of their eldest brother, saying "May the vengeance of the cross fall upon any of us who breaks what he has sworn by the cross." After this, when Vsevolod invited them to dine with him they refused. "You have Kiev," they said, "and we ask for the lands of Chernigov and Novgorod Seversk, not for that of Kiev." Vsevolod would not relinquish the lands of the Viatichians, which evidently he was saving for his sons, and continued to offer them the four towns. "You are our elder brother," they replied, "but if you will not give, we shall take."

Then, breaking off relations with their brother, they went to make war on Viacheslav in Pereiaslavl, no doubt hoping to drive him out of that city as easily as Vsevolod had driven him out of Kiev. They were disappointed, for the city resisted, and Vsevolod sent a force of Pechenegs and men of Kiev under his commander Lazar Sakovsky to Viacheslav's assistance. When Iziaslav Mstislavich heard that the princes of Chernigov were attacking his uncle, he quickly dispatched to Pereiaslavl an army which defeated them. The four princes could not withstand just one prince, each fleeing to his own city. Meanwhile Rostislav appeared at the head of the men of Smolensk and attacked the principality of Chernigov along the Sozha. When Iziaslav heard that his brother had driven out the princes of Chernigov, he attacked their lands from Pereiaslavl, taking the villages along the Desna and around the city of Chernigov, returning home with great honor.

Igor and his brothers wanted to take revenge. They attacked Pereiaslavl again, besieged the city, fought beneath the walls for three days, and again returned empty-handed. Then Vsevolod called his cousin Sviatosha (Sviatoslav Davydôvich, who became a monk under the name of Nicholas in 1106) from his monastery and sent him to his brothers. "Brothers," he urged, "take what I give you with love, Gorodets,[58] Rogachev, Brest, Drogichin and Kletsk, and do not fight the sons of Mstislav any more."

This time, discouraged by their failure at Pereiaslavl, they did as their brother required. When he summoned them to Kiev they came. Vsevolod, who held on to what he had obtained only thanks to the disunity amongst the other princes, was not pleased at their alliance. In order to break it, he offered to reward the sons of Davyd if they would abandon his brothers.

They were seduced by his promises. Breaking their oath to Sviatoslav and Igor, they went over to Vsevolod's side. Vsevolod, pleased at this, gave Davyd's sons Brest, Drogichin, Vshchizh and Ormina,[59] gave Gorodets Ostersky and Rogachev to his brother Igor and Kletsk and Chartoryisk to Sviatoslav. The sons of Oleg had no choice but to make do with two towns each, but complained again when Viacheslav, with Vsevolod's approval, exchanged thrones with his nephew Iziaslav. Vsevolod gave Pereiaslavl to Iziaslav, returning to his old principality of Turov, while Vsevolod moved his son from Turov to Vladimir.

It is understandable that Viacheslav was not happy in Pereiaslavl, where he was besieged repeatedly by the princes of Chernigov, while the bold Iziaslav was capable of dealing with any enemies. Vsevolod's brothers murmured against him for favoring his brothers-in-law, the sons of Mstislav. "These are our enemies," they said, "and he has surrounded himself with them. No good will come of it for us or for him." They kept urging Vsevolod to let them attack the sons of Mstislav, but he would not listen. This all shows that Vsevolod indeed previously promised his brothers the lands occupied by the descendants of Monomakh, but by now they should have understood that this was not an easy promise to keep. However understandable their irritation with their eldest brother, their insistence was a sign of poor judgement. Their hostility concerned Iziaslav Mstislavich, who could see from the way Vsevolod dealt with his brothers what sort of a man he was, how unreliable. He was well aware that Vsevolod tolerated princes of Monomakh's line in major principalities only because he had to. Therefore he decided to attempt reconciliation with his uncle Yury. He went in person to meet him at Suzdal but could not reach any agreement, then went on to his cousin Rostislav in Smolensk, and thence to Sviatopolk in Novgorod, where he spent the winter.

SITUATION IN GALICH

Such were the relations between the two major lines of the descendants of Yaroslav during Vsevolod Olgovich's seniority. Let us now consider the others. Foremost among them were the descendants of Rostislav, called princes of Galich. Rostislav's sons Volodar and Vasilko both died in 1124. Volodar left two sons, Rostislav[60] and Vladimir, better known by the diminutive Vladimirko.[61] The sons of Vasilko were Grigory and Ivan.

Most significant was Vladimirko, Volodar's second son. Despite being surrounded by powerful enemies he not only held onto his throne, he left his son a strong principality, the friendship or hostility of which was to prove of great importance to neighboring lands. Being a weak prince with strong neighbors, Vladimirko was not particular about the means he used to achieve his ends. He used finesse and cunning, not setting much store by oaths. He attacked his elder brother Rostislav in alliance with the Hungarians in 1127, but Rostislav was supported by his cousins, Vasilko's own sons, and by Grand Prince Mstislav Vladimirovich of Kiev. He could not achieve anything against Rostislav, then on the deaths of Rostislav and his two cousins he took both their principalities, Peremyshl and Terebovl, not dividing them with his nephew Ivan Rostislavich who became prince of Zvenigorod.

As a result of the feuding which broke out in Rus after the death of Mstislav the Great, Vladimirko had complete freedom of action. Vladimirko and one of his cousins, Ivan Vasilkovich, assisted Vsevolod Olgovich in his war with the descendants of Monomakh. Their relationship changed when Iziaslav Mstislavich was replaced by Vsevolod's son Sviatoslav as prince of Volhynia. A prince with Vladimirko's character and aspirations could not be a good neighbor, neither were Sviatoslav and his father of a conciliatory disposition. So it is not surprising to read in the chronicles that in 1144 Vsevolod quarreled with Vladimirko on his son's account, that they found further fault with each other, and that Vladimirko dispatched to Kiev a sworn complaint. Vsevolod marched against him with both his brothers, his cousin Vladimir Davydovich, Viacheslav of Turov, Iziaslav and Rostislav, the sons of Mstislav, his own son Sviatoslav, the two sons of Vsevolod of Gorodets, and with Prince Władysław of Poland. They demanded that the *voluble*[62] Vladimirko come and submit to Vsevolod. Vladimirko would not hear of it, calling upon the Hungarians for aid.

Vsevolod advanced upon Terebovl, and Vladimirko came out to meet him, but they could not fight because they were separated by the Seret river, therefore they both marched along its banks towards Zvenigorod. Vsevolod, joined by his cousin Iziaslav Davydovich with a troop of Polovetsians, took up his position on one side of Zvenigorod, facing Vladimirko on the other, so that the two armies were separated by a shallow river. Then Vsevolod made pontoon bridges and sent his troops across the river to cut off Vladimirko's army in the rear, cutting him off from Peremyshl and Galich. This caused despondency among the men of Galich, who feared that their wives would be taken into captivity while they were immobilized.

Then the resourceful Vladimirko found a way out of the situation. He sent to Vsevolod's brother Igor. "If you reconcile me with your brother," said he, "I will help you to become prince of Kiev after his death." Igor was won over by this promise, urging Vsevolod to make peace by alternate pleading and anger. "You wish me no good," he complained. "Why do you appoint me your successor to Kiev if you will not allow me to make friends for myself?" Vsevolod listened to him and made peace. Vladimirko rode out to him in front of his army, submitted to him and gave him fourteen hundred grivnas of silver. In the past he had spoken much, and now he had much to pay, adds the chronicler. Vsevolod kissed Vladimirko. "You have come to no harm," he said, "now do no more wrong." He returned to him the two towns, Ushitsa and Mikulin, that Iziaslav Davydovich had taken. Vsevolod did not keep all the silver for himself, dividing it with all his brothers.

Vladimirko's setback encouraged his enemies at home, who supported his nephew Ivan Rostislavich. That winter, when Vladimirko went hunting, the citizens of Galich sent to Ivan in Zvenigorod and opened their town to him. When Vladimirko heard of this he led his retinue to Galich and attacked it for three days, yet could not take it until one night Ivan made a sortie. Riding out too far from the town, he was cut off by Vladimirko's men. He fought through enemy lines with heavy losses and fled towards the Danube, thence making his way across the steppe to Vsevolod in Kiev. Vladimirko entered Galich and massacred many of the people, putting others to a cruel death, according to the chronicler's expression.

Perhaps the protection Vsevolod afforded Ivan Rostislavich caused a fresh war between the princes of Kiev and Galich. In 1146 Vladimirko took Priluk,[63] on the border of the principality of Kiev. Vsevolod once more assembled his brothers and brothers-in-law. He also formed an alliance with Novgorod, which sent a detachment under their commander Nerevin, with Polish and Wild Polovetsian auxiliaries. Together they besieged Zvenigorod with a very large force. On the first day they burned the fort, and on the next day the citizens of Zvenigorod held an assembly and decided to surrender.

Their commander, Vladimirko's boyar Ivan Khaldeevich, was against surrendering. To terrify the citizens into obedience he seized three of them, killed them and had their bodies cut in two and flung over the walls. He was successful, for the citizens took fright and fought unwaveringly. Seeing this, Vsevolod decided to take the town by storm. On the third day his army launched a mass attack. The fighting continued from dawn to late evening, and the town was set on fire in three places. The defenders extinguished the fires, and Vsevolod was forced to raise the siege. He returned to Kiev, apparently having been impeded greatly by illness in his prosecution of the war.

SITUATION IN OTHER PRINCIPALITIES

As for the other princely lines, the death of Vsevolod Davydovich of Gorodets is recorded in 1141. He left two sons, Boris and Gleb, and two daughters, one of whom was married by Grand Prince Vsevolod to his cousin Vladimir Davydovich, and the other to Yury Yaroslavich. This is the first mention of Yury, who was the son of Yaroslav Sviatopolchich, and thus a representative of Iziaslav's line. It is not known what city he ruled.[64]

The princes of Polotsk took advantage of the disturbances, which weakened the princes of Monomakh's line, to return from exile. Vasilko Sviatoslavich was prince of Polotsk under Yaropolk, and the chronicle records the return of two other princes from exile in 1139. Instead of being enemies of the descendants of Yaroslav, they were now related by marriage to both their principal lines, Monomakh's and Oleg's. Vsevolod married his son Sviatoslav to Vasilko's daughter, and Iziaslav Mstislavich married his daughter to Rogvolod Borisovich. Sviatoslav, son of Yaroslav Sviatoslavich of Murom, died in 1144, being succeeded by his brother Rostislav, who made his son Gleb prince of Riazan.

FURTHER COMMOTION IN NOVGOROD

As for the men of Novgorod, clearly they could not have enjoyed a period of tranquillity while the feuding between the sons of Monomakh and Oleg continued. After Vsevolod expelled Viacheslav from Kiev, as a result of the triumph of Oleg's sons, the citizens of Novgorod found themselves between Scylla and Charybdis, and again were drawn into the conflict. They were forced to draw their swords against the grand prince of Kiev, on whom supposedly they were dependent. As Yury of Rostov made preparations against Vsevolod he demanded troops from Novgorod, but the citizens refused to attack the grand prince, just as previously they refused to march against Yury. Their refusal was the occasion for the departure of Yury's son Rostislav, who went to Smolensk, leaving Novgorod without a prince, while Yury vented his anger by taking Torzhok. In their extremity the men of Novgorod applied to Vsevolod. They were obliged once more to accept Sviatoslav Olgovich, whom they had expelled, which meant reviving all their domestic dissensions.[65]

The men of Novgorod were obliged to take an oath to Sviatoslav. It is not known what its terms were, but disturbances were recorded in the city even before he arrived. Doubtless they were caused by his enemies, the Monomakh party. Sviatoslav also did not forget his enemies, those who had caused him to be ejected. As a result, the citizens in their assemblies complained of his spite, as the chronicle puts it. It was not long before Sviatoslav himself was tired of the situation. "It is hard for me, brother, amongst these people," he said. "I cannot live with them. Send whom you want to be prince here." Vsevolod decided to send his son Sviatoslav, and dispatched Ivan Voitishich to inform them. Probably in order to weaken the Monomakh party and to ensure his son of an easy reign, he instructed Voitishich to ask Novgorod to send its most prominent citizens to Kiev.

This they did, and thus Konstantin Mikulinich, who was mayor under Sviatoslav and later defected to Vsevolod Mstislavich, was exiled to Kiev, as were six other citizens, sent to Kiev in chains. These measures only appear to have made the disturbances worse. Sviatoslav's supporters were beaten at the assembly in revenge for his violent measures, and the chiliarch, his children's godfather,[66] informed him that people were about to lay hands on him also. Sviatoslav slipped quietly out of Novgorod by night with the mayor Yakun. Together with his brother Prokopy, Yakun was captured and brought back to Novgorod, where he was beaten almost to death, stripped naked and thrown off the bridge. He was fortunate enough to reach the bank, after which they did him no more violence but fined him a thousand grivnas. His brother was fined a hundred grivnas. Both had their hands chained to their necks and were exiled to the land of the Chud. Afterwards Yury of Rostov gave them refuge and treated them well.

Meanwhile the bishop of Novgorod arrived at Kiev accompanied by other envoys. "Give us your son," said they to Vsevolod, "for we do not want your brother Sviatoslav." Vsevolod agreed and sent Sviatoslav, his son. Before the young prince reached Chernigov the citizens of Novgorod changed their minds. "We do not want your son," they said, "or your brother, or any of your kin. We want the kin of Vladimir. Give us your brother-in-law, the son of Mstislav."

When Vsevolod heard these demands he made the bishop and the envoys return to Kiev and detained them there. Not wanting Novgorod to pass into Vladimir's line, he sent for his brothers-in-law Sviatopolk and Vladimir, and gave them Brest. "Undertake nothing concerning Novgorod," he told them. "Let them fend for themselves and take whatever prince they like." Novgorod was without a prince for nine months, which was an intolerable situation for its people, says the chronicler, made worse by a cessation of grain supplies.

In these circumstances, naturally the party opposed to Sviatoslav fell, then the opposing side which now gained the upper hand changed its orientation. Yury of Rostov welcomed Yakun and treated him well. Other friends of Yakun and Sviatoslav—Sudila, Nezhata and Strashko—also found refuge in Suzdal. Yury's kind welcome clearly won them all over to his side. Now that their party was in the ascendant they were called back to Novgorod, and Sudila even was elected mayor. Understandably they promoted the interests of their benefactor Yury, all the more so since his support was the only recourse left open to the city. Novgorod sent for Yury, who did not come himself but sent his son Rostislav.[67]

Vsevolod saw that he had miscalculated, and was very angry with Yury. He seized Gorodets on the Oster and other towns of his, together with their horses, cattle, sheep, and whatever else belonged to him in the South. Meanwhile Iziaslav Mstislavich sent a message to his sister,

Vsevolod's wife. "Ask my brother-in-law to give Novgorod the Great to our brother Sviatopolk." She did so, and he finally agreed. Of course he had other reasons for this besides his wife's request. It was better for him to have his brother-in-law, Mstislav's son, in Novgorod than Yury's son. Moreover if Yury's son were driven out in favor of his brother-in-law, the enmity between Yury and his nephews would be intensified, greatly to Vsevolod's advantage.

When the news reached Novgorod that Sviatopolk Mstislavich was coming to them with the bishop and the other prominent citizens detained in Kiev by Vsevolod, the supporters of the sons of Mstislav once more gained the upper hand. In any case there were only two alternatives left. Either they could keep Rostislav and make enemies of the grand prince and the sons of Mstislav, or they could accept Sviatopolk and have only Yury as their enemy. They decided on the latter course. Sviatopolk was received, Rostislav was sent back to his father, and calm returned to Novgorod.

RELATIONS WITH POLAND

Such were the domestic relations while Vsevolod Olgovich was grand prince. Let us now turn to external relations. We left Poland during the reign of Bolesław III Krzywousty,[68] one of the most glorious in the history of Poland in terms of his successful wars against the Pomeranians, Czechs and Germans. He also was involved in a constant struggle with his brother Zbigniew, in which he had assistance from Rus. It is very important, from the point of view of Rus, that Bolesław's energies were largely directed towards the West, and also were restrained by the domestic struggle with his brother. Moreover his contemporaries in Rus were Vladimir Monomakh and his son Mstislav, who were quite capable of resisting Poland should any aggression from its prince arise.

For this reason Bolesław's intervention in the affairs of Volhynia on the side of his relations, the line of Iziaslav, came to nothing. By the time of the troubles that followed the death of Mstislav the Great, when the turmoil in Rus began, the Polish hero was a weary man, and in any case was fully occupied in the West. The feuding between Bolesław's sons after his death not only prevented them from intervening in the divisions between the princes of Rus, but opened the way for intervention in the opposite direction.

Bolesław died in 1139.[69] Relations between his five sons were identical to those existing between the princes or Rus or Bohemia. His eldest son took the senior throne at Cracow, while the younger brothers had their own territories, their relationship towards him being based purely on kinship. The effect of this on Poland is obvious, particularly when there was already a strong aristocracy. Władysław II,[70] the eldest son of Bolesław, was a meek and pacific man, whereas his wife Agnes, daughter of Duke Leopold of Austria, was quite the contrary. To this German princess this relationship between the princes appeared primitive. Outraged by the familial relationship between the princes, her pride would not suffer her husband to be merely the first among his brothers. She called him half a prince and half a man for allowing the existence of so many princes with rights equal to his own.

Eventually his wife's importunities and mockery had their effect on Władysław. He imposed taxes on his brothers' possessions and placed their towns under his rule, betraying his intention of driving them out of Poland altogether. The magnates and prelates stood up for the younger brothers, whereupon Władysław was forced to flee to Germany. He was succeeded by his next brother, Bolesław IV the Curly.[71]

Vsevolod Olgovich took part in these struggles on the side of Władysław, whose son Bolesław was married to his daughter Zvenislava or Veleslava. In 1142 Vsevolod sent his son Sviatoslav, his cousin Iziaslav Davydovich and Vladimirko of Galich[72] to help Władysław against his younger brothers, but they did not save him from exile. Even our chronicle admits that they contented themselves with ravaging the countryside, taking more noncombatants than warriors captive. Władysław took part in Vsevolod's campaign against Vladimirko. In 1145 Igor Olgovich[73] responded to the call of Władysław, who was constantly scheming to get his throne back with the help of the Rus or the Germans, and marched with his brothers against the younger sons of Bolesław. In the middle of the Polish land, says the chronicle, they encountered Bolesław IV and his brother Mieczysław (Mieszko).[74] The Polish princes, reluctant to fight, did obeisance to Igor and agreed to give their eldest brother Władysław four towns to rule, letting Igor and his brothers have Wizna,[75] after which the Rus princes returned home with great booty. That was the sum of their relations with Poland.

RELATIONS WITH OTHER NEIGHBORING PEOPLES

A Swedish prince attacked three foreign merchantmen in sixty flyboats[76] in 1142. He failed to take them, losing a hundred and fifty men in the process.[77] The struggle with the Finnic tribes continued. Also in 1142 the

Häme[78] came from Finland and attacked the lands of Novgorod. Not one returned home, for the men of Ladoga killed four hundred of them.[79] There is record of a Karelian campaign against the Häme the next year.[80] No Polovetsian incursions are recorded for these years. In 1139 the entire Polovetsian nation with all their princes came to make peace. Vsevolod came from Kiev, Andrei came from Pereiaslavl. They met them at Malotin[81] and made peace, which obviously meant buying off the barbarians. The Polovetsians later were to participate in Vsevolod's campaign against Galich.

IGOR OLGOVICH ESTABLISHED AS HEIR TO KIEV

During the Galich campaign Igor Olgovich mentioned his brother Vsevolod's promise that he succeed him at Kiev. In 1145 in the presence of his brothers and cousins and of his brother-in-law Mstislav Iziaslavich, Vsevolod made a public declaration of this arrangement. "Vladimir Monomakh," he said, "placed his son Mstislav on the senior throne after him, and Mstislav left it to his brother Yaropolk. So I too, if God takes me, leave Kiev to my brother Igor."

From the point of view of the sons of Oleg, Mstislav's succession to Monomakh and Yaropolk's to Mstislav were an infringement of the old order, according to which the seniority along with Kiev always belonged to the head of the family as a whole. Since Monomakh's line was the first to abandon tradition to its own advantage, now Vsevolod considered he had the right to do the same and leave Kiev to his brother, even though Igor was not the senior of the descendants of Yaroslav. Although Iziaslav Mstislavich was greatly indignant at this arrangement, there was nothing he could do about it. He was forced to swear to acknowledge Igor's supremacy.

When they were all sitting in the outer hall of Vsevolod's house, continues the chronicle, he said to them "Igor! Swear to love your brethren! You, Vladimir, Sviatoslav and Iziaslav, swear allegiance to Igor and be content with what he gives you of his own free will, not out of necessity." They all swore. When the sick Vsevolod returned from the Galich campaign in 1146 he broke his journey at the island near Vyshgorod, summoning the most prominent citizens of Kiev. "I am very ill," he said. "Here is my brother Igor. Receive him as your prince." "We accept him gladly," they replied. Igor went with them to Kiev, calling all the citizens together. They all swore allegiance to him, saying "You are our prince," but they deceived him, said the chronicle.

The next day Igor went to Vyshgorod, where the citizens also swore allegiance. Vsevolod was still alive. He sent his son-in-law Bolesław of Poland to Iziaslav Mstislavich, and his boyar Miroslav Andreevich to the sons of Davyd to ask whether they would keep their oath to Igor. They replied that they would. Vsevolod died on August 1. He was a clever and energetic prince where his personal interests were concerned, knowing how to turn events to his advantage, without being squeamish about the means he used to achieve his ends.

After burying his brother, Igor went to Kiev, once more assembled all the people on the hill at Yaroslav's Court, and they all took the oath to him again. Then suddenly they all gathered at Turova church and sent for Igor to come to them. Igor went, sending his brother Sviatoslav on ahead to the assembly while he waited with his retinue. The citizens complained of Vsevolod's agent Ratsha and the agent of Vyshgorod, Tudor. "Ratsha ruined Kiev," they complained, "and Tudor ruined Vyshgorod. Now, Prince Sviatoslav, swear to us with your brother that if any of us is wronged, you will redress the matter." "I swear on my brother's behalf," replied Sviatoslav, "that no one will do you any violence, and you shall have whatever agent you desire." He then dismounted and kissed the cross before the assembly. The citizens also dismounted and kissed the cross, saying "Your brother the prince, and you and your children, have sworn not to devise evil against Igor or Sviatoslav." Then Sviatoslav brought the leading citizens to Igor. "Brother," said he, "I have sworn to them that you will love them and judge them justly." Igor dismounted and confirmed with an oath all that they and his brother had done, after which both princes went to dine. The people, leaving the assembly in disorder, went to plunder the houses of Ratsha and the swordbearers. Igor dispatched to them his brother Sviatoslav and the retinue, who with difficulty restrained them.

IZIASLAV MSTISLAVICH SEIZES KIEV

At the same time Igor sent to inform Iziaslav Mstislavich of Vsevolod's death, asking whether he stood by his oath. Iziaslav made no reply, not even allowing the messenger to return. Because Igor broke the promises he made to the citizens of Kiev, they sent to Iziaslav at Pereiaslavl, saying "Come to us, prince, it is you we want."

Iziaslav accepted the invitation, gathered his fighting men and left Pereiaslavl. When he crossed the Dnieper at Zarub he received messengers from the barbarian inhabitants of the marches, the Karakalpaks[82] and the men of the frontier towns along the Ros, who said "You are our prince. We do not want Oleg's sons. Advance quickly, we are with you." Iziaslav went on to Dernovo, where he was joined by the Karakalpaks and the men of the Ros, receiving similar messages from the inhabitants of Belgorod and Vasiliev. Soon new messengers from Kiev came to him, saying "You are our prince. Come, we do not want to pass to Oleg's sons as if we were their inheritance. Where we see your banner, we will be ready to join you."

These are very significant words, showing unfamiliarity with the concept of inheritance in a single family line. Iziaslav assembled all his army in the steppe, Christians and pagans, and addressed them. "Brethren! I held Vsevolod my senior by right, for an elder brother or brother-in-law is as a father to me. As for these people, as God and the power of the cross ordain, so be it. Either I shall lay down my life before you, or I shall attain the throne of my father and grandfather." With these words he advanced on Kiev.

Meanwhile Igor sent to his cousins, the sons of Davyd, to know whether they stood by their oath. They wanted a high price for their loyalty, demanding much territory. In his extremity Igor gave them whatever they wanted so long as they came to his aid, and they set out to join him. It was even more important, though, that Igor be on good terms with his retinue and secure their attachment. He called his chief boyars, Uleb, Ivan Voitishich and Lazar Sakovsky, promising they would enjoy the same favor as under his brother, and confirmed Uleb in his office of chiliarch.

This suggests that every change of prince threatened the boyars with loss of their positions. Igor was anxious to reassure them that they would not lose anything under him. He was too late, for the boyars already had gone over to Iziaslav. Aware of the general disinclination towards Igor, and that all Rus was flocking to the banner of Monomakh's grandson, they hastened to dissociate themselves from a lost cause. They sent a message to Iziaslav urging him to advance more quickly, as the sons of Davyd were coming to Igor's aid. Besides those just mentioned, Sviatoslav's boyars Vasil Polochanin and Miroslav Andreevich, grandson of Khila, went over to Iziaslav. The five boyars met the citizens to discuss the best way of betraying Igor. At the same time they sent a message to Iziaslav, urging him to advance and informing him that they had agreed with the citizens to desert Igor's banner and turn back to Kiev.

Iziaslav advanced on Kiev. He and his son Mstislav took up their position by the earthworks near Lake Nadovo, while the citizens of Kiev stood apart in great numbers at Oleg's Grave.[83] Soon Igor and his army observed that the citizens were in contact with Iziaslav, and had received from him his chiliarch and the standard. Then the Berendey, crossing the Lybed, captured Igor's baggage train in front of the Golden Gates and below the gardens. Seeing this, Igor said to his brother Sviatoslav and his nephew Sviatoslav Vsevolodovich "Go to your men, and God's will be done." He gave the same order to the chiliarch Uleb and to Ivan Voitishich, who as soon as they reached their troops threw down their banners and galloped off towards the Jewry Gate.

The sons of Oleg and their nephew, undismayed, marched out against Iziaslav. Unable to reach him by way of Lake Nadovo, they went across the hills and found themselves in the most unsuitable position, between two ditches leading from the lake and from the dry Lybed. The Berendey attacked them in the rear with their sabres. Iziaslav, Mstislav and their retinue attacked their flank. The sons of Oleg fled. Igor rode into a marsh, where his horse bogged down, and his infirm legs did not allow him to walk. His brother Sviatoslav fled across the Dnieper to the mouth of the Desna. His nephew Sviatoslav Vsevolodovich fled to Kiev and hid in St. Irene's monastery, where he was taken prisoner. Their retinue was pursued as far as the Dnieper, to the mouth of the Desna and to the Kiev ferry.

Iziaslav entered Kiev with great honor and glory. A multitude of the people came out to meet him, together with the abbots of the monasteries and the whole city clergy in their vestments. He went to the Holy Wisdom, prayed to the Mother of God, then sat upon the throne of his father and grandfather. When Sviatoslav Vsevolodovich was brought before him, he called him nephew[84] and kept him under his protection. As for the many boyars loyal to Igor who were captured, Danilo Veliky, Yury Prokopich, Ivor Yurievich, Miroslav's grandson and others, he allowed them to be ransomed. Four days later Igor was captured in the marshes and brought before Iziaslav, who first had him confined in the Vydubits monastery, and then sent in chains to St. John's monastery at Pereiaslavl. Iziaslav and the citizens plundered the houses and villages of Igor's and Vsevolod's retinue, taking much cattle and goods from the houses and monasteries.[85]

VIACHESLAV VLADIMIROVICH'S CLAIM ON KIEV

In this manner the senior throne was restored to the line of Monomakh, though it came to a nephew ahead of his uncles. The reason was that

Iziaslav, who excelled his uncles in his personal merits, was regarded by the people as the chief representative of the line. Initially Iziaslav himself refused to infringe his uncle Viacheslav's rights, declaring at the beginning of his campaign against Igor Olgovich that he intended to return the seniority to Viacheslav.[86] It was a different matter when he was actually in control of the city. If the inhabitants led Monomakh to usurp the seniority of the sons of Sviatoslav, it was they too who made his grandson Iziaslav usurp the seniority of his uncle Viacheslav. Desiring to be rid of the sons of Oleg, they sent directly to Iziaslav and called him their prince.

As will become apparent later, when they summoned him a second time they were to state explicitly that they did not want Viacheslav. Likewise when Yury was prepared to give up Kiev to Viacheslav, his boyars told him that there was no point in so doing, as Viacheslav would be incapable of retaining it. This was the general opinion of the senior prince of Monomakh's line. Yury had to defer to it, so must his nephew Iziaslav.

If Rus rejected Viacheslav, considering him inadequate, this was not the outlook of Viacheslav's boyars, who controlled the weak prince and wished to govern Kiev during his seniority. Persuaded by his boyars, Viacheslav acted as if he were the senior prince. He reoccupied the towns Vsevolod took from him,[87] also seizing Vladimir-in-Volhynia, where he installed his nephew Vladimir Andreevich, son of the late prince of Perciaslavl.

Iziaslav lost no time in demonstrating that the seniority did not belong to his uncle, sending his brother Rostislav and his nephew Sviatoslav Vsevolodovich against him. They captured Turov from Viacheslav, and with it Bishop Joachim and the burgrave Zhiroslav. Iziaslav installed his son Yaroslav in Turov and his eldest son Mstislav in Pereiaslavl. An arrangement of this sort might have been a source of offense to Iziaslav's brothers, particularly the oldest, Rostislav of Smolensk, though probably he was reluctant to exchange a secure for an insecure throne. He expressly refused Pereiaslavl, where he would have been under constant attack from the princes of Chernigov and the Polovetsians. Probably also the frontier principality of Pereiaslavl was not as rich as that of Smolensk, having declined considerably during the troubles of the past few years. Yury of Rostov also declined it in favor of his younger brother Andrei, while the uncle Viacheslav declined it in favor of his nephew Iziaslav. Iziaslav compensated his nephew, his sister's son Sviatoslav Vsevolodovich, for the loss of Vladimir-in-Volhynia with five Volhynian towns. The towns of the southern Dregovichians[88] which Vsevolod Olgovich gave to his cousins remained in the hands of the sons of Davyd.

SVIATOSLAV OLGOVICH ATTEMPTS TO SECURE HIS BROTHER'S RELEASE

So things were arranged in Rus proper. Meanwhile Sviatoslav Olgovich arrived in Chernigov with a small retinue, demanding of his cousins, the sons of Davyd, whether they intended to keep the oath they had sworn five days before. They said they did. Then Sviatoslav, leaving his man Kosniatko with them, journeyed through his own principality exacting oaths of allegiance from the people, first at Kursk, then at Novgorod Seversk.

As soon as he departed the sons of Davyd took counsel without the knowledge of Kosniatko, who nevertheless discovered that they were conspiring to imprison Sviatoslav, and sent to warn him. "Prince," he admonished, "they intend to lay hands on you. When they send for you, do not go to them." The sons of Davyd were afraid that now the sons of Oleg, having no longer any hope of obtaining lands west of the Dnieper, would try to gain possession of Chernigov territories. They decided to ally with the sons of Mstislav against their cousins. They sent to Iziaslav, saying "As Igor was your enemy, so he is ours. Hold him securely." They also sent to Sviatoslav. "Leave Novgorod Seversk," they urged, "and go to Putivl, forsaking your brother." "I do not want lands or anything else," replied Sviatoslav, "only release my brother to me." The sons of Davyd were implacable. "Swear that you will neither ask for your brother nor seek him, but hold your lands." Sviatoslav wept and sent to Yury at Suzdal. "God took my brother Vsevolod," he said, "and Iziaslav has taken Igor. Come to Kiev in the Land of Rus, be merciful and deliver my brother. With God's help I will do what I can to assist you here."

In reality Sviatoslav took action. He sent for help to his wife's uncles the Polovetsian khans,[89] who immediately sent him three hundred men. At the same time Vladimir, son of Sviatoslav Yaroslavich, came to him, fleeing from his uncle at Murom. After Sviatoslav Yaroslavich's death his brother Rostislav became prince of Murom and made his son Gleb prince of Riazan, an arrangement which must have offended Vladimir, who may have been passed over altogether. He was followed to Novgorod Seversk by another exile, Ivan Rostislavich of Galich, known as Berladnik.[90] The town of Bîrlad in Moldavia was, like Tmutorokan, a haven for all kinds of fugitives, prince and commoner alike. There Ivan found refuge and gathered a retinue.

Meanwhile the sons of Davyd tried to dispose of their troublesome cousin. According to the chronicle, they said "We have begun an evil work, so let it end in fratricide. Come, let us make away with Sviatoslav and take his lands for ourselves." They could see that Sviatoslav would stop at nothing to set his brother at liberty. They remembered the trouble Igor and his brother caused by their claims on Chernigov while Vsevolod was alive, when all that restrained them was the promise of Kiev and the lands west of the Dnieper. What was there to restrain them now?

This explains the hostile attitude of the sons of Davyd. They asked Iziaslav's permission for a campaign against Sviatoslav in Novgorod Seversk. Iziaslav met them, and they decided that the sons of Davyd should attack Novgorod Seversk together with Iziaslav's son Mstislav, the men of Pereiaslavl and the Berendey. "Go," Iziaslav told them. "If Sviatoslav does not flee from the town, besiege him there. When you are tired, I will come to you with fresh forces and continue the siege, and you can go home."

The sons of Davyd marched on Novgorod Seversk, encamped by the earthwork and twice made a double attack on the gates. Fierce fighting was in progress when a message arrived from Mstislav Iziaslavich saying that his father forbade them to attack the town without his participation. The sons of Davyd obeyed and waited for Mstislav to arrive. Then the entire army, Christians and Berendey alike, loosed their arrows against the town, attacking it in good order. The citizens were hard pressed and beaten back to the fortress gates, losing many killed and wounded. The fighting continued until evening, but the town was not taken. The besiegers retreated and camped at the village of Meltekovo, where they seized three thousand mares and one thousand stallions from the herds of Igor and Sviatoslav in the forest along the Rakhna river, burning the crops and homesteads round about.

At this point they heard that Yury of Rostov was allied with Sviatoslav and coming to his aid. When he heard his uncle had risen against him, Iziaslav Mstislavich sent a messenger across the steppe to Riazan, asking Rostislav Yaroslavich to attack the lands of Rostov and so distract Yury. Rostislav agreed, for his hostile nephew was with Yury's ally Sviatoslav Olgovich, so it was in his interest to ally himself with the opposing forces. In any case he was hardly likely to be on good terms with Igor and Sviatoslav, who had expelled his father from Chernigov.

Yury had reached Kozelsk when he learned of Rostislav's attack on his territory. The news made him turn back, leaving his son Ivan to bring assistance to Sviatoslav. When Ivan reached Novgorod Seversk, Sviatoslav gave him Kursk and the country along the Seim. Evidently he was determined to spare nothing and give up his last possessions in order to preserve the alliance with Yury and with his help achieve the liberation of his brother.

Giving half his lands to Yury's son, Sviatoslav took counsel with his boyars and decided to make a final appeal to the better feelings of the sons of Davyd. He sent word through his priest, saying "Brothers, you have ravaged all my lands, you have taken my herds and my brother's, you have burned the crops and ruined all my livelihood. All that remains for you to do is to kill me." The sons of Davyd made the same reply as before, that he should forsake his brother, to which Sviatoslav also replied as previously. "Better I die," said he, "than forsake my brother. I shall seek him while my soul is in my body."

The sons of Davyd continued to ravage their cousins' land. They took the village of Igorevo, where Igor had built a fine residence. There was much wine and mead in the cellars, and bulky goods such as iron and copper, so that it was impossible to carry it all. The sons of Davyd had it all loaded onto wagons, then burned the homestead, St. George's chapel and the barn, where there were nine hundred sheaves of grain. Then hearing that Iziaslav was coming from Kiev to reinforce them, they went to Putivl, telling the citizens "Do not fight, for we swear by the holy Mother of God that we will not make you captive." The citizens would not listen, resisting steadfastly until Iziaslav Mstislavich came up with the men of Kiev. Then they did obeisance to him. "It is only you, prince," they said, "that we have been awaiting. Swear to us." Iziaslav took the oath and merely replaced the former burgrave with one of his own.

The action of the men of Putivl is remarkable, for it shows that the grandson of Monomakh was trusted, and the grandsons of Sviatoslav mistrusted, even by the inhabitants of the Chernigov territories. It is not surprising that the descendants of Sviatoslav were so disliked on the other side of the Dnieper. At Putivl Iziaslav and the sons of Davyd took Sviatoslav's court and all the goods therein and divided them into four parts. They took five hundred berkovets[91] of honey and eighty jars of wine, all the furnishings of the church of the Ascension and seven hundred slaves.

Hearing that Putivl was fallen, his possessions plundered, and that Iziaslav was advancing on Novgorod Seversk to besiege him, Sviatoslav called a council consisting of Princes Ivan Yurievich and Ivan Rostislavich Berladnik, his retinue and his Wild Polovetsian uncles, and asked them what to do. "Prince," they replied, "leave this place at once. There is nothing to keep you here, no bread, nothing. Go to the forests, where you can keep in touch more easily with *your father* Yury." Sviatoslav did as they said and fled from Novgorod Seversk to Korachev with his wife and children and his brother Igor's wife. Some of his retinue went with him, others deserted him.

The people of Novgorod Seversk informed Iziaslav and his allies that Sviatoslav had fled from them. This was very displeasing news for the sons of Davyd, who knew that while Sviatoslav was at liberty he would not cease his attempts to set his brother free. "Let me go after him," a wrathful Iziaslav Davydovich said to his brothers. "Even if he escapes me, I shall take his wife, his children and his goods." Taking three thousand mounted and lightly equipped retainers and no baggage, he set off in pursuit of Sviatoslav, who was left with no alternative but to allow his family and retinue to be taken prisoner, or face death himself. After conferring with his allies, the Polovetsians and his retinue, he came out to meet Iziaslav Davydovich and defeated him. Iziaslav Mstislavich and Vladimir Davydovich were following with the army through the woods, and were just about to sit down to dinner when a man came with news of Iziaslav's defeat.

Iziaslav Mstislavich who, the chronicle tells us, was brave and warlike, was greatly displeased by this news. He set his troops in order and pursued Sviatoslav towards Korachev, picking up the remains of Iziaslav Davydovich's retinue on the way, though Iziaslav himself did not appear until midday. The princes marched all day, stopping at nightfall not far from Korachev. Sviatoslav heard of their arrival and went into the land of the Viatichians[92] on the other side of the forest. Then Iziaslav Mstislavich said to the sons of Davyd "I have obtained for you the lands you wanted. Here are Novgorod Seversk and all the lands of Sviatoslav. Whatever belonged to Igor in these lands, slaves or goods, is mine, and whatever was Sviatoslav's we shall divide amongst ourselves."

After making these arrangements, Iziaslav returned to Kiev where Igor Olgovich, who had become seriously ill in his prison, sent to him. "Brother, I am very ill," he said, "and ask to become a monk. I desired it even when I was a prince, and now in my need I have become very ill and do not think that I shall live." Iziaslav had pity on him. "If you are thinking of becoming a monk," he said, "you are free to do so. In any case I will release you because of your illness." They removed the ceiling of Igor's dungeon and lifted him out, putting him in one of the cells of the monastery, where he lay for eight days without eating or drinking, then recovered, and he became a monk of strict observance in the St. Theodore monastery in Kiev.[93]

The war between the sons of Davyd and the sons of Oleg continued in the lands of Novgorod Seversk and of the Viatichians. When Iziaslav Mstislavich left for Kiev he was imprudent enough to leave Sviatoslav Vsevolodovich behind with the sons of Davyd. He was Sviatoslav Olgovich's nephew, his interests being closely bound up with his uncle's and those of Oleg's line. The final defeat of his uncle Sviatoslav and the final triumph of the sons of Davyd deprived him forever of any hope of being prince of Chernigov, though he had every right to it when his turn came, as son of the eldest son of Oleg. For this reason he should have supported his uncle, and indeed instead of pursuing him he kept him informed of his enemy's movements. Notwithstanding the defection of Ivan Berladnik, who took two hundred grivnas of silver and twelve of gold and went over to Rostislav Mstislavich of Smolensk, Sviatoslav's fortunes were improving. This was because Yury of Rostov sent the retinue of Beloozero to his aid. Sviatoslav was preparing to lead it against the sons of Davyd when Yury's son Ivan fell dangerously ill. Sviatoslav would neither leave the sick man nor allow his retinue to go.

For their part, when the sons of Davyd heard that Yury was assisting Sviatoslav, they did not dare attack him. Instead they summoned the leading citizens of Viatka and said to them "Sviatoslav is just as much your enemy as ours. Try and kill him and his retinue somehow by deception, and his goods will be yours." Then they retreated.

On the other side, two of Yury's sons, Rostislav and Andrei,[94] were successful against Rostislav of Riazan, who was forced to flee to the Polovetsians. At this point their brother Ivan, who was still with Sviatoslav, now at the mouth of the Protva river, died. Yury sent comforting words to Sviatoslav. "Do not grieve for my son," he said, "for if God has taken him, I will send you another." At the same time he sent rich gifts of cloths and furs to Sviatoslav, his wife and retinue. These events took place in 1146.

In the spring Yury and his ally began an offensive. Yury himself entered the territories of Novgorod, taking Torzhok and the land along the Msta. Sviatoslav marched against Smolensk, took Goliadey on the upper Protva and distributed the booty amongst his retinue. After this Yury called him to meet him at Moscow, the first time it is mentioned in the chronicles. Sviatoslav went with his son Oleg, Vladimir of Riazan and a small retinue. Oleg rode on ahead and presented Yury with a snow leopard (or more probably with its pelt). Yury and Sviatoslav met like friends and feasted. Yury gave a great banquet for his guests the following day, giving rich gifts to Sviatoslav, his son, Vladimir and all their retinue. Nor did he confine himself to giving presents. He promised to send his son to Sviatoslav's assistance, and did as promised. Sviatoslav also hired some Polovetsian mercenaries, making a successful beginning to his offensive. He sent the Polovetsians against Smolensk, and they devastated the lands about the upper Ugra. Then the burgraves placed in the towns of Viatka abandoned them to be occupied by Sviatoslav.

Meanwhile he was joined by new Polovetsian forces from the steppe and by Yury's son Gleb from the North. Iziaslav Davydovich, no longer feeling secure in Novgorod Seversk, joined his brother in Chernigov, whence they and Sviatoslav Vsevolodovich sent envoys to Sviatoslav Olgovich. "Do not be aggrieved at us," they said, "let us all be as one, forget our malice. Swear peace to us and take your patrimony. Whatever of yours we have taken we will restore to you."

Evidently Sviatoslav Vsevolodovich had established communications with the sons of Davyd. Doubtless he was the prime mover in this action, especially as his earlier exertions on his uncle Sviatoslav Olgovich's account enabled him to act as mediator. It appears they decided to lure Iziaslav Mstislavich onto the eastern bank of the Dnieper, because while they were making peace overtures to Sviatoslav Olgovich, to Iziaslav they were saying "Brother! Sviatoslav Olgovich has taken the lands of the Viatichians, which belong to us. Let us march against him, and when we have driven him out, we shall march against Yury at Suzdal and either make peace with him or fight him." Iziaslav agreed, but Sviatoslav Vsevolodovich had to cross to the eastern bank of the Dnieper before him in order to put the finishing touches to the plan. Therefore he came to Iziaslav and asked his permission to go to Chernigov. "Father," he said, "let me go to Chernigov, where all my wealth is. I want to ask the brothers, Iziaslav and Vladimir, to give me lands." "A good thought" replied

Iziaslav, "go at once!" He went, and final agreement was reached. They decided to invite Iziaslav of Kiev onto their side of the river and take him by trickery, after which, seeing that he was in no hurry to come, they urged haste on him, saying "Our land is perishing, but still you do not come."

Iziaslav called a council of his boyars, his retinue and the citizens of Kiev, and said to them "I have with me my brethren, the sons of Davyd and Sviatoslav Vsevolodovich, and we intend to march against my uncle Yury and Sviatoslav Olgovich in Suzdal, because my uncle has received my enemy Sviatoslav. My brother Rostislav also will march with us with the men of Smolensk and Novgorod." "Prince," replied the men of Kiev, "do not go with Rostislav against your uncle. Rather make peace with him. Do not trust the sons of Oleg,[95] nor accompany them on any campaign." "I cannot do so," replied Iziaslav, "for they have sworn oaths to me, and I have taken counsel with them. I can by no means withdraw from the campaign. Prepare yourselves." "Prince," replied the men of Kiev, "do not be angry with us. We cannot take up arms against the kin of Vladimir [Monomakh]. If it were against Oleg's sons, we would go, we and our children." "He will be a good man who goes with me," replied Iziaslav.

He gathered many such good men, and set out with them, leaving his brother Vladimir in Kiev. He crossed the Dnieper and took up a position on the border of the principalities of Chernigov and Pereiaslavl. From there he sent his boyar Uleb to Chernigov to find out what was happening. Uleb soon returned with the news that the sons of Davyd and Vsevolod had turned against him and were allied with [Sviatoslav] Olgovich. At the same time Iziaslav's friends in Chernigov sent him a message. "Prince," they said, "do not move from where you are. They are deceiving you. They want to kill you or take you prisoner instead of Igor. They have sworn oaths to Sviatoslav, sending to Yury to swear. He too is plotting against you."

Iziaslav returned and sent envoys to Chernigov. "We have undertaken a great campaign," he urged the sons of Davyd, "and confirmed our intention with an oath according to the custom of our fathers and grandfathers. Let us confirm it again, so that afterwards, on the campaign, there be no quarrel or hindrance." "Why should we take another oath needlessly?" they replied. "We have already sworn to Iziaslav. What have we done wrong?" "What sin is it," replied the envoy, "to swear again in love? It is to our salvation." The sons of Davyd would not agree to a second oath. Now Iziaslav instructed his envoy that if they refused, he was to tell them all that was reported to him. The envoy now announced in the prince's name "A report has reached me that you are deceiving me, for you have sworn to Sviatoslav Olgovich to seize me on the road, or to kill me in revenge for Igor. Is this the case, brethren, or is it not?" The sons of Davyd made no reply, but exchanged glances in silence.

Finally Vladimir told the envoy to leave and sit outside until they called him. After long deliberation they called the envoy and sent him back to Iziaslav. "Brother," was their message, "we have indeed sworn friendship to Sviatoslav Olgovich, for we were sorry for our cousin Igor. Now he is a monk of strict observance. Let him go, then we will ride by your side. Would you be content if we were holding a cousin of yours?" In reply Iziaslav sent them written terms and commanded his envoy to say "You swore to be faithful to me unto death, and I have given you the lands of both the sons of Oleg. Together with you I drove out Sviatoslav, obtained his lands for you, gave you Novgorod Seversk and Putivl, and we divided his wealth amongst us, while Igor's I took for myself. Now, brothers, you have broken your oath and brought me here by deception, intending to kill me. God and the power of the life-giving cross be for me, for I shall take redress as God grants me."

Then Iziaslav sent to his brother Rostislav in Smolensk. "Brother, the sons of Davyd swore an oath and took counsel with us to march together against our uncle. They did it all to deceive me, their design was to kill me. God and the power of the cross have made their designs known. Now, brother, whereas we thought to march against our uncle, do not go, instead come to me here. First set the men of Smolensk and Novgorod in readiness to hold Yury back, then send to the men loyal to you in Riazan and elsewhere."

MURDER OF IGOR OLGOVICH

Iziaslav then sent orders to his brother Vladimir, Metropolitan Klim[96] and the chiliarch Lazar in Kiev to call an assembly of the citizens at the Holy Wisdom, for his envoy to deliver his message and reveal to the people the treachery of the princes of Chernigov. The citizens assembled, the lesser and the great, and Iziaslav's envoy addressed them. "Your prince bows to you and commands me to say 'I declared to you before that I took counsel with my brother Rostislav and the sons of Davyd to march against my uncle Yury, and called you to come with me on the campaign. You said then that you would not take up arms against the kin of Vladimir, that is, against Yury, but that you would go against the sons of Oleg, you and your children. Now therefore I declare to you that the sons of Davyd and Sviatoslav Vsevolodovich, to whom I did much good, have sworn oaths to Sviatoslav Olgovich secretly, and have sent messages to Yury, intending to capture me or kill me in revenge for Igor, but God and the Holy Cross, by which they swore to me, have preserved me. Now therefore, brothers of Kiev, do that which you desired, do that which you have promised me, gather together, small and great, and come to me at Chernigov against the sons of Oleg. He who has a horse, let him come on his horse, and he who has none, let him come by boat. For it is not me only that they would have slain. You also would they have destroyed utterly.'"

"We are glad," replied the citizens, "that God has preserved you for us from great danger. We will fight on your behalf, we and our children." "We will follow the prince gladly," said one of the crowd, "but first there is a matter about which we must take thought. In Iziaslav Yaroslavich's time wicked men released Vseslav from prison and made him their prince, which brought great harm upon the city. Now Igor, the prince's enemy and ours, is not even in prison, but in St. Theodore's monastery. Let us kill him, and follow the prince to Chernigov to make an end of them."

At these words the people rushed to St. Theodore's monastery. In vain Prince Vladimir urged them that this was against his brother's orders, which were to come to him, and that Igor was under close guard. The metropolitan also tried to restrain them, as did Lazar the chiliarch and Vladimir's chiliarch Raguilo. The howling mob, bent on murder, would not listen to any of them. Then Prince Vladimir mounted his horse and raced for the monastery. The crowds of people prevented him from crossing the bridge, so he turned right by Gleb's Court. This detour cost him time, so the mob arrived at the monastery first.

They burst into the church, where Igor was attending the liturgy, and dragged him out, shouting "Kill him! Kill him!" At the monastery gates they encountered Vladimir, whom Igor recognized. "O brother," he pleaded, "where are they taking me?" Vladimir leapt from his horse and covered Igor with his mantle, saying to the people "Brothers, do not do this evil, do not kill Igor!" The crowd would not hear, and beat Igor. Some of the blows fell on Vladimir, who tried to defend him and, with the help of his boyar Mikhail, got him into his mother's house and closed the gates behind him. The crowd, killing Mikhail, tore the cross from the chain around his neck and broke down the gates. Seeing Igor in the outer hall, they broke into it and dragged him out, so that he fell unconscious to the ground. They tied a rope round his legs and dragged him from Mstislav's

Court across Babin market to the Prince's Court, where they finished him off. They put his body on a cart and took it to the Podol, where they threw it down in the marketplace.

When Vladimir heard that Igor's body was in the marketplace, he sent the two chiliarchs Lazar and Raguilo. When they arrived they said to the people "Now you have killed Igor, let us bury his body." "It is not we who have killed him," the citizens replied, "but the sons of Davyd and the son of Vsevolod, who devised evil against our prince and wanted to kill him by treachery. God is for our prince and for the Holy Wisdom." Then Lazar commanded that the body of Igor be taken and laid in St. Michael's church, in the Novgorod chapel. Next day he was buried in St. Simeon's monastery.[97]

Iziaslav, on the upper Supoy on the border with Chernigov wept when he heard of Igor's murder. "Had I known this would happen," said he to his retinue, "I would have sent him farther away and so saved him. Now I cannot avoid what men will say, that I had him killed. God is my witness that I did not command or suggest it. Let God judge the matter." "You have not need to worry about what men will say," replied his retinue. "God knows, and indeed everybody knows, that it was not your fault that he was killed, but his cousins'. They took an oath to you and then broke it and tried to kill you." "What's done is done," said Iziaslav. "We must all give our account before God." Yet he did not cease to complain about the citizens of Kiev.

FURTHER PROGRESS OF THE WAR

Meanwhile the war was proceeding. Iziaslav's first move was to take Kursk and the towns along the Seim, thereby cutting off Chernigov from the Polovetsians. His son Mstislav already was installed in Kursk when the town was approached by Sviatoslav Olgovich and Gleb Yurievich. Mstislav told the people of Kursk that the enemy was at hand. They replied just as the citizens of Kiev replied to his father. "We are glad to fight for you against the sons of Oleg," they said, "but we cannot take up arms against the kin of Vladimir, against the son of Yury." At that Mstislav departed and went to his father. The men of Kursk sent to Gleb Yurievich and accepted a burgrave from him.

Evidently Sviatoslav gave Gleb the same lands, Kursk and the country along the Seim, as he previously bestowed on his brother Ivan. For this reason Gleb also placed burgraves along the Seim and the Vyr, where he concluded an alliance with numerous Polovetsian hordes. A number of the towns along the Vyr remained faithful to Iziaslav despite the threats of the princes of Chernigov to give the inhabitants as slaves to the Polovetsians. One such town, Viakhan, successfully withstood a siege while another, Popash, was taken.

When he heard of the movements of Gleb and the princes of Chernigov Iziaslav gathered a large army, including the forces of his uncle Viacheslav and of Volhynia. He went to Pereiaslavl, where he heard that his brother Rostislav was already on the move. "Wait for me," was Rostislav's message. "I have burned Liubech and done great harm to the sons of Oleg. Let us meet and consider what to do next." Receiving this news, Iziaslav then moved off slowly, allowing his brother and the men of Smolensk to catch up with him, which they did at Chernaia Mogila.

The two brothers took counsel with their retinues and the Karakalpaks about their next move. "Now that God has brought us together in one place," said Rostislav, "and delivered you from great peril, we should delay no longer. Let us advance on them now by the shortest way and let God judge between us." This was agreed upon, and the princes marched to the Sula.

When this became known in the Chernigov camp a large part of the Polovetsians deserted and disappeared into the steppe, while the remaining allies fell back towards Chernigov. Iziaslav intended to cut them off from the city at Vsevolozh,[98] but was too late. The sons of Mstislav continued the pursuit, but first *plundered*[99] Vsevolozh, where the citizens of two other towns, evidently less well fortified, also had taken refuge. As in previous instances relating to the borderlands, a number of towns were abandoned at the approach of the enemy. When the fall of Vsevolozh became known, the inhabitants of the other towns in the area all fled towards Chernigov. The sons of Mstislav pursued them and captured some, though not all. Iziaslav had the abandoned towns burned. Only the inhabitants of Glebl were too late to flee. Luckily they repulsed the sons of Mstislav, who went on to Kiev. "Prepare yourselves," they said to their retinues, the men of Kiev and Smolensk, "as soon as the rivers are passable we shall go to Chernigov. God shall judge between them and us."

Taking their ease for some time in Kiev, the two brothers decided to divide their forces. "Brother," said Iziaslav to Rostislav, "God has given you the upper lands, go there against Yury. You have the men of Smolensk and Novgorod and others loyal to you. Use them to hold back Yury while I remain here and deal with the sons of Oleg and Davyd." Rostislav departed for Smolensk.

When the rivers froze over the princes of Chernigov began the attack. They sent their retinue and the Polovetsians to attack the countryside along the right bank of the Dnieper, while their ally Gleb Yurievich took Gorodets Ostersky, which formerly belonged to his father. Iziaslav sent a message inviting Gleb to come to Kiev. At first he was minded to come, then changed his mind because now he was in contact with the men of Pereiaslavl, some of whom were discontented with Iziaslav or his son Mstislav, their prince. They promised to open the town to Gleb, who responded to their call immediately.

At dawn, while Mstislav and his retinue were still sleeping, the sentries ran to him, shouting "Get up, prince, Gleb is attacking you!" Mstislav leapt up. Mustering his men, he rode out of the town to face Gleb. Neither prince made up his mind to give battle. Gleb remained until the morning of the next day, then withdrew. Mstislav summoned the rest of his retinue and the men of Pereiaslavl, gave chase, caught up with them and captured part of Gleb's force. Gleb himself escaped to Gorodets. When Iziaslav heard of these attempts on Pereiaslavl he gathered his retinue and the Berendey and marched on Gorodets. Gleb sent word to Chernigov. "Iziaslav is coming against me," he appealed to the local prince, "help me!" Meanwhile Iziaslav arrived and besieged Gorodets. Seeing no sign of any help, Gleb submitted to Iziaslav and made peace after three days. Apparently Iziaslav allowed him to keep his father's town. Gleb showed no gratitude. No sooner did Iziaslav return to Kiev than he sent another message to Chernigov. "I swore my oath to Iziaslav under duress," he said, "for he besieged me in the town and there was no help from you. Now I want to be your ally again."

In 1148 Iziaslav finally gathered his entire forces, including a contingent from his uncle Viacheslav and another from Vladimir[-in-Volhynia]. He called a Hungarian detachment to his aid, and the Berendey too. He crossed the Dnieper, taking up his position eight versts from Chernigov. He waited there for three days to see if the sons of Davyd and Oleg would venture forth and give battle, but they did not. Meanwhile Iziaslav burned all the surrounding villages. Tired of waiting, Iziaslav said to his retinue "We have burned their villages and taken their goods, yet still they do not come out to us. Let us go to Liubech, where all their wealth is." When Iziaslav approached Liubech the sons of Oleg and Davyd also appeared there with the princes of Riazan and the Polovetsians. The two armies faced each other across the river. Iziaslav would have attacked had not the river prevented him. It was only possible for the archers on both sides to shoot their arrows across it. It rained heavily that night, and the Dnieper flooded. Then Iziaslav said to his retinue and the Hungarians "This river prevents us from fighting here. Over there the water is rising in the Dnieper. We had better cross the Dnieper." The very next day after they crossed the Dnieper the ice broke up. Iziaslav returned safely to Kiev although the ice on the lake broke beneath the Hungarians, a few of whom drowned.

END OF THE WAR

Although the campaign for which Iziaslav had made such great preparations appeared to have come to nothing, the princes of Chernigov could not continue the struggle for long. By devastating their villages Iziaslav was indeed taking away *all their livelihood*, as it was called. They had nothing left with which to maintain their retinues or pay the Polovetsians. The townsmen had little enthusiasm for helping the princes in their feuds, while Yury confined himself to sending his son, having no intention of coming south himself. Without him Chernigov was no match for the sons of Mstislav, consequently the princes of Chernigov sent to Yury, saying "You swore to go with us against Iziaslav, but you did not, while Iziaslav came and burned our towns beyond the Desna and overran the countryside. Then he came again to Chernigov. He burned our villages all the way to Liubech and took all our livelihood. You have not come to our aid, neither have you made war on Rostislav. If it is your real desire to fight Iziaslav, come, and we will be with you. If not, we are absolved of our oath, for it is not right that we die alone in battle."

Receiving no favorable answer from Yury, they made peace overtures to Iziaslav Mstislavich. "In former times," they said, "in the time of our fathers and our grandfathers, peace was followed by war, and war by peace. Do not hold it against us that we started the war, for we grieved for our brother Igor. All we wanted was for you to let him go. Since now he is dead and has gone to stand before God, as we all shall, let God be the judge of all, but now how long shall we destroy the Land of Rus? Should we not make peace?" "Brothers," was Iziaslav's reply, "it is good to preserve the lives of Christians. Since you have all consulted together, I too shall send to my brother Rostislav. We shall deliberate on the matter and send you our answer."

At the same time he sent envoys to his brother. "The two sons of Davyd," he said, "together with Sviatoslav Olgovich and Sviatoslav Vsevolodovich have sent to me asking for peace. I want to consult with you to determine the best course for both of us. Do you want peace? Though they have done us much harm, now they seek peace. If you are for war say this, and I will trust in you in everything." It was clear to Rostislav from these words that his elder brother was in favor of peace. Therefore he sent this reply. "Brother, I greet you. You are older than I, you must do as you see fit, and wherever you lead, I will follow. If you do me the honor of asking my advice, this is what I think. For the sake of the lands of Rus and for the sake of Christian people, peace is better. They began the war, but what good did it do them? Now brother, make peace with them for the sake of the Land of Rus and all Christian people, provided they promise to put aside all enmity they may bear you for Igor's sake, and that they will never more think of doing what previously they sought to do to you. If they continue to bear malice for Igor's sake, better to make war on them, and let God decide the outcome."

Receiving this reply Iziaslav sent Theodore, bishop of Belgorod, and Feodosy, abbot of the Caves, with his boyars to tell the princes of Chernigov "You swore to me that you would leave your brother Igor alone, but you broke your oath, bringing much trouble upon me. Now I forget it all for the sake of the Land of Rus and Christian people. If you yourselves are sending to me asking for peace, and repent of your intentions, swear that you will put aside all enmity on Igor's account, and that henceforth you will not think of doing what you earlier desired to do to me." The princes of Chernigov swore to put aside the enmity they bore for Igor's sake, to care for the Land of Rus, and all to be as one brotherhood. Kursk and the lands along the Seim remained in the possession of Vladimir Davydovich.

VI

IZIASLAV AND YURY STRUGGLE FOR KIEV, 1148-1157

FRICTION BETWEEN IZIASLAV AND YURY DOLGORUKY

About this time Yury's eldest son Rostislav, formerly prince of Novgorod,[1] appeared before Iziaslav. He declared that he had quarreled with his father, who would not give him lands in the territories of Suzdal. Therefore he came and bent the knee to Iziaslav. "My father has wronged me," he said, "by giving me no land. I have come here to entrust myself to God and to you, for you are the eldest of the grandsons of Vladimir. It is my wish to labor for the Land of Rus and to ride at your side." "Your father is the oldest among us,"[2] replied Iziaslav, "but he cannot live in amity with us. God grant that I may do right by you and all our brothers and all our kin as for my own soul. If your father has given you no lands, I will give you some." He gave him the five towns previously held by Sviatoslav Vsevolodovich[3] and in addition Gorodets Ostersk, which Iziaslav no longer wished to see occupied by Rostislav's brother Gleb,[4] whom he told "Go to the sons of Oleg. It was to them that you came, so let them find you lands."

In the autumn Iziaslav Mstislavich met the sons of Davyd near this same Gorodets Ostersk. Iziaslav was accompanied by Rostislav Yurievich, but neither Sviatoslav Olgovich nor his nephew was present. "Your cousin Sviatoslav and my nephew have not come," said Iziaslav to the sons of Davyd, "yet you all swore that if anyone bore me malice you would all be with me against him. Now my uncle Yury of Rostov harms my city of Novgorod. He is seizing the tribute from the men of Novgorod and barring the roads to them. I intend to go and settle my affairs with him either peaceably or by war. You have sworn that you will be with me."

"It does not matter that our cousin Sviatoslav and your nephew are not here," replied Vladimir Davydovich, "since we are here. We indeed all have sworn that when any wrong is done you, we shall be with you." The princes agreed to go to Rostov against Yury as soon as the rivers froze. Iziaslav was to set out from Smolensk, the sons of Davyd and their cousin from the land of the Viatichians,[5] all to meet at the Volga. After their council the princes feasted together and went their ways. On his return to Kiev Iziaslav told Rostislav Yurievich to go to Buzhsk and remain there, guarding the Land of Rus, until Iziaslav settled his differences with his father, peaceably or otherwise.

Iziaslav left his brother Vladimir in Kiev and his son Mstislav in Pereiaslavl. He went to join his brother Rostislav in Smolensk, commanding his army to follow him. The sons of Mstislav took their ease for some time in Smolensk, feasting with their retinues and the men of Smolensk, exchanging rich gifts. Iziaslav gave Rostislav all such goods as were produced by the lands of Rus and the Byzantine empire, receiving in return the produce of the Northern lands and of the Varangians. Even as they prepared for war the brothers did what they could to bring matters to a peaceful conclusion, sending an emissary to Yury, who arrested him instead of sending any answer. Then, commanding his brother Rostislav to lead the army up the Volga and wait for him at the mouth of the Medveditsa, Iziaslav set out with a small retinue to Novgorod.

The citizens of Novgorod were joyful when they heard he was coming. They came out to meet him, some at a day's journey, and others at three days' journey from the city. The prince of Novgorod by this time was no longer Iziaslav's brother Sviatopolk, but his son Yaroslav, for Iziaslav made them exchange principalities and forced Sviatopolk to leave Novgorod for Vladimir-in-Volhynia "because of his wickedness," says the Novgorod chronicle.[6] Iziaslav entered Novgorod on a Sunday with great honor, greeted by his son Yaroslav and his boyars. They all went to the liturgy at the Holy Wisdom. After this they sent the sergeants and criers about the streets to call both lesser and great to the prince's feast. They feasted merrily, returning to their houses with honor.

The following Monday Iziaslav sent orders to Yaroslav's Court to ring the bell to summon the assembly. When the men of Novgorod and Pskov were assembled, he said to them "Brothers, I have heard the complaints that you and my son have sent to me concerning the wrongs done to you by my uncle Yury. Now I have left the Land of Rus and come to you here against him for your sake and because of his wrongs. Take thought therefore, consider how we must go to him, whether we must make peace or settle things by war." "You are our prince," the people replied. "You are our Vladimir, you are our Mstislav. We will follow you anywhere gladly to avenge the wrongs we have suffered. We shall all go, leaving only the clergy to pray to God."

Indeed all the men of the Novgorod lands took up arms, and the men of Pskov and the Karelians[7] went with them. When they reached the mouth of the Medveditsa Iziaslav waited four days for his brother Rostislav. When he arrived with the armies of the South and Smolensk, they all went down the Volga together, and came to the town of Konstantinov at the mouth of the great river Nerl. Since they heard nothing from Yury, they burned his towns and villages and pillaged the country on both sides of the Volga, proceeding to Uglich and thence to the mouth of the Mologa. Here they heard that Vladimir Davydovich and Sviatoslav Olgovich were still in the land of the Viatichians, waiting to see how things would turn out between Yury and Iziaslav, not advancing to the mouth of the Medveditsa as they promised. "Let them stay behind," commented Iziaslav to his brother, "so long as God be with us." He set the armies of Novgorod and Rus to pillage the land in the direction of Yaroslavl.

By the time they returned with great booty it was Palm Sunday and the weather turned quite warm. The water in the Volga and the Mologa rose to the level of the horses' bellies. The sons of Mstislav could stay there no longer. Rostislav returned to Smolensk and Iziaslav to Novgorod and thence to Kiev. Some of the retinue of Rus went with Rostislav, the others where they saw fit. The campaign of 1149 cost the land of Rostov seven thousand inhabitants, taken into captivity by the sons of Mstislav.

Disagreeable news awaited Iziaslav in Kiev. His boyars reported that Rostislav Yurievich was inciting the Berendey and citizens against him. If God had helped his father, he would have come to Kiev to seize Iziaslav's house and family. "Send him back to his father," said the boyars. "He is your enemy and you support him to your own detriment." Iziaslav immediately sent for Rostislav. When he came Iziaslav's boyars said to him in the prince's name "Brother, you came to me from your father because your father wronged you by giving you no lands. I received you like a brother and gave you what your own father did not, telling you to guard the Land of Rus. Yet in return, had God helped your father, you would have ridden into Kiev and taken my house and family." "Brother and father!" Rostislav replied. "I had no such thing in my mind or heart. If anyone has laid such charges against me, if he be a prince I am ready to face him, and if a commoner, Christian or heathen, you judge between us as the senior prince." "Ask for no judgment from me," replied Iziaslav. "I know that you want to make trouble between me and the Christians or the heathen. Go to your father."

Rostislav was put in a barque with four servants and sent up the Dnieper. His retinue were taken prisoner and his goods confiscated. When Rostislav came to his father in Suzdal he bowed down to him, saying "I have heard that all the Land of Rus and the Karakalpaks want you, for they say that Iziaslav has dishonored them. Go and make war on him." It would appear from these words that the charges laid against Rostislav were well-founded, and that Rostislav had made contact with malcontents, or at least they made contact with him.

Yury was deeply distressed by his son's shame. "This way," he said, "neither I nor my sons will have any part in the Land of Rus." He gathered his forces, hired Polovetsians and set out against his nephew. This decision was not only because of his anger at his son's ignominious exile.

Yury had acted slowly and indecisively, even though he might have expected success, thanks to his alliance with the princes of Chernigov. Now he could make his way south in full confidence that he would be met by even more powerful allies, for Rostislav informed him of the dissatisfaction of the citizens and the barbarians settled on the frontiers, even if we suppose that Rostislav was not chiefly responsible for fomenting this dissatisfaction.

Be that as it may, Yury was in the land of the Viatichians when Vladimir Davydovich of Chernigov sent to Iziaslav to warn him that his uncle was advancing on him, and that he must prepare for war. Iziaslav gathered his forces. He and the sons of Davyd sent a message to Sviatoslav Olgovich at Novgorod Seversk to remind him of their agreement. At first Sviatoslav made no answer to the envoys and detained them for a whole week with a guard about their tents so that no one could communicate with them. This gave him time to get in touch with Yury and ask if he was really coming. "Tell me for sure, so that I do not ruin my lands to no purpose." "Why should I not come?" was Yury's reply. "My nephew came, pillaged and burned my lands, and also drove my son out of the Land of Rus. He has given him no lands, he has put me to shame. Either I shall wipe away my shame and avenge my land and win honor for myself, or I shall die in the attempt."

Receiving such a reply, Sviatoslav was reluctant openly to break the oath he had sworn to Iziaslav, so he looked for a pretext. "Give me back my brother's possessions," he demanded of Iziaslav, "then I shall be with you." "Brother," Iziaslav immediately answered, "you swore on the Holy Cross that you would put away all enmity concerning Igor or his possessions. Why do you bring it up again now, when my uncle is marching against me? Either keep your oath in full and support me, or you have broken your oath. When I went to the Volga without you, was I the worse for it? So also now, God and the power of the Cross be with me." Sviatoslav united with Yury. They invited the sons of Davyd to join them against Iziaslav, but they refused. "You swore to be on our side," they said, "but Iziaslav came and pillaged our land and burned our towns. Now since we have sworn an oath to Iziaslav, we cannot gamble with our souls."

Seeing that the sons of Davyd would not join him, Yury went to Old Belaia Vezha[8] and remained there for a month, waiting for the Polovetsians' and Iziaslav's submission. When there was no response from Iziaslav, he moved to the Supoy. Here he was joined by Sviatoslav Vsevolodovich, against his will says the chronicle, because he did not want to break with his uncle Sviatoslav Olgovich, and by a large number of savage Polovetsians. Then Iziaslav sent to his brother Rostislav in Smolensk. "We agreed" he reminded him, "that when Yury went beyond Chernigov you would join forces with me. Now Yury is past Chernigov. Come, let us see together what God will give us." Rostislav and his army moved towards his brother, while Yury moved towards Pereiaslavl, still expecting Iziaslav to make at least some move towards submission. Iziaslav would not bow down to his uncle. "If he came with only his sons," he said, "he could have had whatever principality he wanted, now since he has brought the Polovetsians and my enemies the sons of Oleg upon me, I will fight him."

YURY EXPELS IZIASLAV FROM KIEV

It is clear from these words that Iziaslav felt compelled to find pretexts because now as before the men of Kiev were unwilling to fight against a son of Monomakh. Even if there were not a measure of discontent with Iziaslav in the South, as Rostislav Yurievich reported to his father, the men of Kiev would have found it difficult to take up arms against Yury. First, he was a son of Monomakh. Second, he was Iziaslav's senior, his uncle, and therefore universally was felt to have a better right. Moreover the men of Kiev still had no particular reason to feel hostile to Yury. They refused to march against him, telling Iziaslav to make peace. Iziaslav continued to urge them to go forth, saying "Come with me. Why should I make peace with him when I am undefeated and in a position of strength?"

Eventually the men of Kiev went, though unwillingly, which boded ill for Iziaslav, even though he had considerable forces at his disposal. Both Iziaslav Davydovich[9] and his brother Rostislav [of Smolensk], with a large army, came to his aid. Iziaslav decided to cross the Dnieper and approach Pereiaslavl, where he encountered his uncle's army. The forward detachments, consisting of the Karakalpaks and Iziaslav's young retinue, did battle with Yury's Polovetsians, driving them away from the town. When the main forces met they stood facing each other for a whole day. Only the archers of both sides did any fighting. During the night Yury sent a message to his nephew. "Brother! You attacked me," he said, "you made war on my lands and deprived me of my seniority. Now, brother and son, for the sake of the Land of Rus and Christendom, let us not shed Christian blood, let me place my son in Pereiaslavl, while you remain in Kiev and reign there. If you will not, let God settle the matter between us." Iziaslav was not pleased with this proposition. He detained the messenger and brought all his men out of the town into the open field.

The next day, as he was about to leave St. Michael's church after the liturgy, Bishop Evfimy implored him with tears. "Prince," he said, "make peace with your uncle! You will receive great salvation from God and will save your land from great calamity." Iziaslav would not heed him, relying on the strength of his army. "I won both Kiev and Pereiaslavl at risk of my life," he told the bishop, and left the city. Once more the two armies faced each other all day across the Trubezh river.

Iziaslav took counsel with his brothers Rostislav and Vladimir, his sons Mstislav and Yaropolk, his boyars and all his retinue, considering whether to cross the Trubezh and attack Yury. Opinions were divided. "Prince, do not cross the river," some said. "Yury has come to take your lands, he has labored hard and gained nothing. Now he is turning back and will certainly depart in the night. Do not pursue him." Others urged the contrary. "Go forward, prince! God is giving your enemy into your hand. You must not let him go." Unfortunately Iziaslav, convinced by the more belligerent, led his troops across the river. Next day at noon a deserter rode out of Yury's army with men in pursuit. This alarmed Iziaslav's pickets, who shouted "Battle!" The sons of Mstislav led their troops forward. When Yury and the sons of Oleg saw this, they too advanced, crossed the earthwork and halted. The sons of Mstislav did the same. Again the engagement was confined to an exchange of arrows, because when evening came Yury turned his troops around and returned to his camp.

At dawn on the morning of August 23 the armies engaged in earnest, and there was a fierce battle. The first to flee were the men from the Ros river (who must have included the Karakalpaks), then Iziaslav Davydovich, then the men of Kiev. The men of Pereiaslavl betrayed Iziaslav. As they previously were in contact with Yury's son, so now they were with Yury himself, refusing to take part in the battle. "Yury is our prince," the cried, "we have sought him from afar." The retinues of the sons of Mstislav laughed at these desertions and betrayals. At the beginning of the battle Iziaslav and his retinue engaged Sviatoslav Olgovich and half of Yury's men, then when he drove right through them and was behind them he saw that his own army was in flight.

Now he too fled, crossed the Dnieper at Kanev and reached Kiev with two companions. The fact that the men of Pereiaslavl changed sides and the men of the Ros fled is good evidence in support of the report that Rostislav Yurievich made to his father. In any case, Iziaslav's defeat could have been foreseen, as he was defending his personal rights in the face of generally accepted morality. While the men of Kiev submitted to these personal rights and fought for him against Yury, they went unwillingly, with manifest hesitation and inner conflict. This was not a disposition conducive to fortitude and victory.

Next morning Yury entered Pereiaslavl. After spending three days there he departed for Kiev and encamped in the meadows in front of St. Michael's monastery. "Our uncle has come," the sons of Mstislav informed the men of Kiev. "Can you fight for us?" "Lords and princes," they replied, "do not ruin us utterly. Some of our fathers and brothers and sons are made captive. Some are slain and their weapons taken from them. Us too they will take prisoner. It is best that you go back to your own principality. You know that we cannot live with Yury. When we see your banner, we shall be ready to follow you."

At this the sons of Mstislav departed, Iziaslav to Vladimir and Rostislav to Smolensk, while their uncle Yury entered Kiev. The multitude came out to meet him *with great joy,* and he sat on his father's throne, praising and glorifying God, says the chronicle. First of all Yury rewarded his ally Sviatoslav Olgovich. He sent to Chernigov summoning Vladimir Davydovich and telling him to give him Kursk and the country along the Seim, and Iziaslav Davydovich to give Sviatoslav Olgovich the lands of the southern Dregovichians.[10] Then Yury distributed lands to his sons, installing his eldest son Rostislav in Pereiaslavl,[11] Andrei in Vyshgorod, Boris in Belgorod,[12] Gleb in Kanev and Vasilko in Suzdal.[13]

IZIASLAV PREPARES TO CONTINUE STRUGGLE AGAINST YURY

Meanwhile Iziaslav Mstislavich arrived in Vladimir and sent to his kinsmen the king of Hungary and the princes of Poland and Bohemia for help,[14] asking them to ride in person to Kiev, or if they could not come in person to send armies under their younger brothers or commanders. King Géza II of Hungary[15] at first refused, saying that he was occupied by his wars with Byzantium, but that he would bring or send aid to Iziaslav when he was free of this commitment. The Polish princes replied that, being near at hand, two of them could march, leaving the third behind to look after their own lands. The prince of Bohemia[16] also expressed his readiness to come at the head of an army.

Iziaslav could not be content with promises. He sent further envoys to Hungary, Poland and Bohemia bearing rich gifts. "God reward you," he told the rulers, "for taking it upon yourselves to help me. Ride out at Christmas." They promised to do so, and the king of Hungary sent ten thousand auxiliaries. "I send you my men," he declared, "and I shall ride against the prince of Galich, that he cannot make any move against you. Settle your affairs with those who have wronged you. When the army is exhausted, I shall send you another, even greater, or else I shall come myself." Bolesław of Poland[17] came with his brother Henryk,[18] leaving Mieszko[19] to protect their country against the Prus.

Meanwhile Iziaslav, who was preparing for war and now knew how hard it was for him to struggle against the general conviction that an uncle had a better right than his nephew, turned to old Viacheslav,[20] now prince of Peresopnitsa. "Be a father to me," he told him, "go take the throne of Kiev, for I cannot live with Yury. If you refuse to receive me in love and will not go to take the throne of Kiev, I will burn your lands." Alarmed by this threat, Viacheslav sent to Yury. "The Hungarians are on their way," he warned, "the Polish princes have mounted their horses. Iziaslav is ready to ride out. Either make peace with him and give him what he wants, or else lead your armies to me and defend my principality. Come brother, let us see together what God will give us, good or evil. If you will not come, do not complain of me afterwards."

Yury assembled his whole army together with a Polovetsian force and left Kiev, while Iziaslav and his allies left Vladimir. Viacheslav first was joined at Peresopnitsa by his nephews Rostislav and Andrei, then by Yury himself. Vladimirko of Galich[21] also sent his men, while he himself moved towards the frontier, alarming the Poles and Hungarians. The Polish princes were even more disturbed when they heard from their brother that their country was under attack from the Prus. This news was very little to Iziaslav's liking, as it prevented the Poles from remaining with him any longer. It was decided to send a message to Viacheslav and Yury in the name of all the allied princes in these terms. "You are in place of our fathers, yet now you are at war with your brother and son Iziaslav. Under God we are all Christians and brothers together, and ought all to be as one. Therefore you should come to terms with your brother and son Iziaslav. You should have Kiev, it is for you to decide which of you should rule there. And Iziaslav should have Vladimir, Lutsk and the other towns that he possesses there. Let Yury give back all the tribute that belongs to Novgorod."

"God reward our son-in-law the king," Viacheslav and Yury replied, "and our brother Bolesław and our son Henryk for desiring our good. If you desire to make peace with us, do not occupy our lands, do not destroy our villages and our wealth. Let Iziaslav go back to Vladimir, and every one of you to his own land. Then we shall come to terms with our brother and son Iziaslav." The allies swiftly fulfilled these terms and returned home, while the sons of Monomakh set about coming to terms with their nephew. The chief obstacle was that Iziaslav insisted that Yury return the tributes due to Novgorod, to which Yury would by no means agree. He was particularly urged not to come to terms by Yury Yaroslavich,[22] the great-grandson of Iziaslav I, whose name we have encountered once before.[23] It is not known whether this Yury was offended on some occasion by Iziaslav, or merely considered it to his advantage if the sons of Mstislav were expelled from Volhynia. Be that as it may, his great-uncle Yury[24] followed his advice, especially since Iziaslav's allies now went home, and it seemed that it would be easy for him to deal with his nephew. "I shall drive out Iziaslav and take all his lands," he said, and moved on Lutsk with his brother Viacheslav and all his sons. His two eldest sons Rostislav and Andrei went on ahead with the Polovetsians and stopped for the night at Muravitsy.[25]

For some reason there was panic amongst the Polovetsians during the night and they all ran away. Andrei, who was in front, was not frightened and held his ground, in spite of his retinue, who said to him "What are you doing, prince? Ride away, or we all shall be put to shame." Andrei waited till dawn, when he discovered that he had no Polovetsians left. He retreated towards his brothers and the Polovetsians at Dubno, in expectation of reinforcements from Yury. Then, when they heard that Yury was on his way, they advanced towards Lutsk, where Iziaslav's brother Vladimir shut himself up.

As they approached the town a company of infantry marched out of the gates and shot arrows at them. Andrei's brothers had no idea that he intended to attack this infantry, because his banner was not raised. Andrei had not yet made his name as a great warrior, preferring to seek the praise of God, as the chronicle puts it. Suddenly he rode at the head of his retinue into the midst of the enemy, and a lively skirmish began. Andrei broke his lance and was in great danger. He was surrounded on all sides, his horse was wounded twice by lances, and a third struck his saddle, while stones rained down on him from the walls. A German attempted to stab him with a trident, but God preserved him. Andrei was aware of his peril and thought to himself "I shall die like Yaroslav Sviatopolchich."[26] He prayed to God and St. Theodore, whose feast it was,[27] drew his sword and fought his way out. His father, brothers and uncle were overjoyed to see him alive, and his boyars showered him with praise, for he fought more bravely than anyone in that engagement. His horse, badly wounded, fell as soon as it carried its master out of the battle, and Andrei had it buried above the Styr river.

RECONCILIATION BETWEEN YURY AND IZIASLAV

Yury besieged Lutsk for six weeks and the defenders were worn down by lack of water. Iziaslav wanted to come to their aid from Vladimir. His way was barred by the prince of Galich who preferred the descendants of Monomakh to continue to fight each other rather than that one of them emerge as final victor. It was better for him if the neighboring land of Volhynia belonged to a separate prince. For this reason, when he received a message from Iziaslav saying "Reconcile me with my uncle Yury, for I am guilty before God and before him," Vladimirko interceded with Yury for Iziaslav. Yury Yaroslavich and Dolgoruky's eldest son Rostislav, who hated Iziaslav since his expulsion from Rus, resisted any reconciliation. Yury's second son Andrei inclined towards peace, telling his father not to listen to Yury Yaroslavich and be reconciled to his nephew, and not ruin his patrimony. Viacheslav also urged peace, having his own reasons. "Brother," he said to Yury, "make peace, for if you go away without making peace, Iziaslav will burn my lands." Finally Yury agreed. Iziaslav resigned Kiev to him, restoring to him also the tribute from Novgorod. Iziaslav came to meet his uncles at Peresopnitsa, where it was agreed that each side restore to the other everything captured from the princes or their boyars in the battle at Pereiaslavl. After this Yury returned to Kiev, intending to relinquish it to Viacheslav on account of seniority, but his boyars dissuaded him. "Your brother cannot hold on to Kiev," they said, "and it will be lost to both of you." Then Yury removed his son Andrei from Vyshgorod and gave it to Viacheslav instead.

RENEWAL OF HOSTILITIES

In 1150 Iziaslav sent his boyars and agents to Kiev to recover from Yury his property and herds lost in the war. His boyars also went to recover their property, either in person or through their agents. When they identified their property and demanded it back, Yury refused to let them have it, hence they returned to Iziaslav empty-handed. "Keep your oath," Iziaslav complained to his uncles, "otherwise I cannot allow this wrong to be done to me."

There was no reply. Iziaslav again took up arms, it is said, at the invitation of the citizens of Kiev. Yury's son Gleb, who replaced Viacheslav at Peresopnitsa, was at the time encamped above the town on the Stubla river. Iziaslav made a surprise attack on him and captured his camp, retinue and horses. Gleb himself scarcely escaped into the town, whence he sent a message to Iziaslav, saying "As Yury is my father, so are you, and I bow before you. You can deal with my father yourself, but let me go to my father. Swear by the Mother of God that you will not take me prisoner. If you let me go, I shall come and bow before you." Iziaslav swore, and told him "You are my own cousins, my quarrel is not with you. It is your father who wrongs me, refusing to live in amity with us." After dining with Gleb, Iziaslav sent him to his father escorted by his own son Mstislav, who accompanied him as far as Korchesk, where he told him "Go to your father, cousin. This land as far as the Goryn belongs to my father and me." Gleb went off to his father. Iziaslav set off after him and went to the Karakalpaks, who flocked to him with great enthusiasm.

IZIASLAV'S RETURN TO KIEV AND RECONCILIATION WITH VIACHESLAV

When Yury, hitherto ignorant of Iziaslav's movements, heard that he was already with the Karakalpaks, he fled from Kiev, crossed the Dnieper and went to Gorodets Ostersk. No sooner did Yury leave Kiev than old Viacheslav appeared and took up residence at Yaroslav's Court. The men of Kiev went out to meet Iziaslav in great numbers. "Yury has left Kiev," they said. "Viacheslav has taken his place, but we do not want him. You are our prince, so come to the Holy Wisdom and sit on the throne of your father and grandfather." Iziaslav sent to Viacheslav. "When I called you to take the throne of Kiev," he said, "you refused it. How is it that you sit upon it now that your brother has left the city? Go back to your own city of Vyshgorod." "Though you kill me on the spot, I shall not go," replied Viacheslav.

Iziaslav entered Kiev, worshipped at the Holy Wisdom, and went to Yaroslav's Court accompanied by all his forces and a multitude of the citizens. Viacheslav was sitting in the outer hall. Some of those with Iziaslav urged him to take Viacheslav and his retinue prisoner. Others wanted to break into the hall, but Iziaslav prevented them. "God forbid," he said. "I am not a murderer of my brethren. My uncle is like a father to me, I shall go to him." He took a small retinue and entered the outer hall and bowed to Viacheslav, who rose and kissed his nephew. When they were both seated, Iziaslav spoke. "Father," he said, "I cannot come to any arrangement with you here. You can see what a throng is here, and it is very ill-disposed towards you. Go to your palace at Vyshgorod, then we shall settle matters." "You yourself called me to Kiev, son," replied Viacheslav, "but now I have taken an oath to my brother Yury. Now it has turned out thus, Kiev is yours, and I will go to Vyshgorod." He left Kiev and Iziaslav became its prince again, sending his son Mstislav to Kanev with instructions to regain Pereiaslavl.

Mstislav sent to the retinue on the other side of the Dnieper and to a barbarian tribe settled on the frontier called the Turpei, calling on them to come over to him. The prince of Pereiaslavl was Rostislav Yurievich, who sent to his father in Gorodets for aid. Yury sent his son Andrei to him. When Andrei arrived, Rostislav left him in Pereiaslavl. Setting off after the Turpei, he caught up with them on the Dnieper, captured them and brought them back to Pereiaslavl. Meanwhile Yury joined forces with the sons of Davyd and Oleg, while his daughter's father-in-law[28] Vladimirko of Galich brought assistance from the West.

When he learned that Vladimirko was near, Iziaslav sent to his son to tell him to join him speedily with the Berendey, went to Vyshgorod with his boyars, and said to Viacheslav "You are my father, so take Kiev and whatever else you desire, leaving the rest for me." Viacheslav at first was angry. "Why did you not give me Kiev before," he retorted, "but made me leave it in humiliation? Why do you give it to me now there is one army marching on it from Galich and another from Chernigov?" "I sent to you offering Kiev," Iziaslav replied, "telling you that I could get on with you. It is only your brother Yury with whom I cannot agree. I love you like a father, and I tell you that Kiev is yours, go there." The old man was touched by these words. He swore at the tomb of Boris and Gleb that he would be a father to Iziaslav, who swore to be a son to him, and their boyars swore to seek the princes' common good, guard their honor and not sow dissension between them. Iziaslav bowed down to the holy martyrs Boris and Gleb, then to his father Viacheslav. "I am going to Zvenigorod against Vladimirko," he said, "but you, father, do not weary yourself, let me have but your retinue, while you go to Kiev as soon as you see fit." Viacheslav agreed to let him have his whole retinue.

Having settled matters with his uncle, Iziaslav returned to Kiev, sounded the trumpets, summoned the men of Kiev and went forth against Vladimirko, saying he would first attack the nearest enemy. He first encamped at Zvenigorod. Hearing that the men of Galich were approaching, he moved to Tumashch, where he was joined by the Karakalpaks, who left their wives and children shut up in the towns along the Ros. At dawn the next day Iziaslav set his troops in order and led them against Vladimirko, who was on the upper reaches of the Olshanitsa river. The archers began shooting arrows at each other across the river. The

Karakalpaks, seeing the great number of men of Galich, were frightened and said to Iziaslav "Prince, Vladimirko has a great force, while you have but a small retinue. If he decides to cross the river, it will go ill for us. Do not destroy us and yourself. You are our prince when you are strong. We will be with you then, but this is not your hour. Leave this place."

Iziaslav replied that it was better for them to die than to dishonor themselves in such a way, but the men of Kiev said likewise and fled, followed by the Karakalpaks, who returned to their encampments. Iziaslav, left with only his retinue, had to retreat to Kiev. It was fortunate for him that Vladimirko could not believe that the entire opposing army had run away without a fight. He took it for a feint and forbade his men to pursue Iziaslav, who consequently reached Kiev safely with the loss of only a few from his rearguard. Some of these were captured, others were slain by the troops from Galich.

IZIASLAV AND VIACHESLAV WITHDRAW FROM KIEV

At Kiev Iziaslav found his uncle Viacheslav. After some discussion they were sitting down to dinner when news came that Yury and all the princes of Chernigov were upon them. A large number of the citizens had gone to meet him in boats, while others were ferrying his retinue across the river. "Now is not our hour," said Viacheslav and Iziaslav, leaving the city. Viacheslav went to Vyshgorod, while Iziaslav went to Vladimir, occupying the country along the Goryn and installing his son Mstislav at Dorogobuzh.

The next day Vladimirko of Galich drew near to Kiev and encamped at Oleg's Grave,[29] where Yury and the princes of Chernigov came to meet him and offered greetings without dismounting. Vladimirko brought Yury into Kiev and visited all the holy places of the city, also the tomb of Boris and Gleb at Vyshgorod. He parted with Yury on good terms at the Caves monastery and returned to Galich.

Hearing of his approach, Mstislav Iziaslavich fled headlong from Dorogobuzh to his uncle Sviatopolk at Lutsk. Vladimirko took the towns along the Goryn, giving them to Mstislav Yurievich, whom he brought with him from Kiev. He came close to Lutsk but could not take it. He returned to Galich. Mstislav Yurievich remained at Peresopnitsa. Soon Yury gave this town, together with Turov and Pinsk, to Andrei, who took up residence at Peresopnitsa. The reason for his move and for preferring Peresopnitsa to Turov is clear. Andrei, the bravest of Yury's sons, was to guard the frontier with Volhynia, from which direction Yury could expect his nephew to attack.

That winter Iziaslav sent a message to Peresopnitsa asking Andrei to reconcile him with his father. "I have no inheritance in Hungary or Poland, only in the Land of Rus. Ask your father to give me the land as far as the Goryn." While this was the ostensible reason for his sending to Peresopnitsa, he also instructed his envoy to reconnoiter Andrei's preparations and the situation of the town. Previously he had taken Andrei's brother Gleb by surprise, and hoped to do the same with Andrei. It turned out that Andrei had a strong position and large retinue. Suspecting no guile, Andrei again interceded for Iziaslav with his father, who was unwilling to offer him anything.

IZIASLAV AGAIN PREPARES TO MAKE WAR ON YURY IN KIEV

Iziaslav realized that his uncle would not give him any land, neither did he want to see him in the Land of Rus at all. It was at Yury's behest that Vladimirko occupied his territory and was preparing to attack him in Vladimir. Therefore he sent his brother Vladimir[30] to his brother-in-law the king of Hungary with a message. "You told me that Vladimirko would not dare to show himself, then when I drove Yury from Kiev and he was fleeing before me, Vladimirko in league with the sons of Oleg came and expelled me from Kiev as well. Now, brother, fulfill your promise and ride out." The king immediately summoned his army and set forth, sending on to Iziaslav to say "Your brother Vladimir and I are on our way. Ride forth as well, and Vladimirko shall find out whom he has provoked."

Vladimirko had friends in Hungary. They told him the king was attacking him, so the Galich prince left his baggage at Bełz, where he was encamped. He made haste with his retinue to Peremyshl, where the king opened hostilities. Vladimirko saw he could not hope to fight the Hungarians, therefore he sent to the archbishop and two other Hungarian bishops and the boyars, asking them to persuade the king to return home. He did not spare his gold in this effort and was successful. The king listened to the suborned bishops and boyars, saying "This is not the time to make war, the rivers are only beginning to freeze. When the ice is firm we shall come again." When he dismissed Vladimir Mstislavich to Kiev the king told him "Greet my father and your brother and tell him that the Byzantine emperor is making war on me, therefore I cannot ride out for you this winter or spring. My shield and yours shall not stand apart. If I cannot come myself, I will send help, ten thousand men or more, as many as you like. In the summer, God grant, I shall be at your service, and we will avenge our wrongs."

When Iziaslav received this message he sent Vladimir back to Hungary. "Brother," he told him, "God reward you for laboring for my honor and yours. You have been to Hungary to visit the king, your brother-in-law. You know his counsel and thoughts. So should you labor now. Go there again for the sake of my honor and yours." "This is no hardship for me, brother," replied Vladimir. "For the sake of your honor and that of our brother Rostislav I will go gladly." "If the emperor is making war on you," was the message Vladimir took to the king, "and you cannot come to us in person, send us the help that you have promised, and God will help me against Yury, the sons of Oleg and the prince of Galich. A wrong done to you is a wrong done to me, and a wrong done to me is a wrong done to you."

The king sent Vladimir back with ten thousand men, whom Iziaslav led again to Kiev, heeding the call of Viacheslav's boyars, the men of Kiev and the Berendey. On the way, near Peresopnitsa, hearing that Vladimirko was marching against him, he called a council to consider what to do. "Prince," said his boyars, "you can see that things are going ill for us. You are going against Yury, and Vladimirko is behind you. It will be very hard for us." "You followed me out of the Land of Rus," said Iziaslav, "leaving your villages and wealth. No more can I abandon the land of my father and grandfather. Either I lay down my life, or I shall recover my patrimony and all your wealth. If Vladimirko catches up to me, God means to judge between us. If Yury meets me, I shall see the judgment of God between him and me. As God judges, so be it."

Iziaslav sent back his brother Sviatopolk to guard Vladimir. He advanced to Dorogobuzh with his brother Vladimir, son Mstislav, Prince Boris of Goroden, Davyd Igorevich's grandson, and the Hungarians. The people of Dorogobuzh came out to meet him carrying crosses and bowed down to him. "You are the people of my father and my grandfather," said Iziaslav, "God be your help." "Prince," they replied, "you have foreigners with you, Hungarians. What is to stop them from doing harm to the town?" "I lead the Hungarians and all other foreigners against my enemies, not against my own people," replied Iziaslav. "Fear nothing."

Iziaslav bypassed Dorogobuzh and crossed the Goryn. The people of Korsun also came out joyfully to meet him and bowed before him, and

Iziaslav skirted their town also. Evidently he did not want to alarm the inhabitants or risk causing conflicts by leading a foreign army into their midst. Meanwhile Vladimirko joined forces with Andrei Yurievich, whom he summoned from Peresopnitsa. Iziaslav soon heard that the prince of Galich, Andrei Yurievich and Vladimir Andreevich (a dispossessed prince, the son of the youngest son of Monomakh)[31] were crossing the Goryn with a large army. When the sons of Mstislav crossed the Sluch and the Usha enemy archers appeared on the far bank and harried them from over the river. Some of the more daring even crossed over to the near bank.

One of the Galich archers was captured and brought before Iziaslav. When asked where his prince was, he replied "He has stopped in the forest just beyond the town of Ushesk, for when he heard that you were near, he dared not pass through the wood. 'If we pass through the wood,' he said, 'they will attack us, and our main force is far behind. Let us wait for them here.'" When he heard this, Iziaslav proposed going back to attack them. "Prince," replied his retinue, "you cannot go back, there is a river in the way, a dangerous one. How can you attack him when he is lying in ambush in the woods? Let it be for now, and go to your people in Kiev. We will fight Vladimirko wherever he catches up to us. You said yourself that if Yury meets us, we will fight him too. Now prince, do not delay, press on. When we reach the Teterev, all the retinue there will join you. Then, God willing, we shall reach Belgorod, where you will find even more men, and your strength will be the greater."

Iziaslav did as they said and marched, followed by Vladimirko. By the time Iziaslav was at Sviatoslav's Spring his sentries could see the campfires of the men of Galich. Iziaslav had a large bonfire set to deceive the enemy, moving on by night to the town of Michsk. There multitudes of people from the banks of the Teterev came to him, shouting "You are our prince!" Once across the Teterev, Iziaslav allowed himself and his horses a rest before moving on to Vzdvizhensk, where he took counsel with his retinue.

"Vladimirko is following us," he said, "do you think we should remain here and wait for him, or not spare our strength and move on further by night? If we stay here and wait for Vladimirko, we risk waiting until Yury comes upon us from the other side. Then it will go hard with us. I think that it would be better to press on without rest. If we reach Belgorod, Yury surely will flee immediately. Then we shall go to our own city of Kiev.

If we ride to the strong army of Kiev, I know that it will fight for me. If we cannot go to Belgorod, we shall go to the Karakalpaks. If we join forces with them we need not fear either Yury or Vladimirko."

"We are guests in your land," said the Hungarians. "If you put your trust in the men of Kiev, you should know your own people best. Our horses are beneath us, and it is a good thing when new friends and new forces join us. Let us press on by night." Then Iziaslav said to his brother Vladimir [Mstislavich] "Go on ahead to Belgorod. We will all let you have our younger retinues and come after you. If they resist you at Belgorod, let us know, and fight them from morning until dinner time. Meanwhile I shall either cross over to Abram's Bridge, or else go to the Karakalpaks, join forces with them and attack Yury in Kiev. If you take Belgorod, let us know, and we shall join you there."

Vladimir came to Belgorod, where the local prince Boris Yurievich was feasting quietly in his chamber with his retinue and clergy. Had not the *toll collector*[32] been on guard, had he not raised the drawbridge, the prince would have been taken. When Vladimir's retinue reached the bridge they sounded their trumpets. Boris leapt up in fright and galloped away with his retinue, while the citizens ran down to the bridge, bowing down to Vladimir, shouting "Come in, prince, Boris has fled." They lowered the bridge again. As soon as he entered Belgorod Vladimir sent a messenger to his brother as arranged. "I have entered Belgorod," he said, "and Boris has fled. He knew nothing of my approach, so Yury knows nothing either. Come quickly." Iziaslav marched at once and got his troops across the bridge before dawn. Leaving Vladimir in Belgorod in case the prince of Galich came, he led the Hungarians to Kiev.

IZIASLAV EXPELS YURY FROM KIEV

Meanwhile Boris reached his father to warn him of the approaching armies. Yury was at the Red Court. Too shocked to know what to do, he got into a boat, crossed the river and hid in Gorodets, meanwhile the people of Kiev went out joyfully to meet Iziaslav. Most probably Yury's conduct gave rise to great resentment, angering also the Karakalpaks. Now both these groups started to call on Iziaslav Mstislavich to come to them. After taking Yury's retinue prisoner, Iziaslav went to the church of the Holy Wisdom, thence to Yaroslav's Court, where he summoned the Hungarians and the men of Kiev to a feast. There was great merriment, and after the feast the Hungarians entertained the citizens with a display of horsemanship.

Vladimirko and Andrei Yurievich were at Michsk, knowing nothing about all this, when the news came that Yury was in Gorodets and Iziaslav in Kiev. Vladimirko was greatly displeased. "I do not understand what sort of a prince is your father, my daughter's father-in-law," he said to Princes Andrei and Vladimir Andreevich. "How could he fail to know that an army was marching against him all the way from Volhynia? What about you, his sons, one of you in Peresopnitsa and the other in Belgorod, neither of you raising the alarm? If that is how you and your father rule your lands, sort yourselves out in your own way. I cannot march against Iziaslav by myself. Yesterday he was ready to fight me on his way to attack your father, now he has the whole Land of Rus behind him! I cannot face him alone."

The real reason for Iziaslav's remarkable success was not so much the unreadiness of Yury and his sons, as their general unpopularity and the efforts made by so many to ensure that they would be unprepared.

VLADIMIRKO RETURNS TO GALICH

Vladimirko did as he said. Abandoning Yury's cause, he returned to Galich. He wanted some reward for his pains, hence he demanded a certain amount of silver from the citizens of Michsk, threatening to plunder the town if he did not get it. It was more than they had available, and they were forced to melt down their wives' and daughters' earrings and necklaces to find enough to satisfy him. Vladimirko did the same in every town through which he passed on the way back to his own borders. Andrei and his cousin Vladimir Andreevich went to the mouth of the Pripiat and thence to their father in Gorodets Ostersk.

IZIASLAV OFFERS TO SHARE KIEV WITH VIACHESLAV

The day after Iziaslav arrived in Kiev he sent a message to his uncle Viacheslav. "Father, I greet you," he said. "Since God has taken my father Mstislav, you are my father, and I greet you. I sinned against you once, and I repent. Again, when God gave me victory over Igor at Kiev, I did not do you due honor, and again at Tumashch. Now, father, I repent of everything before God and before you. If you forgive me, father, God too will forgive. I give you Kiev. Come and sit upon the throne of your father and grandfather!"

These words express Iziaslav's complete recognition of the right of family seniority, the precedence of an uncle over his elder brother's children, which neither personal qualities nor popular respect and affection could do anything to alter. "Son!" was Viacheslav's reply. "God reward you for giving the honor due to me, as you ought to have done long ago. If you have honored me, you have honored God. You say that I am your father, and I say to you that you are my son. You have no father, and I have no son. You are my son, you are my brother too." Here the old uncle gives expression to the prevailing notion that an elder brother's sons had a status equivalent to that of younger brothers of their uncles. Viacheslav and Iziaslav swore not to part, for good or ill. This took place in 1150.

In 1151 Viacheslav rode into Kiev. After worshipping at the Holy Wisdom he gave a feast for Iziaslav, the men of Kiev and the Hungarians. The Hungarians were honored greatly by both princes, who gave them rich gifts of plate, clothing, horses, cloth and all kinds of goods. The day following the feast Viacheslav said to Iziaslav "Son, God reward you for the honor you have done to me. I have this to say to you. I am old and incapable of attending to all the business of government. Let us both remain in Kiev. Whatever decision we have to make, concerning Christians or heathen, let us take it together. We shall have but one retinue and one army, and you shall command them. Where both can go, we both shall go, and where both cannot go, you shall go with my troops and with your own." Iziaslav bowed to his adoptive father with great honor and great joy. "Father," said he, "I bow down to you. God grant that it be as we have agreed to the end our days."[33]

FURTHER HOSTILITIES BETWEEN YURY AND IZIASLAV

On the third day they sent the Hungarians home, followed by Iziaslav's son Mstislav with this message for the king. "You have done for us what only a brother can do for his brother, or a son for his father. God grant we always be as one. Where you are wronged, God grant we avenge your wrong, or if not us, our brothers or our sons. We have nothing but our lives with which to pay you for your goodness. Now complete your good work. We do not call upon you, because of your war with the Greeks. Instead send an army to help us, such as you have sent, or better, one still larger, for Yury is strong. The sons of Davyd and Oleg are with him, and the Wild Polovetsians, whom he pays with gold. Now, brother, help us this spring. If we deal with our uncle this spring, we will come to help you with our troops. If you succeed against the emperor, you help us. For the rest, your men will tell you, or your *brother* Mstislav, how God has helped us, how the whole Land of Rus and the Karakalpaks rose up on our side."

At the same time as he sent Mstislav to Hungary Viacheslav sent his boyars to Rostislav Mstislavich in Smolensk. "Brother! God has united us with your brother, my son Iziaslav, for when he won the Land of Rus he did me honor and made me prince in Kiev. I tell you, my son, that as your brother Iziaslav is a son to me, so are you. Do your best to come to us, that we may take counsel together about what to do now." Iziaslav also sent to Rostislav. "Often, brother," he said, "did you urge me to honor my uncle and father. Now that God has restored me to the Land of Rus, I have made our uncle prince of Kiev for your sake and for the sake of all the Land of Rus. Now I say to you that near you in Novgorod is my son, your godson Yaroslav. You have also Smolensk. So when you have set all things in order in the upper lands, come to us here, and we shall consider together what God will give us."

Iziaslav and his uncle were right to summon their allies from all sides, for Yury had no intention of leaving them in peace. He sent to the sons of Davyd and the sons of Oleg saying that Iziaslav was in Kiev, and appealed for help. Sviatoslav Olgovich set out immediately. Joining forces with Vladimir Davydovich in Chernigov, they sailed down the river to Yury at Gorodets. Iziaslav Davydovich went over to the side of Viacheslav and Iziaslav. It would appear that he had no choice but to support Yury hitherto, even though he was angry with him for depriving him of the lands of the Dregovichians to give to Sviatoslav Olgovich.

Rostislav Mstislavich soon arrived in Kiev with the men of Smolensk, while Yury rode forth from Gorodets with his allies, coming to the place where the Radun flows into the Dnieper. There he was joined by many Polovetsians. This time Iziaslav was cautious, not allowing the enemy to cross the Dnieper. Both sides fought in boats from Kiev to the mouth of the Desna. Yury could not succeed in this battle on the river because, as the chronicle said, Iziaslav built his boats with great cunning. The oarsmen could not be seen, only the oars, because the boats were covered with decks, upon which stood the warriors in armor who shot their arrows. There were two rudders on each boat, one at each end, so that they could be sailed in either direction without putting about.

Finding it impossible to cross the Dnieper opposite Kiev, Yury and his allies decided to go downriver to Vitichev ford. Since they dared not try to take their boats past Kiev, they rowed them into Lake Dolobsk, dragged them along the bank to the Zolotcha, then rowed down the Zolotcha into the Dnieper, meanwhile the Polovetsians rode through the meadows. The sons of Mstislav, their uncle Viacheslav, Iziaslav Davydovich, Prince

Boris of Goroden, the men of Kiev and the Karakalpaks all marched parallel to them along the high western bank of the Dnieper, with the boats alongside in the river, hence when Yury and his men reached Vitichev ford the opposing army was waiting for them. The attempt at crossing again resulted in a river battle.

Then Yury called his allies, saying "If we stay here, what will come of it? Better to try and capture the ford at Zarub and cross over there." They all agreed. Yury's sons, the Polovetsians and Sviatoslav Vsevolodovich rode off to take the ford, and the main army marched along the bank level with the boats. Their advance troops reached the ford, guarded by Iziaslav's boyar Shvarn with a small retinue. Seeing that the defenders were few, the Polovetsians rode into the river mounted and in full armor, covering the Rus as they crossed over in their boats. Shvarn took fright and fled back to his prince. The chronicle says that the reason for this disaster was that the ford was defended not by a prince, merely by a boyar, who could not command the absolute obedience of his men. After crossing the Dnieper, Yury's sons sent word to their father, urging him to join them as quickly as possible, lest Iziaslav attack them before they were reinforced. This he did, leading his army over the river at Zarub.

When the news of this reached the sons of Mstislav, they returned to Kiev to consider their next move. They were both for going out and doing battle with their uncle, but not all the princes' retinues were agreed. The Karakalpaks were particularly insistent against it. "Prince," they said, "we cannot go out to meet them because our warriors are not all mounted. If you advance towards them they will ride towards the Ros, then you will have to leave your footmen behind and pursue them with only your cavalry. We believe that you all must go to Kiev, leaving your brother Vladimir over us. He will lead us to our encampments, where we will collect our wives, children and cattle and bring them to Kiev. Wait just until evening, and we shall certainly come, for we are ready to die for your father Viacheslav, for you, your brother Rostislav and all your brethren. We will defend your honor or die, for we want nothing to do with Yury."

The sons of Mstislav and their uncle followed the advice of their retinues, the men of Kiev, and the Karakalpaks. They sent Vladimir to the camps of the Torks, the Koui, the Berendey and the Pechenegs (these are the names of the tribes known collectively as the Karakalpaks).[34] The rest of them went to Trepol, spent the night there, departing for Kiev at sunrise. They did not enter the city, but encamped around it, Iziaslav Mstislavich

before the Golden gates, Iziaslav Davydovich between the Golden and the
Jewry gates, Rostislav and his son Roman before the Jewry gate, Boris of
Goroden at the Polish gates. The men of Kiev, mounted and on foot, were
positioned between the princes.

Soon Vladimir arrived with the Karakalpaks, their wagons and herds.
These allies did as much harm as the enemy, breaking into monasteries,
burning villages and trampling down the gardens. The sons of Mstislav
sent Vladimir with the Berendey and their wagons and herds to Oleg's
Grave, where they were to hold the ground between it and the Ivanovsk
Garden and the Shchekovitsa. The Koui, Torks and Pechenegs stood
between the Golden and the Polish gates and thence as far as Klov,
Berestovo, the Hungarian gate and the Dnieper. In other words, the
princes and their retinues, the citizens and the Karakalpaks decided not to
go out and meet the enemy, letting them approach the city and fight there.
"With God's help we shall repel them," said Iziaslav, "for they are not
birds. Now that they have flown across the Dnieper, they must land somewhere. When they turn away from us, let the outcome be as God ordains."

Old Viacheslav wanted to stage a last attempt at making peace before
the battle, saying to his nephews "Now we are ready to fight, brethren, but
Yury, after all, is my brother, albeit younger. I would like to send to him
and assert my seniority. When God judges between us, He will see who
is in the right." His nephews agreed, and Viacheslav called one of his
boyars. "Go to my brother Yury," he commanded, "and convey to him my
greetings. You, my brothers and sons, Iziaslav and Rostislav, listen, for
this is done in your presence.

"Tell Yury on my behalf 'I have told both you and Iziaslav many times
not to shed Christian blood or destroy the Land of Rus. I have tried to
restrain you from war. I have not thought of myself, or that you both have
wronged me repeatedly. Though by the grace of God I have both armies
and strength, yet for the sake of the Land of Rus and the Christian people
I have not called to mind how when Iziaslav went out to fight against Igor,
he said "It is not for myself that I seek Kiev, but for my father Viacheslav,
who is the eldest brother," nor how when he won Kiev he took it for
himself and moreover took Turov and Pinsk from me. This is how Iziaslav
wronged me. You, brother, when you went to Pereiaslavl to fight your
nephew, you also said "I do not seek Kiev for myself. I have an elder
brother, Viacheslav, who is as a father to me. It is for him that I seek Kiev."
Yet when through God's help you took Kiev for yourself, and moreover

took Peresopnitsa and Dorogobuzh from me, you wronged me, giving me only Vyshgorod. Yet for all that I sought no redress, for the sake of the Land of Rus and the Christian people. It is not in my sight that you have been unjust, but in the sight of God. I still sought to restrain both of you from war, yet you did not heed me. You, brother, said to me "I cannot submit to a younger prince," whereas Iziaslav, though he broke his word twice before, has now won Kiev, and bowed down to me, done me honor, made me prince of Kiev, and called me his father, and I have called him son. You have said that you will not submit to a younger prince but I am older than you, not by little but by much. I had a beard when you were born.[35] If you want to assail my seniority, let God judge between us.'"

"I bow down to you, brother," Yury replied. "What you say is right, and you stand in place of a father in relation to me. If you want to come to terms, let Iziaslav go back to Vladimir and Rostislav go back to Smolensk, then we shall settle matters."

Viacheslav sent a further message. "You have seven sons, and I have only Iziaslav and Rostislav and their younger brothers. I urge you for the sake of the Land of Rus and the Christian people to go to Pereiaslavl and Kursk with your sons. You will still have Great Rostov. Send the sons of Oleg home, then we shall come to terms without spilling Christian blood. If you insist on doing what you intend, Our Immaculate Lady and her Son and our God will judge us in this life and the next." As he said this, Viacheslav pointed to the image of the Mother of God on the Golden gates.

Yury, having made no reply, appeared with his army the next day and took up a position on the far side of the Lybed. There began an exchange of arrows across the river that lasted until evening. Some of Yury's men crossed over. Here, as before at Lutsk, Andrei Yurievich charged forward and galloped almost as far as the enemy when one of the Polovetsians seized his bridle and forced him to turn back, cursing his own people for not keeping up with the prince. When Iziaslav observed that the opposing forces were crossing the Lybed he sent a select retinue chosen from all his forces. They beat the enemy back into the river, killing many and taking numerous prisoners. Among the slain was the Polovetsian Savench Boniakovich who had boasted he would strike his sword against the Golden gates as his father did before him. No one crossed the Lybed after this. Yury turned his regiments about and withdrew. He heard that Vladimirko, his daughter's father-in-law, was marching from Galich, and he went to meet him.

YURY'S RETREAT FROM KIEV

The sons of Mstislav went to their uncle Viacheslav proposing to pursue them, but Viacheslav restrained them. "This is the beginning of God's help to us," he said, "for they have come and achieved nothing, winning only ignominy for themselves. There is no need to hurry. God willing, we shall ride out in the evening, or even tomorrow when we have had time to think." Then Iziaslav turned to Boris [Vsevolodovich] of Goroden,[36] saying "They no doubt will go to Belgorod. Go there with God's help." Boris did so.

Yury indeed went to Belgorod, sending a message to the citizens saying "You are my people. Open the town to me." "Did Kiev open its gates to you?" asked the people. "Our princes are Viacheslav, Iziaslav and Rostislav." At that, Yury rode further. At the same time the sons of Mstislav and their uncle Viacheslav set out from Kiev to prevent him joining forces with Vladimirko. The indifference of the men of Kiev, or their reluctance to take up arms against any of Monomakh's family, was a thing of the past. "Let everyone go who can bear arms," they said to Iziaslav. "If any be unwilling, give him to us and we will kill him."

Such zeal shows how unpopular Yury was. The chronicle says that they were all glad to follow their prince, horsemen and footmen, a great multitude. On the way Iziaslav received news from his son Mstislav. "The king your brother-in-law," he said, "has sent such a force to help you as has never been seen before, a great multitude. I have already crossed over the mountains with them. If you need us soon, let us know and we shall be with you swiftly." "We are on our way to God's judgment," replied Iziaslav, "and we always have need of you. Come as soon as you can."

DEFEAT OF YURY

The sons of Mstislav overtook Yury at the Rut river.[37] Fresh attempts at peace talks again proved vain, because the sons of Oleg and the Polovetsians refused to make peace. Indeed any reconciliation between all the sons of Monomakh would have been greatly to their disadvantage. Yury refused to fight before Vladimirko arrived while Iziaslav, for the same reason, was anxious to begin the battle quickly. When they were all ready dense fog suddenly covered the field, preventing anyone from seeing further than the end of his lance. This was followed by heavy rain. At noon, when the fog cleared, the two armies saw that there was a lake between them. Yury retreated, crossed the Lesser Rutets stream and camped there for the night. The sons of Mstislav and their uncle kept close to him and made their camp for the night at an arrow's flight from the enemy's tents. At dawn the next day Yury's men beat their drums and sounded their trumpets, making ready for battle. Soon the same sounds could be heard in the other camp. Yury and his sons and allies moved towards the head of the Rutets. The sons of Mstislav advanced against him, then when Yury reached the upper reaches of the Rutets he turned his army round and moved towards the Greater Rutets river. He wanted to avoid battle and wait for Vladimirko on the other side of the Rut.

Seeing Yury's retreat, the sons of Mstislav sent their own archers and those of the Karakalpaks after him. They harried his rear, shooting arrows and taking some of his baggage. Then Yury, seeing that the enemy would not let him cross the Rut, was forced to stand and fight. His son Andrei, as the eldest of the brothers (Rostislav had died at Pereiaslavl in 1150), set his father's troops in order. On the other side the sons of Mstislav rode up to their uncle Viacheslav. "You have desired greatly the good," they declared, "but your brother would not agree. Now, father, we are ready to lay down our lives for you or else vindicate your honor."

"Brothers and sons," Viacheslav replied, "I have never been fond of bloodshed, but my brother has brought us into this situation, so let God be our judge." His nephews bowed to him and went to their regiments. Iziaslav ordered that the whole army observe his men and do as they did.

As soon as battle was joined Andrei Yurievich seized his lance and rode forward to be the first to engage the enemy. His lance was broken, his shield riven, his helm fell from his head and his horse, wounded in the nostrils, charged around aimlessly. Iziaslav Mstislavich did likewise and was exposed to similar danger. He was the first to ride into the enemy ranks, broke his lance, was wounded in the arm and thigh and thrown from his falling horse.

After the general engagement there followed a fierce battle in which the army of the sons of Mstislav was victorious. Yury's allies from the steppes, the Polovetsians, preferred to loose their clouds of arrows from a distance and were of little use in the mêlée. They were the first to flee, without so much as taking an arrow from their quivers, followed by the sons of Oleg, then by Yury and his sons. Many of their retinue were killed or taken prisoner or drowned in the marshy Rut. Prince Vladimir Davydovich of Chernigov was one of those killed, while many princes of the Polovetsians were captured.

When the victors returned from pursuit to the field of battle, a man picked himself up out of one of the heaps of wounded. A crowd of footmen from Kiev ran up to kill him, then he suddenly said "I am the prince!" "Then you are just the man we need," said one of the men of Kiev, thinking that he was a son of Yury or Oleg, and struck him on the helm with his sword. Then the wounded man said "I am Iziaslav, your prince," and took off his helm. The men of Kiev recognized him, took him joyfully in their arms as their king and prince, as the chronicle says, exclaiming *"Kyrie eleison!"*

The entire army was overjoyed when they learned that the prince was still alive. Iziaslav Mstislavich was very weak, having lost much blood but when he heard that Iziaslav Davydovich was weeping for his brother Vladimir he summoned all his strength, mounted his horse and rode to mourn with him. He wept for a long time, then said "We cannot bring him back to life. Take his body and go to Chernigov. I will give you aid." The sons of Mstislav sent Roman Rostislavich and his retinue with him. By evening they were at Vyshgorod. They crossed the Dnieper at night, arriving next morning at Chernigov, where Iziaslav buried his brother and took possession of his throne.

Meanwhile Yury and his sons crossed the Dnieper at Trepol and halted at Pereiaslavl. The Polovetsians melted into the steppe and the sons of Oleg crossed the Dnieper above Zarub and fled to Gorodets. Sviatoslav Olgovich, being very fat and weary, could not go further. When he reached Gorodets he sent his nephew Sviatoslav Vsevolodovich on to Chernigov. When Sviatoslav Vsevolodovich reached the Desna he learned that Iziaslav Davydovich was in Chernigov, so he turned back, sending on a message to his uncle that Chernigov was occupied and that he should go to Novgorod Seversk. On the other side Vladimirko of Galich was coming to aid his daughter's father-in-law, but when he heard of Yury's defeat he hurriedly turned back. This meant the sons of Mstislav had nothing to fear from the West. They entered Kiev with their uncle in triumph, living there with great merriment and in great amity.

MASSACRE OF THE HUNGARIANS BY VLADIMIRKO

Their uncle Yury was sti' at Pereiaslavl. Iziaslav could not tolerate his proximity, therefore he and Viacheslav made preparations for war against him, letting Rostislav return to Smolensk. The news from the West was not good. While Vladimirko of Galich was on his way home he discovered that Mstislav Iziaslavich[38] was leading a Hungarian detachment to his father's aid, and decided to attack him. Mstislav, unaware of this, halted at Sapogin, near Dorogobuzh. Vladimir Andreevich, whom Vladimirko evidently installed as prince of Dorogobuzh, sent Mstislav a large quantity of wine and informed him of Vladimirko's approach. Mstislav drank with the Hungarians and during the feast announced that Vladimirko was coming. "Let him come," cried the drunken Hungarians, "and we will fight him."

At midnight, when all the camp was asleep, the sentries came running to Mstislav to tell him that Vladimirko was attacking. Mstislav and his retinue mounted their horses and tried to wake the Hungarians, who were all lying dead drunk after their carousal, without success. At dawn Vladimirko attacked the encampment, slaughtering almost all the Hungarians, taking only a few prisoners, while Mstislav and his retinue fled to Lutsk. When the news of his son's defeat and the massacre of the Hungarians reached Iziaslav in Kiev, he quoted a proverb the chronicler heard him use before. "The place does not become the head, but the head the place.[39] So long as God grants me and the king health, Vladimirko will feel our revenge."

YURY FORCED TO RETURN TO SUZDAL

First of all Yury had to be dealt with. Viacheslav, his nephews Iziaslav and Sviatopolk and the Berendey went to Pereiaslavl, where they fought for two days. On the third day the infantry forced their way into the city and burned the suburbs. Then Viacheslav and Iziaslav sent to Yury, saying "Greetings! Go to Suzdal, and let your son reign here in Pereiaslavl. We cannot have you here, for you will bring the Polovetsians upon us again."

Yury had no hope of any swift assistance although he was in contact with both Vladimirko and the Polovetsians. Because many of his retinue had been killed or captured he replied that he would go to Gorodets and thence to Suzdal. They told him that he might stay a month in Gorodets and that if he did not move to Suzdal by then, they would besiege him there just as they had in Pereiaslavl. Yury had no choice. He swore together with his sons that in a month he would depart for Suzdal, nor would he try to take Kiev from Viacheslav or Iziaslav. He was also compelled to renounce his alliance with Sviatoslav Olgovich, who was excluded from the agreement. Yury left his son Gleb in Pereiaslavl and went to Gorodets, while his eldest son Andrei asked leave to go ahead to Suzdal, saying that they had nothing more to do there and might as well depart while the time was favorable.

When Sviatoslav Olgovich learned that Yury had come to terms with Viacheslav and his nephews, he and his nephew Sviatoslav Vsevolodovich sent to Iziaslav Davydovich in Chernigov. "Brother," he said, "peace endures until war, and war until peace. We are your brethren, so receive us. We have two patrimonies, my father Oleg's and your father Davyd's. You are a son of Davyd, and I of Oleg, take what was your father Davyd's, and give to us what was Oleg's and we shall divide it between us." Iziaslav, says the chronicle, acted in a Christian manner, granting them what they asked on condition they abandon their alliance with Yury and take the side of the sons of Mstislav.

Yury could not bring himself to leave the Land of Rus. He broke his oath and remained at Gorodets more than a month. Iziaslav was true to his word and appeared with a besieging army including the Berendey, Iziaslav Davydovich of Chernigov and Sviatoslav Vsevolodovich. Some auxiliary troops were dispatched by Sviatoslav Olgovich, who was unwilling to ride in person against his old ally. Yury shut himself up in Gorodets and resisted for a long time, but no one came to his aid. Eventually he was forced to swear he would return to Suzdal, which now he actually did. Gorodets was left to his son Gleb, who evidently was deprived of Pereiaslavl in reprisal for Yury's previous oathbreaking, and Iziaslav installed his son Mstislav in Pereiaslavl. Yury proceeded to Suzdal by way of Novgorod Seversk where he visited his old friend Sviatoslav Olgovich, who received him honorably and supplied him with everything he needed for the journey.

FURTHER HOSTILITIES AMONG THE PRINCES

Perhaps this meeting of Yury and Sviatoslav Olgovich was one of the reasons for Iziaslav Mstislavich's meeting with Iziaslav Davydovich of Chernigov and Sviatoslav Vsevolodovich in 1152. At this meeting they decided to rid themselves of Yury's southern outpost between the principalities of Pereiaslavl and Chernigov, and destroyed Gorodets together with St. Michael's church. According to the chronicler Yury gave a heartfelt sigh when he heard of this, and gathered an army. He was joined by the prince of Riazan, Rostislav Yaroslavich,[40] with his brothers and the regiments of Riazan and Murom, by Sviatoslav Olgovich of

Novgorod Seversk[41] and all the hordes of the Polovetsians between the Volga and the Don. "They have burned my Gorodets and the church," said Yury, "so I shall burn their lands in return." He headed straight for Chernigov.

When he knew of his uncle's movements Iziaslav Mstislavich sent to his brother Rostislav in Smolensk. "Your Novgorod and Smolensk are strong," he urged, "gather an army and defend your lands. If Yury attacks you, I shall come to your aid. If he passes you by, come to me here." Finding that his uncle had bypassed Smolensk and was marching directly on Chernigov, Rostislav set out immediately for the same destination. He arrived before Yury and shut himself up in Chernigov with Sviatoslav Vsevolodovich. It was not long before Yury's Polovetsians appeared and burned the surrounding country. Seeing how many they were, the besieged princes ordered the citizens to abandon the outer defenses and take refuge in the citadel during the night.

Next morning Yury and Sviatoslav Olgovich approached with all their regiments. The Polovetsians attacked the town, broke down the outer defenses, set fire to the suburbs and did battle with the citizens, who defended themselves resolutely. Seeing this, the besieging princes decided that they must join the attack in person if their retinues and their Polovetsians were to fight well. As usual, Andrei Yurievich was the first to offer to lead the attack. "I shall begin today's action," said he, leading his retinue against some of the defenders who were making a sortie, driving them back into the town. The other princes, encouraged by Andrei's example, also rode up to the town, so that the men of Chernigov dared no longer make any sorties. After Yury besieged Chernigov for twelve days news came of the approach of Iziaslav Mstislavich and his uncle Viacheslav. The Polovetsians, brave enough when it was a matter of burning the suburbs of Chernigov and shooting at the defenders from a distance, were the first to lose courage and melt away. Their desertion forced Yury and Sviatoslav Olgovich to retreat from Chernigov too. Yury went first to Novgorod Seversk, thence to Rylsk, intending to proceed to Suzdal, then he was halted by Sviatoslav Olgovich. "You want to go away and leave me," he said. "My lands have been laid waste and the Polovetsians have destroyed all the grain. Now that the Polovetsians have gone, Iziaslav will come and destroy everything I have left because of my alliance with you." Yury promised to help him, leaving him his son Vasilko with a retinue of fifty men!

IZIASLAV ACTS AGAINST SVIATOSLAV OLGOVICH AND VLADIMIRKO

Sviatoslav's apprehension was justified. Iziaslav Mstislavich was already at the Alta river with all his forces. He sent the elderly Viacheslav back to Kiev, dispatching his son Mstislav with the Karakalpaks in pursuit of the Polovetsians, probably to prevent them sending any help to the Severian prince. Iziaslav himself advanced on Novgorod Seversk, where he was joined by Iziaslav Davydovich, Sviatoslav Vsevolodovich and Roman, son of Rostislav of Smolensk. On the third day of the siege, when the outer fortifications fell and the people were crammed into the citadel, Sviatoslav Olgovich sued for peace. At first Iziaslav would not hear of it, then considering that it was nearly spring, he made peace and returned towards Chernigov. There he heard from his son Mstislav that he had defeated the Polovetsians on the Ugla and Samara rivers, put them to flight, captured their herds and horses and wagons and liberated a large number of Christians from slavery, sending them home.

After this, in 1154, Yury gathered his forces and made another unsuccessful attack on the Land of Rus. His horses died of a murrain on the way. He halted in the land of the Viatichians before reaching Kozelsk. Here he was joined by the Polovetsians, then on reflection he sent them off into the steppes with his son Gleb, and returned to Suzdal. Some accounts attribute this to the fact that the Polovetsians were far fewer than he expected, and Gleb was sent to hire more barbarians.

This was the end of the wars between Yury and Iziaslav. Yury's chief ally in the East was Sviatoslav Olgovich, who now was forced to make peace on Iziaslav's terms. Yury received more active support from his ally in the West, his daughter's father-in-law Vladimirko of Galich. Iziaslav's wrath must have been greater against him than against Sviatoslav, and he promised vengeance for the slaughter of the Hungarians. As early as 1151, as he was preparing to expel Yury from Gorodets, Iziaslav sent to the king of Hungary, saying "Vladimir of Galich has killed both your retinue and ours. Now, brother, you must consider this matter. God forbid that we leave it thus. We should rather avenge our retinue. Make preparations in your own land, brother, as I shall here. We shall see what God gives us in our struggle." The king replied that he was preparing, at which Iziaslav feared that he would be too long about it and sent his son Mstislav to Hungary to urge his son-in-law on. Géza named a day for them to be ready, and sent a message to Iziaslav, saying "I am on my way, and I bring your son Mstislav with me. Mount up also."

Iziaslav immediately assembled his retinue. Taking with him all Viacheslav's forces, all the Karakalpaks, the foremost men of Kiev and all the retinue of Rus, he set out for Galich. He was joined at Dorogobuzh by his brother Vladimir, at Peresopnitsa by his cousin Vladimir Andreevich and another brother, Sviatopolk, from Vladimir. Iziaslav commanded Sviatopolk to remain in his own town, but took his men with him and advanced. When he crossed the San river he met the king's envoy with a hundred warriors. "Your brother-in-law the king" said the envoy, "greets you. He commands me to say that he has been waiting for you for five days. Make haste to join him!" Iziaslav advanced immediately and approached the Hungarian camp, situated beyond Yaroslavl, the following afternoon. The king and his retinue rode out to meet them, and they embraced, says the chronicle, with great love and honor. They entered the king's tent and considered riding out to give battle early next day at the San river.

DEFEAT OF VLADIMIRKO

At dawn the king ordered the drums beaten, set his troops in order and sent to Iziaslav, saying "Ride with your men beside mine, and stand where I stand, so that we can consider all things together." They came to the San below Peremyshl. Vladimirko awaited them on the opposite bank, and was forced by the Hungarians to give ground. Before the battle began Iziaslav said to his men "Brothers and retinue! God has never let the Land of Rus or the sons of Rus be dishonored. Always have they won themselves honor. Let this be our example now. God grant we win honor in this country and before these foreign armies."

With these words Iziaslav forded the river at the head of his troops. The Hungarians, seeing the Rus already had crossed, followed their example. They attacked the Galich army from different sides and put them to flight. Vladimirko himself, fleeing from the Hungarians, very nearly fell into the hands of the Karakalpaks, barely reaching Peremyshl with one companion. The town certainly would have been taken, for there was no one to defend it. Fortunately for Vladimirko, the prince's court with all its wealth was in the meadows beyond. Here it was that the king's army went, forgetting about the town.

Appreciating the disaster, Vladimirko decided to ask the king for peace. As previously, he sent to the archbishop and the king's officers during the night, pretending to be seriously wounded and at the point of death. "Intercede with the king for me," he told them, "for I am badly wounded. I repent that I grieved him when I killed the Hungarians and by opposing him now. God forgives sins, let the king forgive me now and not give me up to Iziaslav, for I am very sick. If God takes me now, I entrust my son to the king. My lance and my men did great service to the king's father, and I fought for his cause against the Poles. Let the king remember this and forgive me."

Vladimirko sent many gifts of gold, silver, plate and raiment to the archbishop and the Hungarian lords so that they would persuade the king not to destroy him, as Iziaslav's sister the queen would have desired. The next day Géza and Iziaslav met. "I greet you, father," said the king. "Vladimirko has sent to me, pleading and abasing himself, saying that he is seriously wounded and will not live. What say you to this?" "If Vladimirko dies," replied Iziaslav, "it will be God's punishment for his perjury to both of us. Has he ever done anything he has promised you? Furthermore he has put us both to shame, how can we trust him now? Twice has he broken his oath. Now God Himself has given him into our hands, let us take him and his principality."

Mstislav Iziaslavich, who had not forgotten Dorogobuzh, spoke particularly vehemently against Vladimirko, reminding them of his misdeeds. The king, persuaded by the archbishop and lords whom Vladimirko had bribed, would not hear of them. "I cannot kill him," he said, " for he pleads and abases himself and begs pardon for his misdeeds. If he swears now and breaks his oath, either I shall be king of Hungary, or he will be prince of Galich."

Vladimirko also sent to Iziaslav. "Brother," said he, "I bow down to you and repent of everything, I am to blame for everything. Now, brother, receive me and forgive me. Urge the king to receive me, and God grant me to be with you." For his own part Iziaslav would not even hear of peace yet could not oppose the king and his magnates by himself, and had to parlay. The king demanded that Vladimirko return to Iziaslav all the Rus towns he had occupied, and always be his ally in all circumstances, favorable and unfavorable.

When the king was about to send his lords to Vladimirko with the cross that he was to kiss to confirm his oath, Iziaslav said that there was no point in extracting oaths from a man who played with oaths. "This is the wood of the very cross on which Christ our God was crucified," said the king. "It pleased God that it should come into the possession of my ancestor St.

Stephen. If Vladimirko kisses this cross, breaks his oath and remains alive, then I tell you, father, either I shall conquer the land of Galich, or lay down my life in the attempt. Nevertheless for now I cannot kill him."

Iziaslav agreed, but his son Mstislav protested. "You are doing as Christians should," he said, "putting your trust in the Holy Cross and being reconciled with Vladimirko, but I say to you before this holy cross that he will certainly break his oath. Then, O king, do not forget your word, but lead your armies again into Galich." "I tell you truly," said the king, "that if Vladimirko breaks his oath, then as my father Iziaslav has hitherto called upon me for aid, I will call upon him." Vladimirko swore that he would do all that the king commanded. He took the oath in bed, pretending to be suffering from his wounds, whereas in fact he was not wounded at all.

PERFIDY AND DEATH OF VLADIMIRKO

Parting from the king Iziaslav returned to the Land of Rus. While he was at Vladimir he sent his burgraves to the towns which Vladimirko promised to return to him. They all came back because Vladimirko refused them entry to any of the towns. Iziaslav continued on his way to Kiev, sending to the king, saying "Neither of us can turn back now. I only declare to you that Vladimirko has broken his oath. Do not forget your word."

Vladimirko lost no time in breaking another part of his oath. As soon as he heard that his daughter's father-in-law Yury again was marching against Iziaslav he too rode forth, turning back when he discovered that Iziaslav was coming to meet him. Having settled matters with his uncle, Iziaslav sent to Galich his boyar Peter Borislavich, a witness to the oath Vladimirko took on the cross of St. Stephen. He was to tell the prince in Iziaslav's name "You swore to the king and me that you would return the towns of Rus, yet you have not returned them. For now I will not make mention of this. If you are willing to keep your oath and be at peace with us, give me back my towns. If you do not give them back, you are an oathbreaker. The king and I will deal with you as God permits."

"Tell Iziaslav," said Vladimirko, "that he attacked me without provocation and set the king upon me. If I live, I will avenge myself upon him or die in the attempt." "Prince," said Peter, "you swore to Iziaslav and the king that you would make amends and be their ally, which means that you have broken your oath on the cross." "What do I care for a little cross?"

rejoined Vladimirko. "Prince," said the boyar, "though the cross be small, great is its power in heaven and on earth. Did not the king tell you that it was the wood of that very cross upon which Christ was crucified? Were you not told that if you broke your oath on that cross, your life would be forfeit? Did not the king's envoy tell you all this?" "Yes," said Vladimirko, "you told me more than enough then. Now go away and report to your prince."

Peter laid the text of his oath before him and left his presence. When he departed he was given neither carriage nor fodder, having to ride out on his own horses. As Peter left the prince's court Vladimirko was going to vespers in the church. Seeing Peter's departure he laughed, saying "Behold the conquering boyar of Rus going home!" Vladimirko was returning from church after vespers when, passing the spot where he had mocked Peter, he suddenly said "What is this? It is as though someone struck me on the shoulder." He could not move his legs and would have fallen from the staircase had not his men supported him. They carried him into an upper room and laid him upon a bed of herbs. His condition worsened in the evening, and by nightfall he was dead.

Meanwhile Peter Borislavich left Galich, stopping for the night at the village of Bolshovo, where a messenger from Galich found him at dawn, saying that the prince forbade him to ride further. He was to wait there until summoned. Peter, who knew nothing of Vladimirko's death, was dismayed, supposing that he must return and suffer various humiliations. Indeed before noon another messenger arrived with an order from the prince for him to return to the town. Peter set off. When he arrived at the prince's court he was met by the prince's servants all in black. He wondered what this could mean. When he entered the outer hall, he saw Vladimirko's son Yaroslav[42] sitting in the prince's place dressed all in black, with a black cap on his head. All the boyars dressed in black. A chair was brought for Peter. When he sat down, Yaroslav looked at him and wept.

Peter sat in bewilderment, looking from side to side. At length he asked the meaning of what he saw. Then they told him that the prince was dead. "Dead?" he exclaimed. "When I left he was perfectly well!" They exclaimed that he was well, but suddenly clutched at his shoulder, fainted and died. "God's will be done," said Peter. "It will come to us all." "We have summoned you," said Yaroslav then to Peter, " so that God's will be done. Now go to my father Iziaslav, greet him in my name. 'Now that God has taken my father,' tell him, 'be a father to me. As for your dealings with the late prince, God has judged between you. God has taken my father, leaving me in his place. His army and retinue are mine. Only one lance is left by his coffin, and that is in my hands. Now I bow to you, father. Receive me like your son Mstislav. Let Mstislav ride at your stirrup at one side, and I shall ride at the other with all my men.'" This was the message with which Peter departed.

FURTHER HOSTILITIES AGAINST GALICH

Yaroslav or, according to some accounts, his boyars, were merely trying to buy time from Iziaslav, having no intention of returning the towns Vladimirko took. As a result the prince of Kiev undertook another campaign against Galich in 1153, accompanied by his son Mstislav with the men of Pereiaslavl, the men of Iziaslav Davydovich of Chernigov and all the Karakalpaks. On the way they were joined by his brothers Vladimir from Dorogobuzh and Sviatopolk from Vladimir and by Vladimir Andreevich from Brest. Iziaslav encountered Yaroslav's army at Terebovl. Before the battle the Galich boyars urged caution, saying "Prince, you are yet young, ride away and watch us from a distance. Your father fed us and loved us, and we are ready to lay down our lives for his honor and yours. You are the only prince we have. If anything happened to you, what would we do? Go over towards the city, and we shall fight against Iziaslav. If any of us survive, we will come and defend the city with you."

A fierce battle raged from midday till evening, when there was panic on both sides. It was impossible to tell who was the victor. Iziaslav pursued the men of Galich, meanwhile his brothers fled from them. Iziaslav captured some of the boyars of Galich, and the men of Galich captured some of his. It was almost nightfall when the Kievan prince stood with a small retinue on the battlefield and raised the Galich banners. The men of Galich ran to him, thinking that their own men were there, and were taken prisoner. During the night Iziaslav took fright because his retinue was very small, outnumbered in fact by the prisoners. There was also the possibility of Yaroslav's attacking him from Terebovl. On reflection Iziaslav commanded that the prisoners be killed, sparing only the most distinguished. He then retreated towards Kiev because his brothers and retinue had fled in all directions, leaving him no resources to continue the campaign. After this there was great weeping in the land of Galich, says the chronicler.

DEATH OF IZIASLAV

This sad campaign was the last of Iziaslav's career. In 1154, after marrying his second wife, a Georgian princess, Iziaslav buried his brother Sviatopolk. Soon afterwards he himself fell ill and died. The chronicler calls him honorable, noble, pious and glorious, saying that all the Land of Rus and all the Karakalpaks wept for him as for their ruler and lord, but even more as for a father. The reason for the affection in which he was held is that besides his great courage (perhaps the only prince who could compare with him in this respect was Andrei Yurievich), always foremost in battle, pursuing his enemies even when his own forces were in disarray, Iziaslav was also an able tactician and an inventive general. He resembled his famous grandfather in courage and in his kindness to the people, as exemplified by his treatment of them in Kiev and Novgorod. The contrast with the unwelcome rule of his uncle Yury emphasized Iziaslav's good qualities, forcing any who were discontented to hold their peace. Both the citizens and the Karakalpaks, previously indifferent, fought for him with great enthusiasm. His saying, *the place does not become the head, but the head the place*[43] is indicative of his ambition and his position, in all probability serving to justify both his ambitions and the novelty of the position in which they eventually placed him. After all, this proverb justifies placing personal merit above seniority. Indeed, in comparison even with his uncles, who were older, Iziaslav was the only head of the house of Monomakh that suited this place. Nevertheless Iziaslav was forced to give way. He was not successful in asserting his personal qualities or even his right of conquest over the senior throne. Even though he obtained Kiev at risk of his life, eventually he was compelled to recognize the rights and seniority of his uncle Viacheslav, whose head was far from suiting the place.

Iziaslav's premature death dealt an irreparable blow to the rights of the nephews and to Mstislav's line as a whole. None of Iziaslav's brothers was capable of taking his place. His son Mstislav was more energetic and enterprising than any of the uncles, yet could not act without reference to them or against their interests. His position was exactly the same as his father's, only much more difficult. Furthermore the premature death of his father Iziaslav, who had abdicated the seniority in his uncle's favor, must in many people's eyes have disqualified Mstislav as an heir to the throne of Kiev.

DISPUTES OVER THE SUCCESSION

Iziaslav was mourned most of all by his old uncle Viacheslav, who only recently had found peace behind his nephew's shield. "Son," he lamented over his grave, "this should have been my place, but who can oppose the will of God?" All Kiev wept whereas on the other side of the Dnieper there was great rejoicing at Iziaslav's death, and no time was wasted. Iziaslav Davydovich of Chernigov immediately set out for Kiev and at the crossing of the Dnieper he was met by Viacheslav's envoy. "Why have you come," he asked, "and who has called you? Go back home to Chernigov." "I have come to mourn my dead brother," replied Iziaslav. "I was not present at his death, at least let me weep at his grave." Viacheslav, advised by Mstislav Iziaslavich and his boyars, refused to let him enter Kiev.

It his hard to say how justified their suspicions were, though it must be said that in 1153 Iziaslav Davydovich had a meeting with Sviatoslav Olgovich at which the two cousins agreed to make common cause. The arrival of Rostislav Mstislavich from Smolensk[44] was eagerly awaited in Kiev. Meanwhile it was decided to undermine the unity of the princes of Chernigov by winning over Sviatoslav Vsevolodovich, whose family ties, and the fact that only he had any hereditary claim to the throne of Kiev, made it easier for him to side with the sons of Mstislav. "You are Rostislav's beloved son, and mine too," was Viacheslav's message to him. "Come to Kiev and stay here until Rostislav arrives. Then we shall all agree together about the disposition of the principalities."

Sviatoslav Vsevolodovich went to Kiev without telling his uncles, awaiting Rostislav's arrival. When Rostislav arrived, everyone was very glad, says the chronicle, old Viacheslav and all the Land of Rus, and all the Karakalpaks. "Son," said Viacheslav, "I am old, and cannot assume all the burden of government. I give it to you, as your brother held and ruled it. Honor me as your father, respect and treat me as your brother did. My army and retinue are at your disposal." Rostislav bowed to him. "I am heartily glad," said he, "my lord and father. I shall honor you as father and lord, respect you as my brother Iziaslav respected you and obey your will." The citizens, having installed Rostislav, also told him "Treat Viacheslav as your brother Iziaslav treated him, and Kiev will be yours till your death."

Rostislav's first task was to settle with his nephew (his sister's son) Sviatoslav Vsevolodovich, whom he rewarded with Turov and Pinsk for coming to Viacheslav's side and guarding his principality. Sviatoslav gladly accepted this reward. Rostislav had to assure his support with a rich principality because his uncles on the other side of the Dnieper already were acting in concert with Yury of Suzdal, with whom they were in contact even before Rostislav's arrival in Kiev. As a result Yury's son Gleb, who previously was sent to the steppe to recruit as many barbarians as possible, was leading a large force of Polovetsians against Pereiaslavl. He could not take Pereiaslavl, but he took Piriatin on the Uday river. Rostislav and Sviatoslav Vsevolodovich rode out towards the Dnieper and were assembling their retinues when a messenger from Mstislav Iziaslavich of Pereiaslavl brought them news that the Polovetsians were surrounding the city, exchanging arrows with the defenders. Rostislav immediately dispatched his son Sviatoslav, who arrived at Pereiaslavl in time. The next day the Polovetsians began a more serious attack on the town. When they heard that Mstislav had received reinforcements, they were frightened and fled across the Sula. Hearing of their flight, Rostislav took counsel with his brothers and decided to march directly against Iziaslav Davydovich of Chernigov without going back to Kiev. "We must forestall Yury," he said. "Either we must drive him back or make peace with him."

DEATH OF VIACHESLAV

Commanded by the three princes Rostislav, Sviatoslav Vsevolodovich and Mstislav Iziaslavich, the Kievan army and the Torks crossed the Dnieper at Vyshgorod. They were about to set off for Chernigov when a messenger arrived from Kiev bearing tidings of Viacheslav's death. "How can this be?" asked Rostislav. "When we left he was in good health." "Last night he feasted with his retinue," explained the messenger, "he was well when he went to bed, but he lay down never to rise again."

Rostislav immediately rode to Kiev to bury his uncle, distributing all his wealth to the clergy and the poor. Entrusting any remaining business to his mother, Mstislav's widow, he returned to the other side of the Dnieper. When he rejoined his warriors he considered with his nephews and retinue whether he should continue to march against Chernigov. His boyars advised him not to. "Your uncle Viacheslav is dead," they said, "and your position with the citizens of Kiev is unsure. You had better go to Kiev, to confirm your position with the people. Then, if your uncle Yury attacks, you can make peace with him or resist him as you see fit." It is curious that the boyars of Kiev wanted Rostislav to go to the city and arrange his affairs with the citizens, who already had declared that Kiev should be his till his death. In any case, Rostislav had been there just recently. If the people had anything new to tell him, they could have done so after Viacheslav's funeral. The only possible conclusion is that the boyars themselves wanted to go to Kiev and arrange their own affairs after the old prince's death. Perhaps they also wanted the men of Kiev to come to some sort of arrangement with Rostislav concerning the new retinue he brought from Smolensk.

ROSTISLAV MSTISLAVICH ABANDONS KIEV

Whatever the reason, Rostislav did not take their advice, continuing on his way to Chernigov. He sent messengers ahead commanding Iziaslav Davydovich "Swear that you will remain in your patrimony of Chernigov, while we remain in Kiev." "I have done you no harm," replied Iziaslav Davydovich, "nor do I know why you have attacked me. Since you have come, let God decide the outcome." In reality, as the chronicle points out, it was he who sent Gleb Yurievich and his Polovetsians on their way, he who accompanied them to Pereiaslavl. Next day Iziaslav Davydovich, joining forces with Gleb and the Polovetsians, marched against the sons of Mstislav. When Rostislav saw how many they were in comparison with his own small retinue, he was fearful and sent peace proposals to Iziaslav, offering him his own principality of Kiev and his nephew Mstislav's principality of Pereiaslavl.

This unworthy behavior, cowardice and neglect of the interests of his house gave great offense to Mstislav Iziaslavich. "This way neither I shall have Pereiaslavl, nor you Kiev," he said, turning back to Pereiaslavl. Rostislav, abandoned by his nephew, was surrounded by the Polovetsians. After a two-day battle he turned and fled. Pursued by his enemies, he lost his horse. His son Sviatoslav gave him his own and fought off the Polovetsians, thus giving his father time to escape.

Rostislav crossed the Dnieper below Liubech and proceeded to Smolensk. Mstislav Iziaslavich and his cousin Sviatoslav Rostislavich fled to Pereiaslavl, where Mstislav took his wife and went to Lutsk, while Sviatoslav Vsevolodovich was captured by the Polovetsians. Iziaslav Davydovich and his wife ransomed him, and many other Rus besides. They did much good, says the chronicle, for if any prisoner escaped and fled to the town, they did not give him up. Possibly Iziaslav Davydovich did this with a view to gaining popularity in the Land of Rus, where he must have known how strongly disliked his family was. He announced his intention of going to Kiev to appeal to the citizens, who found themselves in an extremely awkward position. Abandoned by Rostislav, they saw that the only thing that could save them from the approaching Polovetsians was to accept Iziaslav Davydovich at once. They sent to him, saying "Come to Kiev, lest the Polovetsians take us. You are our prince, come to us." Iziaslav came to Kiev and sat on the throne, sending Gleb Yurievich to be prince of Pereiaslavl, the lands around which were devastated by their allies the Polovetsians.

YURY DOLGORUKY BECOMES PRINCE OF KIEV

Yury of Rostov would not be content with Pereiaslavl. As soon as he learned of Iziaslav's death and the arrival of Mstislav's other son in Kiev he rode forth towards Smolensk, whose prince was now his chief adversary. Here the news reached him that Viacheslav was dead, Rostislav defeated, Iziaslav Davydovich in Kiev and Gleb in Pereiaslavl. Meanwhile Rostislav, arrived in Smolensk, had time to gather a force and march out against his uncle. Rostislav did not have his brother's courage, nor was he fond of quarrels with his uncles, therefore he sent to Yury asking for peace. "Father," he said, "I bow before you. We were good to each other in former times. Now I bow to you, for an uncle is as a father to me." "You speak truly, son," replied Yury. "I could not get on with Iziaslav, but you are a brother and son to me."

After this exchange the two, in the chronicler's words, swore to love each other. Yury set off for Kiev, Rostislav to Smolensk. Probably his need to make haste to Kiev and his nephew's large army also had some bearing on Yury's peaceful disposition. Not far from Starodub Yury met Sviatoslav Olgovich, his old ally.[45] Sviatoslav Vsevolodovich[46] also came to make his excuses. "I was completely mad," he told Yury. "Forgive me." Sviatoslav Olgovich persuaded Yury to be reconciled with him. Yury compelled him to swear an oath not to desert either himself or his uncle, after which all three went towards Chernigov.

Before they reached the city Sviatoslav Olgovich sent a message to Iziaslav Davydovich in Kiev. "Leave Kiev," he warned, "for Yury is marching against you, and we both invited him." Iziaslav Davydovich did not heed him. Sviatoslav sent to him a second time from Chernigov. "Leave Kiev," he urged, "for Yury is going there, and I am willing to let you have Chernigov for the sake of Christian souls." Iziaslav was very unwilling to leave Kiev, of which, says the chronicler, he had become very fond. Finally he received a message from Yury himself. "Kiev," said he, "is my patrimony, not yours."[47] Since he had neither right nor much popular support on his side, Iziaslav no longer could remain in Kiev. He sent to Yury, saying "Did I come to Kiev of my own accord? It was the people who installed me. Kiev is yours, only do me no harm."[48]

YURY'S ACTIONS AGAINST THE PRINCES OF VOLHYNIA

Yury made peace with him and in 1156 entered Kiev with his four eldest sons, whom he installed in the neighboring principalities: Andrei in Vyshgorod, Boris in Turov, Gleb in Pereiaslavl and Vasilko on the Ros. The descendants of Mstislav, Vladimir and his nephews Mstislav and Yaroslav, reigned in Volhynia. The first of these evidently made peace with Yury, promising to help him fight his nephews, against whom Yury sent his old ally, their enemy Yury Yaroslavich[49] and his grand-nephews, grandsons of his brother Viacheslav. They drove Mstislav from Peresopnitsa to Lutsk. Not even there was he left in peace for long. Yury sent his son-in-law Yaroslav of Galich against him, whereupon Mstislav left his brother Yaroslav in Lutsk, himself riding to seek aid in Poland. The prince of Galich approached Lutsk with Vladimir Mstislavich. After encamping about the town for some time he went away again without doing anything.

YURY COMES TO TERMS WITH OTHER PRINCES

Yury could not continue the war against the sons of Iziaslav because Iziaslav Davydovich, counting on the hostility between Yury and the other members of the house of Monomakh and Yury's unpopularity in Rus, still promoted his own claims. Immediately on his return to Chernigov he tried to persuade Sviatoslav Olgovich to join him in a war against Yury, but Sviatoslav was content to deprive his nephew Sviatoslav Vsevolodovich of three towns (Snovsk, Korachev and Vorotynsk) in exchange for three inferior towns, and had no inclination to take up arms against his old ally.

Yury was probably aware of Iziaslav's intentions. He also was having trouble with the Polovetsians. He sent to his nephew Rostislav Mstislavich in Smolensk. "Son, come to me here," he said, "for I have no one to help me hold onto the Land of Rus." Rostislav came and negotiated a peace between him and his nephews. Vladimir Mstislavich and Yaroslav Iziaslavich even met Yury face to face, but Mstislav Iziaslavich would not, fearing the prince of Kiev might take him prisoner. Having settled his own family affairs, Yury sent an ultimatum to Iziaslav Davydovich. "Come make peace with us," he ordered, "else we shall come to you." Iziaslav Davydovich, seeing that there was now unity within the house of Monomakh, was afraid. He came accompanied by Sviatoslav Olgovich. They came to terms. Yury gave each of them a town on the western side of the Dnieper. Iziaslav got Koretsk in Volhynia, and Sviatoslav received Mozyr in the region of Turov. Yury also married his son Gleb to the daughter of Iziaslav of Chernigov.

FURTHER FEUDING AMONG PRINCES

Though this might have been expected to initiate a reign of peace in all the principalities of Rus, it was not to be. Struggles of the kind that characterized previous years broke out in every corner of the land, feuding between nephews and uncles. In Chernigov, for example, Iziaslav's nephew Sviatoslav, his elder brother Vladimir's son, probably dissatisfied with the lands his uncle gave him, fled from Berezy (near Chernigov) to Vshchizh, seized all the towns along the Desna, cast off allegiance to his uncle and placed himself under the protection of Rostislav Mstislavich of Smolensk. Sviatoslav Vsevolodovich also rebelled against his uncles, who prepared to make war on him. In the event he made peace, although it is not known upon what terms.

At the same time similar events were taking place in Volhynia, ruled by Vladimir Mstislavich and his two nephews Mstislav and Yaroslav Iziaslavich. Mstislav, following his father's example, decided that Vladimir was not suitable for the senior position, for although Vladimir was his uncle, he may well have been younger than Mstislav.[50] Moreover he was the son of Iziaslav's stepmother, Mstislav the Great's second wife, for which reason the chronicles never call him the "uncle" of the sons of Iziaslav, rather their "father's stepmother's son."[51]

Whatever the reason, Mstislav took his uncle by surprise in Vladimir, seized his wife, mother and all his possessions, and forced him to flee to Hungary. Yury, himself a younger uncle, took Vladimir's side and actually undertook a campaign against Mstislav in 1157, on which he was accompanied by his son-in-law Yaroslav of Galich, his sons, his nephew Prince Vladimir Andreevich of Brest, and the Berendey. The princes of Chernigov also wanted to take part, but Yury left them behind on the advice of Yaroslav of Galich.

It soon was apparent that Yury did not begin this war for the sake of Vladimir Mstislavich, rather for his other nephew Vladimir Andreevich. He had sworn to his late brother Andrei,[52] and subsequently to his son, to obtain for him the principality of Vladimir-in-Volhynia. When Yury could not take the city by surprise, he besieged it. While the siege was in progress Vladimir Andreevich obtained Yury's permission to attack the other towns. When he came to Cherven he announced to the citizens "I have not come to make war on you, for you were people beloved of my father, and I am your prince's son. Open the gates to me." In reply one of the citizens loosed an arrow which struck Vladimir in the throat. The wound was not dangerous, and Vladimir repaid the men of Cherven by utterly devastating their lands. Yury besieged Vladimir for ten days without result. Indeed, according to one account, Mstislav mounted a sortie, inflicting a heavy defeat on the Galich regiments. Then, after consulting his sons and retinue, Yury returned to Kiev, Yaroslav to Galich.

Mstislav pursued Yury as far as Dorogobuzh, burning the villages and doing much harm, says the chronicle. When they reached Dorogobuzh, Yury consoled Vladimir Andreevich. "Son," he said, "your father and I swore to each other that whichever of us remained alive would be a father to the other's children and would protect their territory. Later I swore to you to treat you as a son and to obtain Vladimir for you. Having failed to obtain Vladimir, I give you Dorogobuzh for your principality, with Peresopnitsa and all the towns along the Goryn."

DEATH OF YURY AND ACCESSION OF IZIASLAV DAVYDOVICH

The fact that Yury attacked the sons of Iziaslav not for the sàke of Vladimir Mstislavich, and that he deprived them of part of their lands to give to Vladimir Andreevich, could not fail to anger Rostislav of Smolensk, who was obliged to be concerned about the fortunes of the house of Mstislav. This helped Iziaslav Davydovich persuade him to declare war against Yury. It goes without saying that Mstislav of Volhynia needed no encouragement to join the alliance against his great-uncle. Iziaslav Davydovich also tried to persuade Sviatoslav Olgovich to join them, in vain. "I have sworn an oath to Yury," he replied, "so I cannot attack him without cause." This did not prevent the others from continuing with their plans. Iziaslav was to ride out with the men of Chernigov and Smolensk, who were led by Roman, son of Rostislav. At the same time Mstislav Iziaslavich was to strike Yury from the West. The very day that Iziaslav Davydovich intended to set out for Kiev he received a message from the city. "Come to Kiev, prince," it said. "Yury is dead."

This embassy from the citizens of Kiev proves that they were aware of the allies' intentions and that they were ready to accept Iziaslav as their prince. Otherwise they would not have informed him directly of Yury's death or invited him to take the throne. When Iziaslav heard the news he wept. "Blessed art thou, O Lord, " he said, "for judging between us by his death, and not by bloodshed."

On May 10, 1157 Yury was feasting at the house of Petrila the tax collector.[53] He was taken ill during the following night and died five days later. Much evil was done on the day of his funeral (May 16), says the chronicler, for the people plundered the Red Court, and Yury's other court across the Dnieper, which he used to call Paradise, also his son Vasilko's court. The men of Suzdal in the towns and villages were murdered, and their possessions looted. This shows the antipathy felt by Kiev towards Yury and the retinue he brought from the North.[54]

THIRD GENERATION AFTER YAROSLAV

Yury's death marked the end of the third generation of Yaroslav's descendants. This generation was marked by the struggle between younger uncles and their nephews, the sons of their older brothers, and ended in the uncles' triumph, namely the affirmation of the rights of the whole family to succeed to the seniority. During this time both lines of Sviatoslav's descendants, by Oleg and by Davyd, reasserted their rights to the seniority. From events within individual principalities we have noted the activity of Vladimirko and his son Yaroslav in Galich, also of Iziaslav Yaroslavich's descendants, such as Yury Yaroslavich of Turov, of Viacheslav Yaroslavich's grandsons, though it is not known what lands they held. Boris Vsevolodovich, prince of Goroden,[55] a grandson of Davyd Igorevich, also appeared.

EVENTS IN POLOTSK

After Mstislav's death the descendants of Iziaslav Vladimirovich returned to Polotsk from exile, also taking possession of Minsk. Vasilko Sviatoslavich was succeeded as prince of Polotsk by Rogvolod Borisovich,[56] who was married to a daughter of Iziaslav Mstislavich. There is no record of the princes of Polotsk participating in the struggle along the Dnieper, even though Rogvolod might have been expected to take his father-in-law's side. Evidently he lacked either the means or the opportunity to do so. In 1151 the men of Polotsk, not without the other princes' cooperation, seized Rogvolod and sent him to Minsk, where he was confined in considerable hardship. They summoned Gleb Vseslavich's son Rostislav, probably from Minsk, to be their prince. The men of Polotsk evidently were apprehensive that Iziaslav Mstislavich, then at the height of his power, might take steps in support of his son-in-law. They put themselves under the protection of his enemy, Sviatoslav Olgovich of Novgorod Seversk, whom Rostislav Glebovich promised to honor and obey as a father. This alliance between Sviatoslav Olgovich and the prince of Polotsk, the enemy of Iziaslav's son-in-law Rogvolod, may have had some bearing on Iziaslav's hostile actions towards Sviatoslav's friend Yury. It was immediately after this that Iziaslav destroyed Yury's stronghold at Gorodets.

OTHER PRINCIPALITIES

In Murom and Riazan conflict raged between Rostislav Yaroslavich[57] and his nephew Vladimir Sviatoslavich, who was allied with Sviatoslav Olgovich and Yury, while Rostislav was allied with the sons of Mstislav. As a result, Yury's sons drove Rostislav into exile among the Polovetsians in the steppes. It is not known when he returned, but by 1147 the princes of Riazan were subject to Rostislav Mstislavich of Smolensk, regarding him as their father, and placing themselves at his disposal. In 1152 Rostislav Yaroslavich of Murom and his brothers were fighting on Yury's side against his nephews, then in 1154 Rostislav and Yury were enemies once more. Yury, on his way back from Kozelsk, expelled Rostislav from his principality and gave it to his own son Andrei. Rostislav soon returned with a Polovetsian army, attacked Andrei at night and slaughtered his retinue. Andrei himself escaped wearing only one boot and fled from Riazan to Murom, thence to Suzdal. Finally in 1155 Rostislav Mstislavich again swore friendship to the princes of Riazan, who again promised to look to him as a father.

NOVGOROD

Last we saw, the prince of Novgorod was Sviatopolk Mstislavich, and the mayor as before was Sudila. Sviatopolk was made prince of Novgorod by Vsevolod Olgovich, thus he could not dismiss an old friend of the sons of Oleg. Only in 1144, a year or so later, Sudila's comrade Nezhata Tverdiatich was made mayor.[58] The death of Vsevolod Olgovich and Iziaslav Mstislavich's assumption of the throne of Kiev did little to change the course of events in Novgorod. Sviatopolk remained on the throne but Nezhata, a friend of the sons of Oleg, was replaced as mayor by Konstantin Mikulich, a partisan of the sons of Mstislav, who suffered for his allegiance when detained by Vsevolod in Kiev. When Konstantin died in 1147 he was replaced by Sudila Ivanovich, who evidently improved his relations with the Monomakh party.[59]

Meanwhile Novgorod was at war with its neighbor Yury of Rostov. In 1147 Sviatopolk led its entire forces against him, but was forced to turn back at Torzhok because of the state of the roads. The next year Archbishop Nifont went to Suzdal to seek peace with Yury, who received him well and released at his request all the men of Novgorod and merchants whom he had detained. He allowed them to return honorably to Novgorod, but would not make peace. This was the year when Iziaslav removed his brother Sviatopolk from Novgorod "on account of his vindictiveness" and replaced him with his son Yaroslav. Some very credible accounts aver that Iziaslav removed Sviatopolk for allowing the men of Novgorod to conduct peace talks with Yury without his knowledge. This may be connected with the election of Yury's friend Sudila as mayor.

Iziaslav's visit to Novgorod and his campaign against Rostov have been described. It would seem that it won him long-lasting popularity in the city, for during his protracted struggle with his uncle Yury, who frequently had the upper hand, Novgorod remained loyal to Yaroslav Iziaslavich and hostile to Yury, even though this was often to their detriment. For example in 1149 a small company of the men of Novgorod went to collect tribute in the Dvina region. When Yury heard that they were few in number he sent the notorious Ivan Berladnik, evidently in his service at the time, to intercept them. Ivan did not succeed, for the men of Novgorod resisted him and there were many casualties on both sides, considerably more among the men of Suzdal, according to the Novgorod chronicle.[60]

Although the citizens of Novgorod kept Yaroslav as their prince during the period of his father's setbacks, they suddenly expelled him in 1154. The chronicle does not say why, but it appears that Yaroslav broke the peace, that is to say he was the cause of factional strife. To settle this the citizens invited Rostislav Mstislavich of Smolensk to be their prince, which demonstrates that they did not intend a break with the sons of Mstislav or the prince of Kiev. Rostislav could not have taken the throne of Novgorod without his elder brother's agreement.[61]

Rostislav failed to restore order. When, on his brother's death, he was summoned to Kiev, he left his son Davyd in Novgorod in the most unfavorable circumstances. The people were highly dissatisfied with his latest decisions. According to the chronicle, they were angry with him because he stirred even more trouble instead of calming the city. They soon banished Davyd,[62] offering the throne to Yury's son Mstislav. The fact that Yury soon was established on the throne of Kiev meant that his son was firmly established in Novgorod.

Yury did not enjoy his throne in peace for long. Likewise the peace of Novgorod was short-lived. The alliance of all the descendants of Mstislav with Iziaslav Davydovich against Yury was the occasion for their party to take the initiative in Novgorod. In 1156 Yakun Miroslavich replaced Sudila as mayor. In 1157 there was a bitter division within the city, and an attempt to expel Mstislav Yurievich by force of arms. The prince gained his own adherents. The Market Side[63] took his part, and there nearly was bloodshed. The arrival of Sviatoslav Rostislavich and his brother Davyd, and the flight of Mstislav, meant that the party in favor of the descendants of Mstislav Vladimirovich was victorious. Three days later Rostislav himself arrived from Smolensk. This time he could arrange a reconciliation. No harm was done, says the chronicle. When Rostislav departed he left his son Sviatoslav in Novgorod, sending Davyd to Torzhok, evidently to secure the frontier with Suzdal.[64]

RELATIONS WITH NEIGHBORING PEOPLES

As for foreign relations, the conflicts continued with the tribal peoples on the borders, Polovetsians in the South and Finnic tribes in the North. The feud between Yury and his nephew Iziaslav gave the Polovetsians an opportunity to enrich themselves at the expense of Rus. When Yury became prince of Kiev in 1155 the country along the Ros received a prince of its own, Yury's son Vasilko. The Polovetsians were not slow in visiting him in his new dominions, but Vasilko and the Berendey defeated them and he returned to his father with honor and glory, says the chronicle. Soon after this Yury went to confer with the Polovetsian khans at Kanev. They requested the return of the prisoners taken by the Berendey at the recent battle, which the Berendey refused to give up. "We die for the Land of Rus with your son," they told Yury, "and lay down our lives for your honor." Yury did not want to take their captives from them by force, for it would have been dangerous to irritate a people which guarded his borders. He bestowed gifts on the Polovetsians and dismissed them.

This incident sheds light on the relations between the princes and the barbarians of the marches who fought for their honor. The same year, when the Polovetsians again appeared on the frontier to discuss peace, Yury set off to these peace talks as though embarking upon a war. He took both the sons of Mstislav, Rostislav and Vladimir, accompanied by Yaroslav Iziaslavich and a detachment of Galich troops. He sent to the Polovetsians, saying "Come and make peace with me." At first only a small group of Polovetsians came to see the size of Yury's force, telling him they would all come the following day. In fact they all fled during the night. As for the North, in 1149 the Finns (Häme) made war on the Vod region of the Novgorod territories. A company of five hundred men of Novgorod and Vod went out to meet them and killed or captured them all.[65]

BOYARS AND OTHER MEMBERS OF PRINCES' ENTOURAGES

As for the boyars who were active during this period, Monomakh's boyar Ivan Voitishich continued to serve his son Mstislav, accompanied the Torks against the princes of Polotsk, and remained in Kiev under Vsevolod Olgovich, who sent him to restore order in Novgorod. He acted together with the other boyars against Vsevolod's brother Igor and in favor of Monomakh's grandson. In Monomakh's time the chiliarch of Pereiaslavl was one Stanislav. The chronicler mentions a Stanislav Dobry Tukievich as one of the boyars slain at Yaropolk's battle on the Supoy. It is reasonable to assume that this was the former chiliarch of Pereiaslavl, the son of Tuki the brother of Chudin, mentioned earlier. Yaropolk's chiliarch of Kiev, Davyd Yarunovich, fell in the same battle. It is not known who was his immediate successor. Under Vsevolod Olgovich the office was filled by Uleb, who acted in favor of Iziaslav Mstislavich and against Igor Olgovich. He was Iziaslav Mstislavich's envoy to the sons of Davyd in 1147. Uleb's confederates were Lazar Sakovsky, who succeeded him as chiliarch, Vasily Polochanin and Miroslav (Andreevich) the grandson of Khila.

The name of Vasil is recorded as belonging to one of Sviatopolk's boyars. Vasil was for a certain time burgrave of Vladimir-in-Volhynia. If this were the same man he would have been seventy-five or eighty years old in 1146. Miroslav was the name of one of the boyars involved in Monomakh's legislation. After Iziaslav's overthrow of Igor those boyars who supported the sons of Oleg were taken prisoner. These were not necessarily boyars of Chernigov, they may have been old boyars of Kiev who took their part. Their names were Danilo Veliky, Yury Prokopich, and Ivor Yurievich, grandson of Miroslav. In connection with the patronymic of the second, it may be remembered that a certain Prokopy, chiliarch of Belgorod, took part in Monomakh's legislation against usury.

During the siege of Novgorod Seversk by the sons of Davyd and Mstislav Iziaslavich in 1146, Dmitry Zhiroslavich and Andrei Lazarevich were killed. If Andrei Lazarevich was with Mstislav, he may have been the son of Lazar Sakovsky. The account of the murder of Igor Olgovich in Kiev in 1147 mentions the same Lazar Sakovsky, at that time chiliarch of Kiev, Vladimir Mstislavich's chiliarch Raguilo Dobrynich (possibly the son of the Dobrynia or Dobrynka who was a boyar in Iziaslav Mstislavich's retinue), and another of Vladimir's boyars, Mikhail, who helped the prince defend Igor from his assassins.

The envoys whom Iziaslav sent to Kiev on the occasion of the treachery of the princes of Chernigov were Dobrynko and Radil. It is interesting that Lazar became chiliarch during the lifetime of his predecessor Uleb, who was with Iziaslav's army at the time. Perhaps he resigned his office as a result of the men of Kiev refusing to fight for Iziaslav against Yury. Iziaslav Mstislavich's commander Shvarn, who failed to hold the ford at Zarub, is mentioned in 1151. The next year, Iziaslav's boyar Peter Borislavich or Borisovich was sent as Iziaslav's envoy to Vladimirko of Galich. Finally, the chronicle mentions Petrila the tax collector, with whom Yury Dolgoruky was feasting shortly before his death.

Among the boyars of Viacheslav Vladimirovich of Turov, his chiliarch Ivanko, who accompanied the prince on Grand Prince Mstislav's campaign against Polotsk in 1127, is mentioned. He may be identical to the Ivanko Zakharich who has been mentioned before. His son Zhiroslav Ivankovich[66] is mentioned several times. In 1146 Viacheslav was encouraged by his boyars to take on the role of senior prince without consulting his nephew Iziaslav, who had deprived him of Turov, imprisoning both Bishop Joachim and the burgrave Zhiroslav. This suggests that Zhiroslav was one of Viacheslav's chief counsellors. Later, somehow having regained his liberty, Zhiroslav appeared in Yury of Rostov's retinue. He accompanied Yury's son Gleb to the South, urging him to attack Pereiaslavl, asserting that the men of Pereiaslavl would come over to them willingly. He may also have been commander of the Polovetsian troops in Yury's war with Iziaslav in 1149. Finally, in 1155 Yury sent Zhiroslav to expel Mstislav Iziaslavich from Peresopnitsa.

Andrei Vladimirovich's Volhynian boyars include the chiliarch Vratislav. Galich boyars mentioned are Ivan Khaldeevich, who defended Zvenigorod so vigorously against Vsevolod Olgovich in 1146, and Izbygnev Ivachevich, who was Vladimirko's only companion as he fled from the battlefield to Peresopnitsa in 1152. Finally Ksniatin or Konstantin Seroslavich was Yaroslav's envoy to Yury Dolgoruky in 1157.

Sviatoslav Olgovich of Severia had a boyar named Kosniatko, who acted as intermediary between his prince and the sons of Davyd at Chernigov in 1146. There was also Peter Ilyich, who was one of Oleg Sviatoslavich's boyars and who died in 1147 at the age of ninety, too old to ride any more. The chronicler calls him a good old man. Vsevolod Olgovich's agents Ratsha in Kiev and Tudor in Vyshgorod caused great resentment among the people by their depredations. A certain Yury is mentioned as chiliarch of Rostov in 1130. At the battle with Gleb Yurievich at Pereiaslavl in 1118 Mstislav Iziaslavich captured a certain son of Stanislav, whom he put to a cruel death, probably for intriguing with the men of Pereiaslavl. Perhaps this was the son of the earlier chiliarch of Pereiaslavl, Stanislav Tukievich.

VII

FROM THE DEATH OF YURY VLADIMIROVICH TO THE SACK OF KIEV BY ANDREI BOGOLIUBSKY, 1157-1169

IZIASLAV DAVYDOVICH IN KIEV

For the second time a descendant of Sviatoslav, this time of the line of Davyd, inherited the seniority and Kiev. Iziaslav Davydovich's success was due to the same combination of circumstances as brought his cousin Vsevolod Olgovich to Kiev.[1] The senior of the line of Monomakh was Rostislav Mstislavich,[2] who was not at all like his valiant brother, with whom alone he could act successfully. His inadequacy was painfully apparent when he came to act alone as head of the family. His flight before Iziaslav Davydovich's armies after Viacheslav's death hardly augured well for his chances in a renewed struggle with the same prince. There is no doubt that when Rostislav formed his alliance against Yury with the prince of Chernigov he renounced his claims to the seniority in favor of Iziaslav, who did indeed belong to his father's generation. Mstislav Iziaslavich,[3] the most able and energetic of the descendants of Mstislav, could not take unilateral action either in support of his uncle or in opposition to him, still less on his own account. His father's career made it abundantly clear that no good would come of flying in the face of the prevailing understanding of the rights of uncles, particularly the older.

DISPUTES OVER SUCCESSION TO CHERNIGOV

So Iziaslav Davydovich came to Kiev again, this time with the agreement of all the descendants of Monomakh. Nothing was heard, at least, of Yury's son Andrei Bogoliubsky. Iziaslav's translation to the throne of Kiev inevitably brought about changes in Chernigov, which itself should have been inherited by Sviatoslav Olgovich.[4] He was not only the next in seniority in Sviatoslav's line, but also in the whole family. Accordingly Sviatoslav and his nephew Sviatoslav Vsevolodovich[5] appeared before the walls of Chernigov, where they were prevented from entering the city by Iziaslav's nephew Sviatoslav Vladimirovich,[6] whom Iziaslav left there with his entire army when he proceeded to Kiev. It should be noted that the chronicle says that Iziaslav *left* him there, not that he *installed* him, indicating that Iziaslav did not intend to make Sviatoslav Vladimirovich prince of Chernigov. He merely wanted to exclude Sviatoslav Olgovich, with whom he was on bad terms since he had refused to join him in an alliance against Yury. When they were not allowed to enter Chernigov, the sons of Oleg withdrew to the banks of the Svina. Iziaslav Davydovich soon appeared on the opposite bank with his army and Mstislav Iziaslavich.

There was no battle. It would have been hard for Iziaslav to keep Chernigov for himself, and strange for him to have given it to his nephew rather than his uncle. Both courses would have been equally opposed to prevailing notions. Therefore, after an exchange of messages between the cousins, it was agreed that Sviatoslav Olgovich receive Chernigov, and Sviatoslav Vsevolodovich have Novgorod Seversk. Sviatoslav Olgovich did not receive the whole principality of Chernigov, for Iziaslav retained a large part for himself and his nephew Sviatoslav Vladimirovich. Mozyr, which Yury previously ceded to Sviatoslav Olgovich, also was incorporated into the principality of Kiev.

CONTENTION FOR TUROV

Curious events also took place in the West around Turov. When Yury established himself in Kiev, he gave Turov to his son Boris. After Yury's death, given the general disaffection towards him in the South, Boris could not maintain himself there and was replaced, very probably driven out, by Yury Yaroslavich,[7] a descendant of Iziaslav Yaroslavich.[8] Neither Iziaslav Davydovich nor the family of Mstislav were prepared to see such a significant principality in the hands of such a dispossessed prince, especially as apparently they had agreed to give it to Mstislav's youngest son Vladimir, who had no principality. Iziaslav therefore set off for Turov against Yury Yaroslavich, accompanied by Vladimir Mstislavich, Yaroslav Iziaslavich from Lutsk, Yaropolk Andreevich on behalf of his brother in Dorogobuzh, Riurik Rostislavich on behalf of his father in Smolensk, and detachments from Polotsk and Galich. Mstislav Iziaslavich of Volhynia did not participate, presumably because he did not want to help his uncle, with whom he was on bad terms, win a powerful principality, for if the campaign was a success he could turn out to be a dangerous neighbor.

The territories of Turov and Pinsk were devastated, but Yury continued to fight steadfastly in his sorties from Turov. Nevertheless he saw that he could not hope to defeat so many enemies. He sent to Iziaslav, asking to be received in friendship. Iziaslav refused, for he still wanted to take Turov and Pinsk. After ten weeks' fruitless siege he was forced to withdraw because of the onset of a murrain amongst his horses. The dispossessed prince Yury Yaroslavich was left to reign in peace in Turov, while Vladimir Mstislavich remained landless as ever.[9]

IZIASLAV DAVYDOVICH DEFENDS IVAN BERLADNIK

In the following year, 1158, there were disturbances in Galich leading to the expulsion of Iziaslav Davydovich from Kiev and its return to the house of Monomakh. Once again we encounter the exiled prince of Galich, Ivan Rostislavich Berladnik,[10] who was forced to take service under various princes. Last time we saw him in the North serving Dolgoruky, who sent him to intercept the men of Novgorod. When Yury became prince of Kiev he needed the support of his son-in-law Yaroslav of Galich, and agreed to surrender the unfortunate Berladnik. He was brought in chains from Suzdal to Kiev, where Yaroslav's envoys were expected with a large retinue.

The clergy were indignant at such baseness. The metropolitan and all the abbots told Yury that it was a sin for him to inflict such hardship on Ivan, to whom he had sworn his oath, and especially now to send him to his death. Accordingly, instead of handing Berladnik over to the the the men of Galich, Yury sent him back to Suzdal in chains. When Iziaslav Davydovich heard of it, he sent his men to intercept him and brought him to Chernigov. After Iziaslav succeeded Yury in Kiev, Berladnik remained at complete liberty in Chernigov, where he had every opportunity to communicate with the disaffected in Galich. This was obviously disquieting to Yaroslav, who according to the chronicler sought a way to lay hands on his cousin Ivan, persuading all the princes of Rus, the king of Hungary and the Polish princes to assist him.

It is hard to say what moved them all to agree to his request, or why they hated the unfortunate Berladnik, unless perhaps for taking one prince's money and then moving on to a second and a third. It may also be that Yaroslav inherited his father's cunning and promised each something he wanted. Be that as it may, only Iziaslav Davydovich continued to defend Berladnik. When he received an embassy from almost all the princes of Rus (Yaroslav of Galich, Sviatoslav Olgovich, Rostislav Mstislavich, Mstislav Iziaslavich, Yaroslav Iziaslavich, Vladimir Andreevich and Sviatoslav Vsevolodovich), the king of Hungary and the Polish princes, demanding that he hand Berladnik over, he defied them all, sending them on their way with an outright refusal.

Berladnik took fright at the almost universal alliance against him and fled to the Polovetsians in the steppes, with whose help he occupied the towns along the Danube, seized two Galich ships and terrorized Galich fishermen. He attracted many Polovetsians, also six thousand "Berladniks," exiles and cossacks like himself. He led them into Galich, where he took the town of Kuchelmina and besieged Ushitsa. Yaroslav's garrison defended it well, but about three hundred of the common people climbed over the wall and joined Ivan's men. The Polovetsians wanted to take the town, but Ivan would not let them, which made them angry, so the barbarians abandoned him. Meanwhile Iziaslav sent for him to lead the rest of his men to Kiev and join in the preparations for war.

The Southern branch of Monomakh's line, whose effective leader was Mstislav Iziaslavich of Volhynia, found a convenient opportunity to expel Iziaslav Davydovich from Kiev and bring it back into their own family. All the princes were enraged with Iziaslav for his refusal to extradite Berladnik, causing Mstislav and Vladimir Andreevich to ally against him with Yaroslav of Galich. Seeing the danger, Iziaslav did what he could to reconcile himself at least with the princes of his own line. He sent to Sviatoslav Olgovich, ceding to him Mozyr and Chichersk, two towns in the principality of Kiev. "To tell the truth, brother," replied Sviatoslav, "I was angry with you for not giving me the whole principality of Chernigov, still I did not wish you any harm. If they intend to make war on you now, God forbid that I should stay at home. You are my cousin. God grant us a good life together." The princes of Sviatoslav's line, namely Sviatoslav Olgovich and his sons, together with Sviatoslav

Vsevolodovich, Iziaslav Davydovich and Sviatoslav Vladimirovich, all gathered at Lutava, four versts from the Oster. For three days, according to the chronicler, they affirmed their friendship and exchanged large gifts. They immediately sent messengers to Galich and Volhynia announcing to the local princes their close alliance, thereby achieving their aim, in that Yaroslav and Mstislav abandoned their campaign. .

Iziaslav saw he had attained merely a short respite. The news from Vladimir was that Yaroslav of Galich and Mstislav of Volhynia still thought of marching on Kiev. He decided to forestall them. The circumstances were favorable, because Berladnik had just received an invitation from the men of Galich, saying that as soon as they saw his banners they would desert Yaroslav. Only by deposing Yaroslav and elevating Berladnik in his place could Iziaslav feel secure in Kiev. Therefore he sent to the sons of Oleg asking for military assistance. The prince of Chernigov either could not or would not see why Iziaslav needed this war. "Brother," he said repeatedly, "for whom are you seeking a principality, your brother or your son? It would be better for you not to be the aggressor. If they attack you in their arrogance, God will be on your side, and so will my nephews and I." Moreover when Iziaslav despite these admonitions set out, Sviatoslav's envoy came to him at Vasiliev. "Your cousin says that you should not begin a war," was his message. "He says you should go back."

Understandably annoyed, Iziaslav could not restrain his anger. "Tell my cousin," he told the envoy, "that I will not go back once I have set out. Tell him also that if he does not accompany me and let his sons come also, he is not to complain when, God willing, after I have succeeded in my purpose in Galich he finds himself crawling from Chernigov to Novgorod Seversk." Sviatoslav was mortally offended at these words. "Lord," he said, "thou seest my humility. I did not seek my own gain, all I desired was that Christian blood not be spilt and that my patrimony not be destroyed. I accepted Chernigov and seven empty towns inhabited only by kennelmen and Polovetsians,[11] while he holds the whole principality of Chernigov for himself and his nephew. That is not enough for him, for he tells me I must leave Chernigov. So, brother, God and the Holy Cross which you kissed when you swore not to seek by any means to deprive me of Chernigov, will judge between us. I did not wish you ill when I told you not to go to war. I desired only good and the peace of the Land of Rus."

DEFEAT OF IZIASLAV

Meanwhile Iziaslav was joined by his nephew, whom he sent to fetch the Polovetsians. He awaited him a short distance from Kiev. They advanced towards Belgorod, occupied by the Galich-Volhynian alliance. Iziaslav besieged them there, confident of success, for he had twenty thousand Polovetsians, then he was betrayed by the Berendey. Either hoping to profit by the change, or else genuinely well-disposed towards the son of their beloved prince Iziaslav, they communicated with the defenders, sending a message to Mstislav. "Prince," they urged, "your fortunes depend upon us. If you will love us as your father loved us and give us better towns, we shall desert Iziaslav."

Mstislav was delighted with this offer. That very night he swore to do as they wanted. The Berendey wasted no time. At midnight they galloped to Belgorod with loud cries. Iziaslav realized that the barbarians were up to no good, mounted his horse and rode to their camp. Seeing that it was on fire, he turned back. Taking his nephew Sviatoslav Vladimirovich and the landless Vladimir Mstislavich, he fled towards the Dnieper, to Vyshgorod. He waited for his wife to join him at Gomel, and invaded the land of the Viatichians, which he occupied in return for Sviatoslav Vsevolodovich's failure either to lead his men in person or to send his son in support. Sviatoslav took his revenge on his uncle's boyars, seizing their possessions and wives everywhere and holding them to ransom.

ROSTISLAV MSTISLAVICH BECOMES PRINCE OF KIEV

Now that the Berendey had raised the siege, Mstislav and his two allies entered Kiev and seized the possessions of Iziaslav's retinue, which he sent to his own city of Vladimir-in-Volhynia. Then he sent to Smolensk to call his uncle Rostislav to come and take the senior throne, because before the campaign the allies all had sworn to obtain Kiev for him. Rostislav understood how awkward his position would be in Kiev, where he was hardly much loved or respected since he had fled from Iziaslav. The leader of the military operations was his brave and energetic nephew, who like his father before him had obtained Kiev by his own efforts and only resigned it to his uncle out of necessity. Rostislav may well have decided that his nephew intended to treat him as Iziaslav had treated his uncle Viacheslav, displaying outward respect, calling him father, at the same time being the real ruler.

Therefore Rostislav sent this reply. "If you call me in truth and love, I shall come to Kiev to do as I see fit. You must really regard me as a father and obey me. First of all I tell you that I do not want Klim as metropolitan[12] because he has not received the blessing of the Holy Wisdom or the patriarch." Mstislav was firmly on Klim's side, and on no account would acknowledge the metropolitanate of the Greek Constantine, who had anathematized his father Iziaslav. Then Rostislav sent his eldest son Roman[13] to Vyshgorod to reach some agreement with Mstislav about the metropolitan. After long and hard discussion they agreed to depose both Klim and Constantine, and accept a new metropolitan from Constantinople.

RECONCILIATION BETWEEN PRINCES OF KIEV AND CHERNIGOV

Having come to this agreement with his nephew, Rostislav entered Kiev in 1159 and occupied the throne of his father and grandfather. Mstislav received Belgorod, Torchesk and Tripol within the principality of Kiev. Since Iziaslav Davydovich was their common enemy, the princes of Kiev and Chernigov needed to unite against him. Indeed they soon met at Moravsk with great friendship, as the chronicle says. The princes dined together without any particular occasion and exchanged gifts. Rostislav gave Sviatoslav sables, ermines, black martens, arctic foxes, white wolves and walrus tusks. Sviatoslav gave Rostislav a snow leopard and two horses with wrought saddles.

The chronicler found it necessary to add that the princes, descendants of Monomakh and Oleg, entertained each other without any particular occasion, for this alliance seemed strange and suspicious in Kiev. Nothing good was expected of Sviatoslav Olgovich, who was the perpetual enemy of the sons of Mstislav and the ally of Yury. Neither did anyone think he had forgotten his brother Igor's murder. To calm the fears of the men of Kiev and the Berendey Rostislav had to receive Sviatoslav Vsevolodovich's son Vsevolod in exchange for his son Riurik, whom he sent to Chernigov to assist Sviatoslav against Iziaslav Davydovich.

IZIASLAV DAVYDOVICH'S ATTEMPTS TO REGAIN THE THRONE

Iziaslav was not wasting his time in the land of the Viatichians. He recruited a large company of Polovetsians and led them along the Desna. He could do nothing but destroy the villages because Sviatoslav Olgovich's troops would not let him cross the river. Nevertheless Sviatoslav Olgovich and Sviatoslav Vsevolodovich felt that their forces were inadequate, and sent to Kiev for reinforcements. Rostislav sent them Yaroslav Iziaslavich of Lutsk, Vladimir Andreevich of Dorogobuzh and a detachment from Galich. Iziaslav was afraid and retreated into the steppe with his Polovetsians. He was overtaken by a messenger from his sympathizers in Chernigov telling him not to go away. His cousin Sviatoslav Olgovich was ill, his nephew Sviatoslav Vsevolodovich had dismissed his retinue and retreated to Novgorod Seversk. Receiving this news Iziaslav set off with all haste for Chernigov where Sviatoslav, knowing nothing of all this, was sitting quietly in his tents before the walls with his wife and children. Suddenly he received word that Iziaslav was crossing the Desna and the Polovetsians were burning the villages. Sviatoslav immediately set his own troops in order and recalled Vladimir Andreevich and Riurik, who appeared with the men of Galich that very day. Consequently Iziaslav, failing to take Sviatoslav by surprise, found him with a large and well-ordered army.

Meanwhile the Berendey attacked the Polovetsians and defeated them. When Iziaslav saw that some of the Polovetsians were wounded and in flight, and others were drowning in the Desna, he wanted to know why. Told that there was a large army at Chernigov, he made haste back across the Desna and into the steppe. His enemies set about devastating the areas they occupied, then Iziaslav soon returned with a large Polovetsian force, moved from the principality of Chernigov to that of Smolensk, and wrought terrible devastation. The Polovetsians took over ten thousand captives, besides the men they killed.

Finding himself opposed by both Rostislav and Sviatoslav, Iziaslav turned to the northern prince, Andrei Yurievich, who reigned at Vladimir-on-the-Kliazma. Iziaslav sent to him to ask for his daughter's hand in marriage to his nephew Sviatoslav Vladimirovich, prince of Vshchizh, and for aid at the same time, for the bridegroom was besieged in his town by Sviatoslav Olgovich, Sviatoslav Vsevolodovich and Riurik Rostislavich. Andrei sent him his son Iziaslav[14] with his own men and those of Murom. News of the approach of this large force from Rostov first caused Sviatoslav to retreat from Vshchizh. When Andrei's forces returned to Rostov, Sviatoslav and his allies returned to Vshchizh, besieged it for five weeks, and forced Sviatoslav Vladimirovich to renounce the alliance with his uncle. He had to acknowledge the seniority of his cousin once removed Sviatoslav Olgovich, regard him as a father and obey him.

Despite all these setbacks Iziaslav had no thought of surrender. At Kiev and in the steppe borderlands Rostislav's close alliance with Sviatoslav Olgovich was regarded with disapproval and suspicion. Iziaslav could use this malaise to break the alliance between Kiev and Chernigov which had denied him all possibility of success. There is an account according to which he did indeed attempt this, suborning the boyars of both cities to sow discord between the princes. He was unsuccessful. The princes at first did not believe what they were told, remained in communication and grew more firmly allied than ever before. To improve Sviatoslav Olgovich's standing with the men of Kiev and the barbarian inhabitants of the marches, who played such an important part in the affairs of Southern Rus, Rostislav asked the prince of Chernigov to send him his son Oleg. He wished to introduce him to the leading personages among the men of Kiev, the Berendey and the Torks. Sviatoslav, suspecting nothing, agreed and sent his son, who was very well received by Rostislav and dined with him two days in succession. On the third day he left his tents to go hunting, and encountered a certain boyar of Kiev. "Prince," said the boyar, "I have important business with you. Swear that you will say nothing to anyone." Oleg swore, and the boyar warned him that there were plans to take him prisoner. Oleg believed him. On the pretext of his mother's illness he asked Rostislav to allow him to go back to Chernigov. Rostislav, though at first unwilling, let him go.

It should be stressed that the chronicle completely exonerates Rostislav and places all blame on the boyars. The prince, it says, had no evil intentions. It was all the fault of wicked men who did not desire to see good among the brethren. Oleg on his return to Chernigov said nothing to his father, but was secretly angry with him and asked to be allowed to go to Kursk. Sviatoslav, being unaware of anything, let him go. On the way he was met by Iziaslav Davydovich's emissaries with friendly words, inviting him to ally himself with their prince, informing him that his cousins Sviatoslav Vsevolodovich and Yaroslav Vsevolodovich already had done so. Oleg told all this to his boyars. "Prince," said they, "is it good that they wanted to take you prisoner in Kiev, or take Chernigov away from your father? After this you would both be justified in swearing allegiance to him." Oleg took their advice and allied himself with Iziaslav without consulting his father.

When old Sviatoslav was told that the sons of Vsevolod and his own son Oleg had allied with Iziaslav, he was grieved and told his boyars. "It is a wonder to us, prince," they replied, "that you complain of your nephews and Oleg without taking thought for your own safety. It is no lie that Roman Rostislavich sent his priest from Smolensk to say to Iziaslav 'Live in peace with me, for my father gives you Chernigov.' Rostislav himself wanted to take your son prisoner in Kiev. Prince, you have ruined your lands by your alliance with Rostislav, who does not exert himself to aid you."

Thus, says the chronicle, was Sviatoslav reluctantly detached from Rostislav's friendship and won over to Iziaslav, who was not slow in making use of this favorable turn of events. Assembling a large body of Polovetsians he joined forces with the sons of Vsevolod from Novgorod Seversk, with Sviatoslav Vladimirovich and with Oleg Sviatoslavich. In spite of everything, Sviatoslav Olgovich did not march with him but remained in Chernigov. Iziaslav also wanted to bring his son-in-law Gleb Yurievich, prince of Pereiaslavl, into the alliance against Rostislav, but he would not join. Consequently the allies went to Pereiaslavl and wasted two weeks besieging it.

Rostislav made use of this delay to assemble a large army and march towards the Dnieper. When he arrived at Tripol, Iziaslav heard of his approach and fled. All the Polovetsians vanished into the steppes. Probably the defection of the Polovetsians, who never liked to fight against large armies, caused Iziaslav to decamp. As soon as Rostislav returned to Kiev and dismissed his troops, Iziaslav regrouped, crossed the frozen Dnieper at Vyshgorod and appeared before Kiev. There was no one with Rostislav except his cousin Vladimir Andreevich. After a bloody battle which seemed like Armageddon to the chronicler, Iziaslav gained the upper hand, and the Polovetsians were breaking through the palisade into the city. "Prince," Rostislav's boyars said to him, "your brothers are not here, neither are the Berendey or the Torks. The enemy's strength is great. You would do better to go to Belgorod and wait for assistance there." Rostislav did as they advised and took his troops and his princess to Belgorod. There he was joined that very day by his nephew Yaroslav Iziaslavich of Lutsk and his brother Yaropolk, while Vladimir Andreevich went to Torchesk to fetch the Torks and Berendey.

DEFEAT AND DEATH OF IZIASLAV DAVYDOVICH

Iziaslav entered his beloved Kiev for the third time and issued an amnesty for all of its citizens whom he had captured. Immediately he set off to besiege Rostislav in Belgorod. Sviatoslav of Chernigov once more sent to him telling him to make peace. "Even if they will not make peace with you, go back across the Dnieper. Once you are on the other side, you will be in the right." "When my brethren cross the Dnieper," Iziaslav replied, "each will go to his own principality. Where shall I go? I cannot go to the Polovetsians, neither do I wish to starve on the banks of the Vyr. Better that I should die here."

For four weeks he besieged the citadel of Belgorod to no avail, while Mstislav Iziaslavich from Vladimir led the men of Galich to relieve his uncle. Riurik Rostislavich, Vladimir Andreevich and Vasilko Yurievich approached from the other side, from Torchesk, bringing a huge army of Berendey, Koui, Torks and Pechenegs. They joined forces with Mstislav at Kotelnitsa and marched on Belgorod together. As they advanced the Karakalpaks asked Mstislav's permission to ride on ahead to see the extent of the enemy's forces. Mstislav agreed. Iziaslav's Wild Polovetsians also lay in wait for the enemy, returning to him with news that a very large force was moving against him. Iziaslav, fearful, left Belgorod without waiting to see for himself. The besieged princes left the town. The moment their deliverers joined them, they set off in pursuit of the princes of Chernigov. The Torks caught up with them, harried them and took prisoners. One of them, Voibor Negechevich, caught up with Iziaslav himself and struck him about the head with his sabre. Another Tork wounded him in the thigh and unhorsed him. Mstislav found him mortally wounded and sent him to St. Simeon's monastery in Kiev, where he died. His body was taken to Chernigov. These events took place in 1160-1161.

ROSTISLAV'S RESTORATION AND QUARREL
WITH MSTISLAV IZIASLAVICH

This was the second time that Rostislav received Kiev thanks to his nephew Mstislav, which could have been a cause of dissension between them. Perhaps Mstislav considered himself entitled to make considerable demands in return for his services, particularly as he followed his father's saying that the place does not go to the head, but the head to the place.[15] He was also hardly a model of filial humility towards his uncles, since we merely need to recall his behavior towards Rostislav on the matter of reconciliation with Iziaslav Davydovich. Rostislav for his part did not want to be like his uncle Viacheslav. In fact he made it a condition of his acceptance of Kiev that he must be the true head of the family. Therefore it is not surprising to read in the chronicle that soon after Rostislav's second entry into Kiev Mstislav left the city in anger, having quarrelled with his uncle. At the same time one of Rostislav's sons, Davyd,[16] acting on his own initiative, went to Torchesk, where he took Mstislav's burgrave prisoner and brought him to Kiev. Torchesk had to be seized in order to cut Mstislav's lines of communication to the Karakalpaks. Rostislav sent his other son Mstislav to Belgorod.

It was hard for the prince of Volhynia to fight his uncle by himself. He needed to find allies, but went about it in a curious way. He led his army to Peresopnitsa, ordering Vladimir Andreevich to renounce his alliance with Rostislav. Vladimir refused, and Mstislav was obliged to return. Meanwhile Rostislav made peace with Sviatoslav Olgovich and his nephews, also with Yury Yaroslavich who, thanks to the hostilities within the line of Monomakh, established himself at Turov.

HOSTILITIES AGAINST VLADIMIR MSTISLAVICH

There was still Rostislav's younger brother, the landless Vladimir Mstislavich. He was expelled from Volhynia by his nephew Mstislav, campaigned with Iziaslav Davydovich and accompanied him on the retreat from Belgorod across the Dnieper. His next movements are unknown, but in 1162 he was the object of a campaign against Slutsk[17] led by Riurik Rostislavich, Yury of Turov's son Sviatopolk, Sviatoslav Vsevolodovich and his brother Yaroslav of Novgorod Seversk, Sviatoslav Vladimirovich of Vshchizh, Oleg Sviatoslavich and certain princes of the Polovetsians. When and how Vladimir Mstislavich acquired this town is unknown. Unable to resist such a large force, Vladimir relinquished the town and went to his brother Rostislav in Kiev, who gave him Tripol and four other towns. Rostislav finally made peace in 1163 with Mstislav, who probably was made more amenable by the fact that the other princes remained on good terms with his uncle. Rostislav gave him back Torchesk and Belgorod. He also gave him Kanev in compensation for Tripol.

DEATH OF SVIATOSLAV OLGOVICH

While the situation on the western side of the Dnieper was becoming calmer, Sviatoslav Olgovich's death in 1164 gave rise to great disturbances on the eastern shore. By rights his elder brother's son Sviatoslav Vsevolodovich should have inherited Chernigov. Sviatoslav Olgovich's widow, with the connivance of Bishop Anthony[18] and her late husband's chief boyars, kept his death a secret for three days to have time to send for her son Oleg and hand Chernigov over to him. "Come quickly, prince," they said to him, "for the son of Vsevolod has not been on good terms with your father or you, and may have devised some evil against you."

Oleg arrived first. Sviatoslav was informed of his uncle's death by Bishop Anthony, who was involved in the princess's plot and even swore on an icon of the Savior that he would not reveal the prince's death to anyone. This was in spite of the fact that the chiliarch Yury said he ought not be made to swear, being a bishop, and above suspicion on account of his affection for the princes. "God and His Mother are my witnesses," the bishop replied, "under no circumstances shall I send to Sviatoslav Vsevolodovich. Likewise I forbid you, my children, to do so, lest we lose our souls and become traitors like Judas."

These were his words, although he nursed deception in his heart because he was a Greek, says the chronicler. He was the first to kiss the icon, and the first to break his oath, for he sent a letter to Sviatoslav. "Your uncle is dead," he wrote, "and Oleg has been summoned. His retinue is scattered far off in the towns. The princess sits grieving with her children, and has great wealth. Come quickly. Oleg is not here yet, so you can make whatever arrangements you want with him."

When Sviatoslav read the letter he sent his son to Gomel and his burgraves to the other towns. He himself prepared to go to Chernigov. When he learned that Oleg had arrived before him he exchanged messages urging him to come to agreement about the distribution of lands.

Oleg let him have Chernigov, and took Novgorod Seversk for himself. Sviatoslav also swore to provide for Oleg's brothers Igor[19] and Vsevolod from the territories of Chernigov, but he did not keep his word. Oleg evidently passed over this in silence, then a further dispute soon arose. The prince of Vshchizh, Sviatoslav Vladimirovich, died in 1167. As representative of the senior line of Sviatoslav's descendants he had more right to Chernigov than the sons of Oleg. Evidently he did not want to dispute it with them because of his health or some other reasons. The surviving members of the family should have divided his escheated lands but Sviatoslav gave Oleg nothing, gave the best part of the territory to his brother Yaroslav and installed his son in Vshchizh.

Then Rostislav of Kiev, seeing that Oleg was the victim of injustice, intervened on his behalf, especially since Oleg was his son-in-law. He tried repeatedly to persuade Sviatoslav to give Oleg his due. At the same time the men of Starodub, displeased with Sviatoslav for some reason, invited Oleg to be their prince. He would have accepted had not Yaroslav

Vsevolodovich forestalled him, preventing the citizens from carrying out their intention. Oleg, angry at being thwarted, took captive many of the villagers round about. Sviatoslav sent his brother Yaroslav with the Polovetsians to Novgorod Seversk in retaliation, which force turned back more than fifteen versts from the city. Oleg was much too ill to continue his campaign. He easily agreed to Rostislav's proposal that he make peace with the prince of Chernigov in return for four towns.

ROSTISLAV'S VISIT TO THE NORTH

In this way Rostislav made peace amongst all the princes on both sides of the Dnieper. It only remained to deal with the North. He went there in 1168, calling on his son-in-law Oleg in Novgorod Seversk on the way. The chief citizens of Smolensk met him three hundred versts from the city. Then his grandsons came out to meet him, followed by his son Roman, the bishop, the chiliarch and very nearly the entire population. Everyone was delighted at his arrival and gave him many gifts.

From Smolensk Rostislav went to Toropets, whence he sent a message to his son Sviatoslav in Novgorod, telling him to meet him with the leading citizens at Velikie Luki, as he was not well enough to go any further. He settled his affairs with the men of Novgorod, receiving many gifts from them and from his son, but by the time he returned to Smolensk he was seriously ill. His sister Rogneda besought him to remain at Smolensk at the church he had founded. "I cannot lie here," he replied, "take me to Kiev. Should God take my soul on the way, lay me by my father at St. Theodore's. If, God willing, I recover, I shall be tonsured in the monastery of the Caves."

Before his death he told his confessor Simeon he would have to answer before God for not allowing him to become a monk. It was a constant idea of his, which first came to him, as he told Abbot Polikarp,[20] when he heard news of Sviatoslav Olgovich's death. Subsequently he asked Polikarp to prepare a cell for him, for he feared sudden death. Polikarp dissuaded him, saying "God has ordained that you be what you are, see to justice on this earth, judge righteously and keep your oaths." "Father," replied Rostislav, "government and the world cannot be without sin. I have lived long enough on this earth. Now I want to devote myself to holiness." Polikarp resisted no longer. "If you desire it so greatly, prince," said he, "God's will be done." "I shall wait just a little longer," said Rostislav, "for I still have some little business." Now that all his business was done, Rostislav was hurrying to Kiev to die or become a monk. On the road from Smolensk, when he reached his sister's village of Zarub, he felt death approaching and sent for his confessor. He read the prayer for the dying himself and died fully conscious, wiping away his tears.

This son of Mstislav was also remarkable amongst the princes of Rus. He was far behind his brother Iziaslav in energy, courage and strategic ability. His character was essentially conservative. He was always respectful towards his elder brother and obedient to his will. Likewise he was respectful towards his uncles, nor was he pleased at the struggle between them and his brother, whom he urged to give way. When his turn came to be the senior member of the family he demanded the same obedience from the junior members as he himself had been wont to accord his seniors. Once he succeeded to the seniority he would not give way to the evidently excessive demands of his nephew Mstislav. On the other hand, he never gave any cause of offense to him or any of the other junior members of the family. He provided them all with lands and tried to keep them on good terms, and thus by the end of his life there was peace throughout the land. These events occurred in 1168.

ACCESSION OF MSTISLAV IZIASLAVICH

After Rostislav's death the seniority passed to Sviatoslav Vsevolodovich as the representative of the senior line, which the descendants of Monomakh refused to recognize. The most senior in their line was Vladimir Mstislavich, the last son of Mstislav the Great, but this prince was the son of Mstislav's second wife[21] and probably younger in years than his nephew who deprived him even of Volhynia. He could hardly expect that the nephew would let him have Kiev. Finally, the next most senior prince was Yury Dolgoruky's son Andrei Bogoliubsky, but the Northern princes were not popular in the South, while Andrei's behavior towards his brothers did nothing to improve their disposition towards him. Therefore when Rostislav died everyone's attention turned towards his valiant nephew Prince Mstislav Iziaslavich of Vladimir-in-Volhynia, who already had won Kiev twice and given it up to his uncle. He certainly would not be prepared to relinquish it to anyone else. In spite of this, Mstislav's dubious right to the seniority, or even to inherit at all (for his father was not really the senior prince when he died), made his kinsfolk hope that he would reward them generously for letting him have the seniority, giving them whatever they wanted.

They miscalculated for Mstislav, like his uncle Rostislav, wanted to be senior in fact, not in name only. When he received the invitation to go to Kiev from his cousins Vladimir Mstislavich, Riurik Rostislavich and Davyd Rostislavich, together with a separate invitation from the men of Kiev and another from the Karakalpaks, he immediately dispatched his nephew Vasilko Yaropolchich and his agent to Kiev. Vasilko was told in Kiev by Mstislav's supporters that the princes, Vladimir Mstislavich, Vladimir Andreevich, Yaroslav Iziaslavich of Lutsk and the sons of Rostislav, all had sworn to make common cause and to demand their own choice of principalities from Mstislav. Vladimir Mstislavich was to receive Torchesk and the lands along the Ros in addition to Tripol, Vladimir Andreevich was to have Brest, and Yaroslav was to have Vladimir.

Vasilko immediately informed his uncle, passing the news on to his allies, Yaroslav of Galich, the sons of Vsevolod at Goroden, and the princes of Poland. Then he led his troops and his Galich auxiliaries towards Kiev. The chief figure in the princes' plot was evidently Vladimir Mstislavich, an old enemy of his nephew. For this reason, on hearing of Mstislav's approach, he fled with his family from Tripol to Vyshgorod, where he shut himself up with the sons of Rostislav. Mstislav meanwhile entered Kiev, came to an agreement with his cousins, the citizens and his retinue, setting off the same day to besiege Vyshgorod. After some bitter skirmishing they began negotiations and finally came to terms about the distribution of territory. Then Mstislav entered Kiev a second time and occupied the throne of Yaroslav, the throne of his father and his grandfather.

VLADIMIR MSTISLAVICH PLOTS AGAINST MSTISLAV IZIASLAVICH

It can easily be understood that the princes, particularly the older, being disappointed in their hopes, were secretly bitter at heart. Vladimir Mstislavich was particularly resentful. No sooner was the settlement reached than he began hatching new plots against his nephew. This came to the knowledge of Davyd Rostislavich's boyar Vasil Nastasyich, who told his prince about it, and he informed Mstislav. When Vladimir realized that his plot was discovered he came to Kiev to justify himself before Mstislav. They arrived at the monastery of the Caves almost at the same time. Mstislav entered the abbot's cell and told Vladimir to wait in that of the œconomus.[22] Mstislav sent to ask him why he was present, since he had not been summoned. "I have heard that wicked men slandered me to you," replied Vladimir. "It was my cousin Davyd that told me," said Mstislav. They sent to Davyd in Vyshgorod and he sent Vasil, escorted by the chiliarch and another boyar, to give evidence, and the trial began.

Three days later Mstislav returned to the Caves monastery. Vladimir sent two of his boyars, who disputed with Vasil, then a further witness appeared on his side. Eventually Mstislav grew tired of all this, saying to his uncle "Brother, you have kissed the cross, and your lips are not yet dry. This is, after all, what our fathers and grandfathers have determined, that if anyone break an oath, God will judge him. So now, if you had no evil intentions, and have none now, swear." "I shall be glad to swear, brother," replied Vladimir, "for everything is false which they have devised against me." He kissed the cross and went away to Kotelnitsa.

The same year he communicated with the Karakalpaks, inciting them against his nephew. When they agreed to join him he related this to his boyars, but his retinue said "This is something that you have thought up by yourself, prince. We know nothing of it, we will not follow you." Vladimir was angry. Indicating the young men of his retinue, he said "These will be my boyars." Then he went to the Berendey, whom he met below Rostovets. When the barbarians saw that he came alone, they said "You told us all your brethren had made common cause with you. Where is Vladimir Andreevich, where are Yaroslav and Davyd? Neither do you have any retinue. You deceived us, better for us to risk others' lives than our own." They shot arrows at Vladimir, two of which found their mark. "God save us from trusting the heathen," said Vladimir, "for both my life and my soul are forfeit." He fled towards Dorogobuzh, having lost his young servitors, who were killed by the Karakalpaks. Vladimir Andreevich demolished the bridge over the Goryn and would not let Vladimir Mstislavich approach. Now he turned east, traversed the land of the Radimichians,[23] reaching the principality of Suzdal. Here Andrei Bogoliubsky also refused to receive him. "Go to the prince of Riazan," he said, "and I will provide for you." Vladimir did as he was told and set off for Riazan. After this Mstislav of Kiev would not tolerate even Vladimir's mother's presence in Rus. He sent to her, saying "Cross over the Dnieper to Gorodets, and thence go wherever you like. I cannot live in the same place as you because your son is always seeking my life and breaking his oath." She went to Sviatoslav Vsevolodovich in Chernigov.

DISAFFECTION AGAINST MSTISLAV

Once his uncle was removed to the far Northeast, Mstislav might have expected to look forward to a period of tranquillity. Such was not the case. The princes' inability to divide the land when Mstislav assumed the senior throne to their satisfaction left an underlying bitterness which tended to surface at every opportunity. After a successful campaign against the Polovetsians in 1168 the princes' resentment against Mstislav was kindled by the fact that he allowed his servants to plunder the Polovetsian wagons without their knowledge. Soon after, Mstislav again summoned all the brethren to Kiev, proposing a new campaign in the steppe. This scheme met with general approval. They set off and stopped at Kanev. While they were there two members of the retinue, Peter and Nestor, the sons of Borislav, spoke ill of Mstislav to Davyd Rostislavich. Mstislav had dismissed them from his retinue because their bondsmen stole his horses and branded them with their own brands. Now they wanted to seek revenge by slandering him. Davyd believed them and told his brother Riurik that friends had informed him Mstislav intended to imprison them. "Why? For what reason?" asked Riurik. "It is not long since he swore friendship to us!"

To convince the sons of Rostislav further, the slanderers told them it was Mstislav's intention to take them prisoner while they dined with him. If they received an invitation to dinner from Mstislav this would be a sign that they were telling the truth. Indeed the unsuspecting Mstislav did invite Riurik and Davyd to dinner. Their reply was that they would come if he swore he had no evil intentions towards them. Mstislav was horrified and asked his men what it could mean that the brothers were demanding such an oath when he had a clear conscience. "Prince," replied his retinue, "it is absurd that the brothers should ask you to swear. It must be that some evil men, envious of your friendship for them, have spoken wicked words. An evil man is worse than a devil, for not even a devil could imagine the things that evil men devise. You are guiltless before God and man, for you could not have undertaken or accomplished anything without us, and we know your sincere friendship for the brethren. Tell the brothers that you will swear, on condition that they hand over those creating discord between you." Davyd refused to hand over the sons of Borislav, saying that if he did, no one would ever tell him anything again. Nevertheless, Mstislav took the oath. So did the sons of Rostislav, but their hearts were not honestly turned towards him, adds the chronicler.

At the same time Vladimir Andreevich asked Mstislav for additional lands. Mstislav realized that he was doing this deliberately to have a pretext for a quarrel. In reply he asked how long it was since Vladimir swore friendship to him and received his principality. Vladimir returned home to Dorogobuzh in anger.

ANDREI BOGOLIUBSKY ATTACKS MSTISLAV

Now Andrei Bogoliubsky took advantage of the general disaffection towards Mstislav in the South to assert his right to the seniority and to Kiev. He disliked Mstislav as heartily as his father Yury had disliked Mstislav's father Iziaslav. Just like his father, he engaged in open war once he was sure of finding allies in the South. All they needed was an occasion, which was provided when Mstislav sent his son Roman to Novgorod at the citizens' request. Then all the princes allied themselves against Mstislav and confirmed their pact with an oath, declaring Andrei Yurievich to be the senior prince.[24]

Bogoliubsky sent out his son Mstislav and his commander Boris Zhid-islavich with the men of Rostov, Vladimir and Suzdal. This army was joined by ten other princes, namely Gleb Yurievich of Pereiaslavl, Roman of Smolensk, Vladimir Andreevich of Dorogobuzh, Riurik Rostislavich of Ovruch, his brothers Davyd and Mstislav of Vyshgorod, Oleg Sviatoslavich and his brother Igor from Novgorod Seversk, Andrei Bogo-liubsky's younger brother Vsevolod Yurievich,[25] and his elder brother's son Mstislav Rostislavich.[26] Sviatoslav Vsevolodovich of Chernigov did not join the coalition, evidently not wanting to deprive Mstislav of Kiev for the benefit of a prince whose seniority he could not acknowledge. One of Bogoliubsky's brothers, Mikhail Yurievich, also took no part. Mstislav sent him to Novgorod with the Karakalpaks to help his son Roman. The sons of Rostislav, Riurik and Davyd, learning that the army of Andrei and their own brother Roman was at hand, set off in pursuit of Mikhail and took him prisoner near Mozyr, thanks to the treachery of the Karakalpaks.

SIEGE AND SACK OF KIEV

It is hard to say whether Mstislav was aware of the storm about to break over his head. More likely he was not, otherwise he would not have sent the Karakalpaks to Novgorod with Mikhail Yurievich. Mstislav's ene-mies all gathered at Vyshgorod then marched and surrounded Kiev. Msti-slav shut himself up in the city and defended it fiercely. The citizens were persuaded by their love for the son of Iziaslav, perhaps even more by their dislike of the son of Yury, to agree to endure the siege. There is no record of any of them venturing out to meet the besieging princes, or of the assembly telling Mstislav to leave because it was not his hour, as happened in former times. Only the Karakalpaks were unreliable as usual.

After three days the besiegers' retinue forced its way into the town, whereupon Mstislav's retinue said to him "Why do you stay here? Leave the town, for we cannot overcome them." Mstislav took their advice and fled to Vasiliev, pursued by a company of Karakalpaks who shot at him from behind and took many of his retinue prisoner. Mstislav himself met up with his brother Yaroslav. Together they made their way to Vladimir-in-Volhynia.

For the first time Kiev was taken by force of arms against the general resistance of the inhabitants. For the first time the mother of the towns of Rus suffered the fate of a city given over to plunder. The victors sacked the town for two days, sparing nothing and no one. The churches were burned, the citizens beaten and bound, wives were separated from their husbands and taken into captivity. Children wept as they beheld their mothers. A vast quantity of riches was looted. All the churches were robbed. The Polovetsians even would have burned the monastery of the Caves had not the monks put the fire out. There was sorrow and wailing amongst all the people of Kiev, says the chronicler, sadness inconsolable and tears unceasing.[27]

It was not Yury's eldest son, in whose name the campaign was undertaken and the city where his ancestors had reigned was taken and destroyed, not Bogoliubsky who took the throne. Andrei's son Mstislav installed his uncle Gleb from Pereiaslavl, who gave Pereiaslavl to his son Vladimir. The senior prince continued to reside far away in the North at Vladimir-on-the-Kliazma, while his son Mstislav returned to his father with great honor and glory, according to some versions of the chronicle, or according to others with maledictions.

EVENTS AFTER YURY DOLGORUKY'S DEATH

Concerning events in the various principalities after the death of Yury Dolgoruky we note that the descendants of Iziaslav Yaroslavich[28] established themselves in Turov, and those of Igor Yaroslavich[29] continued to rule in Goroden. Yaroslav of Galich finally was rid of his dangerous rival Ivan Berladnik, who died in 1161 in Thessalonika.[30] The chronicle records a rumor that he was poisoned.

There were great disturbances in Polotsk. In 1151 the people expelled Rogvolod Borisovich,[31] replacing him with Rostislav Glebovich,[32] who put himself under the protection of Sviatoslav Olgovich. Rostislav evidently forgot about his obligations to the prince of Chernigov, who received the exiled Rogvolod and in 1158 even lent him his regiments to help him win a principality. Rogvolod approached Slutsk and opened communications with the men of Drutsk, who invited him to their city, saying "Come, prince, without delay, for we are glad that you are come. If we must, we and our children will fight for you." Indeed they sent more than three hundred boats to meet him. The citizens of Drutsk brought him into their town with honor, driving out Gleb Rostislavich,[33] whose court and retinue they plundered. When Gleb came to his father Rostislav in Polotsk with the news that Rogvolod was in Drutsk, there was rioting among the citizens, many of whom were for Rogvolod. It was with great difficulty that Rostislav restored order. He gave gifts, extracted oaths, and marched with all his brethren to Drutsk, where he met fierce resistance. The men of Drutsk fought valiantly, and there were many casualties on both sides. Then Rostislav, realizing that he would gain nothing by force, made peace with Rogvolod, gave him lands and returned home.

This was not the end of the matter. The same year there was a plot among the men of Polotsk to eject Rostislav. Evidently they forgot that when they swore allegiance to him they said "You are our prince. God grant that we may live with you." They sent a secret message to Rogvolod Borisovich in Drutsk. "Prince, we have sinned before God and before you, in that we rose up against you without cause, plundering your goods and your retinue, abandoning you to be tormented by the sons of Gleb. Forget what we did in our madness, and take an oath to us. We will be your people, and you will be our prince. We will deliver Rostislav into your hands. Do with him what you will."

Rogvolod swore he would forget the past, but as usually happened in the towns, Rostislav had many friends who informed him that the others were planning to seize him. It was agreed to invite him to a feast at the old church of the Mother of God on St. Peter's Day [June 29] and seize him there. Rostislav, forewarned by his supporters, donned armor under his clothes. That attempt was foiled.

The next day they again called him to attend the popular assembly, where they said they had things to discuss with him. "Why," asked Rostislav, "did you not say anything to me when I was with you yesterday?" Despite the warnings he received, he rode to the town (he was living at his court at Belchitsa, on the opposite bank of the Dvina three versts from Polotsk). On the way he met his young servitor who told him to go no further, as the assembly had rebelled against him. They were assaulting his retinue and looking to seize the prince himself. Rostislav turned back, gathered his retinue at Belchitsa and marched towards Minsk, his brother Volodar's seat, laying waste the lands of Polotsk and taking the cattle and the people.

Rogvolod, who responded to the invitation of the people of Polotsk and took his place, was in no mood to leave the sons of Gleb in peace. He assembled a large force of the men of Polotsk, asking for assistance from Rostislav of Smolensk, who sent him his two sons Roman and Riurik and his boyar Vnezd with contingents from Smolensk, Novgorod and Pskov. They went first to Iziaslavl, where Vsevolod Glebovich had taken refuge. This Vsevolod previously was a great friend of Rogvolod's. Therefore, relying on their old friendship, he rode out to his camp and bowed down to him. Rogvolod received him well, but did not yield Iziaslavl back to him, as it was rightfully the patrimony of Briachislav Vasilkovich.[34] Instead he gave him Strezhev. Then Rogvolod went to Minsk. Besieging it without success for ten days, he came to terms with Rostislav and went home.

Although the sons of Gleb were forced to give way, they soon renewed activities against their other cousins. In 1159 they once more took possession of Iziaslavl, where they captured Vasilko's two sons Briachislav and Volodar and imprisoned them in Minsk. In response, Rogvolod again was compelled to march against Minsk. Rostislav Mstislavich sent six hundred Torks from Kiev to his assistance. Rogvolod besieged the city for six weeks, making peace on his own terms. In other words, he secured the liberation of the sons of Vasilko. The Torks, having lost their horses and themselves starving, made their way back to the South on foot before the peace was concluded.

This episode was followed by yet another campaign by Rogvolod against Rostislav in Minsk, and yet another peace. In 1161 Rogvolod undertook still another campaign against Volodar Glebovich, now prince of Gorodets. Volodar would not fight during the daytime, but made a sortie by night. With Lithuanian support he inflicted a heavy defeat on Rogvolod, who fled to Slutsk. After three days here he returned to his old town of Drutsk, not daring to show his face at Polotsk after losing so many of its men at Gorodets. The men of Polotsk then made Vseslav Vasilkovich their prince.

Within the territories of Polotsk, the towns of Minsk, Iziaslavl, Drutsk and Gorodets are mentioned as having princes of their own. In days gone by Yaroslav I ceded Vitebsk to Prince Briachislav of Polotsk. It is recorded that in 1165 Davyd Rostislavich of Smolensk[35] became prince of Vitebsk, while the previous prince Roman received the two towns of Vasiliev and Krasny in the principality of Smolensk.

Meanwhile the sons of Gleb could not view with equanimity the fact that Polotsk had passed out of their line, from a son of Boris to a son of Vasilko. In 1167 Volodar Glebovich of Gorodets[36] marched on Polotsk. Vseslav Vasilkovich[37] came out to meet him, but Volodar attacked him suddenly before he had a chance to set his men in order, killing and capturing many. Vseslav was forced to flee to Vitebsk, while according to the chronicler Volodar entered Polotsk and came to terms with the citizens, kissing the cross.

Having established himself here, Volodar went to attack Davyd and Vseslav in Vitebsk. He took up his position on one side of the Dvina and engaged the enemy on the other. Davyd was unwilling to engage in a decisive battle, as he was waiting for his brother Roman and the men of Smolensk. Suddenly one night there was a dreadful clap of thunder which filled the men of Polotsk with panic. "Why are you standing here, prince," said Volodar's retinue, "and not riding away? Roman is crossing the river and Davyd will attack from the other side." Volodar was afraid and fled from Vitebsk. Next morning Davyd, hearing that the enemy had fled, sent men to pursue them. They could not catch up with the prince himself, though they caught many of his warriors who were lost in the woods. Vseslav followed Volodar to Polotsk and once again established himself there.

EVENTS IN NOVGOROD

In 1158 Rostislav restored order to Novgorod, installing his son Sviatoslav there and his other son Davyd in Torzhok. Rostislav himself soon was called upon by his nephew to take the throne of Kiev, which might have been expected to reinforce the peace in Novgorod, where the opposite actually occurred. When Andrei Bogoliubsky intervened on Iziaslav Davydovich's behalf he wanted to strike a palpable blow against Rostislav in the North. He sent to the men of Novgorod, saying "Be it known to you that I shall seek to obtain Novgorod by fair means or foul."

The citizens of Novgorod did not know how to respond to this threat. There were disturbances and frequent meetings of the assembly. Not wishing to offend the prince of Kiev, they decided to resort to half-measures in the hope that Sviatoslav would understand the situation and depart on his own initiative. Therefore they asked him to remove his brother Davyd from Torzhok on the grounds that the maintenance of two princes was a heavy burden on the treasury. Sviatoslav did as they asked, did not get angry with them and remained in the city. More decisive steps had to be taken. It should not be forgotten that in Novgorod there was a faction opposed to descendants of Mstislav, which doubtless was very active now that circumstances had changed in its favor.

Sviatoslav was at Gorodishche near the church of the Annunciation when a messenger came hurrying to him with the news that evil was afoot in the town and that the people sought to lay hands on him. "What evil have I done them?" responded Sviatoslav, "Did they not swear to my father that I would be their prince while I lived? Did they not kiss the image of the Mother of God only yesterday as they swore fealty to me?" The words were not yet out of his mouth when a crowd of people rushed in, seized him and locked him up. The princess was sent to a convent, his retinue put in irons, and his possessions plundered. Then Sviatoslav was sent to Ladoga under heavy guard. When Rostislav heard what happened to his son in Novgorod, he seized all the men of Novgorod in Kiev and threw them into the dungeon at Peresechen, where fourteen died in a single night. At news of this calamity Rostislav repented bitterly and released the rest of them from the dungeon and those detained in the various towns round about.

Meanwhile Novgorod sent to Andrei beseeching him to send one of his sons to be their prince. He offered them his brother Mstislav instead, whom the men of Novgorod did not want because he was their prince before. They finally agreed that Yury's nephew Mstislav Rostislavich come to be prince of Novgorod. Meanwhile Sviatoslav escaped from Ladoga and went to Polotsk, whence Rogvolod Borisovich conducted him to his relatives in Smolensk. The change of prince, as usual, brought about a change of mayor, Nezhata being chosen to replace Yakun Miroslavich. This did not halt the disturbances in Novgorod. Soon Andrei came to terms with Rostislav, agreeing that Novgorod be restored to Sviatoslav.

The people of Novgorod did not like to accept princes who were their princes previously, which was natural, as such a prince inevitably favored his former sympathizers, persecuting his opponents who secured his earlier deposition. This was not conducive to good order in the city, but what could they do against the will of the two most powerful princes of Rus? They were forced to accept Sviatoslav *on his own terms*. It is the first time the chronicler uses such an expression. If Sviatoslav was accepted on his own terms, we must conclude that the princes before him were accepted on terms stipulated by the men of Novgorod. In other words, before Sviatoslav's rule conditions, the style of which may be seen in the later charters, were negotiated between Novgorod and its princes. It could hardly have been otherwise in the troubled years following the death of Mstislav Vladimirovich. Vsevolod Mstislavich's second accession, after he fled from Pereiaslavl, may be considered the time when the first conditions, Novgorod's first contract with its princes, began to be imposed. This second acceptance of Sviatoslav, imposed on the citizens against their will by two princes acting together, violated the order that was beginning to be established. Loss of hard-won privileges resulted in the citizens' violent hatred of Sviatoslav, as subsequent events demonstrated.

The first consequence of the change of princes was a change of mayors. Nezhata was chosen when Sviatoslav was expelled as a result of the triumph of the opposing faction. Now that Sviatoslav was restored, Nezhata was dismissed and his place taken by Zakharia. As might have been expected, a prince forcibly imposed could not have a peaceful reign at Novgorod. Rostislav of Kiev had to visit Novgorod to restore order at the end of his life, knowing that the citizens were on bad terms with his son. Rostislav met the chief citizens at Velikie Luki. He made them swear not to seek to have any other prince than Sviatoslav, and to be parted from him only by death.[38]

Even so, in the very year of Rostislav's death some disaffected citizens assembled secretly in their houses and plotted against his son. Sviatoslav's friends warned him, telling him to be on his guard. Sviatoslav told his retinue. "They have only just taken the oath to you after your father's death," they said. "What shall we do with them? To which of their princes have they been faithful? Let us think about ourselves before other people start thinking about us!"

Sviatoslav left the city, taking up residence at Velikie Luki. From there he sent to the men of Novgorod, telling them he no longer wanted to be their prince. In response they swore on the icon of the Mother of God not to seek to have Sviatoslav as their prince, and went to expel him from Velikie Luki. Sviatoslav departed for Toropets, thence to the Volga, where with Andrei of Suzdal's assistance he burned Novy Torg. His brothers Roman and Mstislav burned Velikie Luki, where some of the citizens shut themselves up in the fortress, while the rest fled to Pskov.

Andrei of Suzdal prepared to attack Novgorod with the men of Smolensk and Polotsk. They cut off all roads and intercepted all messengers, depriving the men of Novgorod of means of sending any message to Mstislav Iziaslavich in Kiev to send them his son. Andrei and the sons of Rostislav wanted to impose Sviatoslav again on Novgorod by force. "There is no prince for you but Sviatoslav," they said. This information given by the chronicler suggests that the citizens were negotiating with Andrei and asking him to give them any prince but Sviatoslav. Andrei's obstinacy only exasperated Novgorod further, hence they killed Sviatoslav's friends, the mayor Zakharia, the distinguished boyar Nerevin, who led them in battle more than once, and the herald Nezda, accusing them of conspiring to betray them to Sviatoslav.

Eventually they found a way to send news south across the territories of the sons of Gleb, princes of Polotsk, who were hostile to the sons of Rostislav at Smolensk because of events described above. Danislav Lazutinich and his companions set out for Kiev to fetch a son of Mstislav. Another commander, Yakun (probably the old mayor Yakun Miroslavich), went out to meet Sviatoslav, who was marching towards Russa with his brothers, together with the men of Smolensk and Polotsk. The enemy did not reach Russa, turning back without accomplishing anything, while the men of Novgorod elected Yakun as their mayor. Under his leadership they waited for Roman Mstislavich to come from the South.

Roman arrived in 1168. The citizens were cheered to have what they wanted, says the chronicler. Having received the prince they wanted, the men of Novgorod set out to avenge their wrongs. First they went with the men of Pskov to Polotsk, where they devastated the countryside, though they returned without coming within thirty versts of the city. Then Roman went to Toropets in the territory of Smolensk, where he burned the houses and took many prisoners. Yet Roman's dispatch to Novgorod merely brought on the storm gathering over his father Mstislav's head. It led the irritated sons of Rostislav to conclude a close alliance with Andrei in order to satisfy their revenge on the prince of Kiev who had forced them and their sons out of Novgorod. Once his father was deprived of Kiev, Roman could not expect a long reign in Novgorod.[39]

EVENTS IN SWEDEN AND RELATIONS WITH RUS

At the same time as the domestic disturbances were taking place during Sviatoslav Rostislavich's second reign Novgorod was plagued by quite a significant external struggle with the Swedes. The Swedes had posed no threat to the territory of Rus since the time of Riurik, thanks to the domestic conflicts arising as a result of the Swedes' conversion to Christianity, leading to decay of the old pagan way of life. Yaroslav I's father-in-law King Olof Skötkonung[40] after his conversion no longer could call himself king of Uppsala because that was the title of the pagan high priest. As a result he lost his status in Upper Sweden, where the majority of the population was still pagan. When the line of the kings of Uppsala, descended from the famous Sigurd Hring, became extinct, Stenkil, the son of Earl Ragnvald and a zealous Christian, was elected king.[41] This suggests that the Christian party by this time was dominant. Nevertheless when Christian missionaries urged him to destroy the pagan shrine at Uppsala, he replied that the consequences of such an action would be their deaths and his exile.

Stenkil's death in 1066 was followed by civil war. Two kings, both called Erik, contested the throne. Both fell in the war, together with their most prominent supporters. During the struggle there was such a strong revival of the pagan religion that no bishop could be persuaded to venture to Sweden for fear of persecution. The war continued until the middle of the twelfth century, ending in the accession of St. Erik to the Swedish throne in 1150, which marked the final triumph of Christianity.[42] It did not mean an end to the feuding between rival claimants. St. Erik was killed fighting Prince Magnus of Denmark, whose claim was based on his kinship with the house of Stenkil. A year later Magnus also was killed, to be succeeded by Karl Sverkersson, king of the Goths, who was the first to call himself king of the Swedes and Goths. He was remembered as a wise and benevolent king. There was no feuding in his reign, which allowed the Swedes to pursue an aggressive policy towards their neighbors.[43]

The Novgorod Chronicle records that in 1164 the Swedes made an attack on Ladoga.[44] The men of Ladoga burned their homes and shut themselves up in the citadel with their mayor Nezhata, calling on Prince Sviatoslav and the men of Novgorod for help. The Swedes attacked the citadel but were repelled with great loss and retreated towards the Voronay river.[45] On the fifth day Prince Sviatoslav and the mayor Zakharia arrived with the men of Novgorod, attacked the Swedes and defeated them. The Swedes lost forty-three of their fifty-five flyboats.[46] Few escaped, and even those were wounded.

WARFARE AGAINST OTHER NEIGHBORING PEOPLES

In the same year as the men of Novgorod repelled the Swedes so successfully, Andrei Bogoliubsky, his son Iziaslav, his brother Yaroslav and Prince Yury of Murom waged a successful campaign against the Kama Bulgars, killed many of them and took their standards.The Bulgar prince scarcely escaped with a small retinue to his chief city. After this victory Andrei took their glorious city of Brakhimov and burned three other towns.

The struggle against the Polovetsians continued in the Southeast. They were defeated at the beginning of Rostislav's reign by the princes of Volhynia and the men of Galich. The attack of the Polovetsians on the Karakalpaks at Yuriev in 1162 also ended unsuccessfully. At the beginning they captured many of the Karakalpaks' wagons, then a united force of the Karakalpaks defeated them on the banks of the Ros, retrieving everything that was captured, and taking five hundred prisoners, some of princely rank. Nevertheless the following year Rostislav considered it necessary to make peace with them and to marry his son Riurik to the daughter of Khan Beluk.

There could be no durable and comprehensive peace with these barbarians, fragmented as they were into many hordes ruled by independent khans. In 1165 Rostislav's nephew Vasilko Yaropolkovich defeated the Polovetsians on the Ros river, taking many prisoners, for whom he exacted a heavy ransom. His retinue acquired many weapons and horses. Next year the Polovetsians suffered defeat at the hands of Oleg Sviatoslavich within the borders of Chernigov. At the same time a separate Polovetsian army defeated Shvarn and shattered his retinue on the other side of Pereiaslavl. Shvarn had to pay a heavy ransom for himself. Some sources call Shvarn one of Prince Gleb of Pereiaslavl's commanders, others call him a warrior hero.[47] After this the descendants of Oleg, Oleg Sviatoslavich and his cousin Yaroslav Vsevolodovich, waged a successful campaign against the Polovetsians in bitter winter weather and captured their wagons.

The barbarians were dangerous not only because of their direct incursions into the territory of Rus. They also hindered trade with the Greeks, which was the main source of Kiev's prosperity and the wealth of the grand prince's treasury. Constantine Porphyrogennetos[48] has described the dangers attending the voyage along the lower Dnieper, where the steppes were full of Pechenegs. The situation was unchanged, only the nomads of the steppes along the Dnieper bore a different name. It was not safe for merchant vessels to make their way up and down the river. In 1166 the Polovetsians encamped at the rapids and plundered the merchants engaged in the trade between Kiev and Byzantium.[49] Rostislav dispatched his boyar Władysław the Pole with an army under whose protection the ships coming from Greece safely negotiated the rapids and sailed upstream to Kiev.

The importance of the Greek trade for the Rus princes, how vital it was to protect this trade from the Polovetsians, is evident from this chronicle entry for the year 1166. Rostislav sent to all his brothers and sons, commanding them to assemble all their forces and join him. Mstislav Iziaslavich of Vladimir, his brothers Yaroslav of Lutsk and Yaropolk of Buzhsk, Vladimir Andreevich, Vladimir Mstislavich, Gleb Yurievich, Gleb of Goroden, Ivan Yurievich of Turov, the sons of Rostislav, Riurik, Davyd and Mstislav, and the men of Galich all came, waiting at Kanev for a long time until the merchants passed through, after which the princes went home.

Rostislav's successor Mstislav continued to organize forays against the Polovetsians for the same purpose. In 1167, says the chronicle, God put into his heart a good thought concerning the Land of Rus and he summoned his brethren. "Let us have pity on the Land of Rus," he said, "the land of our fathers and our grandfathers. Every year the Polovetsians abduct Christians to their encampments, swear that they will not make war on us, and always break their oath. Now they are cutting off all our trade routes. It would be well for us, brethren, to place our hope in God's help and in the prayers of His Holy Mother, seeking to regain our honor and the roads of our fathers and grandfathers." Mstislav's words were pleasing to God, his brethren and their men. "God reward you, brother," said the princes, "for such a good thought. God grant that we lay down our lives for the Christian people and for the Land of Rus and be numbered among the martyrs." Mstislav also sent to the princes of Chernigov. They too were pleased with his idea. Two sons of Rostislav, Riurik and Davyd, four princes of Chernigov, Sviatoslav Vsevolodovich and Yaroslav Vsevolodovich, Oleg Sviatoslavich and Vsevolod Sviatoslavich, Yaroslav Iziaslavich of Volhynia and his brother Yaropolk, Mstislav

Vsevolodkovich of Goroden, Sviatopolk Yurievich of Turov, Gleb Yurievich of Pereiaslavl and his brother Mikhail gathered at Kiev with their troops.

Nine days the princes rode from Kiev along the road to Kanev, when one of the army let the Polovetsians know of their approach. The barbarians fled into the steppe, abandoning their wives and children. Leaving Yaroslav Vsevolodovich with the baggage train the princes pursued them, capturing their wagons along the Ugol and the Snoporod rivers, overtaking the Polovetsians themselves near the Black Wood. They forced the Polovetsians back against the forest's edge, where they slew many and took even more prisoner. All the warriors of Rus were enriched with booty, captives, women and children, slaves, cattle and horses. They liberated all the Christians in captivity, all this for the loss of two men killed and one captured.

Mstislav had no thought of resting on his laurels. He soon called the princes together again, saying "We have done much harm to the Polovetsians, and captured their wagons, their children and their herds, so they will take revenge on our merchants. We must go out and meet the merchants coming from Byzantium." The princes were pleased. "Let us go," they said, "since this is for our good and for all the Land of Rus." They did as in Rostislav's time and *there awaited* the merchants at Kanev.

It was not only the Polovetsians who hindered the Greek trade. In 1159 the Berladniks[50] gained control of Oleshie. Grand Prince Rostislav sent against them along the Dnieper two commanders, who caught up with and defeated them, taking back what they had stolen.

MEMBERS OF PRINCES' RETINUES

The following members of the princes' retinues of the period are mentioned by name. Gleb Rakoshich served in Kiev under Iziaslav Davydovich and was the prince's envoy to his cousin Sviatoslav of Chernigov. Shvarn, possibly identical with Iziaslav Mstislavich's commander, took part in Iziaslav's struggle with Rostislav, as did Stepan Miliatich and his brother Yakun and Nazhir Pereiaslavich. They all were captured in the battle in which Iziaslav was killed. Under Rostislav mention is made of Yury Nesterovich and Yakun, who led the force against the Berladniks who captured Oleshie, and Zhiroslav Nazhirovich, who led the Torks from Kiev to the aid of Rogvolod of Polotsk. Giurata Semkovich was sent by Rostislav to the emperor in Constantinople on ecclesiastical business. Władysław the son of Wracisław the Pole was sent by Rostislav to protect the merchants trading with Byzantium from the Polovetsians. Some sources name the chiliarch of Kiev under Rostislav as Zhiroslav Andreevich. Among those close to Rostislav were his *gentleman of the bedchamber*,[51] Ivanko Frolovich, and Boris Zakharich.

Among the retinue of Mstislav Iziaslavich in Volhynia were Zhiroslav Vasilievich, his envoy to Iziaslav Davydovich in the Berladnik affair, and later during his war with Iziaslav, Kuzma Snovidovich and Olbyr Sheroshevich (who was obviously a foreigner). His burgrave in Torchesk was Vyshko, taken prisoner by Davyd Rostislavich. Władysław the son of Wracisław, previously Rostislav's boyar and commander in Kiev, was sent on ahead to Kiev by Mstislav when he was summoned there by his brethren and the citizens. It may be supposed that he was a member of the delegation sent by the men of Kiev to invite Mstislav to take the throne immediately after Rostislav's death. Finally, these members of Mstislav's retinue are mentioned as having been captured by the enemy at the time of his flight from Kiev: Dmitry the Bold, Alexis Dvorsky, Sbyslav Zhiroslavich (possibly Zhiroslav Vasilievich's son), Ivanko Tvorimirich, and one Rod or Rodion. Amongst the Galich boyars we find Izbignev Ivachevich, who was an envoy to Iziaslav Davydovich, and the commander Tudor Eltsich, who took part in the war against him.

Elsewhere in the Southwest, among the boyars of Vladimir Mstislavich of Trepol, Raguilo Dobrynich and Mikhail are mentioned as having opposed Vasily Nastasich, who accused their prince of evil intentions against Mstislav Iziaslavich. Afterwards these two, together with a third boyar, Zavid, left his service when he plotted against the prince of Kiev without consulting them. The first two, Raguilo and Mikhail, were mentioned earlier when they assisted their prince in his attempt to defend Igor Olgovich from his murderers. Raguilo then held the rank of chiliarch. The boyars Onufry of Lutsk and Gavrilo Vasilievich of Dorogobuzh were their princes' envoys to Iziaslav Davydovich.

One of Sviatoslav Olgovich's boyars at Chernigov was Zhiroslav Ivankovich,[52] who formerly served Viacheslav and Yury. It is natural that after Yury's death he entered the service of Sviatoslav Olgovich, Yury's only constant friend. Georgy Ivanovich, Shakushan's brother, was the envoy whom Sviatoslav sent to Iziaslav Davydovich in Kiev to persuade him not to defend Ivan Berladnik. In all probability he was the chiliarch of Chernigov at the time of Sviatoslav's death. Oleg, Sviatoslav's son, had a boyar called Ivan Radislavich. Amongst Sviatoslav Vsevolodovich's boyars at Novgorod Seversk was one called "the Kievan" (Kiyanin), which shows from where he came. At Pereiaslavl, in the battle with the Polovetsians one Shvarn is mentioned who, according to some sources, was Prince Gleb's commander, according to other sources a warrior hero.[53]

The boyars of Smolensk included Ivan Ruchechnik, the envoy sent by Rostislav Mstislavich to the Southern princes when they called on him to take the throne of Kiev. Vnezd, evidently chiliarch of Smolensk, took precedence immediately after the prince and the bishop. He also took part with the princes of Smolensk in the campaign in support of Rogvolod of Polotsk against his kinsfolk. Some of the boyars of Davyd Rostislavich at Vyshgorod mentioned in the chronicles are Vasil Nastasich, Radilo the chiliarch, possibly the identical with one of the members of Iziaslav Mstislavich's retinue earlier, and Vasily Volkovich. After this the two sons of Borislav left Mstislav of Kiev and took service under Davyd. One may be the same as the Peter Borisovich or Borislavich mentioned earlier as one of Iziaslav's boyars. The commander Boris Zhidislavich who took part in the sack of Kiev was one of Andrei Bogoliubsky's boyars at Suzdal. By reading Zhiroslavich for Zhidislavich, he might very well be the son of Zhiroslav Ivankovich. Finally certain individuals are mentioned in contexts which make it impossible to determine to whose retinue they belonged, such as Davyd Borynich, who corroborated Vasil Nastasich's evidence against Vladimir Mstislavich, or Konstantin Vasilievich, the brother of Yarun, killed fighting the Polovetsians, or Konstantin Khotovich, taken prisoner by them.

1 RUS RULERS, 862-1125

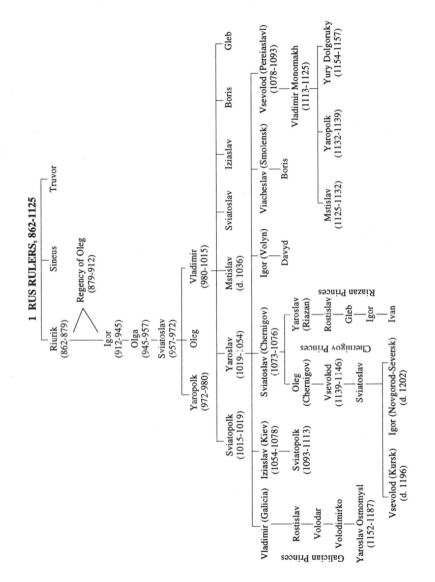

2 DESCENDANTS OF OLEG SVIATOSLAVICH

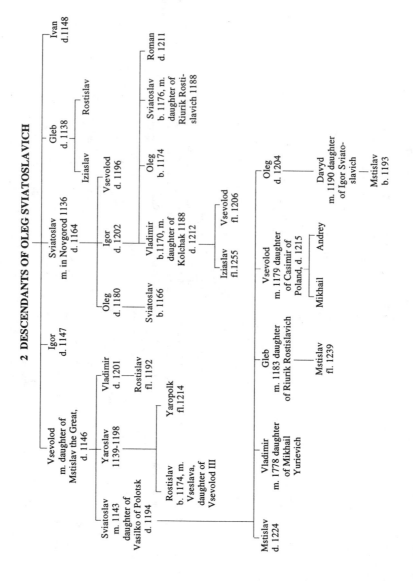

2 DESCENDANTS OF OLEG SVIATOSLAVICH

3 DESCENDANTS OF YAROSLAV SVIATOSLAVICH

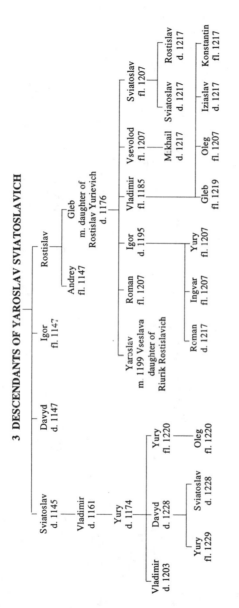

3 DESCENDANTS OF YAROSLAV SVIATOSLAVICH

4 DESCENDANTS OF VSEVOLOD YAROSLAVICH

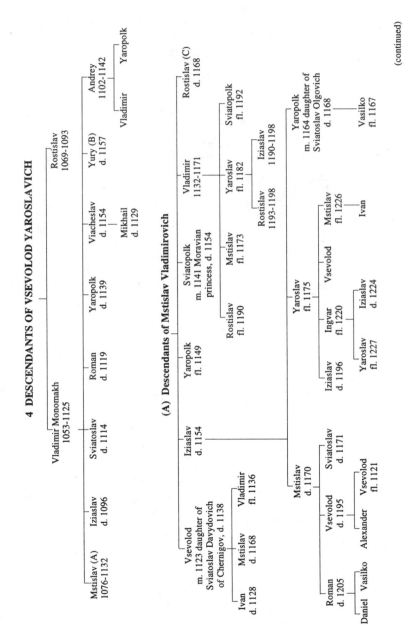

4 DESCENDANTS OF VSEVOLOD YAROSLAVICH

(A) Descendants of Mstislav Vladimirovich

(continued)

4 DESCENDANTS OF VSEVOLOD YAROSLAVICH (continued)

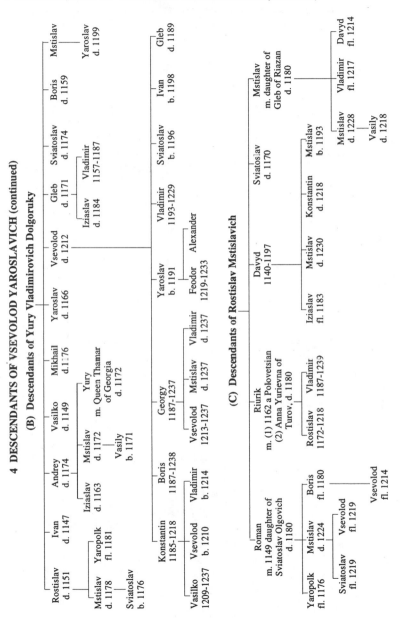

4 DESCENDANTS OF VSEVOLOD YAROSLAVICH (continued)

(B) Descendants of Yury Vladimirovich Dolgoruky

(C) Descendants of Rostislav Mstislavich

5 DESCENDANTS OF IZIASLAV VLADIMIROVICH OF POLOTSK
6 DESCENDANTS OF VIACHESLAV YAROSLAVICH
7 DESCENDANTS OF IGOR YAROSLAVICH

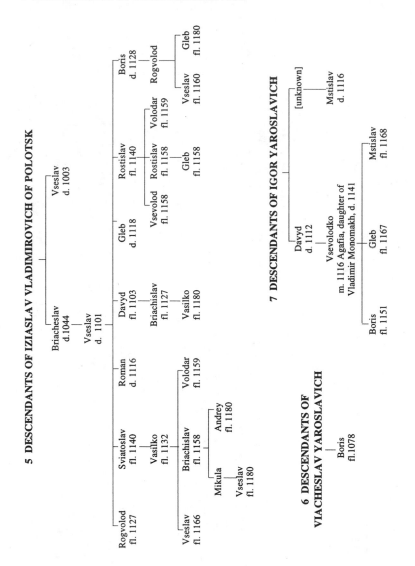

8 DESCENDANTS OF VLADIMIR YAROSLAVICH

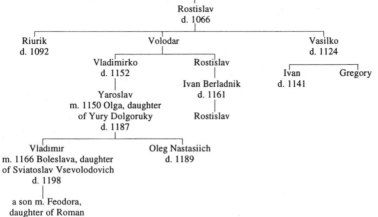

Rostislav
d. 1066

Riurik
d. 1092

Volodar

Vasilko
d. 1124

Vladimirko
d. 1152

Rostislav

Ivan
d. 1141

Gregory

Yaroslav
m. 1150 Olga, daughter
of Yury Dolgoruky
d. 1187

Ivan Berladnik
d. 1161

Rostislav

Vladimir
m. 1166 Boleslava, daughter
of Sviatoslav Vsevolodovich
d. 1198

Oleg Nastasiich
d. 1189

a son m. Feodora,
daughter of Roman
of Volhynia

9 DESCENDANTS OF IZIASLAV YAROSLAVICH

Mstislav
d. 1068

Yaropolk
d. 1086

Sviatopolk
m. a Polovetsian 1094
d. 1113

Rostislav
d. 1093

Yaroslav
d.1102

Viacheslav
d. 1104

Mstislav
d. 1099

Yaroslav
m. 1112
daughter of
Mstislav Vladimirovich
d. 1123

Briacheslav
1104-1127

Iziaslav
d. 1128

Yury
m. 1144 daughter of
Vsevolod of Goroden

Viacheslav
fl. 1127

Ivan
fl. 1168

Yaroslav
fl. 1184

Sviatopolk
d. 1190

Yaropolk
m. 1190

Gleb
d. 1196

10 PRINCES OF PINSK OF UNKNOWN DESCENT

Vladimir
fl. 1204

Alexander Dubrovitsky
fl. 1224

Rostislav
fl. 1228

GENEALOGICAL TABLES

11 DESCENDANTS OF SVIATOSLAV YAROSLAVICH

Gleb	Roman	Davyd	Oleg	Yaroslav
d. 1078	d. 1079	d. 1123	d. 1115	d. 1129

Descendants of Davyd Sviatoslavich

Sviatoslav	Vsevolod	Rostislav	Vladimir
fl. 1142	m. a Polish princess 1124	d. 1120	m. 1144 daughter of Goroden d. 1151

Sviatoslav
m. 1159 daughter of
Andrey Bogoliubsky
d. 1166

NOTES

Additional information on personalities and topics found in the text and notes is available in Joseph L. Wieczynski, et al., eds., *The Modern Encyclopedia of Russian, Soviet and Eurasian History* (MERSH, formerly *The Modern Encyclopedia of Russian and Soviet History*); Harry B. Weber, et al., eds., *The Modern Encyclopedia of East Slavic, Baltic and Eurasian Literatures* (MESBEL, formerly *The Modern Encyclopedia of Russian and Soviet Literatures, Including Non-Russian and Emigré Literatures*); Paul D. Steeves, ed., *The Modern Encyclopedia of Religions in Russia and Eurasia* (MERRE, formerly *The Modern Encyclopedia of Religions in Russia and the Soviet Union*); and David R. Jones, ed., *The Military Encyclopedia of Russia and Eurasia* (MERE, formerly *The Military-Naval Encyclopedia of Russia and the Soviet Union*) all published by Academic International Press.

INTRODUCTION

1. See Nancy Shields Kollmann, "Collateral Succession in Kievan Rus'," *Harvard Ukrainian Studies,* 14 (1990), pp. 377-385.

2. A valuable corrective to Soloviev's "Kievocentricity" is provided by Martin Dimnik, *The Dynasty of Chernigov, 1054-1156* (Toronto, 1994), a book of greater significance for the history of the Land of Rus as a whole than the title would suggest. The Asiatic context is supplied by George Vernadsky, *Ancient Russia* (New Haven, 1943) and *Kievan Russia* (New Haven, 1948), still the most extensive treatment of the period in English, though the author is very uncritical in his attitude to sources. More recent studies include Simon Franklin and Jonathan Shepard, *The Emergence of Rus, 750-1200* (London, 1996), and Janet Martin, *Medieval Russia, 980-1584* (Cambridge, 1995).

3. The religious history of the Land of Rus recently has been treated by Sophia Senyk, *A History of the Church in Ukraine* (Rome, 1993) and J.L.I. Fennell, *A History of the Russian Church to 1448* (London, 1995).

4. For an explanation of this term and of its relevance to the Land of Rus, see Dimitri Obolensky, *The Byzantine Commonwealth* (London, 1971), and also his contribution to *Cambridge Medieval History*, Vol. IV, Part I (Cambridge, 1966), pp. 473-518.

5. For the peoples of the steppe and their image in the chronicles, see Charles Halperin, *Russia and the Golden Horde* (London, 1987), especially Chapter I.

6. See below, p. 128.

7. For a conspectus of modern scholarship on Novgorod, with an excellent bibliography, see Henrik Birnbaum, *Lord Novgorod the Great* (Columbus, Ohio, 1981).

8. P.N. Petrov, *History of the Families of the Russian Nobility* (St. Petersburg, 1886, reprinted Moscow, 1991), Vol. I, p. 12.

9. The best introduction in English to the chronicles and the processes by which they were compiled is still S.H. Cross, "The Russian Primary Chronicle," *Harvard Studies and Notes in Philology and Literature*, 12 (1930), pp. 75-320, which also contains a translation into rather archaic English of the Primary Chronicle itself. A revised version was published as S.H. Cross and O.P. Sherbowitz-Wetzor, *The Russian Primary Chronicle. Laurentian Text* (Harvard, 1953).

10. An English translation of this exists, *The Nikonian Chronicle*, 5 vols., edited, introduced and annotated by S.A. Zenkovsky and B. Zenkovsky (Princeton, 1984-1989). Both the translation and the commentary have been the subject of very severe criticism and should be used with caution.

11. Vasily Nikitich Tatishchev's *History of Russia*, published posthumously between 1768 and 1848, besides the then unpublished chronicles drew upon a significant number of sources which have not survived. Modern historians are agreed that "Tatishchev's material" should be approached with extreme caution when not corroborated by extant sources.

12. Nikolay Mikhailovich Karamzin (1766-1826) was the first official historiographer of Russia. His twelve-volume *History of the Russian State* laid the foundations for all subsequent scholarship. His history is most readily available in a reprint of the 1842-1844 edition (Moscow, 1988).

CHAPTER I

1. Yaroslav I, called the Wise, grand prince of Kiev 1019-1054, after a short period of strife following the death of his father St. Vladimir established himself as the dominant prince in Rus and, after the death of his brother Mstislav in 1036, its undisputed ruler. His long reign was a period of stability and cultural advancement. See Vol. 1, Chapter VIII.

2. Vladimir Yaroslavich, prince of Novgorod, died in 1052. See Franklin and Shepard, pp. 247, 249, and entry by Martin Dimnik, *Modern Encylopedia of Russian and Soviet History* (hereafter MERSH) (Academic International Press, 1976-), Vol. 42, pp. 165-167.

3. Iziaslav Vladimirovich (died 1001), the half-brother of Yaroslav the Wise, was installed as prince of his maternal grandfather's city of Polotsk by his father Vladimir. After his father's death his descendants maintained it as an independent principality. See Janet Martin, *Medieval Russia, 980-1584* (Cambridge, 1995), pp. 23-29.

4. The Russkaia Pravda (Rus Justice) is the first extant East Slavonic legislative code and represents a codification of earlier customary law. It is believed to have received written form first under Yaroslav, and then to have been subjected to some revision by his sons. See Franklin and Shepard, pp. 217-225,

also *Medieval Russian Laws*. Trans. by George Vernadsky (New York, 1947), pp. 26-56, Basil Dmytryshyn, *Medieval Russia. A Source Book, 850-1700*. The Academic International Press Edition (Gulf Breeze, Fla.: 2000), pp. 36-41, and entry by A.A. Zimin, MERSH, Vol. 32, pp. 218-221.

5. *Russian Primary Chronicle*, pp. 142-143; Dmytryshyn, p. 53.

6. Indeed the Russian words for "brother" and "sister" are usually applied without distinction to cousins, second cousins, and so on, and these degrees of kinship are distinguished by the use of an additional adjective when it is felt essential to avoid ambiguity. The nomenclature of family relations is summarized excellently, with useful diagrams, by Genevra Gerhart, *The Russian's World. Life and Language*, 2nd ed. (New York, 1997), pp. 49-51.

7. A useful summary of this phenomenon with a historiographical summary of the subsequent controversy is found in the entry by Edward D. Sokol, "The Rota System," MERSH, Vol. 31, pp. 183-188.

8. Vladimir Vsevolodovich Monomakh, grand prince of Kiev, 1113-1125. See Chapter III, below, and entry by George P. Majeska, MERSH, Vol. 42, pp. 160-164.

9. Sviatoslav, son of Yaroslav the Wise and uncle of Vladimir Monomakh. His sons ruled the principality of Chernigov. See entry by Dimnik, MERSH, Vol. 38, pp. 122-127.

10. Vasilko Rostislavich (died 1124), prince of Terebovl. For the episode of his blinding, see below, pp. 46-51, Franklin and Shepard, pp. 269-270, Vernadsky, *Kievan Russia*, pp. 90-91, Serge A. Zenkovsky, *Medieval Russia's Epics, Chronicles and Tales* (New York, 1963), pp. 73-77 and entry (unsigned) in MERSH, Vol. 41, p. 226.

11. Soloviev supposes erroneously that the Russian word *vnuk* (grandson) is derived from *jun* (young).

12. An *izgoy* (plural *izgoi*) was a *déclassé*, someone who did not occupy that position to which his birth might have been expected to entitle him. Prince Vsevolod of Novgorod's law code lists four classes of izgoi: a priest's son who was illiterate, a manumitted bondsman, an insolvent merchant, and a fatherless prince. Since in this volume the term is applied exclusively to princes, it is translated "dispossessed prince(s)." See entry by Thomas S. Noonan, MERSH, Vol. 15, pp. 85-86, and Vernadsky, *Kievan Russia*, pp. 152-154.

13. See Note 9, above.

14. These were strictly speaking the descendants of Oleg Sviatoslavich, prince of Chernigov, but the term was commonly used both by their contemporaries, and by later historians, to denote all the princes of Sviatoslav Yaroslavich's line who reigned in Chernigov and its subordinate territories.

CHAPTER II

1. Rogvolod (Rognvald), a Varangian prince who established himself in Polotsk, was killed by Vladimir, who married his daughter Rogneda (Ragnheid).

See below, Chapter V, Note 24. Iziaslav (980-1001) was Vladimir's first son from his marriage to Rogneda. He ruled first in Iziaslavl and subsequently in Turov.

2. Iziaslav Yaroslavich (1024-1078) was prince of Turov and from 1054 grand prince of Kiev. In 1068 he was stripped of the grand-princely title as the result of a popular uprising in Kiev. Several times thereafter he sought foreign aid, from the Holy Roman emperor, the king of Poland and the Pope, in an effort to secure allies to assist him in his bid to regain the grand-princely throne. In 1077 he was restored, then the following year lost his life in a fresh outbreak of internecine strife. He was also, with his brothers Vsevolod and Sviatoslav, a participant in the drafting of the so-called Pravda of the Sons of Yaroslav. See Franklin and Shepard, pp. 245-263.

3. Rostislav Vladimirovich (died 1067) according to Tatishchev was prince of Rostov and Suzdal after the death of Yaroslav the Wise (1054), then became ruler of Vladimir-in-Volhynia. In 1064 he expelled Gleb Sviatoslavich from Tmutorokan and subjected local tribes to his authority. As related below, he was poisoned at a banquet given by Byzantine nobles who feared that his growing power would threaten their interests. See *Russian Primary Chronicle*, p. 145.

4. Sviatopolk "the Damned" (978-1019), so called because of the murder of his half-brothers Boris, Gleb and Sviatoslav. See Vol. 1, Chapter VIII, and entry by Walter K. Hanak, MERSH, Vol. 38, pp. 108-110.

5. Vsevolod Yaroslavich (1030-1093), grand prince of Kiev from 1078. Some time between 1046 and 1052 he married Maria, the daughter or niece of Constantine IX Monomachos (reigned 1042-1055), and their son Vladimir took his maternal grandfather's surname. Vsevolod's daughter Evpraksia (in Latin Praxedis, in German Adelheid) was married first to the margrave of Northern Saxony and then, on his death, to Emperor Henry IV. For a comprehensive sketch of Vsevolod, see entry by Sokol, MERSH, Vol. 43, pp. 96-101; also Franklin and Shepard, pp. 261-265.

6. See Chapter I, Note 12, above.

7. The term "mayor" is here and elsewhere, when referring to Novgorod, used to translate posadnik. A posadnik was originally a burgrave placed in a town by a prince to administer it during his absence, which term continued to be used in this sense in the smaller towns of Southern Rus. In Novgorod and other towns of a similar constitution the posadnik soon became the effective head of the civic government, something like a lord mayor, and was appointed by the popular assembly.

8. Soloviev uses the term Kasogi. The Circassians were known in Russian as Cherkesy, in Georgian as Cherkezi, in Abkhaz as Azkwha, in Ossetian as Käsgon and in Arabic and Persian as Kashaki or Kesheki. They consist today of a number of indigenous tribes found on both slopes of the Western Caucasus range and its northern foothills. The Circassians call themselves Adyge (collectively Käsäg), while their largest group, the upland Circassians, are known as Kabardians or Kabardinians. The Adyge dwelling south of the Caucasus in Georgia are called

Abkhazians. A considerable number of Circassians live elsewhere in the Northern Caucasus and also in other countries, corresponding to present-day Turkey, Syria, Israel, Jordan and Iraq. The Circassian language (Adyghebze), along with Abkhazian and Ubykh, belongs to the northwest group of the Caucasian languages and consists of two main dialects, Kabardin (or Kabardo-Circassian) and Adyghian, both of which had the status of literary languages in the Soviet Union, though their fate in the successor states is uncertain. Circassian was written in the Arabic script as early as the nineteenth century, but in 1927 this form of writing was replaced by a modified Latin alphabet and in 1938 by a version of the Cyrillic script. For a detailed history of the Circassians and extensive bibliography, see the entry by Robert H. Hewsen, MERSH, Vol. 7, pp. 131-136.

9. The term Soloviev uses is kotopan, cognate with katepano, variously anglicized as "catapan" or "catepan," a Byzantine official combining civil and military functions. "The term was often used to denote the commander of a military unit...and was identical with *strategos*. By the end of the tenth century, *katepano* became primarily the designation of governors of major provinces, especially Italy...and Mesopotamia, in the eleventh century Bulgaria..., Antioch, etc. The term in the sense of governor-*doux* disappeared after 1100, but it continued as a name for local officials, at least in Smyrna in the twelfth and in Trebizond in the fourteenth. Accordingly the term *katepanikion*, known in both Macedonia and Asia Minor, was used for small administrative units. The term *katepanate*, often employed in scholarly literature, is not found in Byzantine sources, although the Normans created the word Capitanata as a description for southern Italy." *Oxford Dictionary of Byzantium* (Oxford, 1991), p. 1115.

10. Cherson, rendered here as Korsun, earlier known in Greek as Chersonnesos (dry island), was a settlement founded in the fifth century B.C. as a Doric colony of Heracleia in Bithynia. After defending itself from the kingdom of Bosporos and the native Scythians and Tauri, around 115 B.C. the city was forced to call in the aid of Mithridates VI and Diophantos, and submitted to the Pontic dynasty. Regaining nominal independence, it came under Roman suzerainty, receiving an imperial garrison from Nero late in the first century and again from Hadrian in the second century A.D. During the reign of Constantine (324-337) in return for aiding the empire against the Bosporans and other tribes, Cherson regained its autonomy and received special privileges, albeit still under Byzantine rule. Emperor Justinian II (reigned 685-695 and 705 to 711), exiled there between his two reigns, is said to have sacked the city in revenge. Nevertheless it became an important emporium of Byzantine commerce on the northern coast of the Black Sea, through which relations with the Pechenegs and Rus were channelled. Indeed it was in Cherson that, according to some versions of the story, Vladimir received baptism and his "born in the purple" bride Anna. (See Andrzej Poppe, "The Political Background to the Baptism of Rus'. Byzantine-Russian Relations between 986-989 [sic]," *Dumbarton Oaks Papers,* 30 (1976), pp. 197-244. The city's ruin was caused by the rivalry of Genoa, which diverted the Greek merchant shipping to its colonies of Kaffa and Sudak. See *Oxford Classical*

Dictionary, 2nd ed. (Oxford, 1970), p. 229, and *Oxford Dictionary of Byzantium*, pp. 418-419.

11. Vseslav Briachislavich (died 1101), prince of Polotsk from 1044. In 1065 he attacked Pskov but failed to capture it. A year later he attacked Novgorod, plundered the Holy Wisdom cathedral and burned the town. In 1067 he was defeated on the Nemiza river by the brothers Iziaslav, Sviatoslav and Vsevolod Yaroslavich, who treacherously seized him during peace negotiations. In 1068 he was freed from his dungeon by the insurgent townsmen of Kiev, who by a decision of the assembly installed him as prince for seven months. He moved to stem the advance of the former prince Iziaslav Yaroslavich, then secretly fled to Polotsk. He was expelled from there by Iziaslav then in 1070 definitively established himself in Polotsk and struggled against Prince Vsevolod Yaroslavich and his son Vladimir Monomakh to preserve the independence of the Polotsk principality.

12. The Holy Wisdom cathedral of Novgorod, built 1045-1050 in the middle of the Novgorod citadel, was the symbol of the city's identity. For a physical description and summary of its history, see entry by V.S. Rumiantseva, MERSH, Vol. 33, p. 92.

13. *The Chronicle of Novgorod*, translated by Robert Michell and Nevill Forbes (London, 1914, reprinted Academic International Press, 1970), p. 5.

14. The term used is otdali na shchit, literally "gave over to the shield." Soloviev paraphrases the term in parentheses.

15. The Polovetsians, known in Byzantine and Latin sources as Cumans, are first mentioned in the Rus chronicles under the year 1054. After this there occurred a series of raids on the scattered Rus principalities, whose rulers occasionally concluded alliances with the invaders and helped them plunder their rivals. In 1103, after the Dolobsk conference, Vladimir Monomakh organized campaigns into the steppe. The Polovetsians, conceding defeat, retired into Georgia. From the second quarter of the twelfth century Polovetsian raids intensified, and Rus borderlands were devastated. In 1223, during the first Mongol incursions into Eastern Europe the Polovetsians, having betrayed their allies the Alans, were defeated by the Mongols, first in the Northern Caucasus and then on the Kalka river. The eastern Polovetsians, the Kipchak, entered the Mongolian alliance, forming a basic part of the population of the Golden Horde, mostly composed of Turkic peoples like themselves, who eventually assimilated their Mongol overlords. The western group spread into Hungary where, after a further flight into Bulgaria when that country was overrun by the Mongols in 1242, they were welcomed by King Béla IV, who took the title Rex Cumaniae and settled them on his lands. The assimilation was a slow and difficult process, and as late as the eighteenth and nineteenth centuries the inhabitants of Nagykunság and Kiskunság, the Greater and Lesser Cumania, though by now indistinguishable from the rest of the Hungarian population, were still asserting their peculiar privileges. For a detailed historical sketch, see the entry by Noonan, MERSH, Vol. 29, pp. 12-24.

16. The Pechenegs were an alliance of Turkic tribes formed in the eighth and ninth centuries, speaking a language close to Oguz. They also absorbed elements of conquered Sarmatian, Finno-Ugric and possibly Caucasian groups. Until the end of the ninth century they roamed the area between the Aral Sea and the Volga basin, fighting the Oguz, Kipchak and Khazars. At the end of the ninth century, under presssure from the Khazars and Oguz, they crossed the Volga. Having driven the Magyars from their homeland between the Don and the Dnieper, they occupied the northern littoral of the Black Sea as far as the Danube. In the tenth century they divided into ten tribes, each subdivided into five clans. Their livelihood was derived from raids on neighboring sedentary societies such as Rus, Byzantium and Hungary. The Byzantine empire occasionally used the Pechenegs as allies against the Rus, culminating in the death of Prince Sviatoslav Igorevich by the Dnieper rapids in 972. Pecheneg raids on the southern Rus borderlands continued until 1036, when Yaroslav the Wise inflicted a decisive defeat upon them. Under pressure from the Torks and Polovetsians they migrated in the mid-eleventh century to the Carpathians and the Danube basin, their place on the northern Black Sea littoral being taken by the Polovetsians. Some migrated to Hungary and Bulgaria, there to be assimilated, while others settled in the Rus borderlands and became slavicized. For a detailed history, consult the entry by Noonan, MERSH, Vol. 27, pp. 126-133.

17. The Torks were a branch of the Oguz Turks who migrated to the steppes of what is now the Ukraine some time earlier. At the period in question they seem to have been in transition from a nomadic to a sedentary mode of existence. During the tenth century the Torks allied with the princes of Rus in various military campaigns. By the mid-eleventh century they struggled against Kievan Rus, then were driven westwards by the marauding Polovetsians. The Torks ravaged Thrace and Macedonia, then returned to the steppes, settling along the borders of the southern Rus principalities. They then became allies of the Rus in their continuing struggle against the Polovetsians. In the twelfth century the Torks merged into the tribal federation known as the Chernye Klobuki (Black Hoods or Karakalpaks). The Torks eventually were assimilated by the inhabitants of Kievan Rus or by the Polovetsians, passing from history as an independent people. See entry (unsigned) in MERSH, Vol. 39, p. 125.

18. Bolesław II Śmiały (the Bold), also known as Szczodry (the Generous) (1039-1081), was prince of Poland 1058-1077, king 1077-1079. He waged continuous war on Bohemia and conducted two campaigns against Kievan Rus (1069 and 1077). Intervention in Rus affairs distracted his attention from the western borderlands, where Poland lost control over Western Pomerania. He was also blamed for the death of the saintly bishop Stanisław (see Note 47, below), and was ousted by an aristocratic revolt in 1079. He spent the remaining two years of his life exiled in Carinthia. See O. Halecki, *A History of Poland*, rev. ed. (London, 1978), pp. 18-20.

19. The quotation is from the Tale of Igor's Campaign (Slovo o polku Igoreve), possibly the most famous work of Old Russian literature. Its subject is the campaign conducted in 1186 by Igor Sviatoslavich, prince of Novgorod Seversk, against the Polovetsians, but it contains frequent references to earlier history. See Vol. 3 of this series, Chapter VIII. A blank verse translation of this poem is found in Zenkovsky, pp. 137-160 and Dmytryshyn, pp. 77-92. For text and prose translation, see the *Penguin Book of Russian Verse*, rev. ed., Ed. and Introduction by Dimitri Obolensky (Harmondsworth, 1965), pp. 1-22. There has been some controversy concerning the authenticity of this work. For a summary of the scholarly debate, see John Fennell and Antony Stokes, *Early Russian Literature* (London, 1974), pp. 191-206. Henryk Paszkiewicz, *The Origin of Russia* (London, 1954), pp. 336-353, has also subjected this work to critical scrutiny.

20. This refers to Bolesław I's intervention in 1017 in support of Sviatopolk Vladimirovich. See Vol. 1, Chapter VIII.

21. The Vod were a Finnic tribe living to the south of the Gulf of Finland. They gave their name to one of the administrative subdivisions of the Novgorod territories, the Vodskaia Piatina. From about the middle of the first millennium A.D. their burial customs were similar to those of the Estonians and Finns, then between the ninth and the fourteenth centuries they were assimilated to the Slavs, adopting their burial customs and language.

22. For the earlier career of St. Anthony, see Vol. 1, Chapter VIII. Soloviev's account is based on late medieval and early modern sources which are largely fictional. For a modern and more reliable account, see Francis J. Thomson, "Saint Anthony of Kiev. The Facts and the Fiction," *Byzantinoslavica*, 56 (1995), pp. 637-668.

23. In the beginning of his excursus into the history of the Western Slavs Soloviev goes back three generations to the time of Bolesław the Brave (992-1025), the Polish king who had intervened in Kiev on behalf of his son-in-law Sviatopolk in 1018 (see Vol. 1 of this series), and the great-grandfather of Iziaslav's ally Bolesław the Bold. Bolesław the Brave had taken advantage of a local conflict to intervene in Bohemia as part of the expansionist policy that he was pursuing at the expense of the Holy Roman empire. He succeeded in installing himself as prince briefly in 1003-1004, but was expelled by Emperor Henry II, who restored Jaromír. The subsequent conflict between Jaromír and Oldřich may be related to the perennial problem of Bohemia's status *vis-à-vis* the empire.

24. Conrad II (990-1039), king of the Romans 1024, Holy Roman emperor 1027, founder of the Franconian dynasty. In his struggle with the feudal magnates in Germany and Italy he was aided by the lesser nobility, whose fiefs he made hereditary. He consolidated his domination over the church, placing his nominees over bishoprics and major religious houses. In 1032-1034 he annexed the Burgundian kingdom of Arles. Taking advantage of disorders in Poland he took Upper Lusatia away from Mieszko II. Otherwise he was largely unsuccessful in his relations with his eastern neighbors, except Bohemia, where Břetislav, Jaromír's nephew and successor, was his constant ally.

25. Frederick G. Heymann, *Poland and Czechoslovakia* (Englewood Cliffs, N.J., 1966), pp. 34-36.

26. To piece together the rather complicated relations between Germany and Bohemia in the eleventh century, consult the *Cambridge Medieval History*, Vol. 3 (London, 1922, reprinted Cambridge, 1957), pp. 222-226, 299-302; Timothy Reuter, *Germany in the Early Middle Ages, 800-1056* (London, 1991), pp. 260-262; Vernadsky, *Kievan Russia*, p. 73; Heymann, pp. 32-33; Vol. 1 of this series, Chapter VII.

27. Casimir the Restorer (Kazimierz I Odnowiciel, 1016-1058), prince of Poland from 1034. He came to the throne against a background of collapse of centralized power and dissolution of Poland into its component parts. Almost immediately on his accession he was driven into exile by a rebel noble faction. After the suppression of a major peasant rebellion Casimir returned late in 1038 or early in 1039 with the aid of Emperor Henry III. Once restored to the throne he carried out a vigorous policy of reunification of the Polish lands. Concluding a Kievan alliance in 1047 by marriage to Vladimir's daughter Maria-Dobronega, he recovered Mazovia, and in 1054 resumed control over Silesia, which had been seized by Bohemia. He also secured the independence of the Polish clergy from the German hierarchy.

28. See Note 18, above.

29. Henry III (1017-1056), king of the Romans 1039, Holy Roman emperor 1046, son of Emperor Conrad II (see Note 23, above). He placed great reliance upon his ministeriales (unfree military servitors) and knights. During his campaign in Italy in 1046-1047 he deposed the rival popes and imposed his own candidate. Yet by his support of the Cluniac reform movement he unwittingly prepared the ground for the resurgence of papal power. He gave out fiefs for money, arousing indignation among the secular magnates. In his eastern policy he strove to prevent any union between Poland and Bohemia, making Bohemia and Hungary dependent upon the empire.

30. Henry IV (1050-1106), king of the Romans from 1056, Holy Roman emperor from 1086, son of Henry III (see previous note). During his long minority he was under the tutelage, first of Archbishop Anno of Cologne, then of Adalbert of Bremen. Many magnates took advantage of this regency to seize royal lands and offices. Having attained his majority, Henry sought to assert his authority by building a base of strength in Saxony through construction of fortifications and resumption of crown lands. This led to the Saxon revolt of 1073-1075. Henry's attempt to maintain the right of royal investiture to church offices inevitably led to a clash with an increasingly authoritarian papacy, as personified in Gregory VII. In turn his embroilment with the papacy encouraged the German and Italian nobility once again to raise the standard of rebellion. If this were not enough, Henry was faced with revolt by his own sons, Conrad (1093) and Henry (1104).

31. When Stephen I died in 1038 the country refused to accept his designated successor, his half-Italian nephew Peter, and in 1041 put up a rival king, Aba. With German help, in 1044 Peter drove out Aba and then acknowledged Hungary

to be a fief of the Holy Roman empire. The Hungarians then brought back from Polish exile three of Stephen's cousins, Andrew, Béla and Ladislas. Andrew expelled and slew Peter, and assumed the crown in 1046. He married his infant son Salomon to Judith, Henry III's daughter, and had him crowned as his successor. This violated the generally accepted rule of succession and a long struggle ensued in which Béla expelled Andrew with Polish help. He then reigned for three years (1060-1063), but on his deathbed designated Salomon as his heir. See László Makkai, "The Foundation of the Hungarian Christian State, 950-1196," *A History of Hungary*. Edited by Peter F. Sugar, Péter Hanák and Tibor Frank (Bloomington, 1990), pp. 18-19, and C.A. Macartney, *Hungary. A Short History* (Edinburgh, 1962), pp. 18-19.

32. See II Kings 20: 16-18.

33. Gregory VII (Hildebrand), pope 1073-1085, who after 1075 was in constant struggle with Emperor Henry IV (see Note 29, above). The conflict is summed up by Geoffrey Barraclough, *The Medieval Papacy* (London, 1968), pp. 77-90. See also Nicholas Cheetam, *Keepers of the Keys* (New York, 1982), pp. 86-98. Gregory was canonized in 1606, his feast day being May 25.

34. "Red Ruthenia" (in Polish, Rus Czerwona) was the name given to the northwestern edge of what was soon to become the principality of Galich. It included the modern city of Lvov but at this period its most important town was Cherven (now Chervonograd). Soloviev uses the term Chervenskie goroda.

35. The country to the northeast of present-day Volokolamsk.

36. Franklin and Shepard, pp. 262-263.

37. Franklin and Shepard, p. 271.

38. Franklin and Shepard, pp. 263, 269; *Russian Primary Chronicle*, pp. 168-169.

39. Sons of St. Vladimir, killed by another of his sons, Sviatopolk (see Note 4, above), during the power struggle which followed his death. Their unresisting deaths were regarded as emulating the sufferings of Christ, and they were the first native saints to enjoy an extensive cult in Rus. See Vol. 1, Chapter VII.

40. See below, pp. 46-51.

41. *Russian Primary Chronicle*, pp. 174-175

42. ...zaezzhali, *po pozdneishemu mestnicheskomu vyrazheniiu*. Soloviev makes reference to mestnichestvo, the extremely complicated and highly contentious system of precedence in use during the Muscovite period.

43. The quotation is again from the Tale of Igor's Campaign.

44. *Russian Primary Chronicle*, p. 168.

45. The Goliad were a Balt tribe attested in the Rus chronicles of the eleventh and twelfth centuries. They lived in the basin of the Protva river, a right tributary of the Moskva, between the habitations of the Viatichians and Krivichians. By the end of the twelfth century they were completely slavicized.

46. The Sosola was a Finno-Ugric tribe native to Northwestern Rus. *Nikonian Chronicle*, Vol. 1, p. 154.

47. Bolesław II (see Note 18, above) assumed the title of king of Poland in 1077, thus asserting his independence of the emperor.

48. Stanisław (1030-1079) was elected bishop of Cracow in 1072. It is said that he repeatedly rebuked the king concerning irregularities in his private life. According to a commonly received tradition, Stanisław was attacked and hacked to pieces while celebrating mass. He was canonized in 1253 and his feast day is April 11. See Donald Attwater, *The Penguin Dictionary of Saints*, 2nd ed. (London, 1983), p. 303; Norman Davies, *God's Playground. A History of Poland* (Oxford, 1981), Vol. I, p. 70; also Note 18, above.

49. Władysław Herman, prince of Poland, born 1043, the younger brother of the deposed Bolesław II, reigned from 1079 to 1102, but never assumed the royal dignity. He sided with the Holy Roman empire in its struggle with the papacy, contrary to Poland's history and interest. Yielding to ambitious magnates, especially the palatine Sieciech who actually controlled most of the country, he could not even appease the rivalry between his two sons, Zbigniew and Bolesław, who received large sections of Poland during their father's lifetime. Halecki, pp. 20-23.

50. The Pomeranian Slavs (Pomorzanie) inhabited the Baltic littoral (Pomorze) in the north of modern Poland and northeast of modern Germany, and only gradually submitted to Polish rule. See Davies, pp. 28-29.

51. Franklin and Shepard, pp. 262, 286; *Russian Primary Chronicle*, pp. 168, 180-181.

CHAPTER III

1. Sviatopolk Iziaslavich (1050-1113), baptismal name Mikhail, was prince of Polotsk 1069-1071, prince of Novgorod 1078-1088, Turov 1088-1093 and grand prince of Kiev from 1093. He was the son of Iziaslav Yaroslavich. In 1077, together with Vladimir Monomakh, he went against Prince Vseslav Briachislavich of Polotsk. In 1093 he was twice defeated by the Polovetsians, then in 1096 he and Monomakh invaded the steppe. In 1096 he waged war against Prince Oleg Sviatoslavich of Chernigov, who refused to attend the proposed princely conference in Kiev. In 1097 Sviatopolk Iziaslavich attended the Liubech conference after which, in conjunction with Prince Davyd Igorevich of Volhynia he was an accomplice in the seizure and blinding of Vasilko of Terebovl. In 1098, under pressure from Vladimir Monomakh and other princes, he waged war on Davyd Igorevich, whom he expelled from Vladimir, but was defeated in his attempt to seize lands from Volodar and Vasilko Rostislavich. He took part in the princely conferences at Vitichi (1100), on the Zolotcha river (1101) and on the Dolobsk island (1103). In 1103, 1107 and 1111 he participated with Vladimir Monomakh in successful campaigns against the Polovetsians. Towards the end of his reign he engaged in speculation in salt and other commodities, which provoked the

Kiev uprising immediately after his death. Sviatopolk generally has received a negative assessment by historians, for example Vernadsky, *Kievan Russia*, pp. 92-94. On the other hand Franklin and Shepard (p. 276) state "It is easy to underestimate the reign of Sviatopolk Iziaslavich. He is often obscured in the long shadow cast by the more glamorous heroes of epic, ecclesiastical, imperial and nationalist legend: Vladimir Sviatoslavich for the conversion to Christianity, Iaroslav for his glorious city and for refounding the dynasty; Vladimir Monomakh for his military energies and for his self-promoting patronage and writings. Sviatopolk personally did not have a good press even in the earliest sources, whose attitude towards him tends to have been adopted uncritically by subsequent commentators. However, one should look beyond the prejudices of writers loyal to Vladimir Monomakh whose patronage and whose progeny shunted the family and the name of Sviatopolk to the sidelines of dynastic history. The impact and influence of Sviatopolk's twenty-year reign was profound." For a concise biographical sketch, see entry by Dimnik, MERSH, Vol. 38, pp. 105-108.

2. Franklin and Shepard, p. 265; *Russian Primary Chronicle*, p. 276, Note 284; Martin, pp. 31-32.

3. This quotation is taken from the so-called Instruction of Vladimir Monomakh (Pouchenie Vladimira Monomakha), interpolated in the Laurentian Chronicle at the year 1096, with which it has no apparent connection. It is a mixture of autobiography and moral advice addressed to Vladimir's sons. It is firmly within the tradition of early medieval European political thought, which has allowed scholars to suggest many parallels, not only in Byzantine sources, but even in the Anglo-Saxon Fæder Larcwidas, with which, it is alleged, Vladimir could have been acquainted through his English wife Gytha, daughter of King Harold Godwinson. See *Russian Primary Chronicle*, pp. 206-215, reprinted in Dmytryshyn, pp. 65-72. For Soloviev's discussion of this document, see Vol. 3 of this series, Chapter VIII.

4. See Chapter II, Note 15, above.

5. The account of Vladimir's hunting exploits, as well as the direct quotations, are again taken from his Instruction.

6. *Russian Primary Chronicle*, p. 175.

7. See Chapter II, Note 41, above.

8. This is now the village of Torchitsa, on the banks of the Torcha, a tributary of the Ros. (Soloviev's note)

9. The monastery at Vydubichi, built by Vsevolod and dedicated to St. Michael in 1088, is situated on the western shore of the Dnieper about one and a half miles from the Caves monastery. See *Russian Primary Chronicle*, p. 267, Note 222; Fennell, *Russian Church*, p. 69.

10. There is a village called Zhiliane on the little river now called the Borshchagovka between Belgorodka and Kiev. (Soloviev's note)

11. *Russian Primary Chronicle*, p. 178.

12. *Russian Primary Chronicle*, p. 179.

13. "Tugorkan (Tugorkhan) and Bonyak (mentioned under 1096) also figure prominently in Byzantine history of the period. During the reign of Alexius I Comnenus (1081-1118) the rebellious Bogomils in Bulgaria summoned the aid of the Pechenegs, who in 1091 penetrated even to the very gates of Constantinople, and in combination with the Seljuq threat placed the Byzantine Empire in one of the most critical situations of its entire history. Alexius despaired of the issue when the day was saved by the arrival of the Polovetsians under Tugorkan and Bonyak, whose aid was purchased by Alexius so that, on the 29th of April 1091, they administered a crushing defeat to the Pechenegs. The captives from this battle were mercilessly slaughtered by the Greek soldiery during the same night, a bloodthirsty act which so terrified the Polovetsians that they precipitately retired without claiming the promised rewards, which had to be sent after them, and their next exploits took place in Hungary.... Though Svyatopolk and Vladimir scarcely realized it at the time, they were thus fighting against two nomad chiefs whom modern historians class as 'the saviors of the Byzantine Empire.'" *Russian Primary Chronicle*, pp. 276-277, Note 291; see also *Cambridge Medieval History*, Vol. 4 (Cambridge, 1966), pp. 213-214.

14. Oleg Sviatoslavich (died 1115) was prince of Volhynia 1073-1076, Tmutorokan 1083-1094, Chernigov 1094-1096 and Novgorod Seversk from 1097 until his death. In 1076, in alliance with Monomakh he aided the Poles by a raid on Bohemia. In 1078 he tried to establish himself in Chernigov, but failed. In 1079 he was captured by the Khazars and sent on to Constantinople, spending the next four years both there and on the island of Rhodes. In 1094 with Polovetsian help he deprived Vladimir Monomakh of Chernigov. He refused to go to Kiev for a princely conference, then the combined pressure of Grand Prince Sviatopolk and Vladimir Monomakh forced him to yield. As a result of the Liubech conference (1097) Oleg received the principality of Novgorod Seversk. He took part in the Vitichi and Zolotchevsk conferences (1100 and 1101) and in the Polovetsian campaigns of 1107 and 1113. See *Russian Primary Chronicle*, pp. 179-180; Franklin and Shepard, pp. 259-270; and entry by Dimnik, MERSH, Vol. 26, pp. 9-12.

15. *Russian Primary Chronicle*, pp. 180-181.

16. Franklin and Shepard, p. 267; *Russian Primary Chronicle*, p. 181.

17. The *History of Russia* by V.N. Tatishchev (1686-1750), published posthumously in 1768-1848, included material from many sources that have not survived. See Introduction, Note 11, above.

18. *Russian Primary Chronicle*, p. 182.

19. These words do not, as some have suggested, imply direct inheritance. Oleg's position amongst his cousins was the same as his father's amongst the sons of Yaroslav, so he was entitled to all his father's territories. (Soloviev's note)

20. dannikov (sborshchikov dani).

21. *Russian Primary Chronicle,* p. 187.

22. An uncle was also regarded as a father to his nephews. See above, Chapter I. (Soloviev's note)

23. Psalm 51:3 (BCP).

24. Monomakh's words are a direct indication that Iziaslav occupied the territories of the sons of Sviatoslav without his knowledge and agreement. (Soloviev's note)

25. Davyd Sviatoslavich (1050-1123), prince of Smolensk 1093-1097, prince of Chernigov from 1097, was a son of Sviatoslav Yaroslavich of Chernigov. Davyd was a major participant and an active speaker at most of the conferences held by the princes of Rus during the final years of the eleventh century and the early part of the twelfth century. He also played an important role in the efforts made to repulse the destructive raids on Rus made by the Polovetsians. See entry (unsigned) in MERSH, Vol. 8, p. 209.

26. *Russian Primary Chronicle*, pp. 177-178; *Nikonian Chronicle*, Vol. 1, p. 213. For assessments of the Liubech conference see Franklin and Shepard, pp. 265-277; Vernadsky, *Kievan Russia*, pp. 89-91; and entry by Dimnik, MERSH, Vol. 20, pp. 97-100.

27. Vasilko Rostislavich (died 1124), prince of Terebovl from 1084, was the youngest son of Prince Rostislav Vladimirovich. In league with his brother Volodar he carried on determined efforts to maintain his independence from the grand princes of Kiev. The brothers frequently had to contend with Hungary and Poland, with which the grand prince Sviatopolk Iziaslavich had concluded alliances. Vasilko and Volodar formed an alliance with the Byzantine empire and the Polovetsians to oppose a formidable coalition of enemies. After the Liubech conference in 1097 Sviatopolk and Davyd Igorevich had Vasilko blinded, but were unable to seize any of his lands. See entry (unsigned) in MERSH, Vol. 41, p. 226.

28. These are all Oguz Turkic peoples. The Pechenegs, in particular, were the dominant power in the southern steppes until displaced by the Polovetsians. See Chapter II, Note 14, above.

29. Bolesław I, prince of Poland, who marched into Rus in 1017 in support of Sviatopolk Vladimirovich, and his great-grandson Bolesław II, who intervened in 1069 in support of Iziaslav Yaroslavich.

30. A Turkic (Onogur) people who migrated in the mid-seventh century from the eastern steppe to the lands between the Danube and the Balkan mountains. They became the rulers of the local Slavs, thus laying the foundations of the modern Bulgarian nation. In the late eleventh century Bulgaria was under Byzantine rule.

31. This was on November 5, and Sviatopolk's nameday was November 8, his baptismal name being Michael. (Soloviev's note)

32. Possibly the present village of Zdvishka, on the river Zdvizh, in Radomysl district, Kiev province. (Soloviev's note)

33. *Russian Primary Chronicle*, pp. 189-191, reprinted in Zenkovsky, pp. 73-76; also *Nikonian Chronicle*, Vol. 1, pp. 213-217. For commentary, see Vernadsky, *Kievan Russia*, pp. 90-91; Franklin and Shepard, p. 270.

34. This means that relatives never before blinded each other. Princes fell in battle, and there was a suspicion, but no more, that Yaropolk Iziaslavich was murdered by the sons of Rostislav, and in any case there was already an open feud

between them. Vsevolod was taken by treachery, but not blinded. Never before had there been such flagrant perfidy and violence. (Soloviev's note)

35. For the role of Metropolitan Nicholas, see Fennell, *Russian Church*, p. 114.

36. One may wonder why the people of Kiev prevented Sviatopolk's flight when they might have been glad to be rid of such a prince. The reason is that they well remembered the consequences of his father's expulsion, and knew that Sviatopolk would make every effort to regain his throne, which would mean internecine strife that would take a heavy toll of the towns and villages, of their city in particular, and would be all the more terrible for the opportunities that it would give to the Polovetsians. (Soloviev's note)

37. Vasilko is, of course, a diminutive of Vasily.

38. Vsevolozh is perhaps the present village of Volozhki, twelve versts from Kovel in Volhynia. Shepol is Shepel on the Stava, a tributary of the Styr, eighteen versts from Lutsk in the same province. Peremil is in the *powiat* of Duben, north east of Berestechko, on the Styr. (Soloviev's note)

39. *Russian Primary Chronicle*, pp. 192-193.

40. Now Busk, in the Zolochovski district, on the right bank of the Western Bug, in Galich. (Soloviev's note)

41. A little town on the Turie river, Kowel district, Volhynia. (Soloviev's note)

42. *Russian Primary Chronicle*, p. 194.

43. See Chapter II, Note 48, above.

44. *Russian Primary Chronicle*, p. 195.

45. Tatishchev (*Istoriia Rossii*, Vol. II, p. 189) gives the words spoken by the sons of Rostislav to Sviatopolk before the battle. "Our grandfather Vladimir was your father's elder brother, and our father was older than you. After our grandfather Vladimir's death your father and his brothers Sviatoslav and Vsevolod gave Vladimir and the land of Cherven to our father, taking for themselves other lands, greater than that which they gave our father. In confirmation of this we have your father's charters. Though we were still young when our father died, your father and Sviatoslav remembered the promise that they gave our father, and did not take Vladimir from us. But when your father died your brother Yaropolk, in breach of his father's oath and his uncle Vsevolod's testament, deprived us of Vladimir, yet we were content with what we were given then, which your brother confirmed with his oath. We ask no more than that of you. If you are not content with what is yours, and would take away from us that which was our father's, then we leave it to the judgment of God that He will give it to whom He will. As for us, we will not give you so much as a village, while we humbly ask that you remember your father's oath and the promise you made, and leave us in peace. We have done nothing to hurt you and have always honored you as the eldest amongst us. This we promise to observe forever." (Soloviev's note)

46. Kálmán the Bibliophile (Könyves), king of Hungary 1095-1116, evidently was intended to pursue an ecclesiastical career, which probably accounts

for his life-long love of learning. He seized the throne on the death of his uncle Ladislas, overriding the designated successor, his brother Almus. At first Almus accepted the situation, but then the brothers quarrelled. Kálmán had Almus and his infant son Béla blinded. Despite this atrocious crime, he was an exceptionally shrewd and enlightened ruler, among other things banning the trial of witches "because they do not exist." In 1097 Kálmán took possession of the former kingdom of Croatia, and was crowned its king in 1102. He also secured possession of the northern Dalmatian coast through the betrothal of his cousin Piroska to John Comnenus, at that time heir to the Byzantine throne (later reigned as John II, 1118-1143). He also took vigorous steps to secure the resumption of alienated crown lands. See Macartney, pp. 19-28, and Makkai, pp. 19-24.

47. *Russian Primary Chronicle*, p. 196.

48. zastupami, *ili* zastavami.... Soloviev then paraphrases in the manner indicated here.

49. *Nikonian Chronicle*, Vol. 1, p. 223.

50. The Russian chronicles give the highly exaggerated figures of a hundred thousand for the size of the Hungarian army and forty thousand for the number of those killed. The figure of eight thousand for the whole army given by Bielski and Stryjkowski is more credible, though even this seems excessive given the small number of the Rus and the Polovetsians. Their successes may be explained by the information given by Tatishchev, according to which Volodar, on hearing of the arrival of Davyd and Boniak, made a sortie from Peremyshl and attacked the king's camp, throwing the Hungarians into utter confusion. (Soloviev's note)

51. There are a number of places called Suteisk or something similar today, but none of them near to where these events took place. Cherven is assumed to be the modern Chervonogorod, in the Chortov region, near the Dzurosh river, a tributary of the Dniester. (Soloviev's note)

52. *Russian Primary Chronicle*, p. 197.

53. By so doing Mstislav would not only enrich himself, but strike a blow against Sviatopolk by disrupting the trade between Kiev and Byzantium.

54. For an assessment of this princely conference see Franklin and Shepard, pp. 274-275; Vernadsky, *Kievan Russia*, p. 91. The narrative is found in *Russian Primary Chronicle*, pp. 198-199. Soloviev variously uses the forms Vitichi, Vitichev and Uvetichi. For the sake of consistency we have used Vitichi throughout.

55. "There came men sent by my brethren, and met me at the Volga," says Monomakh, "and they said to me 'Join with us, and let us go to drive out the sons of Rostislav, and possess their lands. If you will not go, we shall go our way, and you shall go yours.' 'Though you be wrathful,' said I, 'I cannot go with you, nor break the oath that I have sworn.'" (Soloviev's note, quoting Monomakh's Instruction)

56. *Russian Primary Chronicle*, pp. 199-200, also p. 282, Note 357; Franklin and Shepard, p. 278.

57. *Russian Primary Chronicle*, pp. 199-200.

58. Yaroslav's baptismal name was Yury, or George.

59. *Russian Primary Chronicle*, p. 182.

60. Zadom, "by the back way," and not za dom, "behind the house," as it is printed in PSRL. (Soloviev's note)

61. A princely residence outside the walls. *Russian Primary Chronicle*, p. 183.

62. On the left bank of the Dnieper, not far from Pereiaslavl, possibly the present village of Salkov. (Soloviev's note)

63. These events are dated to 1103 in the Laurentian Chronicle and 1111 in the Hypatian Chronicle. (Soloviev's note)

64. "The assessment was that the potential cost of inaction was higher than the cost of mobilization for a pre-emptive strike." Franklin and Shepard, p. 273.

65. *Russian Primary Chronicle*, pp. 201-202.

66. A regional center in the province of Poltava. (Soloviev's note)

67. *Russian Primary Chronicle*, p. 203; *Nikonian Chronicle*, Vol. 1, pp. 232-233.

68. "On December 2 of this year, Dmitr, the son of Ivor, captured the Polovcian camp beside the Don." *Russian Primary Chronicle*, p. 204.

69. The third Sunday in Lent, not to be confused with the Exaltation of the Cross, which is celebrated on September 14.

70. *Nikonian Chronicle*, Vol. 1, p. 236.

71. The Yatviags were an ancient Prus tribe, ethnically akin to the Lithuanians. They inhabited the area from the middle course of the Neiman to the headwaters of the Narev rivers. In classical times the territory was known as Sudovia, and the Sud tribe is attested by Tacitus in the second century B.C. The first mention of them under the name Yatviag is in the Russo-Byzantine treaty of 944. At that time they were engaged in agriculture, hunting and fishing, with a few crafts. In the tenth century, after the formation of the Kievan polity, campaigns were fought against the Yatviags by the Kievan princes in 983, 1038, 1112-1113 and 1196. In the 1140s and 1150s much of their territory was partitioned between the Galich-Volhynian and Mazovian principalities. Later, in 1283, their lands were annexed by the Teutonic Order.

72. Great Moravia was a West Slavonic state which emerged in the ninth century and extended beyond the borders of present-day Moravia. It reached the height of its power under Svatopluk (870-894), then collapsed at the beginning of the tenth century. The mission conducted there in 863-885 by St. Cyril and St. Methodius provided the Slavs with their first written language, Old Church Slavonic, and their first translations of the Holy Scriptures and the service books of the Eastern church.

73. Leo VI "the Wise," Byzantine emperor, born 866, reigned 886-912. Acclaimed by modern historians as the most prolific lawgiver since Justinian, in 890 he published his law code, the Basilica. In his dealings with the church he was very high-handed. In 886 he deposed Patriarch Photius, and in 907 he dismissed the patriarch Nicholas Mysticus, who denounced him for "tetragamy," in other words, for contracting an uncanonical fourth marriage to his mistress Zoë, daughter of his long-time Armenian adviser Stylianus Zautzes. He fought with varying

success against the Arabs, but was unsuccessful in the Bulgarian war of 894-896. His domestic policies which favored the court bureaucracy and merchant oligarchy of the capital aroused the opposition of the provincial aristocracy, leading to the revolt of Andronicos Ducas in 906 or 908. The military treatise *Tactica* is also ascribed to Leo. Immediately on Leo's death Nicholas Mysticus was restored to the patriarchal throne and Leo's widow Zoë was thrust into a convent. See George Ostrogorsky, *History of the Byzantine State*, 2nd ed. (Oxford, 1968), pp. 239- 247, 254-260; *Cambridge Medieval History*, Vol. 4, pp. 125-134; and *Oxford Dictionary of Byzantium*, pp. 1210-1211.

74. Géza (reigned 972-997) succeeded his father Taksony as prince of Hungary. He sent ambassadors to the court of Emperor Otto I at the imperial diet of 973, and established friendly relations, though it is notable that he did not go in person in order to avoid swearing fealty to the emperor as the Polish and Bohemian princes had done. Missionaries came, led by the Bavarian priests Wolfgang and Pilgrim of Passau, later reinforced by Adalbert of Prague. Géza moved his capital to Esztergom and surrounded himself with Bavarian knights, on whom he bestowed large estates. Progress was delayed by conflicts in Germany, but when Henry II recovered the duchy of Bavaria in 985 the Hungarian alliance was renewed. For Géza the introduction of Christianity was a foreign policy measure, since he still sacrificed to pagan gods. He gave up the Vienna Basin in order to live at peace with the Holy Roman empire. When the Bohemian prince began to extend his realm to the Morava river Géza sought the aid of the Polish ruler, who had married an Árpád princess. Henry III later consented to the marriage of his sister Gisela to Géza's son Vajk, who already was baptized under the name Stephen (István). The marriage took place in 996, a year before Géza's death. Macartney, pp. 11-12; Makkai, p. 16.

75. Stephen (István, pagan name Vajk), born 975, reigned 997-1038, was the son of Géza (see previous note). Having reduced the kingdom to order and consolidated his position, he received from Pope Sylvester II (reigned 999-1003) a royal crown which he assumed on Christmas Day, 1000. He worked energetically to promote the Christian faith, instituting bishoprics and endowing monasteries. Esztergom was established as the primatial see, and Pannonhalma, founded by his father Géza, became the leading monastery. He was canonized in 1083, feast day August 16. Stephen's son predeceased him, and his designated sucessor, Peter Orseolo, soon faced rebellion, After a turbulent reign he was succeeded by Stephen's great-nephew Andrew I, who previously was in exile at the court of Yaroslav the Wise, where he was baptised. Macartney, pp. 12-18, 23; Makkai, pp. 16-18; Attwater, pp. 304- 305.

76. László I (born 1040, reigned 1077-1095) was the son of Béla I and the Polish princess Richeza, and was born in exile, either in Poland or Bohemia. Returning to Hungary, Ladislas and his brother Géza refused to contest the throne against their brother Salomon, whom they served in his campaigns against the Polovetsians (1070) and the Pechenegs (1072). Nevertheless in 1073 they quarrelled with Salomon and expelled him, Géza taking his throne (reigned 1074-1077). László succeeded him, and had a very eventful reign. He defeated an alliance between Salomon and the Polovetsians, and crushed a second Polovetsian invasion, allegedly by divine aid. He

Polovetsians, and crushed a second Polovetsian invasion, allegedly by divine aid. He supported the papacy in the Investiture Contest, marrying the daughter of Henry IV's arch-rival Duke Welf of Bavaria. He is said to have refused the imperial crown for himself. By supporting the widow of Prince Stephen of Croatia he secured that country for Hungary in 1091, promoting Latin Christianity by founding the archbishopric of Agram (Zagreb). He ruthlessly extirpated heathenism in his domains and promulgated an elaborate legal code. He died just as he was to set off on the First Crusade. He does not appear to have been officially canonized as a saint by Rome, but he was certainly the object of local veneration, his relics in 1192 being enshrined in the cathedral he had founded at Nagyvárad.

77. See Note 47, above.

78. Boris "Kalamanos" found refuge in Byzantium, where his father's cousin Irene was empress, and played an active part in the conflicts between Byzantium and Hungary. See *Cambridge Medieval History*, Vol. 4, pp. 580-583; Vernadsky, *Kievan Russia*, pp. 331-332.

79. Stephen (István) II, king of Hungary 1116-1131, who was much involved in the affairs of the Land of Rus. Macartney, pp. 19-20, 25.

80. The entry concerning the eclipse is in the *Nikonian Chronicle*, Vol. 1, p. 237, under the year 1114, followed by only a brief mention of Sviatopolk's death.

CHAPTER IV

1. Oleg Sviatoslavich, nicknamed Gorislavich, "the son of woe." See Chapter III, Note 14, above.

2. See pp. 57-58, above.

3. For an analysis of the events of 1113, see Franklin and Shepard, pp. 278-279; Dimnik, *Dynasty of Chernigov*, pp. 267-272.

4. Gleb Vseslavich (died 1119) was the second son of Vseslav Briacheslavich, said to be the son who most resembled his father. In his youth, in 1067, he was imprisoned together with his father. During his father's lifetime he received Minsk as an appanage. After the death of Vseslav in 1101 his sons fell out among themselves. Gleb's brother Davyd, deprived of his appanage, perhaps by Gleb himself, tried to gain support and protection from the other Rus princes, taking part in their expeditions against the Polovetsians. He gained the favor of Monomakh, then prince of Pereiaslavl. In 1104 Davyd besieged Gleb in his city of Minsk. Grand Prince Sviatopolk sent to aid Davyd an army under the command of his boyar Putiata, while Monomakh sent his son Yaropolk. The reason for this aid to Davyd was probably that Gleb had attacked the Dregovichians, to whose territories the grand princes of Kiev felt they had a proprietary right, and had burned their town of Slutsk. Not only was Gleb unrepentant of this action, he even reproached Monomakh that it was on his account that he had attacked the Dregovichians. Also allied to the enemy princes was Oleg, son of Sviatoslav Yaroslavich. The campaign ended inconclusively when Gleb repulsed the

attackers from the walls of Minsk. The brothers then made peace, and in 1106 waged a campaign against the Lithuanian tribes of Semigallia, formerly tributaries to the Polotsk princes. There was a bloody battle which ended badly for the sons of Vseslav.

In 1108 Gleb founded and built the church of the Mother of God on the Klova river, and donated funds for building the refectory of the Caves monastery in Kiev. Meanwhile Gleb did not cease his attacks on the Kievan principalities, fearing neither Sviatopolk nor Vladimir Monomakh, who became grand prince in 1113. In 1116 Gleb once again invaded and devastated the lands of the Dregovichians. He took the town of Slutsk and burned it despite the threats of Monomakh, who then "trusting in God and his righteousness" advanced on Minsk in alliance with numerous princes of Kiev and Chernigov. He sent ahead his brother Viacheslav, then prince of Smolensk, who took Orsha and Kopys. Meanwhile the main force under Monomakh himself besieged Minsk, where he ordered the construction of sturdy siege quarters to show he meant business. Gleb was suitably intimidated and sent envoys to open peace talks. Since it was close to the Lenten season Monomakh, unwilling to shed Christian blood, received Gleb's submission and restored him to his patrimony. Though Monomakh returned those of Gleb's subjects whom he had rendered captive, Yaropolk did not follow suit, seeing fit to take the inhabitants of Drutsk to populate his new town of Zhelny. Three years later Gleb attacked the Smolensk territory. This time Gleb was deposed and forced to reside in Kiev, where he died September 13, 1119, and was buried within the Caves monastery. See entry (unsigned) in MERSH, Vol. 12, pp. 92-93; Franklin and Shepard, p. 340.

5. A protoslavic tribe whose name may be connected with a word for "marshland." They inhabited the basin of the Pripiat and the upper reaches of the right bank of the Dnieper in the area around Turov. In the tenth century they were absorbed by the Kievan polity, their lands being partitioned between the principalities of Turov and Polotsk. See entry by Noonan, MERSH, Vol. 10, pp. 10-11.

6. A regional center in the province of Minsk. (Soloviev's note)

7. There is a small town of some antiquity called Zhovlin or Zholnin on the river Sula in the Zolotonoshski region of the province of Poltava. (Soloviev's note)

8. According to Tatishchev, Gleb renewed his aggression against Novgorod and Smolensk, so Vladimir sent Mstislav against him and deprived him of Minsk. (Soloviev's note)

9. See Chapter II, Note 48, above.

10. Bolesław III Krzywousty ("Wrymouth"), born 1086, reigned 1106-1138. Having in 1097 received Silesia and Lesser Poland as an inheritance from his father, after a bitter struggle with his half-brother Zbigniew, who was allied to Emperor Henry V, he united all the Polish lands under his authority. He waged war on Bohemia from 1103 to 1110, and intervened in Hungary on behalf of the pretender Boris Kalomanos (see Chapter III, Note 78, above) against the blind king Béla II. As a result of successful campaigns he annexed the western (1106) and eastern (1123) parts of Pomerania. He did not bother to be crowned, but in

1135 he was invested by Emperor Lothar von Supplinburg for his Pomeranian acquisitions. Just before his death he promulgated the so-called Statute, which divided the Polish domains among his sons. See Davies, pp. 71-72, 84, 93.

11. After Zbigniew was driven out by Bolesław and Yaroslav he found refuge at Kiev with Sviatopolk, who later reconciled him with his brother.

12. Piotr Włostowicz (died 1153), palatine of Wrocław in the reigns of Bolesław Krzywousty and Władysław Wygnaniec, was one of the richest and most powerful Polish lords, owing his influence at least in part to his military successes. His ascendancy was evidently too much for Władysław, who had him blinded and banished in 1145 as a result of an accusation of treachery.

13. Romanus IV Diogenes, emperor 1068-1071. He had risen to distinction in the army, then was convicted of treason against the sons of Constantine X. He was pardoned by the empress Eudocia, whom he later married. After his coronation he carried on three successful campaigns against the Saracens and Seljuk Turks, though in a fourth he was soundly defeated by Alp Arslan at Manzikert on the banks of the Araxes, and was taken prisoner. Releasing himself by the promise of a large ransom, he turned his arms against the pretender Michael VII, but was compelled after a defeat to resign the empire and retire to the island of Prote, where he was blinded and died shortly afterwards. Romanus's deposition rendered the treaty he had concluded null and void, consequently the Turks renewed their offensive. It was during his reign that by the surrender of Bari to the Normans in 1071 the Byzantine empire lost its last outpost in Southern Italy. His successor was not of the Comnenos dynasty, as Soloviev states here, but Michael VII Ducas (reigned 1071-1078). Ostrogorsky, pp. 344-345; *Oxford Dictionary of Byzantium*, p. 1807; Michael Psellus, *Fourteen Byzantine Rulers*. Translated by E.R.A. Sewter. Rev. ed. (Harmondsworth, 1966), pp. 350-366. Psellus was a former tutor of Michael, and this bias is reflected in his chronicle.

14. Alexius I, born 1048, reigned 1081-1118, was the founder of the Comnenos dynasty, although there was an earlier ruler from that family, his uncle Isaac (1057-1059). Alexius's main support came from the landed aristocracy in Asia Minor. He was a persecutor of the Paulicians and Bogomils. In alliance with the Venetians, to whom he granted considerable privileges, he successfully fought against the Normans from Southern Italy led by Robert Guiscard. In 1091, with the aid of the Polovetsians, he defeated the Pechenegs, and in 1093 he repulsed the emir Chakha in Asia Minor. When he summoned the crusaders from the West he got rather more than he bargained for, although he did compel them to cede to the empire the coastline of Anatolia which they had conquered from the Seljuks. He is the subject of an adulatory biography by his daughter, *The Alexiad of Anna Comnena*. Translated by Sewter (Harmondsworth, 1969). See also *Oxford Dictionary of Byzantium*, p. 63. Soloviev's chronology is very erratic. Romanus was deposed in 1071, the Comnenoi were established only a decade later, and no less than 45 years elapsed between Romanus's overthrow and the alleged rebellion of his son Leo.

15. "In 1116 Leo Diogenes, the son-in-law of Vladimir Monomach, participated in an expedition of the Rus' against Byz[antium]." "In 1116-1118 [Vladimir
Monomakh] encroached on Byz[antine] interests by sanctioning two attempts to
occupy towns in the lower Danube, the first led by the enigmatic Leo, known to
some sources as 'son of Diogenes,' who was probably related to Vladimir by marriage.... If there was a rift with Byz[antium], it was apparently healed by 1122,
when Vladimir's granddaughter was married into the Komnenian lineage. A later
Muscovite legend casts Vladimir as a powerful tsar who was kept from attacking
Constantinople by rich gifts from Alexius I." *Oxford Dictionary of Byzantium*,
pp. 627, 2184. As can be observed, the source base for this incident is rather
meager. Soloviev has accepted the account in the Laurentian Chronicle rather
uncritically, telescoping events more than four decades apart.

Karamzin (Vol. 2, cols. 91-92) was somewhat more sceptical. "But the
conquest of Thrace appears doubtful, since in the *ancient* chronicles there is only
the following account of Vladimir's relations with the Greeks. 'In 1116 *the
husband of Monomakh's daughter, Prince Leo*, son of the former emperor Diogenes, collected an army on the shores of the Black Sea, invaded the northern
districts of the empire and and occupied the Danube towns, but Emperor Alexius
dispatched against him to the town of Dorostolon two Arabs, who treacherously
assassinated him (August 15). Then Vladimir, either wishing to avenge his son-
in-law's murder, or else to preserve for Maria's young son, called Basil, the towns
taken by Leo, sent his commander Ivan Voitishich, and his son Viacheslav with
another boyar, Foma Ratiborovich. The first actually occupied several of the
towns, but Viacheslav retreated from Dorostolon without success.'

"Contrary to this narration Anna Comnena, relating the life story of her
illustrious father, Emperor Alexius Comnenos, asserted that Leo the son of
Diogenes fell fighting the Turks near Antioch. 'Shortly thereafter,' writes Anna,
'there appeared within the empire an impostor who assumed his name. Banished
to Cherson as punishment, he was freed by the Cumans. Putting himself at the
head of their hosts, he entered Thrace, but was taken prisoner by the Greeks. He
soon found out that impertinence does not go without punishment, for his eyes
were gouged out.' (1096) Other Byzantine chronicles also call him an impostor,
but Monomakh's son-in-law who perished at Dorostolon was of course the true
son of Diogenes for Vladimir, who himself was in close communication with the
court at Constantinople, could not have been taken in by a vagabond impostor.
Leo's widow Maria died as a nun in Russia, where her son Basil devotedly served
the grand prince, and the Danube towns soon were restored to the empire, whether
by force of arms or through a peace treaty." (Italics are Karamzin's) For Anna
Comnena's account of the pseudo-Diogenes incident, see *Alexiad*, pp. 297-304.

16. PSRL, Vol. 3, col. 5. See W. Vodoff, "Remarques sur la valeur du terme
'tsar' appliqué aux princes russes avant le milieu du XVe siècle (Remarks on the
Validity of the Term 'Tsar' as Applied to the Russian Princes Before the Middle
of the Fifteenth Century)," *Oxford Slavonic Papers*, New Series, 11 (1978), pp.
1-41. It does not imply imperial status. It is highly unlikely that this has anything

to do with the story of the presentation of imperial regalia, which Soloviev gives in a version which is entirely legendary.

17. Belaia Vezha was the name by which the early Rus knew the Khazar city of Sarkel, on the lower Don. The term here probably refers to remnants of the Khazar nation.

18. The Häme, known in Russian as Yam or Yem, were a Finnic tribe which during the first millennium A.D. lived inland on a group of islands. Their chief occupations were forestry, fishing and trade. In the Tale of Igor's Campaign the Häme are mentioned as tributaries of the Rus. In the eleventh and twelfth centuries they paid tribute to Novgorod and at the end of the twelfth century they were conquered by the Swedes, who knew them as Tavastians. Together with the Suomi and the Karelians they formed the Finnish nation.

19. Some time after one branch of the Bulgars migrated to the Balkans (see Chapter III, Note 28, above), another branch of the same people settled along the Volga, and became an important power in the region.

20. *Russian Primary Chronicle*, p. 203.

21. See pp. 73-74, and Note 15, above.

22. Torchin means "the Tork," and Kozarin means "the Khazar."

CHAPTER V

1. Mstislav Vladimirovich (died 1132), prince of Novgorod 1095-1117, prince of Pereiaslavl 1117-1125, grand prince of Kiev 1125-1132, eldest son of Vladimir Monomakh. He defeated Oleg Sviatoslavich, whom he compelled to attend the Liubech conference in 1097. He returned Murom to Oleg and reconciled him with the grand prince. In 1107 and 1111 he participated in the campaigns organized by his father against the Polovetsians. In 1113 and 1116 he conducted campaigns against the Finnic tribes bordering on Novgorod. After his father's death Mstislav continued to assert the overall authority of the grand prince of Kiev and to defend the Rus lands against external enemies. In 1129 he pacified the Polotsk princes and placed his own son Iziaslav in Polotsk. In 1130 and 1131 he successfully waged war against the Lithuanians. His name is connected with the oldest surviving original princely document, his charter issued around 1130 to the monastery of St. George in Novgorod. Vernadsky (*Kievan Russia*, pp. 96-98) emphasizes Mstislav's Nordic connections, as the son of Monomakh's first wife Gytha, daughter of Harold Godwinson, king of England, while Mstislav himself was married to Princess Kristina of Sweden. "In leaving Novgorod, Mstislav left behind there his son Vsevolod, whom the Novgorodians gladly recognized as their prince (1117). Thus he did not actually sever his connection with the northern metropolis and it is significant that after his first wife died he married a daughter of the mayor of that city (1122)."

2. See Chapter III, Note 15, above.

3. See Chapter III, Note 26, above.

4. Yaroslav Sviatoslavich (died 1129) was the son of Prince Sviatoslav Yaroslavich of Chernigov. After his father's death he supported his brother Oleg in his struggle against Vladimir Monomakh, attacking the Land of Rostov in 1096. By the decision of the Liubech conference the Chernigov territories were confirmed to him and his brothers. Apparently Yaroslav received Murom, which formerly belonged to his father. Here in 1104 Yaroslav was defeated by the Mordvinians. After the death of his brother Davyd in 1123 Yaroslav occupied the Chernigov throne, then in 1127 was expelled by his nephew Vsevolod Olgovich (see Note 13, below) and again retired to Murom, where he died two years later. Yaroslav Sviatoslavich is regarded as the progenitor of the Murom and Riazan princely dynasties.

5. *Nikonian Chronicle*, Vol. 1, p. 247.

6. Yaropolk Vladimirovich (1078-1139), son of Vladimir Monomakh. In 1107, 1111 and 1113 he took part in his father's expeditions against the Polovetsians. In 1113, after Monomakh was summoned to the Kievan throne, Yaropolk succeeded to the Pereiaslavl principality, continuing to assist the grand prince in his campaigns. After Monomakh's death Yaropolk still retained the Pereiaslavl principality, which on the death of his elder brother Mstislav when he succeeded to the Kievan throne, he yielded to Mstislav's son Vsevolod. See entry by Hugh F. Graham, MERSH, Vol. 55, pp. 122-124.

7. This Yury, named Dolgoruky, "the Long-armed" (born 1100, grand prince 1154-1157), reigned in Rostov and Suzdal (from 1125) at a time when the power of his principality was in the ascendant, eclipsing that of Kiev, and thus was to be one of the most significant figures of his generation. He is also celebrated as the founder of Moscow, by which it is meant that he was the first to fortify the town.

8. Andrei Vladimirovich "the Fair" (1102-1141) was the fifth and youngest son of Vladimir Monomakh. He ruled the principality of Vladimir-in-Volhynia during his father's lifetime, then after his father's death became prince of Pereiaslavl. Andrei participated in the interprincely strife which followed Monomakh's death and sided with his elder brothers Mstislav and Yaropolk against the Chernigov branch of the sons of Oleg. See entry (unsigned) in MERSH, Vol. 1, p. 223.

9. Viacheslav relinquished Pereiaslavl in 1134 in favor of Turov. He also occupied Kiev for a few weeks in 1139, then made way for Vsevolod Olgovich. In 1146 Viacheslav remained in Kiev as the nominal ruler, with Iziaslav Mstislavich exercising the real power. See Franklin and Shepard, pp. 346-349, Martin, p. 106 and Vernadsky, *Kievan Russia*, pp. 97, 210.

10. Vsevolod Mstislavich, baptismal name Gavriil (died 1138), was prince of Novgorod 1117-1132 and again 1132-1136, prince of Pereiaslavl briefly in 1132, of Vyshgorod in 1136 and Pskov in 1137. He was the eldest son of Mstislav Vladimirovich and his first wife, Kristina of Sweden. He undertook a number of military engagements in the Baltic region between 1117 and 1134, primarily against the Chud. He also campaigned in the Land of Riazan in 1134 and 1135. He issued

statutes regulating the ecclesiastical courts (around 1126) and concerning the church of St. John the Forerunner on the Opoki in Novgorod (around 1132), though some scholars relate some of these statutes to the late fourteenth century. Vsevolod distributed lands to monasteries and secular lords, actions which tended to impoverish and enslave the peasantry. As oppression increased, peasants and poor townsmen in the Novgorod region mounted rebellions in 1132 and 1136, during which Vsevolod was banished from the town. In 1136 the accusation was levelled at Vsevolod that "he had no care of the serfs." After he was held in prison with his wife and children for seven weeks Vsevolod was expelled from Novgorod on July 15, 1136. He then was chosen prince of Pskov, thereafter waging an unsuccessful war on Novgorod. See entry by S.M. Kashtanov, MERSH, Vol. 43, pp. 92-93.

11. Rostislav Mstislavich (died 1167), from 1127 prince of Smolensk, grand prince of Kiev 1154 and 1159-1167, grandson of Monomakh, founder of the Smolensk princely dynasty. In his earlier years he fought under the command of his father and brothers against the princes of Polotsk, the Chud, the Lithuanians and Polovetsians. In 1144 and 1146 he participated in the war of the Kievan princes against Prince Vladimir Volodarevich of Vladimir-in-Volhynia. In 1149-1150 he supported his brother Iziaslav in his struggle for the Kievan throne against Yury Dolgoruky, in which the brothers were defeated. Some time between 1133 and 1150 he established an independent bishopric in Smolensk. For further details see entry by Dimnik, MERSH, Vol. 31, pp. 162-165.

12. Iziaslav Mstislavich, baptismal name Panteleimon (1097-1154), was the eldest son of Mstislav Vladimirovich, prince of Novgorod. From 1134 he was prince of Vladimir-in-Volhynia, from 1143 prince of Pereiaslavl. In 1146, taking advantage of the uprising in Kiev against the sons of Oleg, Iziaslav seized the Kievan throne and waged a lengthy struggle against Prince Yury Dolgoruky of Rostov-Suzdal, who was allied to the descendants of Oleg (see Chapter VI). Iziaslav's reign was the subject of a special chronicle written by the boyar Peter Borislavich, later incorporated into the Hypatian Chronicle. See entry by Hanak, MERSH, Vol. 15, pp. 88-89.

13. Vsevolod Olgovich (died 1146), prince of Chernigov 1127-1139, grand prince of Kiev 1139-1146, was the son of Oleg Sviatoslavich, prince of Chernigov. He incited and in other ways exploited interprincely disputes over the Kievan throne. His reign is particularly noted for the increased exploitation of townsmen, especially for the depredations of his stewards Ratsha and Tudor in Kiev and Vyshgorod. Vsevolod regarded Kiev as his hereditary property, which exacerbated the citizens' discontent, fanned by his opponents. Following his death on August 1, 1146 riots broke out in Kiev. "For many historians Vsevolod was a 'usurper', since his father Oleg had never been prince of Kiev and his grandfather Sviatoslav Iaroslavich had himself usurped the throne. But there is no compelling reason for us to interpret rights and wrongs from a purely Monomakhovich perspective. Over the remainder of the twelfth century the house of Chernigov

provided three more rulers of Kiev. Two of them reigned very briefly, but the third—Vsevolod's son Sviatoslav—was prince of Kiev for a total of seventeen years (1176-80, 1181-94), longer than any Kievan incumbent since before the days of Monomakh." Franklin and Shepard, p. 346. For a contrary view, see Dimnik, *Dynasty of Chernigov*, pp. 349-362, and Nancy Shields Kollmann, "Collateral Succession," p. 383.

14. A tributary of the Seim in the province of Kharkov. (Soloviev's note)

15. A tributary of the Vyr. (Soloviev's note)

16. Fennell, *Russian Church*, pp. 115-116.

17. In the vicinity of Pinsk. (Soloviev's note)

18. It is not known whether this was the son of Yaroslav Sviatopolchich or of Yaroslav Yaropolchich. Karamzin inclines to the former, but he was married only in 1112. Even if Viacheslav was his first child and born the following year, in 1127, he would have been only fourteen years old.

19. On the Goina river, a tributary of the Berezina, in the Borisov district. Drutsk is a town on the Drucha in the Mogilev district. (Soloviev's note)

20. Davyd Vseslavich was the fourth son of Vseslav. Shortly after his father's death, being without an appanage or having been deprived by his brothers, Davyd wandered in search of a powerful patron among the princes of Southern Rus. In 1103 he distinguished himself in the battle of Suten against the Polovetsians and gained the favor of the princes. He also married his son to a daughter of Mstislav. In 1104 he was in the army sent under the grand prince's boyar Putiata and Monomakh's son Yaropolk against his own brother Viacheslav. This suggests that the campaign was undertaken for the benefit of Davyd, to regain his appanage from Gleb, or to obtain another. From his perspective the campaign was a failure. In 1106 he took part in the ill-fated Semigallian campaign. Around 1125, at the instigation of Davyd, who had gained the support of a faction in the popular assembly, the citizens expelled Gleb and put Davyd in his place. About that time Monomakh died, and Mstislav succeeded him, according to some contrary to custom. Davyd would not recognize Mstislav's succession, so Mstislav supported Davyd's eldest brother Boris, who apparently was prepared to recognize him. This led to the expedition of 1127, as a result of which the citizens of Polotsk expelled Davyd, but instead of Boris installed Rogvolod in his place. On Rogvolod's death Davyd regained his throne, but refused to heed the summons by Mstislav for an all-Rus expedition against the Polovetsians. Mstislav led a general expedition against the Polotsk princes. The townsmen refused to fight, instead sent their princes to Kiev for judgment. Mstislav exiled all the surviving sons of Vseslav, except for Boris, to Constantinople. There they served the emperor John II Comnenos (ruled 1118-1143) in his wars against the Saracens. Davyd probably died in exile some time in the 1130s, since he is not mentioned among those who returned after the death of Mstislav in 1132 or Yaropolk in 1140.

21. See Chapter IV, Note 4, above.

22. Concerning Briachislav Davydovich there is no information prior to 1127, when Grand Prince Mstislav attacked the Polotsk principality to punish the princes who would not recognize his overlordship. Wishing to help his father, Briachislav gathered his retinue at Lagozhsk but, as related here, to little avail. His captor Iziaslav treated him favorably, possibly because he was his brother-in-law. We have little further information about him although he may have been one of the princes whom Monomakh exiled to Constantinople.

23. Rogvolod Vseslavich (died 1128 or 1129) participated in the Semigallian campaign, though the chronicles do not mention him specifically by name. It is not known what territory, if any, he was assigned as an appanage. It is only mentioned that in 1127, when Mstislav and his allies attacked Polotsk and expelled Davyd, the inhabitants parleyed with Mstislav and proposed Rogvolod as their prince. Apparently Rogvolod was acceptable to Mstislav, although he did not rule for long, since when the following year Mstislav summoned the Rus princes to campaign against the Polovetsians, Davyd was back on the throne. Rogvolod was not among the princes exiled to Constantinople, though his sons Vasily and Ivan probably were.

24. According to the Primary Chronicle, at the time of Vladimir's wars with his brother Yaropolk, Rogneda (Ragnheid), princess of Polotsk, was desired by Vladimir, but his proposal of marriage was rebuffed. She apparently preferred Yaropolk. At this, Vladimir attacked Polotsk, killed her father Rogvolod (Rognvald), and took her by force. The legend, which bears distinct similarities to the story of Olaf Tryggvason's marriage to Gudrun, further relates that she subsequently attempted to murder him. Iziaslav, the founder of the dynasty of Polotsk, was the offspring of this union, while Yaroslav, the ancestor of the other princes, was the son of another of Vladimir's wives. The story is repeated in the *Nikonian Chronicle*, Vol. 1, p. 253.

25. The Krivichians were one of the old East Slavonic tribes inhabiting the area covered by the principality of Polotsk. See entry by Noonan, MERSH, Vol. 18, pp. 70-76.

26. Rostislav Vseslavich was the sixth son of Vseslav. He took part in the 1106 campaign in Semigallia, and was one of the princes exiled to Constantinople in 1129. He was not among those who returned after Mstislav's death, so he probably died there.

27. Sviatoslav Vseslavich, baptismal name Yury, was the seventh son of Vseslav Briachislavich. He took part in the 1106 expedition to Semigallia. He was exiled to Constantinople in 1129 and does not appear to have returned. His main claim to fame is through his daughter Predslava, better known as St. Evfrosinia of Polotsk. Fennell, *Russian Church*, p. 59.

28. The two nephews in question were Vasily and Ivan Rogvolodovich, about which little else is known apart from their exile in 1129. Some chroniclers consider that Vasilko, later prince of Polotsk (see Note 37, below) was the son of Vasily rather than Sviatoslav Vseslavich.

29. The emperor provided for them and sent them to fight the Saracens, in which they acquitted themselves with honor. (Soloviev's note)

30. *Nikonian Chronicle*, Vol. 1, p. 248.

31. See Chapter II, Note 17, above.

32. See Note 6, above.

33. At Polstin, in Piriatin district in the province of Poltava. (Soloviev's note)

34. *Chronicle of Novgorod*, p. 12.

35. Klin in Russian means "wedge," in modern Estonian *vai*. In German it was known as Dorpat or Derpt. Its ancient Rus name was Yuriev, which was revived in late tsarist times. Since Estonian independence in 1918 it has been known as Tartu.

36. See Chapter II, Note 3, above.

37. Vasilko Sviatoslavich was the son of the seventh and youngest son of Vseslav Briachislavich. He was chosen because he was the only scion of the Polotsk family living in Rus at the time. Despite Yaropolk's threats, he returned from Constantinople as soon as he heard news of Mstislav's death in 1132. In the redistribution of principalities after Yaropolk's death (1140) Iziaslav Mstislavich left Polotsk, which then fell to his brother Sviatopolk. The inhabitants of Polotsk, availing themselves of the presence of Vasilko, expelled Sviatopolk and made Vasilko their prince. To strengthen his position, Vasilko sought the support of princes elsewhere in Rus, particularly ingratiating himself with Mstislav's eldest son Vsevolod (see Note 10, above). When that prince in 1138 was expelled from Novgorod and travelled through Polotsk on his way to Pskov, Vasilko not only granted him safe passage, he received him honorably, refusing to take advantage of his pitiful condition. This generosity undoubtedly helped his cause. After 1143 he married his daughter to Sviatoslav Vsevolodovich, grandson of Oleg Sviatoslavich. He died in 1143 or 1144, since in the latter year Rogvolod Borisovich was ruling in Polotsk.

38. There are frequent references in this chapter to the small town of Gorodets Ostersk, which Soloviev variously refers to as "Gorodets" and "Gorodok." For the sake of consistency we have rendered it "Gorodets" throughout.

39. See Chapter IV, Note 14, above.

40. This helps to determine the disputed position of Vyshgorod relative to Kiev. To reach Vyshgorod, Vsevolod, marching north from the Supoy, had to cross the Desna. (Soloviev's note)

41. Michael was metropolitan from 1130 to 1145. Fennell, *Russian Church*, pp. 46-47, 115.

42. Now Morovsk in the Oster district of the province of Chernigov. (Soloviev's note)

43. Posadisha — a plural verb.

44. Mstislav was married in Kiev to the daughter of Dmitry Zavidich of Novgorod.

45. *Chronicle of Novgorod*, p. 11.

46. In the ninth century Novgorod was the seat of Riurik, the first Varangian to rule in Rus and the founder of the dynasty. (Soloviev's note)

47. *Chronicle of Novgorod*, p. 12.

48. The Dubna river flows into the Volga below the town of Korcheva in the province of Tver.

49. Rostov and Suzdal were at this time the two chief cities of a single principality.

50. *Chronicle of Novgorod*, pp. 14-15.

51. a Sviatoslavu Ol'govichu ukazan put' iz Novgoroda, literally "Sviatoslav Olgovich was shown the way out of Novgorod." Soloviev here uses the customary euphemism employed in Novgorod for the rejection or dismissal of a prince.

52. See Note 12, above.

53. See Note 11, above.

54. See above, Chapter II, Note 4.

55. Now Karan, a village on the Trubezh five versts from Pereiaslavl. (Soloviev's note)

56. In the Kobrin district of the province of Grodno. (Soloviev's note)

57. The Viatichians were one of the old East Slavonic tribes whose lands apparently coincided to a considerable extent with the later principality of Chernigov. See entry (unsigned) in MERSH, Vol. 42, pp. 73-74.

58. Gorodets Ostersk, or Yuriev, which belonged to Yury Dolgoruky of Rostov and was taken from him by Vsevolod not long before. Rogachev is the district center of Mogilev province, not the Rogachev in Volhynia. Here it is a question of the division of the principality of Turov and Pinsk amongst the descendants of Sviatoslav, who obtained it as a result of Viacheslav's removal to Pereiaslavl. Vsevolod was distributing the towns of Turov or Chernigov that remained to him. He could not distribute the towns of Volhynia, which belonged to Iziaslav Mstislavich. Chartoryisk may have been on the borders of the principalities of Vladimir and Turov and have belonged to the latter. (Soloviev's note)

59. Vshchizh is a village in Orel province, forty versts from Briansk, and there are villages called Vorshina in Mogilev district. (Soloviev's note)

60. I regard Rostislav as the elder because he received the senior throne of Peremyshl, while Vladimir received Zvenigorod, according to the Polish chronicler Stryjkowski. (Soloviev's note)

61. Vladimirko Volodarevich (1104-1152), prince of Galich, son of Prince Volodar Rostislavich. In 1129, following the death of his brother Rostislav, Vladimirko took possession of Peremyshl. In 1141 he was confirmed as prince of Galich. He also attempted to bring together the lands of Volhynia under his authority, but could not attain this objective through warfare against Grand Prince Vsevolod Olgovich of Kiev. Vladimirko brutally suppressed uprisings by the townsmen against his rule. From 1139 he took part in the internecine strife between the descendants of Oleg and Monomakh, first taking one side in this

conflict, then the other. In 1142 he participated in the war against Poland. In an attempt to expand his holdings Vladimirko after 1149 waged war on the side of Prince Yury Dolgoruky against Prince Iziaslav Mstislavich of Kiev. In 1150 he defeated Iziaslav and forced the inhabitants of Kiev to recognize Yury Dolgoruky as their prince. This action brought about a military campaign against Vladimirko by Izaiaslav's ally King Géza of Hungary. Vladimirko then bribed the archbishop of Hungary and the king's men, who forced the king to return home. In 1152 Vladimirko was defeated by Géza, but was able to achieve peace with him through adroit diplomatic measures. The Russian chronicles observed that Vladimirko displayed a certain degree of freethinking. See entry (unsigned) in MERSH, Vol. 42, p. 168.

62. The term used is mnogoglagolivyi, literally "speaking much."

63. Now Priluki in the Berdichev district, Kiev province. (Soloviev's note)

64. See Chapter VI, Note 24, below.

65. *Chronicle of Novgorod*, p. 16.

66. The term used here is kum, denoting the godfather of one's child or children.

67. *Chronicle of Novgorod*, p. 17.

68. See Chapter IV, Note 10, above.

69. This is an error on Soloviev's part. Bolesław actually died on October 28, 1138.

70. Władysław II Wygnaniec ("the Exile"), prince of Silesia 1138-1146. He was expelled as the result of a concerted effort by his brothers. Through his marriage to Agnes (Agnieszka), daughter of Duke Leopold III of Austria, he was connected to Emperor Conrad III, who led an unsuccessful expedition to restore him. In 1163, following intervention by Frederick Barbarossa, Bolesław IV was obliged to restore Władysław's sons to the duchy of Silesia. See the following note.

71. Bolesław IV Kędzierzawy ("the Curly"), king of Poland 1146-1173. He was married to Princess Verkhuslava of Novgorod. "Bolesław of Poland died in October 1139 [1138], leaving a disposition whereby the country was to be partitioned among his four sons, the eldest of whom, Władysław, was to have a certain pre-eminence with the title of grand duke. This prince at once attempted to use his exalted position to develop his own power at the expense of his brothers, an enterprise in which he confidently relied on the support of Conrad [III] his brother-in-law. Early in 1146 he appeared at the German court and was enfeoffed with the whole of Poland. A strenuous and not unsuccessful resistance was made by his brothers, Bolesław and Mieszko. Posen [Poznań] withstood his attack, the archbishop of Gniezno excommunicated him, his own town of Cracow was taken and destroyed; finally, he himself was driven into exile. Conrad made a campaign into Poland on behalf of his vassal, but, unable to make any headway, entered into negotiations and withdrew to Germany with Władysław, who continued to live in exile while his victorious brothers established their authority securely in Poland. The only result which emanated from Conrad's intervention was the

diminution of German influence in that region." *Cambridge Medieval History*, Vol. 5 (London, 1926, reprinted Cambridge, 1964), p. 351 (spelling modified).

72. See Note 61, above.

73. Igor Olgovich (died 1147), prince of Novgorod Seversk, grand prince of Kiev from 1146. Igor participated in the domestic warfare in Rus during the twelfth century, supporting the princes of Chernigov in these struggles. Igor's attempts to secure the title of grand prince of Kiev as his patrimony from his brother Vsevolod brought about an uprising of the townsmen of Kiev, who objected that they did not wish "to be disposed of as of we were part of the estate of the prince." The boyars of Kiev bestowed the grand-princely title on Igor, but he was killed in another popular rebellion against his rule the following year. See entry (unsigned) in MERSH, Vol. 14, p. 138.

74. Mieszko III Stary ("the Old," 1126-1202), third son of Bolesław Wrymouth, was prince of Greater Poland from 1138, prince of Cracow 1173-1177 and 1191. Having become prince as a result of a partition with his older brothers, he tried to gain supremacy over them. His haughty demeanor provoked an aristocratic revolt which in 1177 led to his banishment and the election of Casimir the Just. Around 1182 he regained a power base around Gniezno from which he extended his sway over much of Greater Poland, and in 1191 he was briefly restored to the throne of Cracow. From 1198 he acted as regent for his minor nephew Leszek I Biały ("the White," reigned 1202-1227). Halecki, pp. 25-28.

75. There is a place called Vizna in the Avgustov district at the confluence of the Bobr and the Narew. (Soloviev's note)

76. The Russian term used is shneka, a craft commonly used in the medieval Baltic. "...the ordinary forty-oar levy ship, snekke to the Danes, snækkja to the Swedes, which the Slavs built somewhat lighter and lower than the Scandinavians. These needed crews of trained warriors, provisions for overseas expeditions, and a complicated technique of building and maintenance; therefore the kings and pirate chiefs who controlled them had to be landowners, lords of retinues, the masters of populous communities. Their ships had room on board for slaves, cattle and loot, but it was restricted, and such cargoes limited the movements of the crew." Eric Christiansen, *The Northern Crusades*, 2nd ed. (Harmondsworth, 1997), pp. 15-16.

77. *Chronicle of Novgorod*, pp. 17-18.

78. See Chapter IV, Note 17, above.

79. *Chronicle of Novgorod*, p. 17.

80. *Chronicle of Novgorod*, p. 18.

81. The village of Maliutentsy twenty versts from Piriatino. (Soloviev's note)

82. The Karakalpaks literally, "Black Hats," in Russian Chernye klobuki, are not to be confused with the modern people of the same name who dwell about the southern shores of the Aral Sea. Like them they were Oguz Turks, and represent a confederation of various branches of that people who earlier migrated west to the steppes of what is now Southern Ukraine, notably the Pechenegs, Torks, Berendey and Koui. See also Chapter II, Note 17, above.

83. In Russian Ol'gova Mogila, the burial place of Oleg, prince of Kiev (882-913), just outside the city. Its exact location is uncertain.

84. Sviatoslav's mother was Iziaslav's sister.

85. *Nikonian Chronicle*, Vol. 2 (Princeton, 1984), pp. 22-23.

86. See Note 9, above.

87. Presumably those which Vsevolod distributed to his brothers. (Soloviev's note)

88. See Chapter IV, Note 5, above.

89. "Vladimir [Monomakh] and Davyd and Oleg went to Aepa and to the other Aepa, and Vladimir married Yury to the daughter of Aepa the son of Osen, and Oleg married his son to the daughter of Aepa the son of Girgen." Chronicle entry for 1107. (Soloviev's note)

90. Berladnik was the sobriquet of Prince Ivan Rostislavich, son of Prince Rostislav Vladimirovich of Peremyshl. Prior to 1144 Ivan Rostislavich ruled in Zvenigorod. In that year the inhabitants of Galich, angered at the frequent absences of their prince Vladimir Vladimirovich on hunting expeditions, invited Ivan to be their prince. He accepted with alacrity, but faced with an uneven contest with the ousted prince, he was forced to abandon both Galich and Zvenigorod. He fled to Bîrlad on the Danube and then, in 1145, by way of the steppe to Grand Prince Vsevolod, an implacable enemy of the Galich prince. The Kievan prince employed Ivan, but not for long, since in the following year he is found in the ranks of the army of Prince Sviatoslav Olgovich of Novgorod Seversk, at that time fighting against Iziaslav Mstislavich. This was the beginning of his nomadic career. Many historians see him as the prototype of the "service princes" who became common during the Muscovite period, selling their services to the highest bidder.

After Iziaslav's attack on Sviatoslav Olgovich, Berladnik accepted from prince Rostislav of Smolensk two hundred grivnas of silver and twelve of gold. He was captured and handed over to Yury Dolgoruky, who sent him under armed escort to Kiev. He was saved from extradition to Galich by the entreaties of the metropolitan and abbots of the leading monasteries. Instead he was sent to Suzdal and on the way he was rescued by the followers of Prince Iziaslav Davydovich of Chernigov. He was to be used as a weapon against Yaroslav of Galich, who in 1157 persuaded the Polish king and the Rus princes to send emissaries to Iziaslav urging him to give up Berladnik. Iziaslav refused, and Berladnik returned to the steppe, establishing himself in the Danube towns. From there he launched raids against Galich fishermen and traders, later making war on Yaroslav himself. He reached the small town of Uchitsa but, deserted by his nomadic allies, he gave up the campaign and in 1159 appeared at Kiev, where again Iziaslav Davydovich gave him a cordial welcome. He demanded that Yaroslav give Berladnik an appanage and, when he refused, made war on him. This was disastrous both for Iziaslav and for Berladnik. Having lost his chief supporter, Berladnik left for Greece. According to tradition he met his death by poison at Thessalonika.

91. A berkovets was equal to ten puds, that is to say, four hundred Russian pounds, which would be 163.8 kilograms or about 360 English pounds. Five hundred berkovets therefore was over eighty tons, or nearly 82,000 kg. Professor Robert de Lossa has calculated that if Sviatoslav had barrels of approximately forty gallons, this would amount to a total of 450 barrels of honey. This may represent goods that had been paid to him as a form of tribute or taxation.

92. See Note 57, above.

93. *Nikonian Chronicle*, Vol. 2, p. 25.

94. This is the first mention of Andrei Yurievich, called Bogoliubsky (1111-1174), who later was a dominant figure in twelfth-century Rus. He acquired his surname of Bogoliubsky from his favorite residence at Bogoliubovo, within the principality of Vladimir-Suzdal.

95. By "sons of Oleg" they mean Sviatoslav's line as a whole, Oleg being its most prominent member. Davyd was by no means so well known. (Soloviev's note)

96. For details of the Klim Smoliatich affair, see Fennell, *Russian Church*, pp. 46-48; also Chapter VII, Note 12, below.

97. Hypatian Chronicle, PSRL, Vol. 2, 2nd ed. (St. Petersburg, 1908, reprinted Moscow, 1962), cols. 352-354.

98. Now Sivolozh in the Borzin district of Chernigov province. (Soloviev's note)

99. The term used is vziali na shchit, literally "took onto the shield."

CHAPTER VI

1. Rostislav Yurievich, prince of Novgorod, then of Pereiaslavl, was the eldest son of Yury Dolgoruky. The date of his birth is unknown. The first mention of him in the chronicles is for the year 1138, when he was called to be prince of Novgorod in an effort to gain the friendship of the Suzdal ruler. Rostislav stayed for a little over a year, and left in 1139 angered at Novgorod for not rendering aid to Dolgoruky in his struggle with Vsevolod Olgovich, the incumbent grand prince of Kiev. In 1141 Novgorod invited Yury Dolgoruky to be their prince. He refused, sending Rostislav in his stead. This second reign lasted less than a year. Hearing that Vsevolod was sending Sviatopolk Mstislavich to be their prince, Novgorod placed Rostislav under house arrest in the bishop's palace, then when Sviatopolk arrived sent Rostislav back to his father. In 1147 Rostislav and his brother Andrei were sent by their father, who at that time was in alliance with Sviatoslav Olgovich of Chernigov, to aid the latter in his struggle with Iziaslav Mstislavich, by now grand prince of Kiev. They soundly defeated the retinue of Iziaslav's ally Prince Rostislav Yaroslavich of Riazan, who was forced to flee to the Polovetsians.

In 1148 Rostislav Yurievich once again was dispatched by his father to Southern Rus to aid Sviatoslav Olgovich and also win himself a patrimony, for Yury would not give him an appropriate appanage in Suzdalia. When he arrived in the South he saw that things were going badly for the Chernigov prince, who was being forced to make peace with Iziaslav. Rostislav therefore thought it best to request an appanage from the Kievan ruler. "I have come," said he to Iziaslav, "trusting in God and you, since you are the senior prince among us grandsons of Monomakh. I wish to strive for the Land of Rus and ride alongside you." "Your father is the oldest among us," replied Iziaslav, "yet he cannot live in amity with us." Iziaslav gave Rostislav six towns in Volhynia, including Buzhsk, Mezhibozh, Kotelnitsa and Gorodets Ostersk. This last-mentioned was the site of a princely conference which decided to punish Dolgoruky for his alleged repression of the people of Novgorod. Rostislav attended this meeting but Iziaslav would not take him on campaign, instead ordering him to Buzhsk to guard the allies' rear.

When Iziaslav returned from campaign in the spring of 1149 the boyars accused Rostislav of conspiring against the grand prince and the Berendey, whose families and possessions he intended to seize. Despite Rostislav's strenuous denial, Iziaslav believed these charges. He sent Rostislav home in disgrace to his father, confiscating all his possessions. Returning home, Rostislav persuaded his father that both the inhabitants of the Kievan land and the Karakalpaks were disaffected with Iziaslav, and wanted Yury in their place. Angered at the ignominious expulsion of his son, Yury declared war on Iziaslav, defeated him near Pereiaslavl and expelled him from Kiev. Yury placed Rostislav in Pereiaslavl, where he reigned for the rest of his life. In 1150 he participated in another of his father's wars against Iziaslav, and virulently opposed making peace with him.

Peace was nevertheless concluded at the insistence of Andrei Yurievich, as Iziaslav renounced the grand-princely dignity in place of Viacheslav. When shortly afterwards Iziaslav once again broke the peace and seized Kiev, his son Mstislav sought to deprive Rostislav of Pereiaslavl. In response Rostislav called to his aid his brother Andrei and the nomadic Torks. They defeated and captured Mstislav's allies the Turpei, forcing Mstislav to abandon his designs on Pereiaslavl. Rostislav died on Good Friday of 1151. He was buried by his brothers Andrei, Gleb and Mstislav in the cathedral of St. Michael, close to his uncles Andrei and Sviatoslav Vladimirovich. His daughter Evfrosinia was the wife of Prince Gleb Rostislavich of Riazan.

2. Curiously, he does not even mention Viacheslav, showing how little his relations thought of him. (Soloviev's note)

3. Franklin and Shepard, pp. 346, 349.

4. Gleb Yurievich is first mentioned in the chronicle for the year 1146, on the occasion of the death of his brother Ivan. In 1147 he took part in his father's campaign in alliance with Sviatoslav Olgovich against Iziaslav, who was his father's nephew and his own first cousin. At that time Iziaslav's son Mstislav was prince of Kursk. As Gleb and Sviatoslav approached the inhabitants of Kursk declared that they would be glad to fight against Sviatoslav, but not against Gleb,

he being a descendant of Vladimir Monomakh. Mstislav had no alternative but to return to his father. The inhabitants of Kursk acknowleged Gleb as their prince and accepted his burgrave. Previously Kursk and all the Seim basin was given by Sviatoslav to Gleb's brother Ivan, on whose death Sviatoslav granted these lands to Gleb, who even appointed burgraves to the towns along the Seim and Vyr rivers, concluding also alliances with several Polovetsian hordes. Only a few towns remained loyal to Iziaslav.

With the onset of winter the retinues of the Chernigov princes, with the help of the Polovetsians, seized various territories on the right bank of the Dnieper. Gleb, as their ally, occupied Gorodets, which previously belonged to his father. Instead of obeying Iziaslav's summons to Kiev Gleb set off for Pereiaslavl, where some citizens who were disaffected at the rule of Iziaslav and his son Mstislav declared in his favor. Hearing of Gleb's approach, Mstislav came out with his retinue, but neither side was prepared to hazard battle. The following day Gleb withdrew. Mstislav set off in pursuit and captured Gleb's rearguard, but Gleb himself escaped to Gorodets. Igor's attack on Pereiaslavl encouraged Iziaslav, with his retinue and the Berendey, to attack Gorodets. Despite his appeals none of the Chernigov princes came to Gleb's aid. Having withstood a three-day siege, Gleb proposed peace with Iziaslav, who agreed. He left Gleb in possession of Gorodets, and himself removed to Kiev.

Gleb did not cease communication with the Chernigov princes, saying that he had kissed the cross to Iziaslav under duress, and now wished to renew the alliance. For this Iziaslav deprived Gleb of Gorodets, which he gave to Gleb's elder brother Rostislav, who had come from Novgorod bitterly complaining about his father. In 1150, having seized Kiev, Yury Dolgoruky distributed territories to his sons, Gleb receiving Kanev. In his effort to regain the grand-princely throne Iziaslav called on his relatives in Hungary, Bohemia and Poland. Gleb, who at that time was encamped by the Stubla river upstream from Peresopnitsa, suddenly was attacked by Iziaslav, barely escaping into the town. He made his submission to Iziaslav, who received him graciously, escorted him to Korchesk and bade him go to his father, while he himself went to the Karakalpaks. Shortly thereafter, when Kiev was under the joint rule of Viacheslav and Iziaslav, the two princes sent to Dolgoruky, asking him to remain in Suzdal and send his sons to rule in Pereiaslavl. Dolgoruky asked grace to stay in Gorodets for a while in order to wind up his affairs in the South. Viacheslav and Iziaslav gave him a month's period of grace.

Leaving Gleb in Pereiaslavl, Yury proceeded to Gorodets, but outstayed the time alotted. Iziaslav therefore besieged Yury in Gorodets. Though he held out for a time Yury did not receive help from any quarter, he had to swear to return to Suzdal, leaving Gleb in charge of Gorodets. Yury apparently had forfeited Pereiaslavl by violating his original oath. In 1154 Yury again undertook a campaign in the South then was forced to abandon his plan even before he had reached Kozelsk, because murrain had broken out among the horses and Polovetsian help had fallen short of what was anticipated. Consequently Yury forces, Gleb approached Pereiaslavl. He failed in his main objective, but seized Piriatin, on the Uday river. Shortly thereafter he received Pereiaslavl from his ally, Prince Iziaslav Davydovich of Chernigov, who temporarily seized the Kievan throne after Viacheslav's death. In 1156 Iziaslav Davydovich had to concede the Kievan throne to Yury Dolgoruky, while Gleb retained Pereiaslavl and also married the daughter of Sviatoslav Davydovich. In 1157 Yury died, after which the Kievan throne changed hands constantly.

In 1168 the disaffection of the Southern princes towards Mstislav Iziaslavich was exploited by Yury's eldest surviving son Andrei Bogoliubsky, as he asserted his claims to the seniority and to Kiev. Gleb took part in this campaign. After the capture and sack of Kiev Gleb was placed in charge, yielding his principality of Pereiaslavl to his minor son Vladimir. Shortly after Gleb's accession to Kiev the Polovetsians invaded the Land of Rus. One group halted at the Pesochna, the other crossed the Dnieper and deployed near Cherson. They demanded parlays. Gleb agreed but on the advice of his counsellors he first went to Pereiaslavl to make dispositions for the care of his twelve-year-old son. He proposed to make peace first with the Polovetsians in Pereiaslavl territory. Only then would he negotiate with the other group at Cherson. Having made peace with the Pereiaslavl group, he set off with his brother Mikhalko and his retinue towards Cherson. Meanwhile the other Polovetsian group, convinced that Gleb was stalling at Pereiaslavl, set off for the Volhynian town of Polonny, a property of the Tithe church of Kiev, in search of booty. They seized many prisoners and much livestock, then set off for their own land. When Gleb heard of this, he wanted to strike out at the Polovetsians. His Berendey allies restrained him, saying "Do not go, prince. It is befitting for you to ride only with a large army and accompanied by other princes. Better to send your brother and some of the Berendey." Gleb sent Mikhailko and fifteen hundred Berendey. These defeated the Polovetsians and rescued many captives.

In the meantime, while Gleb was preoccupied at Pereiaslavl, Mstislav Iziaslavich, who had not lost hope of recovering Kiev, approached it with a large army and took it by surprise. Then Mstislav advanced on Davyd Rostislavich in Vyshgorod, which siege was unsuccessful because Davyd had a large retinue, supplemented by aid from his brothers and Gleb Yurievich. While Mstislav was besieging Vyshgorod Gleb with his Polovetsian auxiliaries hastened to Kiev. Mstislav also came then, observing the treachery of his allies, fled to Volhynia, where he died in 1170. Gleb died on January 20, 1171, and was buried within the Savior monastery of Kiev.

5. See Chapter V, Note 57, above.
6. *Chronicle of Novgorod*, p. 19.
7. A Finnic people, inhabitants of Karelia, east of present-day Finland.
8. See Chapter IV, Note 16, above.
9. Iziaslav Davydovich (died 1161) lived at the time of the bitterest struggle for the Kievan throne between the descendants of Monomakh and Oleg. In 1139 he is mentioned as having supported Vsevolod Olgovich against Iziaslav Msti-

he is mentioned as having supported Vsevolod Olgovich against Iziaslav Mstislavich, attacking the lands of Vladimir-in-Volhynia and Turov. He then threw
his support behind Vsevolod's brothers Igor and Sviatoslav, who rebelled against
their elder brother over the assignment of appanages. In 1142 he again supported
the grand prince, but in 1146 allied himself with Iziaslav Mstislavich, who shortly
thereafter seized the Kievan throne. The emissaries of Iziaslav Mstislavich and
the sons of Davyd demanded of Igor's brother Sviatoslav that he surrender them
Novgorod Seversk and cease support for his brother. Sviatoslav refused, and the
allies invaded his lands. When Vsevolod fled from Novgorod Seversk, Iziaslav
pursued him but was defeated. Having received from Iziaslav Mstislavich all the
lands conquered from Sviatoslav except for Kursk, the sons of Davyd expelled
Vsevolod from Briansk and Kozelsk. Receiving news that help was on its way to
Sviatoslav, the allies withdrew to Chernigov, offering a reward for whoever
would kill Sviatoslav.

Shortly afterwards the sons of Davyd switched their support to Sviatoslav
Olgovich and Yury of Suzdal, leading directly, in 1147, to the murder of Igor
Olgovich in Kiev. Yury sent them his son Rostislav, who soon after sided with
Iziaslav Mstislavich, followed in 1148 by the Chernigov princes. Iziaslav Davydovich stayed loyal to his namesake until 1150, when he threw in his lot with Yury
of Suzdal. Yet again he is found on the side of Iziaslav Mstislavich in the conflict
leading to the battle on the Rut (1151), in which his brother Vladimir fought on
the other side and was slain. Shortly thereafter Iziaslav Davydovich made an
amicable agreement with Sviatoslav Olgovich, each to rule his father's former
domain. Meanwhile Yury of Suzdal advanced on Kiev, on his way, in 1152, besieging Chernigov. Iziaslav Davydovich was assisted by the grand prince's
brother Rostislav Mstislavich, and Chernigov held out. In 1154 Grand Prince
Iziaslav Mstislavich died. Iziaslav Davydovich visited Kiev for the funeral but
was denied entry into the city. Iziaslav Davydovich and Sviatoslav Olgovich then
concluded an alliance with Yury.

In 1155 Viacheslav died and Rostislav, having become grand prince, approached Chernigov, demanding of Iziaslav that he recognize his rule. Iziaslav
rejected his demand. Allying with Gleb Yurievich and the Polovetsians, he came
out and deployed along the Belous river. Some disaffected citizens of Kiev sent
a delegation led by Bishop Damian to ask Iziaslav to be their prince. Yury of
Suzdal, hearing of this turn of events, immediately sent to demand that Iziaslav
leave Kiev. He demurred, saying that the people had chosen him. Eventually on
the advice of Sviatoslav Olgovich and also through lack of confidence in his own
forces, he withdrew to Chernigov, and Kiev was occupied by Yury. Iziaslav
contemplated trying to regain Kiev by force, and made preparations for war, then
decided prudence was the better counsel. Peace was sealed by the marriage of
Yury's son to Iziaslav's daughter, who received Korchesk as a dowry.

Nevertheless Iziaslav could not forget Kiev, so he sought allies. At considerable sacrifice he made peace with his nephew Sviatoslav Vladimirovich and
attracted Mstislav Iziaslavich of Volhynia to his side. They were just about to

advance on Kiev when, in 1157, Yury died. The Kievans, under pressure from the Polovetsians, summoned Iziaslav on May 19 and he at last assumed the Kievan grand-princely throne. Preferring to have Sviatoslav Olgovich as a friend rather than an enemy, Iziaslav voluntarily gave him Chernigov, while Novgorod Seversk he surrendered to his nephew Sviatoslav Vsevolodovich. Thus Iziaslav ruled over the principality of Kiev in its narrowest limits, with the addition of only a few of the Chernigov towns. His attempt to gain for Vladimir Yaroslavich the Turov appanage, ruled by Sviatopolk's grandson Yury Yaroslavich, proved unsuccessful. In 1158 he fell out with the princes of Galich-Volhynia for not surrendering Ivan Berladnik, who was a pretender to the Galich throne (see Chapter V, Note 90, above). Prince Yaroslav of Galich, with his allies, declared war on Iziaslav and occupied Belgorod. Iziaslav had a large army, but the Torks and Berendey betrayed him. He was defeated, fled to the Sozha river. There he was joined by his wife, who had fled Kiev. Blaming Sviatoslav for his misfortune, he seized the land of the Viatichians and threatened the towns of the Kursk principality. Sviatoslav was driven into an alliance with Rostislav, who by now had occupied Kiev (1159).

Two attempts by Iziaslav to regain control of Chernigov were unsuccessful even though he received considerable help from Ivan Berladnik and his band of mercenaries. They ravaged the Smolensk territory, and the Polovetsians took many captives. Iziaslav nevertheless saw he was outnumbered and sought an alliance with Andrei Bogoliubsky. The Suzdal prince's daughter married Iziaslav's nephew Sviatoslav Vladimirovich, who came over to his side, accompanied by a faction of the Kiev boyars. In 1160 Iziaslav attacked Pereiaslavl but was defeated. Then with fresh allies he crossed the Dnieper and decisively defeated Rostislav. He proceeded to the Holy Wisdom cathedral and asked pardon of the citizens for any offenses he might have committed against them. Sviatoslav urged him to be reconciled with Rostislav. He refused and attacked Belgorod, but Rostislav began to gather help from all quarters. While retreating from Belgorod, Iziaslav was slain by Voibor, a Genoese mercenary, in the sight of Rostislav and Mstislav. He was buried first in the St. Simeon monastery in Kiev, later his remains were transferred to the church of St. Boris and St. Gleb in Chernigov.

10. See Chapter IV, Note 5, above.

11. See Note 1, above.

12. Boris Yurievich (died 1159), prince of Belgorod, later of Turov. In 1146 he travelled to Koltosk, where his brother Ivan died, and took the body to his father in Suzdal. In 1149 he received Belgorod as his appanage. In the same year he participated in the siege of Lutsk, where his brother Andrei distinguished himself. Boris was not one of the more illustrious princes, neither was he particularly favored by his father. In 1150, in the course of Yury's struggle with Iziaslav, Boris was sent in pursuit of Iziaslav. He gave chase as far as the Chortov wood, then turned back. The same year he was almost captured by Prince Vladimir Mstislavich, who attacked Belgorod while Boris was feasting with his retinue and clergy. He was warned by his tax collector who gave the alarm and raised the

drawbridge. Subsequently he travelled from Belgorod to Kiev to warn his father that Iziaslav was on the move again. In 1151 he again participated in Yury's war against Iziaslav, who once again had seized Kiev. In 1154, after a series of inter-princely struggles, together with his father he re-entered Kiev and subsequently received the principality of Turov. Boris apparently was unpopular in the South and, under circumstances which are rather obscure, was deprived of Turov, which passed to Prince Yury Yaroslavich. In any event, Boris died in the North. His body was buried in the church of St. Boris and St. Gleb at Kideksha, on the Nerl river.

13. Vasily (Vasilko) Yurievich, prince of Suzdal 1162.

14. Mstislav's younger sister Evfrosinia was married to the king of Hungary, the Polish princes were related to him because of the marriage of his niece, Vsevolod Olgovich's daughter, to Bolesław the son of Władysław, and the prince of Bohemia was related to him by virtue of Sviatopolk Vsevolodovich's marriage to a Czech princess. (Soloviev's note)

15. Géza II, king of Hungary, born 1129, reigned 1141-1161, died 1162. He was the son of Béla II (reigned 1131-1141). His reign was marked by the struggle with both the Holy Roman and the Byzantine empires, as well as the dynastic wars in Galich. Apart from a brief period of vassalage to Frederick Barbarossa, Géza was able to maintain Hungary's independence. During his reign Saxon immigrants received privileged status.

16. Vladislav II, duke of Bohemia, date of birth uncertain, reigned 1140-1175. He was the eldest son of Vladislav I (reigned 1109-1125). He was elected with the help of Emperor Conrad III, his brother-in-law. He was also on good terms with Frederick Barbarossa, whom he assisted in his Italian campaigns. Vladislav was named king, and was crowned at Milan in 1158.

17. See Chapter IV, Note 10, above.

18. Henryk was a son of Bolesław Wrymouth by his second marriage, to Salomea, daughter of Count Heinrich of Berg. He was regarded as too junior to take part in the share-out of principalities among his half-brothers following his father's death.

19. See Chapter V, Note 73, above.

20. See Chapter V, Note 9, above.

21. See Chapter V, Note 61, above.

22. Yury Yaroslavich, prince of Turov, son of Yaroslav Sviatopolchich (also referred to as Yaroslavets) of Vladimir-in-Volhynia (died 1123), great-grandson of Grand Prince Iziaslav Yaroslavich. He was born in 1119, probably of his father's third marriage. First mention of him in the chronicles is in connection with his marriage in 1144 to the daughter of Prince Vsevolodko Davydovich of Goroden. Where he ruled at this time is unknown. At the time of Yury Dologruky's struggle with Iziaslav, Yury Yaroslavich was an ally of the Suzdal prince. In the peace talks he urged Dolgoruky not to make peace with his nephew. It is not known whether this was because Yury Yaroslavich was personally offended by Iziaslav, or whether he merely sought to take advantage of the expulsion of

Mstislav's sons from Volhynia, where Iziaslav had gained control over Vladimir and a number of other towns. Perhaps also Yury Yaroslavich's enmity towards Iziaslav was part of a family feud. His father's second marriage was to one of Iziaslav's sisters. This marriage was dissolved in 1118, following which Yaroslav Sviatopolchich fled to Hungary before the avenging forces of Monomakh, grandfather of his former wife.

In any case Dolgoruky heeded the advice of Yury Yaroslavich and continued the struggle with Iziaslav. When Iziaslav once again was about to achieve peace through the mediation of Yury's ally Vladimirko of Galich, Yury Yaroslavich, together with Dolgoruky's eldest son Rostislav, did their best to hamper the peace negotiations. Despite this, Dolgoruky's second son Andrei told his father not to heed Yury Yaroslavich's advice, and counsels of peace prevailed. In 1155 or 1156 Dolgoruky sent Yury Yaroslavich to make war on Iziaslav's sons, Mstislav and Yaroslav. In 1157 Yury Yaroslavich replaced Boris Yurievich as prince of Turov, perhaps at Dolgoruky's instigation.

Nevertheless Grand Prince Iziaslav Davydovich and Mstislav would in no way tolerate the possession by this dispossessed prince of such a key principality. They proposed to give it to Vladimir Mstislavich, who as yet did not have a throne. In 1158 a grand coalition of princes attacked Yury Yaroslavich in Turov. The districts of Turov and Pinsk were devastated, but Yury fought hard, leading sorties out of the city. Nevertheless he saw he could not stand alone against such formidable forces, and sent peace overtures to Iziaslav. These proposals were rejected. Iziaslav besieged Turov and Pinsk, then the campaign had to be called off because of the outbreak of murrain among the horses. Yury Yaroslavich remained as prince of Turov. In 1160 he campaigned against Putivl. Taking advantage of his absence, during the winter of that year Mstislav Iziaslavich with several of his allies advanced on Turov, invested it for two and a half weeks, then lifted the siege. In 1162 Yury Yaroslavich concluded peace with the new grand prince of Kiev, Rostislav Mstislavich, thus averting further attacks on his principality. The date of his death is uncertain.

23. See p. 104, above

24. Yury Yaroslavich's mother was the daughter of Yury Vladimirovich's brother Mstislav, which also, incidentally, makes him a nephew of Iziaslav Mstislavich.

25. In the powiat of Dubno in Volhynia. (Soloviev's note)

26. "Prince Yaroslavets…rode around the city of Vladimir and loudly threatened Prince Andrei and the citizens, saying 'On the morrow I will take your city and torture all of you mercilessly.' And so, on the morrow when the sun rose many warriors began preparing [to attack the city]; but Prince Yaroslavets, not waiting for his troops, alone with but two soldiers, went to the city. Some citizens, however, had left the city secretly at night and had hidden themselves along the route on which Yaroslavets was supposed to go. When Prince Yaroslavets passed them, they leaped up unexpectedly and struck him with a lance. His troops hurried up to him, took him already dying, and bore him to camp, to his tent, where he died." *Nikonian Chronicle*, Vol. 1, pp. 244-245 (spelling modified).

27. Of the numerous saints called Theodore the most widely venerated, and the most appropriate patron for Andrei, is Theodore Stratilates, whose feasts are kept February 8 and June 8. He was a commander in the Roman army martyred for his faith, though the details given in extant accounts of his life are unreliable to the extent that some modern scholars have postulated that his life and that of Theodore Tyro (feast day February 17) are two different elaborations of the same martyr. Theodore Stratilates is honored with the title of Great Martyr, and together with St. George, St. Demetrius and St. Mercurius, is one of the four military saints very prominent in the East.

28. Soloviev uses the term svat, denoting the father-in-law of one's son or daughter.

29. See Chapter V, Note 83, above.

30. Vladimir Mstislavich, prince of Dorogobuzh, died 1171.

31. The youngest son of Monomakh was Andrei Vladimirovich, sometime prince of Vladimir-in-Volhynia and Pereiaslavl, died 1141.

32. mytnik (sborshchik podatei).

33. For a discussion of these events, see Franklin and Shepard, p. 349.

34. See Chapter II, Note 17 and Chapter V, Note 82, above.

35. Neither Viacheslav's date of birth nor Yury's may be determined with any accuracy from the surviving chronicles. Vladimir Monomakh's eldest son Mstislav was born in 1076, and his youngest, Andrei, in 1102. Even if we assume that Monomakh's older sons were born at yearly intervals this would mean that Iziaslav was born in 1077, Yaropolk in 1078, Sviatoslav in 1079, Viacheslav in 1080, and Roman in 1081, thus Yury must have been born between 1081 and 1102. For Viacheslav to have had a beard by the time Yury was born, even if it was only just beginning to grow (at the age of about fifteen), Yury must have been born in 1096, but he was married in 1107. Does this mean that he was married at the age of ten? His brother Andrei was fifteen when he married in 1117, so this should not be a problem for us, as Konstantin Vsevolodovich was married at the age of eleven, and Vsevolod III gave his eight-year-old daughter Verkhuslava in marriage to Rostislav Riurikovich. Tatishchev says that Yury was sixty-six when he died in 1157, which means he was born in 1091. It would be strange if Viacheslav had a beard at the age of ten (or eleven, if we suppose that he was in fact older than Sviatoslav). A mistake on Tatishchev's part seems more likely. (Soloviev's note)

36. Boris Vsevolodovich, son of Prince Vsevolod Davydovich, dates of birth and death unknown. In 1141 his father died, leaving him his appanage of Goroden. In 1144, together with Grand Prince Vsevolod Olgovich, he campaigned against Vladimirko of Galich. In 1150 he supported Iziaslav Mstislavich in his quest for the Kievan throne, and accompanied him on his advance to Dorogobuzh, subsequently taking part in the princely conference at Vshchizh. In 1151 Boris participated in Iziaslav's second seizure of Kiev, after which Iziaslav sent him in pursuit of Dolgoruky, who had set off in the direction of Belgorod. In 1169 Boris helped Iziaslav's son Mstislav to capture Kiev after the death of Grand Prince Rostislav. When Mstislav was driven out of Kiev by the other princes, Boris

rallied to him and participated in his victory over Gleb Yurievich, and in his second occupation of Kiev.

37. The Rut river has two main tributaries, the Great and Lesser Rutets.

38. Mstislav Iziaslavich (died 1170), prince of Pereiaslavl from 1151, and of Volhynia from 1154. He took part in his father's wars against the princes of Chernigov and Yury Dolgoruky. In 1152 he twice defeated the Polovetsians. Having established himself in Volhynia, he opened the struggle for the possession of Kiev. In 1160 he seized the town and placed upon the throne his uncle Rostislav Mstislavich of Smolensk, after whose death in 1167 or 1168 he himself became grand prince. He continued the struggle with the princes of Vladimir-Suzdal for supremacy in Rus. In 1169 he fortified the city against Andrei Bogoliubsky and his allies. After the fall of Kiev he left for Volhynia, where he died, though in the final year of his life he briefly reoccupied Kiev. See entry by David M. Goldfrank, MERSH, Vol. 23, pp. 151-153

39. Ne idët mesto k golove, a golova k mestu. In other words, it is not a person's position that determines his qualities, but his abilities that determine the position he can obtain.

40. Rostislav Yaroslavich was prince of Riazan from 1129 to 1155, son of Prince Yaroslav Sviatoslavich of Murom. Under his rule Riazan became definitively detached from the principality of Murom. In his struggle with the Rostov-Suzdal principality Rostislav Yaroslavich formed close links with Smolensk and some of the more conservative elements of the Rostov nobility. In 1153 he founded the town of Rostislavl. See entry (unsigned), MERSH, Vol. 31, p. 165.

41. Sviatoslav Olgovich (died 1164) was prince of Novgorod Seversk 1136-1138 and again in 1139, of Belgorod 1141-1154, and of Chernigov from 1154 until his death. He was a grandson of Prince Sviatoslav Yaroslavich of Chernigov. In 1139 he helped his brother Vsevolod Olgovich to seize the Kievan throne. He then tried to expel Andrei Bogoliubsky from Pereiaslavl, but without success. From 1146 he engaged in the interminable struggle of the princes for Kiev, having declared himself an ally of Yury Dolgoruky, with whom he met at the famous banquet in Moscow in 1147. He helped obtain the Kievan throne for Dolgoruky, after whose death he supported Iziaslav Davydovich, from whom he received the principality of Chernigov. See entry by Sokol, MERSH, Vol. 38, pp. 117-122.

42. This is one of the earliest references to Yaroslav Vladimirovich Osmomysl ("of the Eight Senses"). He was born some time in the 1130s and died in 1187. He was the son of Vladimir Volodarevich, prince of Galich. He is first mentioned in 1150 in connection with his marriage to Olga, daughter of Yury Dolgoruky. He succeeded his father to the throne of Galich in 1152, at a time when his principality was surrounded by enemies. Yaroslav concluded peace with Iziaslav Mstislavich of Kiev, acknowledging himself as subordinate to Iziaslav. The war between Kiev and Galich was renewed in 1154. Iziaslav defeated the Galich forces at Terebovl, but sustained heavy losses and had to withdraw to Kiev. Vladimir then gravitated towards Rostov-Suzdal. This alliance lapsed with the death of Yury Dolgoruky. From 1158 to 1161 Yaroslav fought against the Kievan

prince Iziaslav Davydovich. In the course of this struggle Yaroslav established closer ties with the Hungarian king. Relations with Rostov-Suzdal deteriorated in 1170, when Yaroslav repudiated his wife Olga and their son Vladimir in favor of his concubine Nastasia and her son Oleg. The princess and her son fled to Poland, accompanied by a faction of boyars. Within Galich the boyars loyal to Olga seized the prince, defeated his Polovetsian allies, eliminated the rival boyar faction and burned Nastasia at the stake. A reconciliation was contrived with Olga and Vladimir, though the following year they fled again, on this occasion to Prince Yaroslav Iziaslavich of Lutsk. This time the boyars sided with Osmomysl, who hired a Polish army to drive his wife and son out of Lutsk. They first sought refuge with Prince Mikhail Yurievich of Torchesk, then in the principality of Chernigov. Olga returned home to Suzdalia, where she entered a convent. She died at Vladimir-on-the-Kliazma in 1182. Despite the crisis of 1170-1171, for most of his reign Yaroslav enjoyed the confidence of his boyars, as the principality prospered. On his death bed he bequeathed Galich to his illegitimate son Oleg, and Peremyshl to his legitimate but dissolute son Vladimir. Yaroslav was buried in the Dormition cathedral of Galich, which he himself had built in 1157. See entry by Dimnik, MERSH, Vol. 44, pp. 229-233.

43. See Note 39, above.

44. See Chapter V, Note 11, above.

45. See Note 41, above.

46. See Chapter V, Note 37 and Chapter VI, Note 9, above.

47. Laurentian Chronicle, col. 345.

48. "In March 1155, after the death of his older brother Viacheslav and after more than fifteen years of intermittent frustration, Iurii of Suzdal—now the only surviving son of Vladimir Monomakh—was at last able to brush aside the local princelings...and enter Kiev relatively unopposed." Franklin and Shepard, p. 349

49. See Note 22, above.

50. Vladimir was born in 1132, so at this time (1156) he was only twenty-four, and in 1146, when Iziaslav first took possession of Kiev, he would have been fourteen. Nevertheless, he is recorded as having been in command of the auxiliary force which Iziaslav sent to Chernigov, while his younger brother Yaropolk was prince of Turov. Could they really have held these positions at such a tender age? Their sister married a Polovetsian prince in 1144. (Soloviev's note)

51. ne diadeiu (stryem), a macheshichem.

52. See Note 31, above.

53. The term used is osmenik, presumaby the official responsible for collection of the os'mina (eighth tax).

54. "Opposition to Iurii was already mounting before his death. One source was the Mstislavich branch of the dynasty. Its leaders were Rostislav of Smolensk and his nephew, the Volynian prince Mstislav, son of the late grand prince. The second source of opposition was the Chernigov line. Its senior member, Iziaslav Davydovich, had briefly seized the Kievan throne after Grand Prince Iziaslav's death (1154), but had been displaced by Iurii. When Iurii died, the Kievan boyars

invited Iziaslav Davydovich to return. The Chernigov prince represented Iurii's, i.e., the senior, generation of the dynasty; he also offered a compromise between the fractious branches of the Monomashichi. But his father had never served as grand prince of Kiev; hence, according to dynastic tradition, he lacked legitimacy. The new grand prince was neither able to extend his authority to key strongholds nor hold his Kievan position for long. Novgorod accepted a representative of the Smolensk line of Mstislavichi (Sviatoslav Rostislavich) as its prince in 1157. The Iur'evichi retained Pereiaslavl', which continued to be ruled by Gleb, and Suzdalia, where Iurii's son Andrei Bogoliubskii assumed the throne. In 1158 Rostislav Mstislavich of Smolensk, the senior, fully eligible, and therefore legitimate heir, supported by both the Volynian and Galician princes, easily took the Kievan throne. His reign lasted until 1167." Martin, pp. 110-111.

55. See Note 36, above.

56. See Chapter V, Note 37, above.

57. See Note 40, above.

58. *Chronicle of Novgorod*, p. 18.

59. *Chronicle of Novgorod*, p. 19.

60. *Chronicle of Novgorod*, p. 20.

61. *Chronicle of Novgorod*, p. 21.

62. See Chapter V, Note 51, above.

63. One of the two main divisions of medieval Novgorod. The Market Side (torgovaia storona) was situated on the opposite bank of the Volkhov river from the Holy Wisdom Side (Sofiiskaia storona), which contained the main cathedral and the political-administrative center of the city.

64. *Chronicle of Novgorod*, pp. 21-22.

65. *Chronicle of Novgorod*, p. 20.

66. Here in the text his patronymic is given as "Ivanovich." Elsewhere in the text, as well as in the index, it is rendered as "Ivankovich." Either Soloviev regards the two forms as variants of the same thing, or "Ivanovich" is a misprint.

CHAPTER VII

1. See Chapter V, Note 13, above.

2. See Chapter V, Note 11, above.

3. See Chapter VI, Note 38, above.

4. See Chapter VI, Note 41, above.

5. See Chapter V, Note 37, and Chapter VI, Note 9, above.

6. See Chapter VI, Note 9, above.

7. See Chapter VI, Note 22, above.

8. To be precise, his great-great-grandson. Boris died in the North in 1159. See Chapter VI, Note 12, above.

9. See Chapter VI, Notes 12, 22 and 30, above.

10. See Chapter V, Note 90, above.

11. tol'ko psari da polovtsy. It is not clear what Sviatoslav meant by this expression.

12. Klim Smoliatich, whose surname has been taken by some to mean that he was a native of Smolensk, in 1147 through the influence of Iziaslav Mstislavich was consecrated metropolitan of Kiev, only the second native prelate after Hilarion in 1051 to occupy the see. There was much opposition to his election among some members of the clergy who considered it uncanonical because it was effected locally, without the approval of the patriarch of Constantinople. He also was criticized for making use of secular philosophy in his writings. His tenure of the metropolitanate did not survive the death of Iziaslav in 1154. See Franklin and Shepard, pp. 358-362, and Fennell, *Russian Church*, pp. 46-48.

13. Roman Rostislavich in 1149 married a daughter of Sviatoslav Olgovich. He died in 1180.

14. Iziaslav Andreevich died either in 1163 or 1165. There is little information concerning him.

15. See Chapter VI, Note 39, above.

16. Davyd Rostislavich, later prince of Smolensk and Vyshgorod, born 1140, died 1197.

17. Or, according to other sources, Lutsk, which is also quite probable. (Soloviev's note)

18. Concerning Bishop Anthony, see Fennell, *Russian Church*, pp. 49-50.

19. This Igor, later prince of Novgorod Seversk, is the prince whose attack on the Polovetsians later was commemorated in the Tale of Igor's Campaign.

20. Polikarp was abbot of the Caves monastery, the first head of that institution to be accorded the title of archimandrite. Fennell, *Russian Church*, p. 67.

21. See Chapter VI, Note 51, above.

22. The œconomus, in Russian ekonom, was the steward or manager of the temporalities of the monastery. The kelar (cellarer) was responsible for the monastery's supply of food and drink. Subordinate to them were the dokhar (in charge of clothing and work tools) and the ksenodokh (hospitality official).

23. Radimichians was the name given to an early Rus tribal confederation which existed during the final centuries of the first millennium A.D. Their lands lay in the eastern portions of the upper Dnieper region, along the Sozh river and its various tributaries. The early chronicles report concerning the Radimichians that they and the Viatichians were "from the Liakhi." This statement is taken frequently as reference to genetic ties with the Western Slavs, a hypothesis not corroborated by archeological evidence. In the middle of the ninth century they are known to have paid tribute to the Khazars. In 885 they were annexed to the Kievan realm by Prince Oleg. Later they are mentioned as part of the armed forces under Oleg which campaigned against Constantinople in 907. They finally lost their independence in 984 when they were defeated at the Pishchana river by Prince Vladimir's commander whose *nom de guerre* was "Wolf's Tail." Later the territory inhabited by the Radimichians became part of the principality of Chernigov and, to some extent, that of Smolensk. The Radimichians are mentioned by name

for the last time in the chronicle entries for the year 1169. For further information, see entry by P.N. Tret'iakov, MERSH, Vol. 30, pp. 144-145, also Vol. 1 of this series, Chapter I, Note 45.

24. *Chronicle of Novgorod*, p. 26.

25. This is Vsevolod III Bolshoe Gnezdo ("of the large nest," 1154-1212), subsequently (from 1174) grand prince, from whom the grand princes of Moscow were descended.

26. Mstislav Rostislavich, grandson of Yury Dolgoruky, in 1176 married a daughter of the Novgorod boyar Yakun Miroslavich, and died in 1178.

27. *Nikonian Chronicle*, Vol. 2, pp. 140-142.

28. See Chapter II, Note 2, above.

29. Igor Yaroslavich (died 1147), prince of Volhynia and Smolensk, son of Yaroslav the Wise.

30. Solun' in the original.

31. Rogvolod was the son of Boris Vseslavich (died 1128). In 1143 he married a daughter of Iziaslav Mstislavich, by whom he had two sons, Vseslav and Gleb, mentioned in 1160 and 1180 respectively.

32. Rostislav, mentioned elsewhere under the year 1144, was the son of Gleb Olgovich (died 1138).

33. Gleb Rostislavich, prince of Drutsk, was the son of Prince Rostislav Glebovich of Polotsk.

34. Briacheslav Vasilkovich, prince of Vitebsk, son of Vasilko Sviatoslavich, prince of Polotsk.

35. Davyd Rostislavich (1140-1197), prince of Smolensk and Vyshgorod, son of Prince Rostislav Mstislavich.

36. Son of Prince Gleb Vseslavich of Minsk (died 1118).

37. Vseslav Vasilkovich, prince of Vitebsk, son of Vasilko Briacheslavich.

38. Curiously there is no mention of this oath in the Novgorod Chronicle. (Soloviev's note)

39. *Chronicle of Novgorod*, pp. 25-26.

40. Olof Skötkonung ("the Tax King") reigned 990-1022. Son of Erik the Victorious, he opposed the formation of a strong Norwegian kingdom, and joined forces with King Svein of Denmark and his allies in a victorious war against Norway in 1000. Olof subsequently married one of his illegitimate daughters, Holmfrith, to Earl Svein, one of the Danish viceroys in Sweden. Initially opposed to Olaf II Haraldsson of Norway, eventually he made peace with him by bestowing upon him the hand of Astri, his other illegitimate daughter. His only legitimate daughter, Ingigerd, married Yaroslav the Wise. Olof was a committed Christian but was prevented by the magi of the Uppsala pagan cult from effecting a mass conversion of the Swedish people, although Christian missionaries from various nations ministered under his protection.

41. Stenkil was son-in-law of Emund, king of Sweden, who succeeded him in 1060 and died in 1066. Inge and Halstan were sons of Stenkil, reigning around

1081. Inge was a Christian but was expelled by his brother Svein, called Blot-svein since he reinstituted the sacrifices to the pagan gods. Blotsvein retained the kingship for three years until Inge returned and slew him.

42. Erik IX, king of Sweden, died at Uppsala around 1160, feast day May 18. He became king of a considerable part of Sweden in 1150, and designed to conquer and convert to Christianity the neighboring Finns. He was killed when the Danish prince Magnus, reinforced by Swedish rebels, attacked Uppsala. To help consolidate his own position, Erik's son Canute encouraged the cult of his father as a martyr, and Erik was venerated as the national saint of the Swedes. The ancient belief in a special heavenly destiny, Valhalla, for those killed in battle doubtless had a part in the idealization of Erik and other Scandinavian heroes. Attwater, pp. 116-117. There is some affinity between the accounts of the Scandinavian royal saints and those of the martyred princes Boris and Gleb, the first saints of Rus. See R.M. Price, "Boris and Gleb. Princely Martyrs and Martyrology in Kievan Russia" in *Martyrs and Martyrologies. Papers Read at the 1992 Summer Meeting and the 1993 Winter Meeting of the Ecclesiastical History Society*. Ed. by Diane Wood (Oxford, 1993), pp. 105-115.

43. Karl VII was the son of King Sverker (reigned 1134-1155). In 1164 he established the archbishopric of Uppsala, previously the residence of the pagan high priest.

44. *Chronicle of Novgorod*, p. 24. See also *Nikonian Chronicle*, Vol. 2, p. 132.

45. Now the Voronovka or Voronega, which flows into Lake Ladoga between the Pasha and the Sias. (Soloviev's note)

46. See Chapter V, Note 76, above.

47. The term used here is bogatyr. Of Turkic origin, it originally became known to the Rus as referring to mighty or valiant warriors amongst their neighbors on the steppes. During the medieval period they began to apply it to fighting men of outstanding prowess from their own people, and now it denotes the traditional heroes of the epic songs of Russian folklore.

48. Constantine VII Porphyrogennetos, emperor 913-959 but effective ruler only from 944, compiled, among other things, the treatise *De Administrando Imperio* (Concerning the Administration of the Empire) which devotes much attention to conditions prevailing in neighboring countries.

49. The term used is grechniki, which Soloviev paraphrases as "either Greeks, or generally merchants engaged in commerce with Greece."

50. Freebooters from Bîrlad. See above, pp. 114-115.

51. pokladnik, ili spal'nik.

52. See Chapter VI, Note 66, above.

53. See Note 47, above.

INDEX

Saint Boris and St. Gleb, church of
(Kideksha), 255
Saint George, monastery of (Novgorod),
239
Saint John the Forerunner on the
Opoki, church of (Novgorod), 240
Saint Michael's monastery, Vydubichi,
228
Saint Michael, cathedral of, 250
Saint Peter's church, Kiev, 25
Saint Simeon monastery, Kiev, 254
Sakov (mod. Salkov?), 61, 233
Salomea, wife of Bolesław III, 255
Salomon, king of Hungary, 226, 234-235
salt, 227
San, river, 54
Sapogin, 154
Saracens, 237, 242, 244
Sarkel, Khazar city, 239
Savench Boniakovich, Polovetsian, 150
Savior monastery, Kiev, 252
Saxony, Saxons, 225, 255; margrave
of, 17; revolt of 1073-1075, 225
Sbyslav Zhiroslavich, 207
Sbyslava, daughter of Sviatopolk, 70
Scandinavia, xiv
Scythians, 221
Seim, river/region, 78, 86, 116, 123, 127,
134, 251
Seljuq (Seljuk) Turks, 229, 237
Semigallian campaign, 236, 243
seniority, 2-7, 22, 68, 72-73, 109; ex-
clusion from, 88, 94; respect for,
34, 67, 145
Senyk, Sophia, author, 217
Seret, river, 103
Setomlia River, 11
Sewter, E.R.A., translator, 237
Shakhmatov, A.A., historian, xxviii
Sharukan, 63
Shchekovitsa, 149
Shepard, Jonathan, co-author with S.
Franklin, 217-220, 226-230, 233,
235-236, 240, 242, 250, 257, 259,
261
Shepol, 50, 231
Sherbowitz-Wetzor, O.P., author, 218

Shvarn, another boyar, 204, 208
Shvarn, boyar, 148, 176, 206
Sieciech, palatine of Poland, 29, 227
Sigurd Hring, king of Uppsala, 203
Silesia, 225, 236, 246
Simeon, priest, Rostislav Mstislavich's
confessor, 190
Slavata, boyar, 76
Slavs, xiv, xxi
Slovo o Polku Igoreve, see Tale of
Igor's campaign
Slutsk, Minsk Province regional center,
235-236
Smolensk, xvi, xxii, 6, 9-10, 20, 27, 40,
88, 113, 119, 128, 190, 236, 241,
254, 258, 261
Snov River, 13
Snovid Izechevich, groom, 48-49
Snovsk, 13, 168
Sokol, Edward D., author, 219-220,
258
Soloviev, Sergei M., historian, xvi,
xix-xxix, 217, 220-222, 224, 226,
228, 232, 237-239, 244-246, 257,
263; notes by, 228-233, 236, 242,
244-250, 256-257, 259, 262-263
Sosola, Finno-Ugric tribe, 29, 226
Sozhitsa (Orzhitsa) River, battle on
the 20, 30, 101
Spytihněv I, prince of Bohemia, 16
Stanislav Tukievich, 76, 175, 177
Stanislaw, bishop of Cracow, 29, 223,
227
Starodub, 41, 100, 167
Stavr, hundredman of Novgorod, 89
Stenkil, king of Sweden, 203, 262
Stepan Miliatich, 206
Stephen I (pagan name Vajk), saint,
king of Hungary, 65, 160, 225, 234
Stephen II, king of Hungary, 66, 72,
235
steppes, 9, 11-12, 19, 22-23, 60, 64, 81-
82, 152, 157, 180, 186, 205, 217,
223, 227, 230, 247, 263; movements
in, 74
Stokes, Antony, author, 224
Strashko, 106

THE EDITOR AND TRANSLATOR

Ralph Cleminson is Professor of Slavonic Studies at the University of Portsmouth and visiting professor at the Central European University, Budapest. Educated at Manchester Grammar School and University College, Oxford, he wrote his doctoral dissertation on the inflectional morphology of Church Slavonic as exemplified by the Russian recension of "Stefanit i Ichnilat." He has compiled descriptive union catalogues of cyrillic manuscripts in the United Kingdom, Ireland and Slovakia, and was also one of the compilers of the catalogue of cyrillic early-printed books in the British Isles. He is currently working on manuscripts in Hungary and elsewhere, and is taking a leading role in the application of the new technology to medieval Slavonic texts and in the development of international standards for the machine-readable encoding of medieval cyrillic and glagolitic material.

FROM ACADEMIC INTERNATIONAL PRESS*

THE RUSSIAN SERIES

*Request catalogs. Sample pages, tables of contents, more on line at www.ai-press.com